RADICAL KABBALAH

Other works by Dr. Rabbi Marc (Mordechai) Gafni:

Your Unique Self: The Radical Path to Personal Enlightenment
Soul Prints
The Mystery of Love
The Erotic and the Holy (audio)
Soul Print Workshop (audio)

Published in Hebrew:
Reclaiming Uncertainty as a Spiritual Value
Re-defining Certainty from "It Is True" to "I Am True"
Lillith: Re-Reading Feminine Shadow
First Steps in Judaism

Forthcoming:
World Spirituality Based on Integral Principles with Ken Wilber
The Dance of Tears and Rosh Hashanah: First Steps Toward
        an Integrally Informed Judaism

RADICAL KABBALAH

The Wisdom of Solomon as the Matrix
of the Enlightenment Teaching of Nondual
Acosmic Humanism and Unique Self

The Great Teaching of Ethics and Eros
of Mordechai Lainer

Book 2

by Dr. Rabbi Marc (Mordechai) Gafni

FIRST EDITION

Revised

Designed by Kathryn Lloyd
Crafty Coyote Book Design

Radical Kabbalah Two Book set ISBN: 978-1-4675-2274-8

Radical Kabbalah Book One ISBN: 978-1-4675-2275-5

Radical Kabbalah Book Two ISBN: 978-1-4675-2276-2

Printed by Lightning Source. Lightning Source is
♦ Sustainable Forestry Initiative® (SFI®) certified and their certificate is active.

♦ Programme for the Endorsement of Forest Certification™ (PEFC™) certified and their certificate is active.

♦ Forest Stewardship Council™ (FSC®) certified and their certificate is active. FSC® C084699

Table of Contents Book 2

VOLUME 2

The Wisdom of Solomon as the Matrix of Lainer's Theology
of Nondual Acosmic Humanism   xxiii

    Introduction   xxv

Section 1: Lainer's Code for the Wisdom of Solomon   3

    Four Methodological Caveats   5

Section 2: The Solomon Sources   9

    Cluster 1: The Goddess Sources   11

      Source 1: *MHs vol. 1* Vayeira s.v. *ki ʿatzor*   11

      Source 2: *MHs vol. 1* Melakhim 1 *s.v. veha-melekh*   14

      Source 3: *MHs vol. 1* Toldot s.v. *vayeishev*   14

      Source 4: *MHs vol. 2* Ki Tisa s.v. *elohei maseikhah 1*   17

    Cluster 2: The Personal Intuition Sources: On Smell, Intuition,
and Truth Beyond Truth   21

      Source 5: *MHs vol. 2* Behaʿalotekha s.v. *im yihyeh*   22

      Source 6: *MHs vol. 2* Devarim s.v. *havu*   27

      Source 7: *MHs vol. 1* Shoftim s.v. *shoftim 2*   29

      Source 8: *MHs vol. 1* Sanhedrin 104b s.v. *amar Rav Yehudah*   31

    The Judah Archetype   33

      Source 9: *MHs vol. 1* Vayeishev s.v. *vezeh*   33

      Source 10: *MHs vol. 1* Emor s.v. *vahaveitem*   34

      Source 11: *MHs vol. 2* Mishlei s.v. *ki vaʿar*   35

      Source 12: *MHs vol. 2* Devarim s.v. *ahad ʿasar*   36

The Messianic Tension in *MHs*   39

Source 13: *MHs vol. 1* Va'et'hanan s.v. *vehayu*   40

Summary of Clusters 1 and 2   43

Section 3: Additional Sources   53

Cluster 3: The David Sources   53

Source 14: *MHs vol. 2* Re'eh s.v. *va'akhaltem*   53

Source 15: *MHs vol. 2* Va'eira s.v. *vayikah*   54

The Two Hands Sub-Cluster   57

Source 16: *MHs vol. 2* Tehilim s.v. *yadekha 'asuni*   57

Source 17: *MHs vol. 1* Likutim s.v. *Hashem YKVK*
and s.v. *ule'atid*   58

Source 18: *MHs vol. 2* Ketubot s.v. *darash Bar Kapra*   67

Source 19: *MHs vol. 1* Tzav s.v. *hamakriv*   72

The Face-to-Face Sub-Cluster   75

Source 20: *MHs vol. 2* Korah s.v. *vayikah 1*   75

Source 21: *MHs vol. 2* Likutim Pinhas s.v. *bayom ha-shemini*   78

Source 22: *MHs vol 1* Kedoshim s.v. *kedoshim 1*   79

Source 23: *MHs vol. 2* Ki Tisa s.v. *vayedaber Hashem
el Mosheh lekh reid*   80

Cluster 4: The Moon Sources   83

Source 24: *MHs vol. 1* Emor s.v. *vahaveitem*   84

Source 25: *MHs vol. 2* Ki Teitzei s.v. *ki teitzei 2*   86

Section 4: Integration and Ecstasy   97

Cluster 5: The Idolatry Sources   97

Strand 1: Paganism as a Phenomenon Whose Time Has Not
Yet Come   98

Source 26: *MHs vol. 1* Vayikra s.v. *'al kol* and Gilyon Vayikra
s.v. *'al kol*   98

   Strand 2: Reclaiming the Energy of the Feminine: The Many
   Faces of the *Shekhinah*   107

   Source 27: *MHs vol. 1* Ki Tisa s.v. *elohei maseikhah*   108

   Source 28: *MHs vol. 2* Vayeira s.v. *vayikra*   110

The *Teva'-Nukva-'Igulim* Sub-Cluster   115

   Strand 3: Paganism in Relation to Unmediated *Shekhinah*   116

Source 29: *MHs vol. 1* Megilah 12 s.v. *veha-karov* and vol. 2
Megilah 12b s.v. *bise'udato*   116

   Source 30: *MHs vol. 1* Vayehi s.v. *uvedam*   122

Cluster 6: The Wine Sources   125

   Source 31: *MHs vol. 2* Shemini s.v. *yayin 2*   126

   Source 32: *MHs vol. 2* Shelah s.v. *vehikriv*   128

   Source 33: *MHs vol. 1* Shabbat s.v. *vehineih*   129

   Source 34: *MHs vol. 2* Mishlei s.v. *hokhmot*   131

   Source 35: *MHs vol. 1* Vayehi s.v. *uvedam*   132

The *Tovat 'Ayin* Sub-Cluster   135

   Source 36: *MHs vol. 1* Rosh Hashanah s.v. *amar leih Rabi*   135

   Source 37: *MHs vol. 2* Eruvin s.v. *amar Rabi*   136

   Source 38 *MHs vol. 2* Pesahim s.v. *tanu rabanan*   137

   Source 39: *MHs vol. 1* Megilah 7a s.v. *tani Rav Yosef*   138

The *Menutzah* Sub-Cluster   139

   Source 40: *MHs vol. 2* Va'eira s.v. *vayikah*   139

   Source 41: *MHs vol. 2* Shelah s.v. *ahar*   142

   Source 42: *MHs vol. 1* Shelah s.v. *beha-sidrah*   144

   Source 43: *MHs vol. 2* Ki Tavo s.v. *arur ha'ish*   146

Source 44: *MHs vol. 1 Vayeishev s.v. vayeishev 1*   148

Conclusion   151

VOLUME 3

The Sources and Evolution of the Wisdom of Solomon in Kabbalah
and *Hasidut*   163

Part One

Introduction   165

Zoharic Sources for the Wisdom of Solomon   169

   Solomon in Rabbinic Literature   173

      Source 1: *bRosh Hashanah* 21b   173

      Source 2: *bMakot* 23b   175

      Source 3: *Shemot Rabbah* 6:1   176

      Source 4: *Shemot Rabbah* 15:26   179

   'Solomon' means God   181

      Source 5: *Shir Hashirim Rabbah* 3:24   181

      Source 6: *Bamidbar Rabbah Naso* 11:3   181

      Source 7: *bMegillah* 11b   183

      Source 8: *bHulin* 60b   184

   The Texts of the *Zohar*   189

    Zivug   191

      Source 9: *Zohar* 1:216a   191

    Solomon and Moses   193

      Source 10: *Tikunei Zohar* 28a   193

      Source 11: *Zohar* 2:140b   194

      Source 12: *Zohar Hadash Shir Hashirim* 4b   197

Source 13: *Tikunei Zohar* 24b   199

The Wisdom of Solomon Texts   201

Source 14: *Zohar* 1:149b–150a   201

Source 15: *Zohar* 1:223b   206

Source 16: *Zohar* 1:49a   214

Sihara – The Moon   217

Source 17: *Zohar* 1:225b   217

Source 18: *Zohar* 1:248b–249a   217

Solomon and David   221

Source 19: *Zohar* 1:249b   221

Source 20: *Zohar* 1:249b   224

Source 21: *Zohar Hadash Sitrei Otiyot Bereishit* 13b   229

Mikdash   233

Source 22: *Zohar* 2:257b–258a   233

Source 23: *Zohar* 3:297a   235

Source 24: *Zohar* 2:235b   236

Integrating the Darkness   239

Source 25: *Zohar* 3:46b   239

Source 26: *Tikunei Zohar* 95b   242

The Judah Archetype   247

Source 27: *Zohar* 1:236b–237a   247

Source 28: *Zohar* 1:237a   251

Source 29: *Zohar* 1:237   253

Source 30: *Zohar* 2:85a   255

The Wine Sources   259

Source 31: *Zohar* 1:238a   260

Source 32: *Zohar* 1:238a–b   263

Source 33: *Zohar* 1:240a   265

Source 34: *Zohar Hadash Hukat Maamar Lamenatze'ah 'Al Shoshanim*   267

Source 35: *Zohar* 3:40b   269

Sitra Ahra   273

Source 36: *Zohar* 2:103   273

A Concluding Passage   281

Source 37: *Zohar Hadash Midrash Rut Ma'amar Zuhama Dehavya*   281

Cordovero, Luria, and Hasidism   283

Cordovero   285

Source 38: *Pardes Rimonim Shaar* 22 Ch. 3   285

Source 39: *Pardes Rimonim Shaar* 23 Ch. 13   286

Luria   289

Source 40: *Shaar Ma'amrei Rashbi Peirush 'Al Zohar Shir Hashirim*   289

Source 41: *Likutei Torah Sefer Melakhim* 1   289

Tikun Ha-nukva   291

Source 42: *Eitz Hayyim Shaar* 36 ch. 1, 42   291

Simcha Bunim   295

Source 43: *Sefer Kol Mevaser vol. 1* Va'eira s.v. *ramatayim tzofim, 15:42*   295

Other Hasidic Sources   299

Source 44: Degel Mahaneh Efrayim Hayei Sarah s.v. *ve-Avraham zaken ba' beyamim*   299

Source 45: *Meor Eynayim Bereishit*   302

Source 46: *Oheiv Yisrael Shemot*   304

    Source 47: *Likutei Moharan* 2:91   305

Part Two

Tzadok Hakohen of Lublin   315

    Source 48: *Tzidkat Hatzadik* 229   316

    Source 49: *Peri Tzadik Shemini Atzeret* 38   318

    Source 50: Dover Tzedek 4 s.v. *ushelomoh*   319

    Source 51: *Tzidkat Hatzadik* 198   320

    Source 52: *Tzidkat Hatzadik* 198–9 (part 2)   322

    Source 53: Dover Tzedek 4 s.v. *veRabi Eliezer*   325

    Source 54: Tzidkat Hatzadik 249   326

    Source 55: Mahshevot Harutz 20 s.v. *vekol*   327

    Source 56: Mahshevot Harutz 20 s.v. *ve'azharta*   328

    Source 57: Dover Tzedek 4 s.v. *vehineih*   329

Index   333

Works Sited   343

About the Author   376

Table of Contents Book 1

VOLUME 1

Mordechai Lainer of Izbica's Theology of Unique Self and Nondual
Acosmic Humanism

Preface by Michael D. Zimmerman	xxv
Foreword by Gabriel Cousens	xxvii
Acknowledgements	xlv
Introduction	xlix
Notes on Transliteration, Style and Citation	lxix
Introduction to Volume 1	lxxiii
The Paradox of Mordechai Lainer's Thought	lxxiii
Levels of Consciousness	lxxiii
The Acosmic Dimension	lxxiv
The Scope and Plan of This Work	lxxv
Precedents for Lainer's Thought	lxxvii
Intellectual Biography	lxxviii
Secular Influences	lxxix
Historical Context	lxxx
The Direct Influence of Kotzk	lxxxi
Personal Revelation	lxxxii
Messianic Self-Understanding	lxxxiii
Textual Issues	lxxxv

Part One

Uniqueness and Individuality as a Theme in *Mei Hashiloah*   1

Chapter One

    Individualism in Context   3

    The Unique Self, Dignity, and Redemption   5

    'Igulim (Circles) and *Yosher* (Straight Lines)   6

    Individuality in Time and Place   8

    The Unique We, Conflict, and Judgment   8

    Berur (Clarification) and Uniqueness   9

    The Desire to Know One's Story   9

    The Unique *Mitzvah* (Commandment)   10

    Uniqueness and Joy   10

    Uniqueness and Sin   10

    Uniqueness and Healing   12

Chapter Two

    Personal Revelation and the Personalized Torah   19

    Uncertainty   20

    The Individual's Unique *Helek* (Portion) of Torah   21

    The Metaphysics of Individuality   21

    Uniqueness and Law   23

    Unique *Mitzvah* and Unique Torah: The Matrix
    of Antinomianism   24

Chapter Three

  The Way of *Hisaron* (Spiritual Pathology)   31

  Three Readings of *Hisaron*   32

  Hisaron Meyuhad - Unique Shadow   33

A Phenomenology of *Hisaron*   38

Hisaron and Uniqueness   39

Part Two

Precedents for the Theory of Uniqueness in *Mei Hashiloah*   45

Chapter Four

Introduction and Overview   47

Strand One: *Mitzvah Ahat* (Unique Mitzvah)   48

Strand Two: The Hermeneutic One-Letter Tradition   50

   Luria and Lainer: Provisional Conclusions   56

Strand Three: Soul Sparks and *Tikun* (Repair)   64

   Revisiting Individuality in Luria and Lainer   67

   Hisaron, Tikun, and Kabbalistic Theories of Evil   72

Strand Four: Prophecy and Uniqueness   75

   Moses, Uniqueness, and Prophecy: A Radical Reading
of Revelation   78

   The *Shekhinah* Speaks Through the Voice of Moses   85

Part Three

Acosmic Humanism in the Religious Theology
of Mordechai Lainer of Izbica   103

Chapter Five

Overview   105

Chapter Six

The General Themes of Acosmic Humanism   111

   First Major Theme: Acosmism and Uniqueness   111

   Second Major Theme: Empowering Acosmism   111

   Third Major Theme: Affirmation of Human Activism   111

Fourth Major Theme: The Ontic Identity of Name and Will   112

Fifth Major Theme: The Ontological Dignity of Desire   112

Sixth Major Theme: *Lema'alah Mida'ato* (The Suprarational)   112

Seventh Major Theme: The Human Being as a Source
of Revelation   113

Eighth Major Theme: The Judah Archetype
and the Democratization of Enlightenment   113

Conclusion   114

Chapter Seven

Texts of Acosmic Humanism   117

One: Acosmism, Unity Consciousness, and Redemption   117

The Experience of Interconnectivity   118

Acosmism and *Mikdash* (The Jerusalem Temple)   118

Participation Mystique   120

Two: The Reality of Love in Lainer's Theology   120

Three: Shadows of Union and Activism   123

Chapter Eight

The Will of God and Radical Freedom   129

Empowering Acosmism and *Tekufot* (Personal Audacity
and Determination)   129

Uniqueness and Acosmism   134

Acosmism and Will   136

The Qualities of Will and the Freedom of the Individual   139

The First Quality of Will: Will and Uniqueness   139

The Second Quality of Will: Eros and the Will of God   140

The Third Quality of Will: Radical Freedom   140

Freedom and Law: *Kelalim* (General Principles)

and *Peratim* (Particulars)   141

Radical Rereading   146

Revelation and Trust   147

Acosmic Humanism and Idolatry   152

The Democratization of Enlightenment   152

Three Qualities of Consciousness   154

    Hitpashtut (Expanded Consciousness)   154

    No-Boundary Consciousness   155

    The Suprarational and the Unconscious   157

Chapter Nine

Name, Activism and Acosmic Humanism   167

All is in the Hands of Heaven: A Humanist Agenda   167

    Called by the Name of God   177

    Called by the Name, Ontology, Uniqueness, and Unique Will   182

    The Dialectical Dance of Acosmic Humanism   185

    Some Concluding Remarks on the Identity of Names   188

The Paradox of Human Activism: Levels of Consciousness   188

Activism Passages not Linked with Name   200

Divine Animation of Human Action   201

Models of Activism: Pre- and Post-*Berur* Consciousness, Linear and Dynamic Models   204

Chapter Ten

The Nature of *Berur*   215

Chapter Eleven

The Way of *Teshukah*   219

Chapter Twelve

The Judah Archetype   227

No-Boundary and Judah   227

Paradox, Activism, and Judah   228

The Will of God, Judah and the Name   228

Judah, Uniqueness, and Individuality   230

Chapter Thirteen

Paradox in *Mei Hashiloah*   235

Laughter and Paradox in *Mei Hashiloah*: An Excursus   239

Part Four

Models for Acosmic Humanism Within the Tradition of Kabbalah   247

Chapter Fourteen

Introduction   249

Post-*Berur* Consciousness vs. Unio Mystica: The *Berur* and *Bitul* Models   249

The Matrix of Apotheosis   254

Model One: The Name of God   258

     Source One: *Zohar*   260

     Source Two: *Avodat Hakodesh*   261

     Source Three: Degel Mahaneh Efrayim   262

     Earlier Kabbalistic Sources for the Phrase *Nikra 'Al Shemo*   263

Model Two: God, Torah, and Israel are One   265

Model Three: The *Tzadik* and the Democratization of Enlightenment   273

Model Four: *Shekhinah*, The Eros of the Will of God   278

     The Face-to-Face Encounter   286

Yihud Ha-sheimot (Unification of the Names)   288

Model Five: The Wisdom of Solomon   290

Summary   291

Part Five

Choicelessness, Continuing Revelation, and Theology in the Context
of Lainer's Zeitgeist   307

Chapter Fifteen

Introduction   309

Lainer and Choicelessness   309

Lainer and the Idealists   311

Lainer and the Romantics   315

Part Six

Echoes of Izbica in Modern Jewish Thought   323

Chapter Sixteen

Introduction   325

Lainer and Abraham Isaac Hakohen Kook   325

Lainer and Abraham Joshua Heschel   329

Lainer and the Neo-Hasidic and Jewish Renewal Movements   331

On the Dangers of High States and Stages   332

Index   337

Afterword   343

Excursus - On Scholarship and Methodology   347

Our Methodology for Reading *Mei Hashiloah*   348

On Acosmic Humanism vs. Autonomy   348

Notes on Transliteration, Style and Citation

The edition of *Mei Hashiloah* cited herein is the most recent edition, which has become the standard. It differs from a commonly available edition cited in some scholarly articles in several significant ways. It includes an index compiled by Lainer's descendants, as well as several new sections of comments at the end of the second volume, including a second section of Likutim, which we have noted herein as 'vol. 2 Likutim 2'. In addition, the first volume adds additional headings for comments that appear at the very end, in particular separating Likutim that are not connected to particular Biblical or rabbinic texts from the preceding sections of Likutei Hashas; comments from that section are noted herein as 'vol. 1 Likutim'.

The method of transliteration for Hebrew terms and passages this work follows is a modified version of the rules for general (as opposed to scientific) transliteration found in the *Encyclopedia Judaica*. A forward or reverse apostrophe respectively indicates the letters א (') or ע ('), while the *tserei* vowel is indicated by either 'e' or the combination 'ei'. The indicator for א is omitted from the beginning and end of words (e.g., *eilav* and *vayikra*). For book and article titles and for names, indications of the letters ע ('), א ('), and of הידיעה ה' (*ha-*) have been left out. An apostrophe has also sometimes been used to separate vowels where its lack might create confusion for the English-speaking reader.

Quotation style follows British conventions, reflecting the fact that the main volume of this work was originally written as a dissertation at Oxford University. Concerning extended quotations from *Mei Hashiloah*, I have frequently included a larger portion of the Hebrew text than what has been translated in the English. The purpose of this is twofold: the English is kept more succinct in order to focus the reader on the most salient points, while the Hebrew provides a slightly more in-depth picture for the reader who can master the texts in the original language.

VOLUME TWO

The Wisdom of Solomon as the Matrix of Lainer's
Nondual Acosmic Humanism and Unique Self

INTRODUCTION TO VOLUME 2

In this volume, we explore in detail the Wisdom of Solomon matrix, which contains the hidden principles underlying Lainer's spirituality. For the most part, this matrix emerges from sources on the Wisdom of Solomon in *MHs* which have not been addressed in previous scholarship.[1] This volume will focus on *MHs*, while the next volume will show that there exists a distinctive Zoharic genre about the Wisdom of Solomon, which served as the direct source for Lainer.

In Part Four of volume 1, we outlined five different models for Lainer's nondual acosmic humanism, the final one of which was the Wisdom of Solomon, which comprises its own thematic expression of the more general model of merging with the *Shekhinah*. In fact, the term חכמת שלמה *hokhmat Shelomoh*, 'Wisdom of Solomon', is one of the *Zohar*'s expressions for *Shekhinah*.[2] Lainer understands his own thought to be to an intentional unfolding of a very specific body of esoteric wisdom, namely, the Wisdom of Solomon. As we will see, the Wisdom of Solomon is virtually synonymous with Lainer's nondual acosmic humanism as we have illuminated it in volume 1. Connected with this wisdom are all the principles which fall under the rubric of nondual acosmic humanism. These principles include:

1) the ability to gain unmediated access to the divine will, which is defined by Lainer as the essence of Israel.[3]

2) the ability of every person, to, on occasion, access a truth higher than the law;

3) *hitpashtut*, the expansion of consciousness that allows transcending of the law;

4) the Judah figure as the paradigm of acosmic humanism;

5) radical individualism;

5) the eros-laden themes of *teshukah* 'desire' and erotic merger with the *Shekhinah*;

6) the Izbica theory of unique *hisaron*, i.e., that every person has a unique personal pathology whose recognition and transcendence (*berur*) is what makes a person whole;

7) the ontic identity of names between human and God.

The core content of the Wisdom of Solomon is essentially equivalent to what we have outlined in these principles in volume 1. Once we decode the symbology of Lainer's Wisdom of Solomon genre with its interrelated key terms, it will become apparent that allusions to this specific esoteric knowledge refer to what Lainer understood to be an esoteric tradition, and that he drew on it consistently in both explicit and implicit ways throughout his work.

Lainer viewed himself as the inheritor and teacher of the Wisdom of Solomon, and he viewed his teaching as a continuation of the Wisdom of Solomon. In this volume we will establish the parameters of the Wisdom of Solomon genre in *MHs*, and in the next volume we will establish that Lainer's theology has deep roots in the *Zohar*. Lainer was aware of these roots and refers to them, sometimes more and sometimes less elliptically, in key passages throughout *MHs*. In volume 3, we will analyze key passages that form the core of the *Zohar* tradition upon which Lainer is drawing. In that volume, we will also analyze passages from Luria, the Hasidic masters, and Lainer's student Tzadok Hakohen that draw on or explicate the same body of wisdom.

What all of these sources share in common is the understanding that Solomon's wisdom is an attempt to embrace the *Shekhinah*, the erotic feminine manifestation of the divine, in a direct and unmediated fashion. All of these sources indicate Solomon's greater attraction to the *Shekhinah* in her different expressions than to the masculine pole of divinity. In some sources this preference is viewed as appropriate, while in others it is viewed as a tragic mistake because the integration of the two poles is regarded as the preferred goal, as opposed to the privileging of one pole over the other.

Notes for Introduction

1 On the Wisdom of Solomon in other sources, see Klein-Braslavy, *Shelomoh*. See also Berger, 'The Wisest'; Charlton, 'Christian'; Sasson, *Yahasam*; Yasif, *Sipur* 595 nn. 20, 29; 615 n. 84.

2 In his classic essay on *shekhinah*, Scholem notes the symbolic identity between the Wisdom of Solomon and the *shekhinah* in the *Zohar* ('Shekhina' 191). To the best of our knowledge, scholarship on the *Zohar* contains no substantive discussion of the Wisdom of Solomon.

3 Lainer's beliefs about the capacity to access the divine presence without mediation, and to know the divine will, were examined extensively in volume 1; see especially the sections 'Two: The Reality of Love in Lainer's Theology' and the sections 'Acosmism and Will' and 'Freedom and Law'.

Section One

LAINER'S CODE FOR THE WISDOM OF SOLOMON

LAINER'S CODE FOR THE WISDOM OF SOLOMON

In his introductory essays to the *Zohar*, Isaiah Tishby has already pointed out that ideas in the *Zohar* are often expressed by multiple interrelated symbols.[1] Rather than one symbol alluding to a concept, a cluster of symbols is used, sometimes with specific intent and sometimes interchangeably with other symbols, which together express the full richness of an idea or experience in a way that could never be expressed in a single term or word. This is of course true not only of the *Zohar* but of mystical texts in general. Elior has implicitly shown that this is particularly the case in the work of Lainer.[2] Her premise, which we accept, is that *MHs* can only be understood by identifying clusters of associated terms, each in their own way expressing different facets of the same basic idea. In this volume, we will outline and analyze the core *MHs* terms that express the hidden Wisdom of Solomon strand of thought.

Judah is the most common term. However, while the Judah passages paint a complete picture of the archetype of acosmic humanism (as we have already outlined in the first volume), they do not in and of themselves reveal the sources from which Lainer emerges. The Judah archetype involves particular qualities, including radical individualism, the ability to access *binah kavu'a balev* (i.e., to transcend the law for higher forms of immediate knowledge), unmediated access to *retzon Hashem*, being *menutzah*, overpowered by God, and a merging with the divine name and will. Only when the reader begins to realize that all of these qualities are expressed in *MHs* using the same clusters of terms, all relating to the Wisdom of Solomon, does one sense that Lainer understands himself—in contradistinction to Faierstein's view—to be part of a larger tradition. As one closely reads these texts, one realizes that these 'Solomon clusters' are not passing remarks. In fact, these text clusters form a coherent body of passages within *MHs*, presenting a consistent pattern in which Lainer, in veiled form, opens to the reader the sources of his tradition. These clusters are closely associated with Judah, and they all point towards the Wisdom of Solomon. Some of the key terms that are analogues for Judah which appear in these text clusters are:

3

1) King David; Kingdom of David; House of David;

2) King Solomon;

3) *sihara* (moon); *sihara bisheleimuta* (the moon in her fullness);

4) wine;

Each of these terms is found in multiple passages which are linked intertextually. Themes directly related to the Wisdom of Solomon are signaled by discussions of:

5) *mikdash* (the Jerusalem Temple);

6) *'avodah zarah* (idolatry) or *yitzra de'avodah zarah* (the pagan desire for idolatry);

7) *Shekhinah*.

The next set of terms appears less often, but wherever they appear they create a fuller picture of the Wisdom of Solomon genre in *MHs*. They are generally representative of the *Shekhinah*:

8) *'igulim*, a Lurianic term referring to the feminine face of divinity;

9) *ti'uvta denukva*, a Zoharic term that can be roughly translated as the erotic passion of the feminine;

10) *teva'* (nature);

11) *menutzah*, the feeling of being seduced and overpowered by the divine.

All of these terms, taken together, form a well-developed matrix from which Lainer's understanding of the Wisdom of Solomon emerges.

Four Methodological Caveats

Four methodological caveats are necessary before we turn to the texts.

First, it will not be immediately clear to the reader that these texts refer to a unique body of knowledge called the Wisdom of Solomon.[3] This will become clearer gradually as we present the texts from *Mei Hashiloah*, and will become fully apparent in volume 3, where we present Lainer's sources in the *Zohar*, as well as teachings related to this theme which Lainer passed on to his student Tzadok Hakohen.

Second, in the few instances where Lainer cites a key source from the *Zohar* that relates directly to the Wisdom of Solomon, we will defer quoting the *Zohar* passage until the next volume, unless it is vital to understanding the text of *MHs*. In that context, it will be clear how these *Zohar* references are part of a broader genre that forms the underlying matrix of Lainer's Wisdom of Solomon genre.

Third, we have chosen to err on the side of organization. In other words, we will cite and analyze separately the set of passages relating to each primary Wisdom of Solomon code-word. Since one passage may contain several of these terms (e.g., David, Solomon, moon, and idolatry), it would be inaccurate to quote only a small piece of the passage. In these cases we will note the different terms, but return to the passage in more depth when we analyze that specific term.

The last caveat is of a more essential nature. While not relevant to our scholarly agenda, it has great contemporary theological relevance. Lainer's acosmic humanism, as we have already pointed out, is highly chauvinistic, and the same is true about the Wisdom of Solomon matrix: for Lainer, only Jews have access to the consciousness and freedom represented by the Wisdom of Solomon. However, a simple theological rereading that transforms Lainer's Jew and non-Jew into the non-chauvinistic categories of 'levels of consciousness' reclaims his central relevance for contemporary theology. We have already shown in volume 1 how this rubric of 'levels of consciousness' is integral to Lainer's thought.

Notes for Section One

1 See, for example, *Wisdom* 269–366.

2 See Elior, 'Temurot'.

3 Indeed, the phrase חכמת שלמה *hokhmat Shelomoh* appears only infrequently in *MHs* (*vol. 1* Bo s.v. *kadesh*; Hukat s.v. *vezot*; *vol. 2* Likutim s.v. *shama'ti*—the latter example coming from Tzadok Hakohen). This possibly reflects the fact that the Wisdom of Solomon is presented as an esoteric, hidden doctrine.

Section Two

THE SOLOMON SOURCES

THE SOLOMON SOURCES

Lainer describes the Solomon archetype in several dozen passages scattered throughout *MHs*. The passages are not easy to locate because often the major topic of the passage is not Solomon; in some cases, Solomon is a secondary, almost passing reference. Closer reading, however, reveals that the Solomon reference is key to understanding the profound intent of the passage.

Within these passages, we encounter two sets of sources, each of a different type. We refer to the first set of sources as the Goddess sources, and to the second set as the Personal Intuition sources. Each of these terms will become clearer as we explain the actual sources. However, we may already state at the outset that these two types of Solomon sources seem to reflect two general concepts of *Shekhinah* that appear within kabbalistic literature. Gershom Scholem has noted that in Lurianic Kabbalah and in earlier sources, *Shekhinah* appears both as 'an impersonal symbol for God's immanence in the world' and in a more personal cast as 'a symbol of the pure inwardness of the divine within man'.[1] Scholem points out that these symbols were often conflated in Lurianic Kabbalah, i.e., the impersonal *Shekhinah* force was conflated with the more personal image of the *Shekhinah* mother or lover with whom the kabbalist longed to merge. He also suggests, citing the Hasidic scholar and initiate Hillel Zeitlin, that in early Hasidism an 'expression of pantheistic feeling' expressed in the notion of the *Shekhinah* 'as the divine life force (חיות *hiyut*) intrinsic to the universe' that also flows through man, becomes the dominant motif.

Returning to Lainer, it is plausible that his concept of the Wisdom of Solomon emerges directly from these early Hasidic notions. This *Shekhinah* idea is expressed in *MHs* in what have called the Goddess sources, which equally refer to a kind of pantheistic, divine life force. In what we have termed the Personal Intuition sources, this divine life force is conceived of as the essential personal identity of the individual. A person can naturally access the unmediated will of God, beyond the law, because the will of God (*retzon Hashem*) is in fact an expression of the personal life force of the *Shekhinah* that courses within the person. This is the identification of

9

Shekhinah and *ratzon* to which we referred above. The Unique Self, which is the incarnation of the *Shekhinah* as the Judah archetype access the unique expression of the divine will, beyond the general principles of the law. Critically, for Lainer, the two sets of sources are merely different expression of *Shekhinah* energy. The Wisdom of Solomon is the realization that these two *Shekhinah* manifestations—first, that which flows through the human being as 'pure divine inwardness', to use Scholem's language, which according to Lainer is expressed as unique personal will; and second, the impersonal 'pantheistic' *Shekhinah* expression that according to Lainer is accessed in paganism, in the Jerusalem Temple, and in the ecstasy of wine—are in fact one and the same. Ultimately, as close reading of the sources will reveal, the drive in Izbica to reconnect with the unmediated *retzon Hashem* is in large measure a clarified version of the ancient pagan drive to embrace and be embraced by the Goddess. What has changed in Izbica is that the great pagan eros has been identified, sublimated, and re-expressed by Lainer as the desire to access the unmediated will of God. For Lainer the unmediated will of God is not generic and not limited by the law. The will of god is in potential alternatively both hypernominan and antinomian. The will of God is uniquely manifest in the unique eros and ethics of the unique individual, singularly expressed beyond the limitations of the law, *as* the life of every person who personally incarnates the *Shekhinah*, the Judah archetype of Unique Self. This understanding which is elucidated in volume one, will become more implicitly and explicitly clear as we analyze these passages.

We begin our discussion with the cluster of sources relating to the archetype of Solomon himself. These texts, as we will see, very quickly bring us face-to-face with the Goddess. In the course of adducing these sources, we will also encounter the *mikdash* cluster, which is comprised of many of the same texts. All of the *mikdash* texts, as we have already noted in Chapter Eight of volume 1, are expressions of acosmic humanism, which we have also termed *mikdash*-consciousness.[2]

Cluster 1: The Goddess Sources

In the first set of Solomon passages, the 'Goddess'[3] sources, *MHs* defies the simple reading of both biblical and classical Talmudic traditions,[4] providing a dramatic new interpretation of Solomon's having many wives. The biblical text states unequivocally that Solomon 'did evil in the eyes of God' (1 Kings 11:6) and that his wives 'turned his heart away from God' (1 Kings 11:4). The Talmudic and kabbalistic approaches to this issue, marshaled extensively by Ginzberg, suggest two basic interpretations.[5] One interpretation follows the lead of the biblical authors and emphasizes the gravity of Solomon's sin. The second, found in both Talmudic and kabbalistic sources, attempts various strategies to mitigate Solomon's sin.[6]

In *MHs*, however, Lainer's understanding of Solomon and his wives goes well beyond any of the sources that Ginzberg adduces. According to Lainer, as we shall see below, Solomon's involvement with his foreign wives was part of a deliberate spiritual project to expand the realm of the holy by integrating the many faces of the *Shekhinah*, especially those manifested in the pagan goddesses. Of course, Lainer never dreamed of integrating pagan goddesses into the Temple. Rather, he refers to the integration of their כח *ko'ah*, which can be termed the energy of paganism. This was not merely a hidden project for the elite; according to several passages in *MHs*, sharing this spiritual project with the people was an essential goal of Solomon's spiritual initiative.[7] We now turn to the texts.

Source 1: *MHs vol. 1* Vayeira s.v. *ki 'atzor*

וה׳ פקד את שרה כו׳ במדרש, אני ה׳ הובשתי עץ לח הפרחתי עץ יבש,
הובשתי עץ לח זה אבימלך הפרחתי עץ יבש זה אברהם...ולכן כח הגבורה
הלזה ניתן לאברהם, וכאשר ניתן לאברהם היא בלי שום גבול, כי כל כחות
האו״ה אצלם הוא בגבול ולזאת יתפזרו ישראל לבין האומות כדי שיקבלו כל
כחותם שנמצא אצל כל אחד מהשבעים אומות, ואצלם יהי׳ בלי גבול, וכן
כתיב בשלמה המלך ע״ה שלקח נשים מהרבה אומות, כי כל תוקף שנמצא
בין כל אומה היא העיקר בנקיבות ובפרט אצל בת מלך, ולכן כאשר יכבשו
כל הכחות האלו יצמח מהם טובה אצל ישראל נצר מטעי

11

'And God remembered Sarah, etc.' The *Midrash* comments: 'I, God, have caused a lush tree to wither and a dry tree to bloom' (Ezek. 17:24). 'I caused a lush tree to wither'—this refers to Avimelekh. 'I caused a dry tree to bloom'—this refers to Abraham…Therefore, the power of this strength *ha-gevurah halazeh* was bestowed upon Abraham, whereupon it was without any limitation *beli shun gevul*. For all the powers of the nations of the world are limited. It is for this reason that Israel is dispersed among the nations, in order to receive the powers inherent in each of the seventy nations; however, among Israel, these strengths will be without any limitation. Thus it is written about King Solomon, of blessed memory, that he took wives from many nations, for the power of each nation is manifest in its women *nekeivot*, particularly in the king's daughter. Therefore, when all these powers will be subdued, goodness shall grow from them in Israel, the 'crown of my plantings' (Is. 60:21).

In this dramatic passage, Lainer introduces the image of two trees. The dry, barren tree, or Abraham, is made to blossom by God. The wet and fertile tree, Avimelekh, is made dry by God. While it might be tempting to gloss over this image as a mere midrashic device to introduce the Abraham-Avimelekh contrast, a closer reading suggests that this image has more significance. If one thinks associatively in the manner of Hasidic texts, one cannot help but relate the image of fertile and barren trees to the fertility trees of Canaanite idolatry, specifically, the *Asheirah* and Astarte trees.

That of course, given only the beginning of this passage, would at best be a midrashic reading. However, Lainer's ambivalence and even sympathy with regard to idolatry makes this the best reading. In the same passage, Lainer goes on to explain that the essential reason for the exile was to allow Israel to collect a kind of sacred power from each of the other nations.[8] This sacred spark is the essential *ko'ah*, the power, energy, or metaphysical quality that sustains each one of the seventy nations. By absorbing this energy into Israel's spirit, that quality which was previously one of *gevul* (limited, bounded, and finite) is transformed into being *beli gevul* (limitless, unbounded, and infinite). As we have seen in volume 1, *beli gevul*, no-boundary consciousness, is an essential part of Lainer's acosmic humanism.

In this passage, every element serves as the background for Lainer's major claim about Solomon. Solomon marries many wives as part of a grand spiritual project: acquiring the *tokef* (essential spiritual power) of the nations, which is found in the feminine, specifically in the בת מלך *bat melekh* 'daughter of the king'.[9] Therefore, 'when all these powers will be subdued or acquired, that is, when all the different metaphysical qualities of the spirit that are presently spread throughout the seventy nations are gathered and integrated by Israel through their exile, then 'goodness shall grow from them in Israel, the "crown of my plantings".[10] Although this is a description of the eschaton, Solomon apparently moves toward realizing this messianic goal even in the pre-eschaton reality by seeking to redeem the sacred spark of paganism found in the feminine, particularly among the daughters of the king. We are drawn to the conclusion that the metaphysical power of the nations of the world, according to Lainer, really refers to the religions of the world, that is to say, the idolatries of the world, as we will continue to see below.

Of course, it is the biblical text itself that explicitly links the daughter of Pharaoh and the other foreign wives married to Solomon with particular Canaanite pagan goddesses, including Astarte, the daughter of *Asheirah* (1 Kings 11:5), while *Asheirah* is of course linked with trees. At this point our initial reading of Lainer's distinction between the two types of trees becomes clearer. The power which makes the tree grow and bear fruit is the sacred spark in paganism, and it will be redeemed and integrated in Israel, just as the power moves from Avimelekh to Abraham. Moreover, there is an exact parallel between the trees and the wives, which is the framework of this passage. In Jewish mysticism and Hasidic literature, *bat melekh* is a *terminus technicus* for the *Shekhinah*, appearing as such from *Sefer Habahir* onward[11] through the well-known story of the *bat melekh* told by Nahman of Braslav,[12] a Hasidic master active only a generation or so before Lainer.

This is not an isolated text in *MHs* but one of a cluster of passages, each of which, in a different way, reinforces the same fundamental idea. The equation of the *bat melekh* with a feminine aspect of God occurs not only in Jewish mysticism. In world religion and myth, the daughter of the king may similarly represent the feminine goddesses, including *Asheirah* and Astarte,[13] both of whom who played a pivotal role in ancient Israel.[14] It is to these goddesses that Lainer is referring, at least in part, when he brings up Solomon's marriage to foreign wives as a project aimed at redeeming the sacred sparks contained in the feminine, particularly in the daughter of the king.[15]

13

Solomon is engaged in a deliberate spiritual adventure whose objective is to redeem the sacred energy of the pagan Goddess and to integrate it into the fabric of the Hebrew spirit.

Source 2: *MHs vol. 1* Melakhim 1 s.v. *veha-melekh*

In this passage, commenting on the verse 'Solomon loved foreign women, and the daughter of Pharaoh' (1 Kings 11:1), Lainer is even more explicit: Lainer writes that Solomon 'chose to take daughters of kings in order to subjugate (that is, integrate) all of their power under the realm of the sacred'.

כל כח או״ה ביותר הוא בנקבותיהם ובפרט בבנות המלכים, ולכך בחר
ליקח בנות מלכים כדי להכניע כל כחותם תחת הקדושה, מואביות הוא כח
אכילה ושתי׳, עמוניות הוא כח התאוה, צידוניות כחם היא בממון, חתיות
בכח וגבורה

> For all the *ko'ah* (power) of the nations is in their females and specifically in the daughters of kings. Therefore, [Solomon] chose to take daughters of kings, in order to subjugate [and hence, integrate] all of their power under [the realm of] the sacred: [from] the Moabites the power of food and drink, [from] the Ammonites the power of sexual desire, [from] the Sidonians the power of Mammon (capital) and [from] the Hittites [physical] power and heroism.

It is clear from this passage that the powers that Solomon wants to integrate into the sacred are precisely the erotic, sensual, earthy powers archetypically incarnated in ancient Canaanite paganism. In fact, the goddess of the Sidonians, whom Solomon worshipped,[16] is none other than Astarte, daughter of the king.[17]

Source 3: *MHs vol. 1* Toldot s.v. *vayeishev*

In the next source in the Solomon-Goddess cluster, we see that Lainer is aware of the radical nature of his own position. The major portion of the next passage only mentions Solomon in passing in the few lines we quote here. Lainer uses the greater portion of this passage to explain that Isaac resents Avimelekh for exiling him and for not recognizing Isaac's spiritual superiority as the son of Abraham. Isaac, however, התישב בדעתו *hityasheiv beda'ato*, returns to his higher, settled awareness (i.e., moves beyond his annoyance

14

and relocates his inner center) when he realizes that Avimelekh is playing an unconscious part in divine history by pointing out to Isaac that Isaac's quality of love is deficient. This is considered a *hisaron* 'lack' on the part of Isaac. Only through Avimelekh's agency does Isaac's awareness of his lack deepen his love and engender חשק חדש *heshek hadash*, new passion, for Torah.

Similarly, Lainer claims, the daughter of Pharaoh engendered new passion for Torah in Solomon, thus elevating Solomon's marriage from what appears to be sin to the level of divine service. Lainer presents what prima facie might seem to be an ambivalent stance towards Solomon and his embrace of the spiritual power of paganism. However, upon close reading, the passage is not only consistent with earlier passages, but even goes one step beyond them.

וזה הי׳ ענין בשלמה המלך ע״ה כמו שאיתא בגמ׳ אין כסף נחשב בימי שלמה למאומה וכתיב ויתן שלמה את הכסף כאבנים ומשני כאן קודם שנשא את בת פרעה כאן לאחר שנשא את בת פרעה, כי תחילה מחמת שהי׳ לו השפעה הרבה בד״ת ע״כ לא הי׳ אצלו כ״כ חשק לד״ת הנקרא כסף כי כסף היינו חשק ולאחר שנשא את בת פרעה אשר זאת הי׳ נחשב אצלו לחסרון וממילא נתהוה לו חשק חדש ע״כ לא נאמר כאן למאומה כי אח״כ נתהוה לו חשק

This was the case with King Solomon, of blessed memory, as one finds in the Talmud, '[In one place it is written,] "Silver was counted as nothing (i.e., worthless) in the time of Solomon" (2 Chron. 9:20), while [elsewhere] it is written, "And Solomon made silver like stones" (1 Kings 10:27). And the distinction is, here [when silver was as nothing] was before he married the daughter of Pharaoh, and here [when silver was like stones] was after he married the daughter of Pharaoh' (bSanh. 21b). For at first, since he had a great influx of words of Torah, he did not have so much *heshek* passion for words of Torah, which is called 'silver', for silver connotes desire. However, after he married the daughter of Pharaoh, this was counted as a *hisaron* deficiency in him, and this necessarily generated new passion for him. Thus it did not say 'as nothing' here, for after this he experienced passion.

The parallel between Isaac and Solomon makes it clear that Lainer is not adopting a milder version of the more classic position that views Solomon's

15

marriage to Pharaoh's daughter as a sin. Lainer draws a structural analogy between Avimelekh and the daughter of Pharaoh, both of whom cause the protagonists of their respective stories, Isaac and Solomon, to uncover a deeper and more powerful well of *teshukah* than they had previously been able to access.

As we have noted, in a superficial reading of this passage, Solomon's marriage to Pharaoh's daughter is considered a lack or *hisaron*, i.e., sinful. However, here as throughout *MHs*, *hisaron* plays an essential role in every person's spiritual development and unique relationship with divinity.[18] First, Lainer interprets the Sanhedrin passage positively: Pharaoh's daughter engendered new *teshukah* in Solomon. In Chapter Eleven of volume 1, we saw that the affirmation of the centrality and ontological dignity of *teshukah* is a demarcating characteristic of Lainer's acosmic humanism. Solomon does not develop new *teshukah* in a generic sense; rather, it is new *teshukah* for *divrei Torah*[19]—broadly, for spiritual service. Moreover, *teshukah* is not a small detail in the life of Solomon. In another important passage[20] from the Wisdom of Solomon genre, Lainer suggests that Solomon's ability to be connected to his essential *teshukah* was the primary quality of his kingship which allowed him to recover his kingdom after his fall. In this highly original reading, *teshukah* is viewed not as the source of Solomon's fall, but quite the opposite, as the quality that allows him to rise again and reclaim his spiritual stature and kingship.[21]

Teshukah is thus the essence of Solomon's spiritual service. The daughter of Pharaoh is the one who allows him to reconnect to *teshukah* after an apparent period of faltering. Thus, while marrying the daughter of Pharaoh may have been a sin, as a simple reading of the passage suggests, it seems to fall into the category—so important for Lainer—of *'aveirah lishmah*, sinning for the sake of God.[22]

As we proceed in our discussion of the relevant *MHs* passages, and particularly as we dissect the Zoharic and Lurianic antecedents to *MHs*, it will become clear that Solomon's marriage to the daughter of Pharaoh seems to have involved no less than *zivug* (sexual intercourse) with the *Shekhinah*.[23] From the sources adduced so far, it is clear that Solomon needs to marry the daughter of Pharaoh, for in doing so he both fulfills his *Shekhinah* project—including the many faces of the *Shekhinah* within 'the realm of the holy'[24]—and he ipso facto re-engages his own passion (eros).[25] This passage identifies the essential spiritual quality of Solomon as his *teshukah*

16

and is suffused with eros, which, as we shall continue to see, is one of the demarcating features of the Wisdom of Solomon in virtually all of its incarnations. We shall see further that in the work of Tzadok Hakohen, Lainer's most important disciple, the eroticism of *teshukah* plays an even more pivotal role than it does in Lainer's work; Tzadok received this lore from his master and explicitly termed it 'the Wisdom of Solomon'.[26]

Source 4: *MHs vol. 2 Ki Tisa s.v. elohei maseikhah* 1

The text we will now adduce, which is the next major source in the cluster of *MHs* texts endorsing Solomon's involvement with the daughter of Pharaoh and the pagan cults, advances well beyond the Talmudic traditions that attempted to mitigate the sin of Solomon.[27] The text is instructive both because it adds something important to our knowledge of Lainer's understanding of Solomon, and because its literary form typifies an attempt (possibly by the editor, Lainer's grandson Gershom Henokh) to soften and even hide Lainer's radical teaching from the casual reader. At first glance, this text reads like a standard condemnation of Solomon. Like many passages or snippets of passages in *MHs*, it can be read more moderately; only when one understands the full passage or the cluster of passages and their internal code does its full radical nature becomes apparent.

אלהי מסכה לא תעשה לך. שלא יהיה האדם קל בדעת שהנאות וחדות מעוה"ז יטה דעתו, כי זה נקרא מסכה, כמו שמצינו אצל שלמה המלך שכתיב (מ"א ז) ובית יעשה לבת פרעה שרצה להרחיב קדושת השי"ת בעולם אף שלא יהיה לב ישראל מבורר ועומד נגד השי"ת, ולכן כתיב (מ"א יא) בנה את המלוא, ולעתיד יגמור, ולכן נאמר ובית יעשה לשון עתיד, כי כשנגמר בית המקדש אז היה בדעת שלמה שכבר הגיע העת, כי שלמה בבנותו המקדש כדי שיכנסו קדושת כל הכלים בו לכן היה אז זך לב ומבורר ולא עשה בו שום רושם כל האלף מיני זמר שנזכר בגמ' (שבת נו):

'Do not make *elohei maseikhah* molded (or 'molten')[28] gods for yourself' (Exod. 34:17). This means that a person should not be frivolous, allowing worldly pleasures and joys to turn his head *yateh da'ato*, for this is called *maseikhah*. As we find regarding King Solomon, as is written, 'And he would make a house for the daughter of Pharaoh' (1 Kings 7:8), because he wanted to expand God's holiness in the world, even though Israel's heart was not yet clarified and capable of standing before God. It is therefore written, 'He built the *milo'* (lit.,

17

'fullness')' (1 Kings 9:24[29]). For in the future he will complete it. This is why 'And he would (will) make a house' is written in future tense. When the Temple was completed, Solomon thought that *higi'a ha-'eit* 'the time had come' (cf. Cant. 2:12). This is because when Solomon built the Temple in order to contain the holiness of all the vessels, he had a clarified and-pure heart, and the thousand forms of music mentioned in the Talmud (*bShab.* 56b) made no impression on him.

Lainer comments, importantly, on a verse outlawing paganism. The language 'should not יטה דעתו *yateh da'ato* turn his head' evokes the phrase ויטו נשיו את לבו 'His wives *vayatu* turned his heart' (1 Kings 11:3, 4), which is used when Solomon's wives influence him to commit idolatry. Lainer continues, 'for this is called *maseikhah*'. If the passage had ended here, it would have been a classical condemnation of Solomon as the archetype of one who lets the pleasures of this world (his wives) turn his heart from God, and as a result worships *elohei maseikhah* (molded gods).

A cursory perusal of this part of the passage indicates nothing amiss. A literary device is employed by Gershom Henokh—or perhaps by Lainer himself—in the presentation of this homily, apparently to mitigate the radical nature of Lainer's teachings.[30] The remainder of this passage reverses its initial reading and returns us to the radical view of Solomon that we saw in the earlier passages.

There, Lainer reveals more clearly his view of Solomon's *Shekhinah* project, adding several pieces of information. First, Solomon knew that the people were not yet ready, not מבורר *mevurar* (clarified) enough to assimilate his *Shekhinah* project. 'This is why "And he would make a house" is written in future tense'. Solomon's goal is to expand the realm of the sacred (God) in the world.[31] Solomon thought, however, that the building of the Temple would signal that העת *ha-'eit* 'the time', i.e., the future or the eschaton, had arrived. Here, as we have seen before, Lainer affirms his belief that the eschatological future could become accessible in the present. In fact, according to this passage, Solomon believed that the *mikdash* could 'contain the holiness of all the vessels', i.e., all the forms of worship, including, perhaps especially, the pagan. Solomon himself was *mevurar*;[32] that is, he was clarified, purified, and thus was already living in that future eschatological place; therefore, the pagan songs of Pharaoh's daughter 'made no impression on him'.[33]

Critical for our purposes in this passage is noting that the nature and intent of Solomon's project are clear. The desire to redeem paganism and make room for it in purified form within the Temple is an essential part of that project. It is implicit that the Temple is an essential vehicle in accomplishing that goal. Solomon thought that the Temple would be the place that would allow for the expansion of the holy in such a way that there would be room for paganism, purified of its dross.[34]

This completes the first part of our discussion of the Solomon sources within the broader Wisdom of Solomon genre. In the passages above, we were particularly interested in Solomon's relationship to what we call 'Goddess energy'; this brought us to sources that obliquely or overtly discuss paganism. We will return to some other important passages on paganism, which do not involve this Goddess energy, in Cluster 5 below.

Cluster 2: The Personal Intuition Sources:

On Smell, Intuition, and Truth Beyond Truth

At this point we turn to a second set of passages in *MHs*. These passages are also part of the Solomon sources. The difference is that in these passages, Lainer begins to relate the spiritual project of Solomon to the core principles of his theology, namely, non-dual acosmic humanism, as outlined in volume 1 of this work. It is critical to note that while upon initial reading this set of Solomon passages might seem to have nothing to do with the Goddess passages cited above (other than the fact that Solomon appears in both sets), upon closer reading it is apparent that they are part of one conceptual literary cluster.[35] The two sets of passages express different manifestations of the yearning for *Shekhinah*, which is basic to the Wisdom of Solomon genre.

Three major passages deal with the same theme: the ability of Solomon in particular and the Judah archetype in general to intuit truth that is beyond the law, i.e., to access *retzon Hashem* (divine will), based on one's deep connection to the feminine (which we will term one's *Shekhinah*-consciousness). As we have detailed in volume 1, Lainer's theory asserts that one can access and be guided by the unmediated *retzon Hashem* even when it contradicts *kelalei divrei torah*. This is a cornerstone of Lainer's acosmic humanism and radical individualism. In effect, this theory is the precise intention of the Solomon project: accessing a level of consciousness in which one realizes one's merger with *Shekhinah*, expressed in the ontic identity between the will of God and the human will. In fact, we have already seen that for Lainer, *ratzon* means *Shekhinah*. Moreover, the notion of uniqueness and individuality, which is a key portal through which one accesses the unmediated divine will, is also a fundamental dimension of Solomon's project.

By accessing one's unique divine point—the *Shekhinah* point in the human being—and expressing it in full form, one naturally accesses the unmediated will of God. When a person settles fully into their own uniqueness, they merge with the One, who is able to include and make room for every individual's uniqueness. Both Solomon, master of feminine wisdom, and Moses, who in some passages is viewed as parallel to Solomon and part of

21

the Judah archetype, are so merged with divinity that they include all souls within them and are thus able to address the uniqueness of each individual soul. This is the paradox of uniqueness according to Lainer. According to Lainer, this is the great spiritual achievement of Moses and Solomon, and, in potential, of every person who incarnates the Judah archetype.

Let us now turn to these texts.

Source 5: *MHs vol. 2 Beha'alotekha s.v. im yihyeh*

In the first source, Lainer wrestles with a Talmudic text in tractate *Yoma* which suggests that although the members of the tribe of Judah are called מחוקקים *mehokekim*, they are paradoxically unable to correctly determine the law. The notion that Judah cannot determine the law is untenable for Lainer. So, in an audacious hermeneutical move flies in the face of classic Talmudic commentary,[36] Lainer suggests that it means that Judah is beyond the law. Lainer's interpretation is that the Talmud can only mean that Judah is *not limited* by the narrow law, based as it is on the *kelalim*.[37]

אם יהיה נביאכם ה' במראה אליו אתודע בחלום אדבר בו, לא כן עבדי
משה בכל ביתי נאמן הוא פה אל פה אדבר בו ומראה ולא בחידות ותמנת
ה' יביט. להבין החילוק בין במראה אליו אתודע בין ומראה ולא בחידות,
אכן הענין בזה כדאיתא בגמ' (יומא כו.) לא משכחת צורבא מרבנן דמורי
אלא דאתי משבט לוי או משבט יששכר וכו' ואימא יהודה נמי דכתיב
(תהלים ס) יהודה מחוקקי אסוקי שמעתא אליבא דהילכתא קאמינא,
וחלילה לומר על שבט יהודה אשר מלך המשיח יצא משבטו שהוא יאיר
וישלים רצון השי"ת והוא מורח ודאין, שאינו יכול חלילה לאסוקי שמעתתא
אליבא דהילכתא, ובאמת הלא מצינו בגמ' (ב"ק נב.) שמשה רבינו התפלל
עליו ועזר מצריו תהיה שיהיה יכול אסוקי שמעתא אליבא דהילכתא

'When there will be a prophet of *Hashem* for you, *bemar'eh* in a vision I will make Myself known unto him, in a dream I will speak with him. Not so my servant Moses. He is trusted in all My house; I speak with him mouth-to-mouth, *umar'eh* [through] a vision, and not with *hidot* riddles, and he beholds a picture of God' (Num. 12:6–8). [How should we] understand the difference between 'in a vision I will make Myself known unto him' and 'a vision, and not with riddles' (since both use the term 'vision' but mean contrary things)? This is like what is found in the Talmud: 'Among the rab-

22

bis who teach, there is no scholar who does not come either
from the tribe of Levi or from the tribe of Issakhar, etc. And
if you would say Judah, too, as it is written, "Judah *mehokeki*
my lawgiver" (Psalms 60:9)—here we are talking about those
who interpret tradition according to *halakhah*' (*b Yoma* 26a).
[This is also a contradiction, because] Heaven forfend that we
should say about the tribe of Judah from whom the Messiah
will come, who will enlighten and realize God's will, who
'smells' certainty, that he is incapable, heaven forbid, of interpreting tradition according to *halakhah*! In fact, we find in the
Talmud that our teacher Moses prayed for [Judah], 'and You
will be a help against those who trouble him' (Deut. 33:7),
meaning that he would be able to interpret tradition according to *halakhah* (*bBaba Kama* 92a).

Lainer, guided as he is by his understanding of the Judah archetype, cannot
even entertain the possibility that Judah would not be able to determine
the law. After all, writes Lainer, Judah is described by the Talmud as מורח
ודאין *morei'ah vada'in*: one who can smell the law with absolute certainty
(smell is a form of spiritual intuition higher than logic and precedent). Furthermore, Lainer asserts that this quality of Judah is messianic in nature,
based on the verse in Isaiah that describes the Messiah's legislative ability
as based on smell, pointing out that the Talmud itself explicitly identifies
morei'ah vada'in as the unique quality of the Messiah.

אכן הענין בזה כמו שנתבאר בחלק ראשון (ליקוטי הש"ס יומא) שמה
שנקרא בכל השבטים אליבא דהילכתא אינו נקרא עדיין אצל יהודה אליבא
דהילכתא, כי כופר הכל הוא פטור מטעם חזקת ממון וחזקה אין אדם מעיז
פניו בפני בעל חובו, אבל אצל יהודה אינו מבורר עוד לפניו שהוא פטור כי
יכול להיות שבאמת חייב לו, ולכן מלך המשיח שיבוא משבט יהודה שהוא
ישלים רצון השי"ת בבריאת עולם יהיה מורח ודאין כמו שכתיב (ישעיה יא)
והריחו ביראת ה' שיריח לעומק האמת

This matter [can be understood] in reference to what was
explained in *MHs vol. 1* Likutim Yoma (s.v. *lo ati*), that what
is called 'according to *halakhah*' for all the other tribes cannot
yet be called 'according to *halakhah*' concerning Judah. For if
someone denies an entire claim, he is declared exempt, as regards a financial claim, and it is presumed that a person would
not be so brazen in the face of his creditor. This exemption

23

is, however, not so obvious to Judah, since the person may in fact owe the money. This is why the Messiah-king, who comes from the tribe of Judah, who will realize God's intention in creating the world, will 'smell certainties'. As it is written [concerning the Messiah], 'And he will *vehareiho* breathe into him the awe of God' (Isa. 11:3) (the word *vehareiho* 'breathe into him' might also derive from the word *rei'ah*, smell)—[meaning] he will 'smell' *yariah* the deepest truth.

The phrase from Isaiah והריחו ביראת ה' *vehareiho beyir'at Hashem* is understood by Lainer to mean that the Messiah shall smell—i.e., intuit the true judgment—through the consciousness of God, and shall not judge merely by sight (i.e., by the logic of the law). Lainer then explains that both Moses and Judah (who in this passage are both Judah figures, unlike other passages in which they are contrasted) are not *peratei nefashot*. They are not individuals in the sense of other prophets, but have merged with divinity sufficiently to contain within themselves all individual souls:

וזה שמשבח השי"ת את משה רבינו אם יהיה נביאכם ה' במראה אליו
אתודע, היינו שכל הנביאים המה פרטי נפשות ואין השי"ת מאיר להם רק
כפי בחינת נפשם וזה נקרא במראה אליו כפי שורש בחינת נפשו, וגם זה
ההארה אינו מפורש לפניו היטב רק בחלום אדבר בו, אבל במשה רבינו פה
אל פה אדבר בו, היינו שבשעת התגלות הוא רואה הדבור מפורש יוצא מפי
השי"ת באתוון גליפין, ומראה ולא בחידות שהוא כלל כל נפשות ישראל,
לכן מראה לו השי"ת כל חילוקי דעות שנמצא בישראל, וזה נקרא ולא
בחידות, היינו לא דעה אחת לבד רק כל הדעות

This is why God praised Moses, saying, 'When there will be a prophet of *Hashem* for you, in a vision I will make Myself known unto him'. This signifies that the prophets are *peratei nefashot* unique individual souls, and God only illuminates for them according to the contours of their [unique] soul. This is described as 'in a vision unto him *eilav*'—[meaning] according to the root of the dimensions of his soul, and even this illumination is not made clearly explicit for him—rather, 'in a dream I will speak with him'. Concerning Moses, however, it is written, 'I speak with him mouth-to-mouth', that is, at the moment of revelation he sees clearly the word coming from God's mouth in formed letters: [hence] 'a vision, and not with *hidot*', for he is the totality of *kol nafshot Yisra'el* all the souls

24

of Israel. Therefore, God shows him all the different opinions of Israel, which is described as 'not with *hidot*' (that is, not one perspective alone, but all possible perspectives.

This is how Lainer interprets the verse describing Moses' prophecy: 'through vision and without *hidot*'. Lainer is most likely associating *hidot* with יחיד *yahid* 'individual' (Hebrew) or with חד *had* 'one' (Aramaic), though he does not make this explicit.[38] Moses, like Solomon after him, is not limited to one individual view (i.e., *hidah*) or even some limited number (i.e., *hidot*) but holds all individuals and all views within him. This is a kind of hyper-individuality, in which the person becomes so completely realized that their uniqueness is fully inclusive instead of being exclusive, aperspectival instead of being from one limited perspective. Now Lainer explains how this works on an ontological level:

כי משה רבינו היה כלל כל הששים רבוא נשמות מישראל, וזה שכתיב
(שמות כב) אם שכיר הוא בא בשכרו, ולא נתפרש דינו ונחלקו בזה
התנאים אם דינו כשומר חנם או כשומר שכר וזה נקרא בא בשכרו, היינו
שאני יודע היטיב היטיב שיש בזה מחלוקת התנאים, ותמנת ה' יביט שיודע עומק
האמת ומכיר רצון השי"ת בכל פרט לכן יכול לאסוקי שמעתא אליבא
דהילכתא כעומק

For our teacher Moses incorporated all six hundred thousand souls of Israel. And this is [the meaning of] the verse, 'If he be hired, he came with his wages' (Exod. 22:15), without explicating the verdict [of what kind of wages should be owed], which gives rise to an argument between the Talmudic sages as to whether he is to be regarded as one who guards something for free or one who is hired to guard something. This is [the meaning of the purposely vague] phrase, 'he came with his wages': it means, 'I (i.e., Moses) know well that there is a disagreement concerning this among the sages.' 'And he beholds a picture of God' means that he knows the depth of the truth and recognizes God's will in every specific detail. Therefore he is able to interpret tradition according to *halakhah* according to the depth [of truth].

This expansiveness and inclusiveness of soul allows Moses to 'behold God's picture', that is, to constantly access the level of divine will that can apply to every unique situation for every individual, not based on the general principles of law, which cannot afford such depth or breadth, but based on deep connection and virtual identification with the divine.[39]

This is the messianic Judah quality of Moses and Solomon. It is also true for Rava, an incarnation according to Lainer of the Judah archetype, as we see in the continuation of the passage:

ובזה התפאר עצמו שלמה המלך ע״ה (משלי ל) נאם הגבר לאיתיאל לאיתיאל ואכל, נאם הגבר הוא כמו פה אל פה אדבר בו שראה הדיבור באתוון גליפן, לאיתיאל לאיתיאל הוא כמו במראה ולא בחידות שראה כל הפלוגתות שבש״ס בין כל הפוסקים, ולכן כתיב שני פעמים לאיתיאל, ואכל הוא כמו ותמנת ה' יביט שיודע עומק רצון השי״ת לכוון ההלכה אמת לאמתו כרצון השי״ת, כי שלמה המלך ע״ה היה גם כן כלל כל נפשות ישראל. וכן מלך המשיח יהיה מורח ודאין, וכמו שנתבאר בחלק ראשון (בפרשת שופטים ובליקוטי הש״ס שם) על ענין קניא דרבא (נדרים כה.) שהוא היה שפיר משתבע אך רבא הריח לעומק רצון השי״ת והרגיש שהדין דין אמת אבל לא לאמתו ולא היה יודע היאך לברר, ובעסקא כזה צריך האדם לצעוק להשי״ת הושיעה ה' וכן עשה רבא, והשי״ת גמר בעדו ונתברר שנשבר הקניא ואסיק ליה השמעתא לעומק האמת

And in this King Solomon, of blessed memory, glorified himself, 'So speaks the man *le'itiel, le'itiel*, to Itiel (Itiel could be a person's name, but the word *le'itiel* can also mean 'I am weary, God'), and I am consumed' (Proverbs 30:1). 'So speaks the man' is like 'I speak with him mouth-to-mouth', that is, he saw the Word in formed letters. *Le'iti'el le'iti'el* is like 'through vision, and without riddles', for he saw all the arguments in the Talmud among all the halakhic authorities, and this is why *le'iti'el* is repeated twice. 'And I am consumed' is similar to 'and he beholds a picture of God'. That is, he knows God's deepest will, and may direct *halakhah* to be really true, like God's will, for King Solomon also incorporated all the souls of Israel. Likewise, the Messiah-king will 'smell' certainties, as was explained in volume 1 (in Shoftim and Likutei Hashas)[40] concerning Rava's cane (*bNed.* 25a), that [the defendant's] oath was true [on the surface], but Rava could smell the depth of God's will, and felt that the verdict might be *emet aval lo le'amito* a true verdict, but not really true, and that he would not know how to clarify the matter. In such a case, a person must cry out to God, 'Save me, O God!' which is what Rava did. And God completed [the judgment] for him, and it was proven by the cane breaking,[41] so the tradition was interpreted according to the depth of the truth.

Rava knows intuitively that there is a truth in this case beyond the law. This level of understanding is referred to by Lainer as not merely truth, but *emet le'amito*, the depth or truth of the truth, or the highest truth. *Emet le'amito* is precisely, writes Lainer, what it means to access the unmediated will of God.[42] Here we see the dimension of radical uniqueness merging with *retzon Hashem*, the unique divine will, in the form of Solomon. Solomon is the penultimate manifestation of the Judah archetype who has realized his ontic identity with the *Shekhinah*.

Before proceeding to a parallel passage in *MHs* that will confirm and amplify our understanding of Source 5, two brief notes are in order. First, in regard to individuality, Lainer refers to at least two different levels of individuated consciousness. The first level, that of the prophets and judges other than Moses, is that of individual consciousness, or what we might term the ego or persona level; this refers to the individuality that separates people.[43] This level does not separate but, quite the contrary, is the portal to the divine. As we saw in volume 1, according to Lainer, it is singularity that leads to the single and all-encompassing One.[44] When a person deepens their individuality through *berur*, paradoxically, the walls drop between the single one and the One. Lainer's great contribution is precisely this paradoxical notion in which radical subjectivity leads to the One. This is how Lainer interprets the non-Mosaic prophets in this passage.

Second, note that in this passage and many others, messianic consciousness and agitation are integral features of Lainer's theology. This is a point to which we shall return again below.[45]

Source 6: *MHs vol. 2 Devarim s.v. havu*

Our reading of the aforementioned passage is affirmed and amplified by a parallel comment on Deuteronomy. Lainer notes here that the *Zohar* tells us that Moses was able to judge without witnesses, meaning that the judgment of Moses is like that of Judah, who is *morei'ah vada'in*. Here Lainer dramatically rereads the classic rabbinic interpretation on which the *Zohar* and *MHs* are based, which is found in the *Sifrei* and brought by the biblical commentator Rashi.[46] That interpretation suggests that Moses chose people who were 'known to you, because if a person would come before me wrapped in his *tallit* (shawl), I (Moses) would not know from what tribe or from what place he is, but you do recognize him', implying that Moses cannot recognize a person's individuality. Lainer, however, cannot entertain the possibility that Moses, an archetype of *Shekhinah* and radical individuality, could not discern the uniqueness of every person. According to Lainer, Moses, like Judah and Solomon, transcended the limited grasp of normative legal procedure; thus, their ability to judge could certainly not be thought to be in any way inferior to the ability of lesser judges. Thus Lainer reinterprets the passage to mean:

ואם יבוא לפני משה הכל לא יהיה מקום לכללי תורה כי תיכף היה רואה
ומכיר שורש כל נפש, ולכן ניתן להם המשפט לישראל, וזה שאמר להם
שלפני משה אין מקום לשום לבושים לדון על פיהם והרי שבא לפני מעוטף
בטליתו איני יודע איזה שבט הוא היינו שאני איני מסתכל לחזקתו כלל רק
לשורשו אבל אתם שאתם במדרגות נמוכים ממני לכם נמסר המשפט לדון
על פי כללים

[I]f anyone would come before Moses, the general principles of Torah would have no place (purpose), for immediately [Moses] would see and recognize *shoresh kol nefesh* the root of every soul. Therefore he gave judgment to Israel, and this is why it says that before Moses there was no place to don garments—[meaning] to judge according to them. 'For when he would come before me (Moses) wrapped in his *talit*, I would not know which tribe he was from'—this means, 'I do not look to assumptions at all, only to his root, but you who are on a lower level from me, you are granted the [power of] judgment, to judge according to principles.

Moses says to his appointed judges, 'You judge people based on their *levushim* (external garb),[47] according to general principles, but I will judge according to the individual'. As in the *Beha'alotekha* passage, Moses is parallel to Solomon in his ability to access the unmediated and radically individual will of God (*retzon Hashem*); they both personify our definition of acosmic humanism. The difference between the Devarim and Beha'alotekha passages is that in the Devarim passage, Lainer softens his position somewhat by adding that even though regular judges lack the ability to judge *le'amito*,[48] nonetheless God approves their judgment even when based on *kelalim* and causes it to be not only *emet* but *emet le'amito*.

28

The acosmic humanism personified by the Solomon figure is crystallized in the next passage, where, unlike in the texts we have seen thus far, a distinction is drawn between Moses and Solomon.[49]

Source 7: *MHs vol. 1* Shoftim s.v. *shoftim 2*

אע״פ שהמלך יותר גדול מחכם, רק בהתחל׳ אין ממנין למלך רק ע״פי
סנהדרין ואח״כ כהן גדול ואח״כ נביא, אבל אחר שנתמנה למלך קודם
לחכם, כי מלך כל היוצא מפיו הם דברי אלקים כמו שמבואר בגמ׳...ואף
שנראין לדברי חולין הם מהש״י, כ״הג הוא מרגיש בבינה איך הוא רצון
הש״י, נביא בעת שיאמר כה אמר ה׳ אז הכל צריכין לשמוע דבריו אבל
כשאינו אומר רק מדעתו אינו רק כחכם, והנה שופטים מרמז על מר״עה כי
הוא הי׳ שופט ולא מלך...ופרשת המלך רומז לשה״עה, ואלו השניים היו
המעולים שבכל הדורות משה הי׳ המעולה שבשופטים, ושלמה הי׳ המעולה
שבמלכים, וסדר ההנהגה שכתב מר״עה בפ׳ האזינו כתב שה״עה בשיר
השירים בענין אחר, ויש הפרש ביניהם, כי שניהם כתבו ההנהגה מראש ועד
סוף כל הדורות

Although a king is greater than a sage, a king is appointed at first only by the Sanhedrin, then by the high priest, then by a prophet. Once he is appointed king, however, he takes precedence over a sage, for all words that come out of his mouth are words of the living God, as explained in the Talmud, and even if [his words] appear to be *divrei hulin* idle words, they are from God. A high priest senses God's will through *binah* (intuitive understanding). When a prophet says, 'So speaks the Lord,' everyone must heed his words, but if he speaks for himself, he is no better than a sage. 'Judges' alludes to our teacher Moses, for he was a judge rather than a king...And the section on the king alludes to King Solomon, of blessed memory. These two were superior among all the generations—Moses was the ultimate [judge] of all judges, and Solomon was the ultimate [king] of all kings. The *seder ha-hanhagah* (order of the world's conduct), that Moses described in *Ha'azinu* was described by Solomon in Song of Songs in a different manner, and there is a difference between them. [But] both wrote of how things will be conducted from the beginning to the end of all generations.

29

Moses and Solomon are each the ultimate personification of their respective models of spiritual leadership. According to Lainer, while each model has its place, ultimately the Solomon model represents the highest level. Moses is the *shofet* 'judge' and Solomon is the *melekh* 'king'. At a certain point in history, the judge has priority over the king: the judge, personifying the law, is a requisite for appointing the king, who cannot be appointed without the Sanhedrin (high court). However, once the king is appointed, teaches Lainer, he surpasses the judge, the law, and the sage.

The qualitative distinction between these models is based on the extent to which they internalize their essential divinity, and are therefore expressions of the divine (in other words, incarnations of non-dual acosmic humanism). The judge in this passage apparently operates based on the law (i.e., what *MHs* terms *kelalim* in other passages). Two other models introduced here, the priest and the prophet, each have access to a source beyond the *shofet* (i.e., beyond the law), namely, *retzon Hashem* (the will of God). Yet neither of them has fully internalized the divine will. There is not yet a merging of wills which reveals their essential oneness. Therefore, only when the prophet is in a particularly attuned state, marked by when he says 'So speaks the Lord' do we treat his words as *retzon Hashem*. Similarly, the priest feels *retzon Hashem* through his sacred intuition. However, when he is disconnected from that intuition, we do not heed his words as *retzon Hashem*. In contrast, the king, who according to Lainer is archetypically expressed by Solomon—the highest manifestation of the king principle—is a virtual incarnation of the divine will. 'All words that comes out of his mouth are words of the living God…and although his talk may seem to be *divrei hulin*, it is from the Holy One, blessed be He.

The Moses and Solomon personae are understood by Lainer not merely as two personalities, but as two religious models, each with their own *seder hanhagah* (order of the world's conduct, or spiritual order). Each model, says Lainer, represents a different approach to history and each has its own guiding text.[50] The text of Moses is the biblical portion of *Ha'azinu*, in which God is seen as transcendent, calling on nature and the human being to obey His will. This is the classic duality of theism. The guiding text for Solomon is the Song of Songs. This is the nondualism of acosmic humanism. Indeed, Solomon is the מלך שהשלום שלו *melekh sheha-shalom shelo*, literally, the 'king to whom peace belongs', that is, God.[51] The story of the Song of Songs is the story of Solomon's erotic merging with the divinity and particularly with the erotic divine feminine. In the erotic matrix of the Song of Songs, Lainer sees Solomon as the incarnation of *retzon Hashem*, which he asserts in countless passages as the essence of the Judah archetype.[52]

Because duality may still be a necessary prism, God affirms the path of Moses. But in the *'atid*, the eschaton (which for Lainer is available in the present to those who have undergone *berur*) God will affirm the truth of the path of Solomon as well. Lainer calls this דבר עמוק *davar 'amok*, a profound idea, which is a code phrase in *MHs* for a particularly radical passage. The passage continues:

ולע״ע הסכים הקב״ה למר״עה כי הקדים שופטים לפרשת המלך, אך לעתיד
בתחיית המתים יברר הקב״ה שדעת שניהם אמת, והוא דבר עמוק

> [A]nd for the present God agreed with Moses, who put [the section on] judges before the section on the king, but in the future, at the resurrection of the dead, God will clarify that the *da'at* of both is true, and this is a deep matter.

Here there is no suggestion that in the eschaton, whether accessed in the present or the future, the Solomon model will render the Moses model irrelevant. Quite the contrary; the dialectical movement between the two models is presented as an essential feature of reality, including redeemed reality. Here again we see that *avodah*, human activism, which is represented by the Moses model, has real ontological weight.

Source 8: *MHs vol. 1* Sanhedrin 104b
s.v. *amar Rav Yehudah.*

This idea that Solomon is beyond משפט *mishpat* (law; from the same root as *shofet* judge) allows Lainer, in yet another passage in the Personal Intuition cluster, to creatively reinterpret a Talmudic quandary in a way that is uniquely endorsing of Solomon:

והראה להם הקב״ה כי על שלמה המלך אין כח המשפט מגיע עד
למדרגותו... כי הוא למעלה מכח משפטים ולכן הוצרך להיות כך כי ע״פ
המשפט בטח הי׳ להם טעם מפני מה חשבוהו, אך הוצרך להיות כך כי זאת
הי׳ מדרגתו של שהע״ה

God showed them that with regard to Solomon, the power of *mishpat* does not reach his level…for Solomon is beyond the power of *mishpatim*…for in accordance with *mishpat* certainly they [the Men of the Great Assembly] had reason that they thought [Solomon should be deprived of his share in the world-to-come]…but it had to be thus, for that was the level of King Solomon.[53]

The Men of the Great Assembly, writes Lainer, who were given the power of *mishpat* to decide who has a share in the world-to-come, wanted to deny Solomon his share in the world-to-come. According to the Talmudic passage Lainer comments on, a *bat kol* emerged with a vague pronouncement that seemed to object to their decision. Lainer clarifies the intent of the divine voice as meaning that Solomon transcends the *kelalim* which are the basis for judgment and moves beyond even the normative truth.

Combining all these elements, we see that for Lainer, Solomon is guided by the acosmic model of Song of Songs, which is beyond judgment in that it does not obey but rather incarnates *retzon Hashem*. The same concept of transcending classical *mishpat* lies at the crux of the *emet le'amito* passages that we analyzed. Solomon operates from a higher model and is thus able to reveal, through the depths of his divine person, the unique *retzon Hashem* for every individual, and the 'emet le'amito' stratum of reality for every unique situation.

The Judah Archetype

The unique quality of *morei'ah vada'in* is what allows Solomon and the other Judah archetype figures to judge *emet le'amito*. This, as we have seen in Source 5, is an integral feature not just of Solomon's wisdom, but also of the Judah archetype. The essential figure in the *emet le'amito* passages is really Judah and not Solomon. The discussion there begins with Lainer rereading the Talmudic passage that seems to say—and in fact is so interpreted by classical Talmudic commentary—that Judah cannot make proper legal decisions. To this Lainer responds by saying that this does not mean that Judah is less than qualified to determine the law; rather, he is more than qualified. Rather, his perceptions transcend the standard rule of law and he has the ability in every situation to determine the precise divine ethic that needs to be applied. Judah is not limited to the formal, rule-driven legal *emet*; Judah is connected to and expresses *emet le'amito*.

Source 9: *MHs vol. 1 Vayeishev s.v. vezeh*

This idea appears not only in the *Beha'alotekha* passage analyzed above (Source 5), but also in what is widely regarded among students of Izbica as the *locus classicus* on Judah in *MHs*.[54]

> ושורש החיים של יהודה הוא להביט תמיד להש"י בכל דבר מעשה אע"פ
> שרואה האיך הדין נוטה עכ"ז מביט להש"י שיראה לו עומק האמת בהדבר
> כי יוכל להיות אף שהדין אמת הוא לפי טענות בעלי דינים אך אינו לאמיתו
> כי פן יטעון אחד טענת שקרית כמו שמצינו בקני' דרבא, וכמו כן נמצא בכל
> עניינים, וזאת הוא שורש החיים של יהודה להביט לה' בכל דבר ולא להתנהג
> ע"פ מצות אנשים מלומדה אף שעשה אתמול מעשה כזו מ"מ היום אינו
> רוצה לסמוך על עצמו רק שהש"י יאיר לו מחדש רצונו ית' וענין הזה יחייב
> לפעמים לעשות מעשה נגד ההלכה כי עת לעשות לה'

The root of the life of Judah is that he must look to God in
every action. Even though he knows how the law inclines,
nonetheless he looks to God to show him the depth of truth
in the matter. For it is possible that while the judgment may
be true according to the claims of the litigants, it is not *le'amito*

(the truth of the truth, the innermost truth), since one could make a false claim, as we found in [the case of] Rava's cane,[55] and as could happen in all matters. This therefore is the root of the life of Judah: to look to God in all matters and not to be guided merely by a commandment as people have taught it. Even though he may have acted this way yesterday, nonetheless, today he does not want to rely on himself (i.e., on what he thought was God's will yesterday). Rather, he desires that God grant him a new revelation of His will. This means that he is sometimes compelled to act against the *halakhah* (law), for '[It is] time to act for God' (Psalms 119:126).

This classic passage on Judah actually revolves around *emet le'amito*. When Judah acts against the law it is because he is moving beyond the *emet* and accessing *emet le'amito*. In fact, this passage cites the same Talmudic case of Rava's cane that appears in all three of the later *emet le'amito* passages.[56] In this story, Rava is able to move beyond the legal requirements in a case and access *emet le'amito*. In one version of the story, Lainer even informs us that Rava was descended from the tribe of Judah.[57]

Source 10: *MHs vol. 1* Emor s.v. *vahaveitem*

The essential Judah archetype is driven by the need and capacity to ascertain the inner truth, *emet le'amito*, through direct intuition or *rei'ah* 'smell'. As we shall see in the next two passages, Lainer equates the consciousness of the Judah archetype with the moon. The moon is of course a classical Goddess-*Shekhinah* symbol for Lainer (as it is for the traditions he draws on),[58] and both the moon and *Shekhinah* are equated with the Judah quality of being *morei'ah vada'in*, able to smell certainty. Thus the personal intuition sources are bound together with the Goddess sources in these two passages. All are expressions of the Wisdom of Solomon, as we will see below when we unfold the *yarei'ah* passages from *MHs* in Cluster 4. At this stage, we will cite only a small part of a central passage discussed below[59] that indicates that this Judah level is accessible to everyone:

שהש״י קובע בינה בלב כל אדם שיבינו בנפשם רצון הש״י, וזה הבינה...
נקראת ירח וירח מורה על בינה בלב ... כי ירח היא מלשון ריח שישראל
יריחו בכל דבר את שורשו מחיי עולם הבא

[F]or God fixes *binah balev* understanding in the heart of every person, that they should understand God's will in their own soul. This understanding is called *yarei'ah* moon, and moon indicates the understanding in the heart….for *yarei'ah* moon comes from the language of *rei'ah* smell, for Israel smells (intuits) in everything the root of life of the world-to-come.

God establishes *binah balev*, wisdom in the heart. *Binah balev*, as we have seen, is a *terminus technicus* in Izbica for the Judah archetype, who is 'drawn after the will of God'—that is to say, who realizes the ontic identity between one's own human will and the unique will of God. This *binah*, which is *rei'ah*—both intuitive and messianic—is called *yarei'ah*.

The moon, of course, is understood by virtually every mythical system to be a symbol of the divine feminine.[60] *Yarei'ah*, as we shall see below and in the next volume, is one of the core symbols for the *Shekhinah* and for the Wisdom of Solomon, both in Lainer and in his source texts. What emerges, therefore, is that the primary element of Lainer's thought—accessing the unmediated will of God as the goal of religious service—is deeply rooted in the *Shekhinah* matrix of the Wisdom of Solomon.

Source 11: *MHs vol. 2 Mishlei s.v. ki va'ar*

We will now turn to a *locus classicus* that expresses the Judah archetype, through the character of Solomon and his unique wisdom, using the symbol of the moon.

Here Lainer interprets Proverbs 30:2–3, 'I have not learned wisdom, [but] I will know knowledge of the holy', to indicate the unique nature of Solomon's knowledge, which went beyond normal forms of human cognition (i.e., beyond *binat adam*, *hokhmah*, and *da'at*).[61] Rather, to use Solomon's words,[62] the nature of his knowledge is that דעת קדושים אדע *da'at kedoshim eida'* 'I will know knowledge of the holy'. According to Lainer, Solomon says:

כי בער אנכי מאיש ולא בינת אדם לי ולא למדתי חכמה ודעת קדשים אדע. ששלמה המלך ע״ה התפאר עצמו אף שנעלם ממנו החכמה והבינה כמו שאיתא בגמ' (ראש השנה כ״א:) בקש קהלת להיות כמשה אף שלא בינת אדם לי ולא למדתי חכמה, מכל מקום דעת קדושים אדע שאני מכוון לרצון השי״ת בעומק אפילו בלי דעתי, יען שלבי מקושר בהשי״ת שזה הוא בחינת

35

סיהרא ואיתא בזוה״ק (פקודי רנח. חקת קפא:) ביומין דשלמה מלכא
קיימא סיהרא באשלמותא, וזהו ודעת קדושים אדע

> King Solomon glorified himself, even though wisdom and
> understanding were hidden from him—as it says in the
> Talmud, 'Kohelet sought to be like Moses' (bRosh Hashanah
> 21b)—[saying] even though I have no human understanding
> 'and I have not learned wisdom', in any case, 'I will know *da'at
> kedoshim* knowledge of the holy', for I intend God's deepest
> will—even without my knowing—since my heart is bound
> to God, which is the aspect of the moon. And one finds in
> the holy *Zohar*, 'In the days of King Solomon the moon was
> always in her fullness' (2:258a and 3:181b), which is the
> meaning of 'I will know knowledge of the holy'.

Solomon affirms that he knows in a direct and concrete way because he
is intrinsically bound up with God; this is what allows him to intend the
unmediated will of God. His knowledge participates directly in divinity,
and does not come through *hokhmah* and *da'at*. This is the essence of the
Judah archetype. What allows Solomon to contact *da'at kedoshim*? Lainer
answers, based on a *Zohar* passage, *sihara*, the moon, i.e., the image of the
Goddess, of *Shekhinah*. We will analyze this *Zohar* reference in volume 3.[63]
For now we will focus on what Lainer draws from this passage: that the
Zohar identifies the full moon (*sihara bisheleimuta* or *sihara be'asheleimuta*)
as the essence of Solomon's wisdom. This motif is one of the most important threads that ties together the Wisdom of Solomon. The conclusion of the passage relates the concepts of *teshukah/heshek*, *ratzon* will, and
name—all essential dimension of Lainer's acosmic humanism—directly to
the Wisdom of Solomon genre he has been discussing.[64]

Source 12: *MHs vol. 2 Devarim s.v. ahad 'asar*

Two more passages will serve to complete our picture of Solomon within
the Wisdom of Solomon sources. As we saw earlier, the quality of *emet
le'amito* emerges directly from *rei'ah*. The spiritual faculty of *rei'ah* is fostered by Torah that is קבוע בלב *kavu'a balev*, 'permanently affixed in one's
heart'. The quality of Torah being *kavu'a balev* is understood by Lainer to
be the defining characteristic of Solomon. Lainer writes that the Torah of
the land of Israel, in contradistinction to the Torah of the desert, is בקביעות
גמור *bekevi'ut gamur* 'completely fixed' in the heart, fully internalized. This

Torah is fixed not only in the mind but also בגוף כיתד שלא תמוט...ואין שום מרחק בין המוח להלב 'in the body, like a stake that can never be removed... and there is no distance between the brain and the heart'.

Lainer portrays a Torah in which there are no decisions to be rendered; rather, Torah is an integral part of the human being which wells up naturally from the divine heart of the person. At the end of the passage, Lainer refers to Solomon and understands him to be describing himself as one who has Torah with *kevi'ut gamur*, complete internalization. The phrase from Psalms (127:2), כן יתן לידידו שנא 'to his beloved *yedido* he gives sleep', is taken by Lainer to refer to Solomon:

לידיד ה' משפיע השי"ת דברי תורה בלבו אף בעת שהוא ישן ואינו מיגע עצמו כל כך ועל עצמו אמר זה

To God's beloved, God *mashpi'a* emanates Torah within his heart, even when he sleeps, and he does not need to exert himself so much, and [Solomon] said this about himself.

In the parallel passage from volume 1, Lainer adds:

קודם שלב האדם נזדכך צריך ליגיעה...אך אחר שנקבע ד"ת בלבו אז משפיע לו הקב"ה ד"ת אף בלי יגיעה ואף בעת שינה

Before a person's heart becomes purified, he requires *yegi'ah* effort...but after the words of Torah are affixed in his heart, God emanates Torah to him without any effort [on his part], even in his sleep.[65]

The purification described in the passage is the dispelling of the opaque illusion that the human is separate from God. In a third passage,[66] where Solomon is explicitly identified as a Judah figure, he is depicted as one who moves beyond אור זרוע לצדיק *or zaru'a latzadik* '[the] light sown for the righteous', which Lainer interprets as the principle of the law, and has the character of ולישרי לב שמחה *uleyishrei lev simhah* 'for the straight of heart there is joy', i.e., *retzon Hashem*. Joy, as we saw in Chapter One of the first volume, is an expression of unique individuality, which is understood here to be referring to David and Solomon. Lainer asserts that even though Solomon committed deeds which were not seemly על הגוון *'al ha-gavan* on the surface, in reality כוון לרצון השי"ת בעומק *kivein leratzon Hashem be'omek* 'he intended the depth of God's will'.

37

The Messianic Tension in *MHs*

We complete our discussion of the Solomon-Personal Intuition texts by discussing the explicitly messianic nature of the texts. This is particularly important in the light of Faierstein's rejection of the notion of messianic tension in *MHs*.[67] In the *rei'ah* passages, we see explicit refutation of this thesis. Lainer explains the Talmudic term *morei'ah vada'in* in overtly messianic terms. In the primary passage, he actually refers to Judah as יהודה מלך המשיח *Yehudah melekh hamashi'ah*, the only appearance of this phrase in *MHs*.[68] Later in the passage, Lainer cites Isaiah's prophetic description of the messiah והריחו ביראת ה' and explicitly states that this is a reference to *melekh hamashi'ah*. Finally, towards the end of the passage, Lainer repeats the phrase *melekh hamashi'ah* a third time, reminding the reader that the role of *morei'ah vada'in*, which he attributes to Judah, is the specific quality of *melekh hamashi'ah*. Given that we know from this and from many other passages that the Judah archetype is in theory fully realizable before the eschaton, it seems clear that the repeated unusual use of the term *melekh hamashi'ah* marks this discourse as overt messianic agitation, consistent with Gershom Henokh's attribution of messianic character to Mordechai Joseph's spiritual project. The Judah archetype, which, as we have seen, is realizable by every person in potential, is the manifestation of messianic consciousness.

The conscious messianic nature of Lainer's spiritual project will become even clearer when we consider his Zoharic and post-Zoharic sources. Lainer views himself as expressing the esoteric teachings of the Wisdom of Solomon. However, even before a more extensive consideration of his sources, the messianic nature of the project becomes clear based merely on the Zoharic passages that Lainer explicitly cites. In one passage cited by Lainer, Solomon's project, expressed by the symbol of the moon's fullness, *sihara be'ashleimuta*, is clearly messianic in nature.[69] In the Zohar, *sihara bisheleimuta* is generally a code word for messianic consciousness. However, even without knowledge of the underlying symbolism of *sihara bisheleimuta* in the *Zohar*, a careful reading of *MHs* reveals that Lainer was fully conscious of the messianic nature of his own project.

This becomes evident when we look at his commentary on the inhabitants of יריחו *Yeriho* 'Jericho'. Lainer suggests that the faculty of *rei'ah* was essential to the spiritual abilities of the people of Jericho. He suggests that the Hebrew word ריח *rei'ah* is the etymological and conceptual source for the name Jericho and the spiritual quality of her people. According to Lainer, this quality is expressed when Torah is נקבע בלב ישראל *nikba' belev Yisrael* (fully and permanently internalized in the hearts of Israel). This was the quality of the people of Jericho.[70]

כי יריחו רומז על ריח וגם נקרא עיר התמרים היינו שהבינו לעומק...והם
הבינו כי לאחרית יקבע ד"ת בלב ישראל כרצון הש"י וע"ז אומרים היום על
לבבך היינו שד"ת אינם רק היום על הלב אבל מחר יהי' נקבעים בתוך הלב,
וחכמים לא הסכימו לזה לפי שאין בכח האדם לקרב הישועה בלתי רצון
הש"י, ולפיכך היתה זאת באנשי יריחו כי יריחו מורה על ריח כנ"ל היינו
שמריח מרחוק את הישוע', וגם נקראת עיר התמרים ותמרים היא הסוף
שבשבעת המיני', והיינו שהיו מביטים לאחרית הדבר

For Jericho (Heb. *Yeriho*, like *rei'ah*) alludes to scent, and is also called the city of date palms, signifying that they understood deeply... And they understood that eventually the words of the Torah would be fixed within the hearts of Israel as the will of God. This is why today we say 'upon your heart', meaning that today the words of the Torah are only 'upon the heart', but tomorrow they will be fixed within the heart. The sages did not agree with this, for a person cannot hasten the redemption unless it be God's will. This is why the people of Jericho were thus, for Jericho alludes to smell, as previously mentioned, meaning that they could 'smell' deliverance from afar. It is also called the city of date palms, for dates are the last of the seven species of the land of Israel; that is, they looked towards the ultimate end of all things (lit. 'the thing').

Clearly this passage, which discusses accessing *retzon Hashem* as the demarcating characteristic of the eschaton, belongs to the Wisdom of Solomon genre in *MHs*. What is fascinating about the passage, however, is the messianic tension it sets up between the people of Jericho and the sages.

The people of Jericho used to link the two words in the *shema'* prayer על
לבבך *'al levavekha* (on your heart), pronouncing the phrase as *'alevavekha'*;
this close linking indicates, according to Lainer, the messianic consciousness which will be achieved when Torah is *kavu'a balev*. This was their
way of expressing in liturgical code the idea that one can act לקרב הישועה
lekareiv hayeshu'ah to bring near (or, agitate for) redemption. Similarly,
in his concluding phrase, Lainer describes the people of Jericho as מביטים
לאחרית הדבר *mabitim le'aharit ha-davar* 'looking towards the ultimate end
of all things'. This is a clear indication of spiritualized messianic agitation
in the present. The sages, however, insist that the phrase *'al levavekha* be
pronounced as two distinct words when recited in prayer, in order to indicate that not only have we not reached the eschaton, but that it is wrong
to agitate for it; it will come when the divine will decides it is time, and we
humans should not be engaged in trying to draw it closer.

A close reading reveals clearly that Lainer identifies with the people of
Jericho and not with the sages. He repeats twice, in the introduction and
conclusion to the passage, that the people of Jericho are the people of *rei'ah*.
In fact, it is this very quality of *rei'ah* that moves them towards messianic agitation, because each one מריח מרחוק את הישוע *meiri'ah meirahok et
hayeshu'ah* 'smells the redemption from afar'. Furthermore, it is clear from
all the passages we have cited on *emet le'amito* and *morei'ah vada'in*, as well
as the passages we have cited thus far on *yarei'ah*, that the Judah archetype—in which Lainer clearly views himself as participating—is defined
in large part by its ability to be *meiri'ah*; that is to say, by its ability to access
the higher spiritual intuition of *retzon Hashem* which derives from its conscious knowledge of participating in divinity. Moreover, given the passages
we have seen, which indicate that Lainer blurs the boundaries between the
eschaton and the present, it seems fairly clear that Lainer views himself as
a man of Jericho.

Summary of Clusters 1 and 2

To briefly recapitulate: We have seen to this point that the two clusters forming the Solomon sources are woven from several strands of interlocking themes. Solomon reclaims sacred sparks of paganism; this is an expression of the *Shekhinah*-consciousness that Solomon seeks in the *nekeivot*, the females, of the Goddess cultures. This is the same *Shekhinah* project which manifests itself in Solomon's marriage to the pagan daughters of the king. It is also the essence of Solomon's *mikdash* project. In a very profound sense, these projects are both part of the same overarching metaphysic which seeks the unmediated embrace of *Shekhinah*. It is the very same sense of *yarei'ah* (moon)-consciousness that drives Solomon to move beyond the *kelalim* to access *retzon Hashem*. Solomon is unsatisfied with *emet*; he seeks *emet le'amito*, the deeper truth. He is able to access this deeper truth because he has actualized his divine self, integrating not only the divinity of occasional peak moments of clarity in the way of the priest and the prophet, but rather integrating his divinity into the very fabric of his entire being, even on the level of subconscious and nonintentional behavior. He is the king whose *divrei hulin* (mundane words) are in and of themselves considered *retzon Hashem*. All of his words are the word of God. This is the essential expression of the major Izbica theme of acosmic humanism.

The following various strands of the Solomon genre are all essentially the same quality: the redemption of the sacred sparks of paganism, the ontic identity of names inherent to acosmic humanism, and the ability to access unmediated *retzon Hashem*—not only for oneself, but for the sake of judging others beyond the *kelalim* in accordance with *retzon Hashem*, which according to Lainer is rooted in Solomon's god-like ability to incorporate within himself *kol nafshot Yisra'el*. These strands are woven together by the themes of the *bat melekh* and of *rei'ah*, and they express the fulfillment of the yearning for the unmediated embrace of the *Shekhinah*, which lies at the very core of the Wisdom of Solomon genre.

This consciousness is expressed by the *Zohar* as *sihara bisheleimuta*, 'the moon in her fullness', which is cited by Lainer in his explanation of the uniqueness of Solomon's wisdom, which is *da'at kedoshim*.

According to Lainer, the major goal of the religious consciousness is to realize the Judah archetype—symbolized by Solomon in the pre-eschaton reality—through the process of *berur*. It is possible for every person to realize their Judah nature, that is to say, their divine nature. This nature is the fullest expression of the radical uniqueness of every person's divine imprint; each person has the ability to manifest this in the world not through the *kelalim* of Torah but through the *peratim*, which are refracted through their *perat nefesh Yisrael*, which is able to access the *retzon Hashem* addressed specifically to them.

This is the deep intent of the Torah of the name. A person's name is actually the unique manifestation of their *Shekhinah* identity. When a person accesses their unique name, the boundaries between the divine name and the human name—as we have demonstrated—begin to blur. This is precisely the meaning of acosmic humanism. This is accomplished through an activist posture of *'avodah*, which effects *berur. Berur*, for Lainer, is an expansion of consciousness accomplished though a process of ethical, psychological, and ritual cleansing, resulting in all of a person's actions being *nikra' 'al shemo*, called by his name—which for Lainer is essentially the same as the name of God.

A particularly powerful idea of overwhelming ethical import that emerges from these passages is found in the *emet le'amito*/cane of Rava references. In fact, the Talmudic case of Rava's cane, which we explained above,[71] is the example of higher judgment which comes from a place of *rei'ah, Shekhinah*, and eros. It is striking in *MHs* that the full power of what may be called Goddess-consciousness is directed not towards sensual or ecstatic goals but rather towards being able to judge a case according to its deep truth and not superficially, that is, in order to decide a claim according to the highest ethical standard, which cannot be embodied merely by the letter of the law. It is here that eros and ethics merge in Lainer. All of the power of the pagan goddesses is integrated into the holy in order to deepen ethics.

Notes for Section Two

1 Scholem, 'Shekhina', 192–193.

2 Although we will not gather the *mikdash* sources in a separate section, we ask the reader to note them here and in volume 1. In addition to Chapter Eight, see also the sections 'Three: Shadows of Union and Activism' (Chapter 7) and 'The Paradox of Human Activism: Levels of Consciousness' (Chapter 9) in volume 1.

3 The term 'Goddess' was employed by Raphael Patai to refer to yearning for the *shekhinah* within Hebrew religion in his classic work *The Hebrew Goddess* (see esp. 23–33). More recently, it has been used by Idel to describe the erotic relation to divinity in Jewish mysticism (*Absorbing Perfections* 29). See also Ezrahi and Gafni, *Mi*.

4 See 1 Kings 11:1–11 and classical commentary *ad loc.*

5 See Ginzberg, *Legends* vol. 4, the section on Solomon, 280 nn. 12–18. The rabbinic literature does not have a uniform view of Solomon.

The *Zohar*, which we explore further in the next volume, suggests in several passages a spiritual rationale for Solomon's sin, but nonetheless regards his actions as sinful and deems Solomon's rationale to be wrong. All the Zoharic ambivalence in regard to Solomon disappears in Lainer, who dramatically endorses Solomon's taking of many wives as an expression of Solomon's *shekhinah* project, as we will explain below.

6 The classic example of this is *bShabbat* 56b, where the Talmud suggests that it is a great mistake to suggest that Solomon sinned. According to the Talmud, he flirted with sin: he did not reproach his wives for their idolatrous practices, and he listened patiently and voiced no objection when the daughter of Pharaoh danced a thousand idolatrous dances before him, each one being a different ritual dance in pagan ritual. Yet Solomon himself did not sin.

7 In one source, Lainer bases the distinction between Moses and Solomon on this issue: Moses has the *hokhmah* to understand this wisdom but not to impart it. In contrast, Solomon wanted to teach 'before the eyes of everyone'. See the end of *MHs vol. 1* Hukat s.v. *zot hukat*. A different view of Moses is found in *MHs vol. 1* Shoftim s.v. *shoftim* 2 (Source 6 below). For other sources indicating that this was not merely a theory of Solomon's but an activist project, see *MHs vol. 1* Likutim Shabbat (Perek Bameh Madlikin) s.v. *'ad dekalya riglei detarmoda'ei* and *vol. 2* Likutim s.v. *shama'ti*.

8 This contrasts with a more traditional interpretation that the dispersion allows Israel to collect proselytes, as the Talmud would have it (*bPesahim* 87b).

9 Cf. *MHs vol.1*, Melakhim 1 s.v. *veha-melekh* (Source 2 above)

10 The compelling validity of this interpretation will become clear in the context of the idolatry passages in *MHs* (Cluster 5, below).

11 See the discussion of the *Bahir shekhinah* sources in Scholem, 'Shekhina' 162–170.

12 R. Nahman's works were already part of the Hasidic canon in Lainer's time. On this story, see for example Steinsaltz, *Beggars and Prayers* 9–16, or Aryeh Kaplan,

Rabbi Nachman's Stories (31– 54). On the almost immediate canonization of some Hasidic books, particularly R. Nahman's, see Idel, *Absorbing Perfections*, 471–475.

13 See Langdon, *Tammuz* for a presentation of the texts and rituals concerned with the Akkadian goddess Ishtar and her antecedents in Sumer.

14 On the relation between the *shekhinah* and the Canaanite goddesses of *Asheirah* and Astarte, see Patai, *The Hebrew Goddess*, 35–66.

15 This will become clearer below in our discussion of other passages.

16 1 Kings 11:5.

17 See Patai, *The Hebrew Goddess* (41) who claims that this was not Astarte but her mother *Asheirah*.

18 See Chapter Three in volume 1.

19 As we pointed out in volume 1, the term *divrei Torah* includes far more than the study of Torah text; it indicates spiritual service in the broadest sense. See volume 1, 'Unique Mitzvah and Unique Torah' (Chap. 2) and 'The Way of Teshukah' (Chap. 11).

20 *MHs vol. 1* Hayyei Sarah s.v. *veAvraham* and Gilyon Hayyei Sarah s.v. *veAvraham*. According to Lainer's interpretation of the Talmud there, even after Solomon lost his kingship and everything else, he retained his 'ko'ah of life', which according to Lainer represents his *teshukah*, explained as the desire to grow, to always attain more.

21 *MHs vol. 1* Hayyei Sarah s.v. *veAvraham* and Gilyon Hayyei Sarah s.v. *veAvraham*.

22 For a discussion of sinning for the sake of God in *MHs* and in the work of his student Tzadok Hakohen, see Gellman, *The Fear* 45–71. Brill also examines this idea specifically with respect to precedents for Lainer's thought, *Thinking* 138-146. His reading of this theme (146-168) in *MHs* minimalizes what for us is a far more substantial and radical motif. See volume 3, Source 15 (endnote 1736).

23 The classic—but not the only—Zoharic model for *zivug* with the *shekhinah* is, of course, Moses, who is called *ish ha-Elohim*, 'the man of God' (based on Psalm 90:1), with the sense that he is the husband or lover of the *shekhinah/Elohim*. For a discussion of this strand in *Zohar*, see, for example, Wolfson, *Through* 336–338, and Liebes, 'Hamashiah' 185, 205–207.

24 See *MHs vol. 1* Kings s.v. *veha-melekh* (Source 2).

25 In this and other passages, Lainer uses the term *heshek* for passion. Elsewhere he uses the term *teshukah*.

26 See our discussion of Tzadok in volume 3 (Source 53 and 57).

27 E.g., Source 7 in volume 3.

28 *Elohei maseikhah* is generally translated as 'molten', but in several passages Lainer uses the term *maseikhah* to refer to what is fixed and stultified, a meaning which is better reflected in the term 'molded'.

29 The printed text cites 1 Kings 1:27, which also includes this phrase, but given the reference to Pharaoh's daughter's house, this must be the verse that was intended.

30 Often in *MHs*, a radical claim made only at the end of a passage turns around everything that was stated until then.

31 *MHs vol. 1* Kings s.v. *veha-melekh* (Source 2), and in the section on Source 3.

32 We see here the implicit manifestation of messianic consciousness in successful *berur*, which brings the future eschaton into the present. See volume 1, esp. the section 'Hisaron Meyuhad'.

33 This position is somewhat modified elsewhere in *MHs*. In *MHs vol. 1* Shoftim s.v. *ki teitztei*, Lainer implies in regard to Solomon's marriage to Pharaoh's daughter that Solomon was not purified in regard to *lo tin'af* (the commandment against adultery), unlike Jeroboam, who was from the tribe of Joseph. Lainer's suggestion is not that Solomon committed adultery, but rather that he was not *mevurar* with regard to the feminine.

34 For the ontological intertwining of *mikdash* and Solomon, see *MHs vol. 1* Likutim Menahot s.v. *amru lei*, where Solomon is the paradigm of one who engages in a *mitzvah* that is *la'ad* 'forever', which in *MHs* is a *terminus technicus* for ontological reality. That which is *la'ad* is not an epistemological illusion but ontological reality.

35 See Source 10 and 11 below.

36 See the commentaries to *bYoma* 26a.

37 See the parallel passage *MHs vol. 1* Devarim s.v. *havu*, where Lainer describes the non-Judah method of judgment (i.e., that which is employed by the standard court system) as *kelalim*, in contradistinction to Moses, who is described as following the *perat*, the unique divine revelation that goes beyond the *kelal*.

38 This was drawn to my attention by David Seidenberg (personal communication, 2008).

39 This is roughly parallel with what is termed second-tier consciousness in the field of spiral dynamics, developed by sociologist Clare Graves and expanded upon by his student Don Beck. A core characteristic of second-tier consciousness is its ability to hold many perspectives simultaneously, while still being able to render clear judgments, or take decisive action. For an accessible overview of spiral dynamics, see Wilber, *Boomeritis* 22–39.

40 *MHs vol. 1* Shoftim s.v. *titein lekha* and Rosh Hashanah s.v. *shanim atah*

41 The case is as follows: A man owes a second man a sum of money, which has hidden inside his cane. He will be cleared of all financial obligations if he swears in court that he does not owe the claimant any money. He hands the claimant his cane while he is taking his oath, and says, 'all the money that I owe you is already in your hands'. Technically the oath is true: all of the money owed to the claimant is indeed in his hands. Rava senses that while all is technically correct, the deeper truth is being lost. The cane breaks open, the money spills out, and justice (*emet le'amito*) is done.

42 See *MHs vol. 1* Shoftim s.v. *titen lekha*, where *emet le'amito* refers directly to the will of God: אצל השי"י יש עומק עמוק יותר מהבנתו כמו דאיתא בגמ' הדן דין אמת לאמיתו 'God has a depth beyond the depth of human grasp, as it says in the Talmud: One who judges *emet le'amito*—according to the truth of the truth (*bShab.* 10a)'.

43 Regarding this level of individuated consciousness, see the parallel passage to Source 6, *MHs vol. 1* Devarim s.v. *havu*. See the final sections of Chapter Four in

volume 1.

44 See the discussion of *peratei nefashot* and *peratei divrei Torah* in Part One of volume 1.

45 See 'Summary of Clusters 1 and 2' below.

46 *ad* Deut. 1:13.

47 See *MHs vol. 2* Megilah 12b s.v. *bise'udato* and *MHs vol. 1* Likutim Megilah 12b s.v. *veha-karov* (Source 20), where Lainer reads *levushim* as the externalities that block the unmediated embrace of *shekhinah*—in those passages, personified by Vashti.

48 This is because Lainer views these judges, like the prophets described in the Behaalotekha passage, as trapped in their *peratei nefashot*. As we saw, this is a lower level of individuality than the Judah archetype in the sense of ego or persona, which prevents the person from attaining the unity consciousness necessary to apprehend the unique *retzon Hashem*.

49 The tension between Moses and Solomon and, particularly, the desire of Solomon to be like Moses, is a theme that appears already in rabbinic sources. See, for example, *bShabbat* 21a: 'Solomon desired to be like Moses'. Rabbinic sources also suggest that Moses desired to be connected to the energy of the Solomon archetype. See Ginzberg, *Legends*, sections on Moses and Solomon.

50 The kingship model is found in earlier Hasidism as well. See Green, 'Typologies' 127–156, esp. 142–146, where Green discusses 'The Tzadik as King'.

51 See volume 3. The interpretation of Solomon as a divine figure is found as metaphor already in rabbinic sources (Sources 4 and 5 in vol. 3). However, the blurring of the line between Solomon's divinity and humanity is expressed fully in the Zoharic view of Solomon (e.g. Source 12 in volume 3).

52 See Chapter Twelve in volume 1.

53 *MHs vol. 1* Likutim Sanhedrin 104b s.v. *amar Rav Yehudah*.

54 I taught this passage for many years before realizing the significance of the *emet le'amito* reference, which is easy to miss. In an informal survey of friends who comprise most of the serious *MHs* teachers in Israel, I found that none of us had noted the reference and indeed no one was aware of the major *emet le'amito* theme in *MHs*. This is not insignificant. I have found that both the non-academic teachers and the academic scholars of Izbica focus on the obviously provocative themes and on a very narrow range of passages where these themes are raised. However, in re-reading *MHs* in preparation for writing this work, the painstaking process of collecting all the references in the lesser-known passages revealed a far clearer picture of Lainer's theology and allowed less obvious themes to come to the foreground.

55 See endnote 1423.

56 *MHs vol. 1* Yoma s.v. *lo ati*; *vol. 2* Behaalotekha s.v. *im yihyeh* (Source 5); Devarim s.v. *havu* (Source 6).

57 *MHs vol. 2* Behaalotekha s.v. *im yihyeh* (Source 5).

58 See e.g. *Zohar* 1:181a–b; 1:199a; 3:181b; 3:248b.

59 See Source 24.

60 See Eliade, *Patterns* 157–187; also Eliade, 'The Moon'; Lewy, 'The Late'; Pritchard, *Ancient*; Stone, *When*; Neuman, *The Great*; Campbell, *The Masks*; Bachofen, *Myth* (while Bachofen and Stone's theories of matriarchy are dated, the material is still useful).

61 Here Lainer interprets the verse as a general reference to standard knowledge, with *binah* almost a synonym for *hokhmah* and *da'at*. This *binah* is not to be confused with *binat ha-lev*. *Binat ha-lev*, a *terminus technicus* in *MHs*, becomes *kavu'a* in a person; it allows a person to access *retzon Hashem*, which is far beyond knowledge accessible through the standard forms of cognition and the classical *kelalim* of Torah. What *MHs* usually refers to as *binat ha-lev* is called in this passage *da'at kedoshim*.

62 That is, according to the traditional view that Solomon wrote Proverbs.

63 See Source 22 there.

64 See esp. Chapter 9, 'Called by the Name, Ontology, Uniqueness, and Unique Will', and the end Chapter 11, 'The Way of Teshukah' in volume 1, where these parts of the passage are quoted.

65 *MHs vol. 1* Devarim s.v. *ahad 'asar*.

66 *MHs vol. 2* Va'eira s.v. *vayikah* (see below Sources 15 and 40).

67 See the introduction to volume 1, 'Messianic Self-Understanding'.

68 *MHs vol. 2* Behaalotekha s.v. *im yihiyeh* (Source 5).

69 Source 27 in volume 3.

70 *MHs vol. 1* Va'et'hanan s.v. *vehayu*. As we saw earlier, the quality of *emet le'amito* emerges directly from *rei'ah*. The spiritual faculty of *rei'ah* is fostered by Torah which is *kavu'a balev*. The quality of Torah being *kavu'a balev* is understood by Lainer as the defining characteristic of Solomon.

71 Sources 5 and 7, and endnote 1423.

Section Three

ADDITIONAL SOURCES

Cluster 3: The David Sources

Source 14: *MHs vol. 2 Re'eh s.v. va'akhaltem*

David is in many ways a figure virtually identical to Solomon in manifesting the Judah archetype. In fact, in some *MHs* texts, Solomon and David are actually interchanged; for example, a verse that in one passage that is said to refer to David is in the parallel text said to refer to Solomon.[1] Like Solomon, David is described as a great lover of the feminine and the *mikdash*. In one source, these two loves of David are, as in the case of his son, explicitly linked.

The basis of this comment is a comparison between a verse describing the pilgrimage to Shilo, where there is only a general reference to 'you and all your house' (Deut. 12:7), and another verse describing the Jerusalem pilgrimage, where 'your servant and maidservants' (Deut. 12:12)[2] is added. According to Lainer, this addition indicates that King David, through his פעולות *pe'ulot*, that is, his intentional spiritual activism, was able to clarify and purify גשמיות וגופים מגושמים *gashmiyut vegufim megushamim* 'materiality and the physical body', which is represented by the maidservants, and thereby reveal the קדושה נפלאה *kedushah nifla'ah* 'wondrous holiness' in them.

This, says Lainer, is the meaning of what David says to Michal when she greets him with great sarcasm as he returns from ecstatic dancing while accompanying the Ark back to Jerusalem. The story is shot through with sexual undertones. In his dancing, David is exposed: 'You have been revealed before the *amhot*' says Michal to David, which in the simple sense of the text suggests a tone of disgust and anger. David replies:

ועם האמהות אשר אמרת עמם אכבדה היינו שזה הוא הכבוד וההתפארות
שלי שנכתב עלי בתורה ואמהתיכם שזה היא הנקודה שלי

'[T]hrough those very *amhot* which you spoke of, through them I will be honored' (2 Sam. 6:21)—meaning, 'this is my (i.e., David's) glory and beauty, about which it is written in the

53

Torah, "[You shall rejoice before the Lord your God]....with your maidservant", for this is my very essence.'

Both the Deuteronomy verse being interpreted and the Michal story are about the Temple, the former referring to the pilgrimage to the Jerusalem Temple, and the latter revolving around the consecration of the ark when it was first brought by David to Jerusalem. David says that his honor is related to the *amhot*, which in this story is directly connected to bringing the ark into the *mikdash*. Finally, David is committed to revealing the *kedushah nifla'ah*—a highly unusual and therefore striking phrase for Lainer—in those very *Shekhinah* figures, the *amhot*.[3]

Source 15: *MHs vol. 2 Va'eira s.v. vayikah*

Like Solomon his son (or vice versa), David is able to move beyond *kelalei divrei Torah* and access the unmediated will of God. The text we will discuss now, which we mentioned above in our discussion of Source 12, interprets the well-known verse אור זרוע לצדיק ולישרי לב שמחה 'Light is sown for the *tzadik* righteous one, and for *yishrei lev*, those straight of heart, there is joy' (Psalms 97:11). The righteous are those who follow the general principles of Torah, but the higher level of service is those who are 'straight of heart', i.e., according to Lainer, those that look to the immanent will of God.[4] This verse is taken by Lainer to mean that although both David and Judah appear to sin, that is only a superficial reading (*gavan*), for anyone who says that David sins does not realize the deeper truth that 'his heart is drawn נמשך *nimshakh* after God', which, as we have noted in volume 1, is the essential formulation of the Judah archetype.

At the end of this passage,[5] Lainer touches on another essential theme of the Judah archetype, that of name, which, as we have seen, is often an allusion to acosmic humanism.

חלק אהרן בעוה"ז הוא שלימות בכל מעשה ומעשה שלא יסור מכללי דברי
תורה...ולפי שהשי"ת רצה להטעימו מחלק דוד המלך שנקרא ולישרי לב
שמחה, לכן היה זיווגו לשבט יהודה...אבל באלעזר כתיב לקח לו מבנות
פוטיאל לפי שלא היה זיווגו לבנות פוטיאל מיופה כל כך על הגוון כדאיתא
במדרש (תנחומא פנחם)...ועל זה כתיב (משלי יח) מגדל עז שם ה' בו
ירוץ צדיק ונשגב. מי שחוסה ובא בשם ה' יש לו מגדל עז אפילו שעושה
מעשה שאינו מיופה על הגוון שנדמה שעושה במרוצה מכל מקום יש
לו תקופות ומגדל עז כיון שהוא שם ה'. אף שבו ירוץ, מכל מקום מכוון

54

לעומק רצון השי"ת, כיון שאינו עושה רק מה שהוא רצון השי"ת, וזה ונשגב
שהמעשה הזה הוא למעלה מהשגת תפיסת האדם בעוה"ז

The *helek* (vocation) of Aaron in this world is wholeness in
every single action, that he should not stray from the principles of Torah... And since God wanted him to taste the
helek portion of David, which is called *uleyishrei lev simhah*
'and for the straight of heart there is joy', therefore his marriage was to [Elisheva from] the tribe of Judah... However,
regarding Elazar (Aaron's son) to the daughters of Putiel,
his mate was not seemly on the surface (i.e., it seemed to be
a sin)... About this it is written, 'The name of the Lord is a
migdal 'oz, a tower of strength; the righteous person *bo yarutz*
runs into it and is lifted up' (Prov. 18:10). One who flees and
comes in (i.e., 'into') God's name has *migdal oz* 'a tower of
strength'—even when he does something that is not right on
the surface, something which he does *bimerutzah* in haste. He
nevertheless has *tekufot* sacred audacity and *migdal 'oz*, since
he is *shem Hashem* the name of God. Thus even as 'he runs
into [the name]' (i.e. merges with it), he nevertheless intends
the depth of God's will, since he does nothing except what is
God's will. And this is the meaning of *venisgav* 'and is lifted
up'—that this action is beyond the reach of a person's grasp in
this world.

Elazar, the product of the tribe of Levi and the tribe of Judah, embodies in
this moment of his story the Judah archetype, 'for he is the name of God'.
Here, as we have seen in volume 1, the David archetype is intimately connected with and merges with the name of God, which is the *Shekhinah*-
consciousness of the Wisdom of Solomon.

David's ability to access *retzon Hashem* beyond the *kelalim* is intimately
connected to the *Shekhinah*. Similarly, the key notion of radical individualism within the David sources, as with the Solomon sources, is directly tied
to *Shekhinah*-consciousness. The hidden genre of the Wisdom of Solomon
is the matrix for both the David and Solomon text clusters as well as for
two key notions in the religious theology of Lainer: radical individualism
and unmediated access to *retzon Hashem*, and their ontological grounding
in acosmic humanism.

All of these themes crystallize in a set of four interlocking passages unnoted by previous scholarship. These passages are both part of the David cluster and at the same time form a cluster of their own. These texts will clarify a notion that we began to see in adducing some of these passages in our discussion of activism in Chapter Nine; that is, Lainer's suggestion that the statement 'All is in the hands of heaven, even the fear of heaven'—ostensibly, an extremely theocentric passage—actually means that 'the hands of heaven' are the 'hands of man', in a state of post-*berur* consciousness.

The Two Hands Sub-Cluster

The following texts, which we term the Two Hands (שתי ידים *shetei yadayim*) passages, were analyzed in volume 1 under the heading 'All is in the Hands of Heaven: A Humanist Agenda'. They all revolve around the distinction, based on biblical verses, between that which is described as being the result of one hand of God, and that which is described as being the result of two hands of God.

Source 16: *MHs vol. 2* Tehilim s.v. *yadekha 'asuni*

ידיך עשוני ויכוננוני הבינני ואלמדה מצותיך...בצדיקים איתא בגמ'
(כתובות ה.) גדולים מעשי צדיקים יותר ממעשה שמים וארץ, דאלו בשמים
וארץ כתיב (ישעיה מח) אף ידי יסדה ארץ וימיני טפחה שמים, ואלו
במעשה צדיקים כתיב (שמות טו) מקדש ה' כוננו ידיך בשתי ידים

> 'Your hands made me and fashioned *vikhonenuni* (estab-
> lished) me. Make me understand and I will learn Your com-
> mandments' (Psalms 119:73)...[C]oncerning the righteous,
> [it says] in the Talmud (*bKetubot* 5a): 'The work of the righ-
> teous is greater than the creation of heaven and earth. For
> regarding heaven and earth it is written, *yadi yasdah aretz*
> 'Even My hand founded the earth, and the heavens were
> spanned by My right hand' (Isa. 48:13), while regarding the
> work of the righteous it is written, *mikdash Hashem (sic) kona-
> nu yadekha*, 'Your hands established the sanctuary of God'
> (Exod. 15:17)—'with two hands'.

As we analyzed in volume 1, the plural 'hands' indicates two hands and hence a more evolved level of spiritual consciousness.[6] Here, we emphasize that the paradigmatic expression of *ma'aseh tzadikim* is the building of the sanctuary or Temple.[7] In relation to *ma'aseh tzadikim*, which 'Your hands established', David says, 'Your hands have made me and established me', since David is identified with the hands of God. David transcends *yir'ah*, the quality of the heavens; he is born naturally into *ahavah*.[8]

All of this is linked by Lainer back to the *Shekhinah* sources. The love that expresses itself in David's feeling of being fashioned by the two hands of God is David's participation in the *Shekhinah*, symbolized by the moon, as explained in the continuation of our passage:

וזה שאמר דוד המלך ע"ה ידיך עשוני היינו שמתאחד בשורשו למעשה צדיקים וכמו שנקרא על שם הירח שלית ליה מגרמיה כלום, ולכן התפלל הבינני ואלמדה מצוותיך, יען שמחצבו הוא ממקום גבוה יותר ממעשה שמים וארץ לכן לא יבוא לו יראה בהביטו לשמים לכן ביקש הבינני בדברי תורה ומדברי תורה יתבונן לירא את ה' וזה ואלמדה מצוותיך

And this is what King David said: 'Your hands made me'—he meant that at his very root, he is united with the work of the righteous. Similarly, he is called by the name of *ha-yarei'ah* 'the moon', for *leit leih megarmeih klum* he has nothing at all (i.e., no light) for himself. He therefore prayed, 'Make me understand and I will learn Your commandments', since he is hewn from a place more lofty than the creation of heaven and earth. Consequently, no fear comes to him when he looks to the heavens (i.e., he has no 'fear of heaven'), therefore he sought [that God would] 'make me understand' the words of Torah and through the words of Torah he would understand to fear *Hashem*, and this is [the meaning of] 'and I will learn your commands'.

The *Shekhinah* symbolism and the two hands motif are thoroughly intertwined here. David, born in love, participates in *Shekhinah*-consciousness. He is of God's hands. He is not motivated or connected to *yir'ah*, because his soul comes from a higher place. Unlike the earth and the sky, David's soul allows him to transcend his sense of separateness from the divine.

Source 17: *MHs vol. 1* Likutim s.v. *Hashem YKVK* and s.v. *ule'atid*

This theme plays itself out in one long but essential passage which Gershom Henokh chose as one of the closing texts of *MHs*, perhaps because it reveals much of the hidden Torah of Solomon that the Lainer is flirting with throughout the book.

השם י״ק״ר״ק, האות יו״ד הוא הנקודה הנאצלת מהמאציל ב״ה וב״ש.
הנקודה הזו הוא אות יו״ד, אח״כ התפשט הנקודה הזו עד שנתהוית בלב
האדם לרצון ולחשק הוא האות ה׳, אח״כ נמשך בזה יראה בלב האדם שלא
יהי׳ הרצון והחשק הלב נוטה מן רצון הש״י זהו אות וא״ו, וזה בא לישועה
שמאיר לו הש״י שהרצון והחשק הלז מציאותו מאתו ית״ש ושהוא מכוון
לרצון הש״י עד המעשה זהו אות ה׳ האחרונה זהו השם של אהרן הכהן

> The name *YHVH:* the letter *yod* is the point emanating
> from the Emanator, blessed be He and blessed be His name.
> This point is the letter *yod.* This point then expanded until it
> became desire and passion in the heart of man, which is signi-
> fied by the letter *heh.* Fear was then drawn into the heart of
> man, so that desire and passion of the heart would not stray
> away from God's will—this is signified by the letter *vav,* from
> which he comes to salvation. God shows him that the essence
> of his desire and passion are from Him, may He be blessed,
> and that his intention is aligned with God's will, even [his]
> action—this is signified by the last *heh.* This is the name of
> Aaron the Priest.[9]

The passage is divided into two sections. The first section focuses on David
and the Divine name he represents, and is replete with hints and implications of acosmic humanism. The second section brings this idea back to
the Two Hands theme.

Lainer begins by explaining how the Tetragrammaton represents the
unfolding of divinity in human action. The first *yod* is the source or the
point of the action in the process of emanation. This point expands to the
first *heh,* generally understood by the kabbalists to be the higher mother
binah; in this stage, the initial point expands until it becomes a *ratzon* and a
heshek in the heart of a person. Here already, some of the essence of Lainer's
thought is revealed. Both *ratzon* and *teshukah* are ontologically affirmed
and embraced by Lainer as the unfolding of divinity within the human
heart. At this juncture, the stage of *vav, yir'ah* is introduced into the heart,
to ensure that the *ratzon* accurately expresses the *retzon Hashem* without
deviation. Finally, we reach the fourth letter, which is the fourth stage. This
stage is the source of redemption, the lower *heh,* virtually always identified by the kabbalists as the lower mother, *Malkhut* or *Shekhinah.* This is
of course the same quality of *yarei'ah,* with which Lainer identifies David
in the previous passage. David is *yarei'ah,* 'as he has nothing on his own

account'. In this fourth stage, God enlightens David with the conscious-ness that the *ratzon* and *teshukah* are indeed from the divine source and that he is *mekavein*, aligned with, *retzon Hashem*, thus the action which he will perform will necessarily express the will of God.

King David, however, manifests a unique צירוף *tzeiruf* (permutation) of the divine name. The name of David is unique in that, at every moment of emanation of the first point, (the *yod*), before its expansion to *ratzon* and *teshukah*, a higher *yir'ah* is drawn down. This *yir'ah* ensures that only the pure *ratzon* of *Hashem* will unfold.

Our passage continues:

ושל דוד המלך תיכף בהרגש נקודה הנאצלת טרם התפשטותה לרצון וחשק
בלב נמשך לו יראה עילאה שלא יתפשט חלילה הנקודה הזו בשום צד נטיה
מרצון הש"י וזהו אות וא"ו אחר אות יו"ד

And [this is also the name] of King David, [meaning] as soon as he felt the emanated point, before its expansion into desire and passion in the heart, *yir'ah* higher awe was drawn to him, so that this point would not expand, heaven forfend, to any side that would incline away from God's will—this is signified by the letter *vav* following the letter *yod*.

The *vav* and the *heh* switch positions, which indicates that everything that the David archetype does is *retzon Hashem*. This expresses the same idea we have seen many times in reference to David. Up to this point in our text we have explained the first two letters of the unique David permutation of the divine name, *yod* and then *vav*. Two *heh* letters remain.

The text continues:

ואח"ז כשבא לו תוקף מרצון הש"י בלבו היינו אות ה' אחרונה תיכף סמוך
לבו לא ירא עוד רק נכון לבו בטוח שחשקו ורצונו אינו נוטה מרצון הש"י
רק זה הוא רצון הש"י, ולכן הציירף בו שני ההין ביחד וגם ה' אחרונה תהי'
אז בראשונה כי ה' אחרונה היא מצד תפיסת האדם כשיכוון בשלימות
לרצון הש"י

Afterwards, when empowerment came to [King David] from the will of God within his heart, signified by the last *heh* [of

60

the divine name], he immediately relied on his heart; he was no longer afraid. His heart was steadfast, certain that his desire and his will could not stray from God's will, for exactly this <u>was</u> God's will. Thus in this combination [of the letters of the divine name] the two *hehs* are together, and the latter *heh* is even first; for the latter *heh* comes from the side of the human perspective *mitzad tefisat ha-adam*, when a person wholly intends [to embody] the divine will.

The last letter *heh*, that is to say *Malkhut* or *Shekhinah*, is called in this text the experience of *tokef*, i.e., what Lainer usually calls *tekufot*.[10] The person described in this passage thus acts with complete certainty that he or she is manifesting and incarnating *retzon Hashem*. Then Lainer takes a subtle but critical step in which the two *heh* letters collapse into each other.

What this means is implied in the text. The fourth *heh*, the *Shekhinah*, represents the perspective of the human being מצד האדם *mitzad ha-adam*.[11] This merges with the higher *heh*, which must be *mitzido*, that is, it represents God's perspective. In the David–Solomon–*retzon Hashem*–*yarei'ah* model, a person moves from *mitzad ha-adam* to *mitzido* by realizing his participation in divinity. This is, of course, strikingly similar to the model of Habad mysticism which views the movement from *mitzideinu* to *mitzido* as the essential goal of spiritual practice.[12] The difference, however, is that in Izbica this move radically empowers the human being. It affirms a person's dignity as fundamentally rooted in divinity, and says that they can trust their deepest intuitions both on the level of *ratzon* and *teshukah*. This is so true that a person who has accomplished *berur* can even trust themselves to go against normative law in the fulfillment of *retzon Hashem*—a conclusion that Schneur Zalman of Liadi would never have countenanced.

At this point Lainer dramatically concludes the first section of the passage. The conclusion sets the stage for the second section of the passage:

ועל ד״ה ע״ה יחתום הש״י תיכף את שמו על כל מעשיו קודם שיצא
להתפשטות, ולכן יהי׳ הצירוף לעתיד יו״ד וא״ו ה״א, והשם י״ק״ו״ק הוא
ברזא דארבע, ושלמה המלך עשה ספר משלי ברזא דארבע ארבע להרות כי
לא נעלם ממנו גם אור צירופי שם ה״ו״י״ בצירוף של אהרן הכהן

Regarding King David, of blessed memory, God will immediately seal His name on all his deeds before he moves

61

into expansiveness (i.e., moving from desire into action). Therefore, in the future the combination will be *YVH*. The name *YHVH* pertains to *raza de'arba* the mystery of the four. King Solomon created the Book of Proverbs according to the mystery of the four—four to show that the light of combining the name of [the letters] *HVY* was not hidden from him, as combined in the name of Aaron the priest.

Lainer states that all that has been said up to this point in the passage is what we mean when we say that 'God will immediately seal His name on all the deeds' of the David archetype. Nonetheless Lainer remembers, even in this ecstatic passage, the dialectical tension inherent in acosmic humanism and the need for the pendulum to swing back and forth between *mitzido* to *mitzideinu*, from the future to the present, from love to fear, and from a pre- to a post-*berur* state of consciousness. Thus he adds before his grand conclusion that the Tetragrammaton in its classical order *YHVH* is 'the mystery of four', and that Solomon—interchangeable with David in the archetype—wrote the Book of Proverbs 'according to the mystery of the four', for he was not unaware of the dialectic between Aaron and David, between *yir'ah* and *ahavah*, between *mitzido* and *mitzideinu*.

Now we turn to the second section of the passage:

ולעתיד ישלוט השם ע״פ צירוף השמות היוצאים מברכת כהנים היינו הכ״ב
אותיות של דהע״ה היינו בתחל׳ יק״ו״ק א״נ״ק״ת״ם היינו בעוד שלא זכה
האדם לבוא לשורשו וחלקו בד״ת הוא נואק בצעקה תמיד להש״י לעזרו
מן רצונות ומחשבות זרות המציקים לו ומנגדים ומבלבלים אותו להורידו
ממקומו

And in the future, God will rule according to the combination of the [divine] names that emerge from the priestly blessing—these are the 22 letters of King David, starting with *YHVH ANKTM*. This represents that as long as a person has not merited arriving at his root and portion in the Torah, he cries out with a constant call to God to save him from the desires and strange thoughts that disturb him and oppose and confuse him, lowering him from his place.

The *tzeiruf* in the eschaton לעתיד לבוא *le'atid lavo* will be that of David. This is the human incarnation of the divine name, which as we have seen, lies at the heart of Lainer's acosmic humanism.

Lainer continues the underlying theme of names, introducing a second major component of acosmic humanism, namely, radical individualism. Relating to the names of God that are based on the permutations of the letters of the biblical verses comprising the priestly blessing, Lainer suggests that one name refers to the period in a person's life before they have identified their unique *helek* (vocation), i.e., what we have termed 'soul print'.[13] The second name refers to the period in a person's life after they have identified their 'soul print'. The first name, *ANKTM*—which Lainer understands as corresponding to the Hebrew word צעקה *tza'akah* (shout or cry)—is, according to him, an existential cry of distress. It derives from the existential distress engendered by lack of participating in and living one's own story. This is a radically different kind of acosmism than, for example, the type discussed by Schatz[14] and Weiss[15] in early Hasidism, or Elior[16] in reference to Habad, where acosmism undermines the legitimacy and dignity of existential angst, and certainly leads to a rejection of angst of the radically self-centered nature that is described in this passage. Here again we have not merely acosmism but, unique to Lainer, acosmic humanism.

The passage continues:

> אח"כ כשזוכה לישועת הש"י ומתחיל לבוא למקום חפצו זהו פ"ס"ת"ם פס
> מורה על הרחבה כמו יהי פסת בד כו' שנרחב לו מהמציקים ואויביו נופלים
> תחתיו, אח"כ פ"ס"פ"ס"י"ם היינו שמשתדל להרחבת גבול לא מן המציקים
> לו, רק בשפע רב שמשפיע לו הש"י בשתי ידים וזהו פ"ס"פ"ס, אח"כ
> ד"י"נ"ס"י"ם היינו שזוכה להתנשאות בנשיאות ראש

> After that, when he merits God's salvation and begins to approach his desire, this is *PSTM. PS* indicates *harhavah* expansion, as if there were a piece (*pesat*) of linen that is stretched wide for him due to (or, beyond) disturbances, and his enemies fall under him (or, it). After that, there is *PSPSYM*, that is, he strives to expand boundaries, not because of [needing to overcome] those disturbances, but rather through *shefa' rav* the great effluence that God showers upon him with two hands—this is *PSPS*. After that [is] *DYNSYM*, meaning that he merits *hitnas'ut* exaltation, raising high [his] head.[17]

63

The second name affirms the humanistic nature of Lainer's acosmism. Divine redemption occurs when a person expands into the parameters of their story. God flows into the person with a great effluence. The phrase used to describe this stage is הרחבה *harhavah*, (expansion), which is a term that has clear associations for readers of *MHs*. We saw[18] that Lainer interprets the verse כי ירחיב ה' אלקיך את גבולך *ki yarhiv Hashem et gevulekha* 'When God will expand your boundaries' as referring to the no-boundary consciousness that one can attain when one realizes the acosmic nature of the universe. The term *harhavah* in *MHs* almost always refers to acosmism. It is therefore significant that Lainer uses this term to describe this unique stage of acosmic humanism, in which the expansion to no-boundary consciousness is paradoxically identical with the affirmation of individuality. In other words, realizing that in reality we are all part of the great quilt of the divine does not nullify the reality that we are each unique patches in the quilt. This is what it means, according to Lainer in the passage, to receive the 'two-handed' divine effluence.

This is precisely the phrase with which we opened our discussion of the Two Hands passages. In the *MHs* commentary on the passage in Psalms, Lainer stated that the two-handed effluence from God that David experienced was precisely his *yarei'ah* nature of having 'nothing of his own'. This is 'the great effluence that God showers upon him with two hands'. This 'two-handed' divine effluence gives a person נשיאות ראש *nesi'ut rosh*, the experience of being raised up, or exalted by God, a term that in *MHs* is covalent with radical individualism and uniqueness.[19] In Lainer's theology, unique individuality and absorption in the divine merge.

The continuation of the passage analyzes this concept of *hitnas'ut*:

והענין מדות התנשאות הוא באמת למעלה מן השכל האיך מדת הש״י ליתן התנשאות לצדיקים האיך מנשא שני צדיקים בדור אחד וכ״א זוכה שחלקו מתנשא על כל ראש ואין שני לו, והשני כמו כן מתנשא ואין שני לו כמו משה ואהרן שהי' כ״א מהם חד בדרא וזהו ד״י״נ״ס״י״ם היינו שנים שהש״י נותן להם נשיאות בעולם כאחד זהו בדרך נס

[The nature of] this quality of being raised up truly transcends reasoning: How does God's attribute grant exaltation to the righteous? How can two righteous people be exalted in one generation, [even though] each one merits that his portion be lifted up above all, and there is no one comparable

64

to him, while the other is also lifted up, and there is no one comparable to him, as with Moses and Aaron, for each one was unique in that generation...that is, [when] there are two whom God grants being exalted in the world as one, this is a kind of miracle.

The concept of *hitnas'ut*, which is extremely paradoxical, defines Lainer's system. Lainer emphasizes the apparent contradiction between his acosmism and the individuality that defines his humanism, saying in this passage that this reality is beyond human reason. He expresses this paradoxical nature by pointing out that two *tzadikim* righteous people can coexist in one generation. The *tzadik* is not nullified before God, but rather is so radically actualized that his name is merged with the name of God. Since radical uniqueness comes from its root in divinity, it can naturally embrace more than one person. Two people can each be 'the most unique'.[20]

Our passage concludes:

לזה על השני שמות שלחג הסכות והם א"נ"י ו"ה"ו הקשה התוי"וט שהשם
ו"ה"ו הוא ראשון בע"ב שמות והשם א"נ"י היא שם הל"ז שבע"ב שמות
ולמה מקדימין א"נ"י ל"ו"ה"ו, אך האמת הוא כי נמצא בע"ב שמות של
ו"ה"ו אחד הוא השם ראשון שמקשה עליו התוי"וט והשני הוא השם מ"ט
והראשון יוצא מפסוק ואתה ה' מגן בעדי כבודי ומרים ראשי, והשני יוצא
מפסוק גדול ה' ומהולל מאוד ולגדלתו אין חקר כמבואר בהאריז"ל, וזהו
השם ו"ה"ו שלחג הסכות הוא השם השני המאוחר לשם א"נ"י, וזהו השם
הראשון א"נ"י היא על התחלה שלא זכה לשרשו וחלקו ורצוניות ומחשבות
המתנגדים מציקים לו כנ"ל גבי שם א"נ"ק"ת"ם לזה הוא יוצא מפסוק ואתה
ה' מגן בעדי כו' שעזרו השי"י בהגנה שלא יזיקו לו המציקים האלה, אבל
השם השני ו"ה"ו הוא יוצא מפסוק גדול ה' ומהלל מאוד שזכה להתגלות
אור שפע השי"י לנגד עיניו והשי"י נותן לו התנשאות לזה הוא מאוחר

This is why the *Tosafot Yom Tov* asks about the two names of the Sukkot holiday, which are *ANY* and *VHV*: If the name *VHV* is the first of the 72 names, and the name *ANY* is the 37th of the 72 names, why does *ANY* precede *VHV*? However, the truth is that among the 72 names, there is a *VHV* which is the first about which the *Tosafot Yom Tov* asks, [while there is a] second [*VHV*] which is the 49th name. The first is derived from the verse, 'You, God, are my shield, my honor and You lift up my head' (Psalms 3:4),

65

while the second is derived from the verse, 'Great is the Lord and exceedingly praised, and there is no inquiry concerning His greatness' (Psalms 145:3), as explained by the Ari (Isaac Luria), of blessed memory. The *VHV* name, which relates to the Sukkot holiday, is the second name preceding the name *ANY*. The name *ANY* regards the beginning, when he has not yet arrived at his root and his portion, and the desires and the thoughts of those who oppose him confound him, as we previously mentioned concerning the name *ANKTM*. This is why [this name] derives from the verse, 'You, God, are my shield', [meaning] that God should help him and protect him, that these *matzikim* disturbing forces not cause him harm. However, the second name, *VHV*, is derived from the verse, 'Great is the Lord and exceedingly praised', for he has merited that the light of God's *shefaʿ* be revealed before his eyes, and God has lifted him up, which is why it comes afterwards…

Lainer reformulates the same idea he has already expressed, using different names of God. One of the 72 three-letter names[21] of God is *ANY*, a second is *VHV* and a third is *VHV* as well. The first *VHV* and the *ANY* names are parallel to the name *ANKTM* which began the passage and describes a person who had not identified their soul print—what Lainer terms *shorsho* and *helko* in this passage and throughout *MHs*.[22] Thus the verse that expressed these names is one of angst and anxiety. It is a prayer that God will help him overcome the מציקים *matzikim* (literally, the damagers), that is to say, the internal processes that prevent him from living his unique story. The verse representing the second *VHV*, the 49th of the three-letter names, which comes after *ANY* (which is the 37th), refers to the time after a person has identified and is living their *shoresh* and *helek*, and is thus expressed by an ecstatic verse. That ecstatic verse גדול ה' ומהולל מאד ולגדולתו אין חקר 'Great is the Lord and exceedingly praised', might itself be understood as an expression of Lainer's acosmic humanism. The verse, which is supposed to express a human being's embrace of their uniqueness, praises the infinite depth and grandeur of divinity, for indeed, one is rooted in the other. Lainer concludes: the revelation of personal uniqueness—*hitnas'ut*—is the great revelation of God to man.

This concludes the passage, which, as we have seen, revolves around the David–yareiʾah–Shekhinah–Two Hands cluster of terms. All of these terms, as we noted, are clearly part of the Wisdom of Solomon tradition in Izbica, expressions of both the Judah archetype and acosmic humanism.

There are two more key passages in the Two Hands sub-cluster of passages. Not surprisingly, one passage deals with the idea of name and acosmic humanism and the other deals with uniqueness and radical individualism. Both merit close reading.

Source 18: *MHs vol. 2* Ketubot s.v. *darash Bar Kapra*

The next passage begins:

דרש בר קפרא גדולים מעשה צדיקים יותר ממעשה שמים וארץ דאלו
במעשה שמים וארץ כתיב (ישעיה מ״ח,י״ג) אף ידי יסדה ארץ וימיני טפחה
שמים ואלו במעשה ידיהם של צדיקים כתיב (שמות ט״ו,י״ז) מכון לשבתך
פעלת ה' מקדש ה' כוננו ידיך. הענין בזה כי בריאת שמים וארץ היה כדי
שיכיר האדם שהשי״ת נמצא בעולם, ואם היה מפורש זאת בהתגלות, אין
שום מקום לפעולות אדם לכן הסתיר השי״ת זאת והלביש זאת בלבושים

Bar Kapra expounded: The deeds of the righteous are greater than the creation of heaven and earth, for concerning the creation of heaven and earth it is written, 'My hand founded the earth, and My right hand spanned the heavens' (Isa. 48:13). In comparison, concerning the deeds of the righteous it is written, 'You fashioned, O God, Your dwelling place, the sanctuary of God which was accomplished by Your hands' (Exod. 15:16). The point of this is that the creation of heaven and earth happened in order that a person would know that God is in the world, and were this clearly revealed, there would be no place for the work of man. God therefore concealed this, clothing it in garments.

In this passage, Lainer comments on the Talmudic text that distinguishes between one-handed and two-handed divine effluence.

This passage is especially interesting because one could easily misread it as a passage affirming the radically theocentric nature of Lainer's theology.[23] This reading denies the ontological reality of any kind of human activism in the world. According to this reading, the human experience that actions are real and do matter is a divine gift to humans, but it is ultimately an illusion. In the final analysis, the attribution of independent agency to the human being is based on an epistemological error.

A careful examination of the passage, however, reveals that it is another Two Hands passage and another strand in the fabric of Lainer's underlying theory of acosmic humanism. Lainer begins his interpretation of the Talmudic passage with the following premise: The purpose of creation was to make recognizable that God is *in the world*, that is, immanent. If this revelation were explicit, there would be no room for human activism, for their actions would be meaningless. Therefore God wraps the radical immanence of the divine in לבושים *levushim* garments. Up to this point, we would have the classical reading advocated by Weiss and others.

The passage continues:

ולכן נדמה שעולם כמנהגו נוהג ואינו נראה הכרת השי״ת מפורש, רק ע״י
מעשה המצות אז נתראה התגלות אור השי״ת בעולם, וכל זה הוא שהשי״ת
חפץ להצדיק בריותיו, לכן נתן מקום שע״י פעולות ישראל נתגלה זאת

> It therefore seems as if the world behaves in its customary fashion (i.e., according to the natural order), and the recognition of God is not shown explicitly. It is only through the work of the commandments that God's light is then shown in the world. All this is so because God desires *lehatzdik* to vindicate His creations. He therefore made room for this to be revealed through Israel's actions.

At this point in the passage, Lainer takes a step in precisely the opposite direction. He suggests that the way God accomplishes His goal of revealing His immanence in the world is by allowing His light to be revealed through human actions of man. It is not that human activism, i.e. the *mitzvot*, are not ontologically real. Quite the contrary: human activism is what makes the manifestation of divine immanence real. Thus, while prima facie 'the world looks like a natural order', independent of the divine, *ma'asei hamitzvot*—that is to say, human activism—reveals God's light.

Lainer has not said here that human action is an illusion. Moreover, his acosmism does not foster quietism; exactly the opposite is true. Human action has been unfolded by God as the manifestation of divinity in the world. Clearly, God could have chosen a different path. The reason God decided to reveal His divine immanence through human beings is because of a divine desire *lehatzdik* to vindicate, or 'make righteous', human beings. The illusion that needs to be dispelled in this passage is not the ontological significance of human action but the illusion that human beings are separate from God and that their actions are meaningless.

In Lainer's acosmism, human actions are ultimately meaningful, dignified, and powerful because they are the *levush* through which God expresses divinity in the world. Here Lainer would subscribe to Schneur Zalman of Liadi's formulation early in the *Tanya* that the garments of the king are like the king.[24] Moreover, passages in which Lainer expresses the desire to see past the garments[25] do not undermine the ontology of the garments; rather, they are distinguished in two ways. First, one can mistake the garments as being *separate* from God. Second, the garments can be used to express a desire for intimate connection to God, i.e., to encounter the *Shekhinah* without her *levushim*.

The text continues:

וכמו שמצינו בעת שנגמר בנין בית המקדש היה כל האומות מכירים
התגלות השי״ת בעולם וזה נקרא בשתי ידים היינו בשלימות הגמור

As we found at the time when the building of the Temple was completed: all the nations recognized the revelation of God in the world. This is what is called 'with two hands', meaning, in complete *sheleimut* perfection.

Lainer concludes that it is none other than the *mikdash*, the Temple in Jerusalem, fashioned by 'yadekha', that is, God's two hands, that symbolizes acosmic humanism. Once again the Temple is an essential part of the cluster of concepts and terms that form Solomon's wisdom of acosmic humanism. The entire set of ideas, as in the previous passages, is associated with God's 'two-handed' effluence.

Next, Lainer links Solomon directly to this level of realization.

ועל זה אמר שלמה המלך ע״ה (קהלת א) מה יתרון לאדם בכל עמלו
שיעמל תחת השמש, כי שמש נקרא בהירות היינו אור מפורש ותחת
השמש, היינו שנסתר אור הבהיר כדי שיהיה מקום לפעולות אדם, וכיון
שעיקר מעשיהם של צדיקים להאיר ולהוסיף על מעשה שמים וארץ
ולהראות מפורש שהשי״ת נמצא בכל העולמות, א״כ כיון שמעשיהם אינם
מבוררים בשלימות מה יתרון בכל עמלם, כיון שכל מעשיהם הוא להאיר
את ההעלם שנקרא תחת השמש ואם אין מעשיהם מבוררים בשלימות אם
כן מה יתרון בפעולתם

Concerning this, King Solomon said: 'What profit is there for a person from all the toil of his labor in which he would toil under the sun?' (Eccl. 1:3). The sun denotes brilliance, that is, explicit light, and *tahat hashemesh* 'under the sun' indicates that the brilliant light is concealed so that there will be room for man's actions. And since the main task of the righteous is to enlighten and expand upon the creation of heaven and earth, to show explicitly that God *nimtza'* exists (i.e., is immanent) in all worlds, then if their deeds are not completely *mevurarim* clarified, 'what profit is there from their toil?'— since all their deeds are for the sake of illuminating the hiddenness, which is called 'under the sun'. So if their deeds are not completely clarified, 'what profit is there' in their action?

This part of the passage confirms our interpretation. The topic of Solomon's verse is the ontology of human activism. In Lainer's reading, Solomon is saying that if human actions are *tahat hashemesh*, that is to say, if they are not clarified, then what value do they have? The word *berur* with respect to action has a precise meaning in Izbica: the clarification that human actions require is that they are a manifestation of divine will.[26]

Lainer then explains how this theology empowers the human being. First he states:

ונתבאר בחלק זה (קהלת) שזה הפסוק מאיר ג"כ תקופות לאדם, כיון שהשי"ת חותם על זה שבפעולתם יכוונו את עומק רצונו

...and it was explained in this volume (Eccl.) that this verse also shines (i.e., emanates) *tekufot* strength to a person, since God seals (affirms) that their actions will align with the depth of His will.

For Lainer, there is no contradiction between human freedom and divine will. God assents to all the details of human action and is present within them. Lainer does not resolve the antinomy between freedom and divine will philosophically, but rather with a parable.

אם כן בטח גם על הסדר הפעולות בפרטים גם כן יסכים השי"ת, כמשל המסדר עטרה למלך והיה מסופק אם כיון בסדרו לרצון המלך, ואח"כ עלה בדעתו גם על עצם האבנים טובות אולי אינם אבנים טובות, ואז לא פחד כלל כיון שהמלך יסכים על עצם האבנים טובות בטח יסכים על הסדר

70

שסדרם כעומק רצון המלך, ולכן העצה לזה שיקבע אותם כפי כוחו וחכמתו
ובטח המלך זה השי״ת יסכים על הכל

> If so, then God will certainly agree also to the order of specific
> actions as well, as in the parable of one who arranged a crown
> for the king and was not certain if his arrangement was in ac-
> cord with the king's desire. Afterwards it occurred to him that
> the precious gems might not, in fact, be precious gems. Then
> he was no longer afraid whatsoever, for if the king had agreed
> to the [value of] precious gems themselves, he would certainly
> agree to the order in which he arranged them, according to
> the depth of the king's will. Therefore, the lesson is that he
> should set them according to his ability and wisdom, and the
> king, that is, God, will surely agree to it all.

In the parable, Lainer makes a great leap when he suggests that divine will is
invested in human freedom. In the parable, the fine stones to which the king
has already agreed represent human activism. The person who is unsure if he
is doing the will of the king is able through reflection, that is, through *berur*, to
embrace his own will without fear, knowing that the king has already done so.

In this succinct parable, Lainer seeks to free the religious persona from the
constant fear and anxiety inherent in the uncertainty as to whether or not
the divine will has been fulfilled. The passage concludes:

כיון שכל עיקר הרצון בפעולת אדם גם כן הוא מחסדי השי״ת שחפץ...
שמעשה צדיקים יאירו הכרת השי״ת בכל העולמות, לכן בטח יסכים השי״ת
על כל פעולתם

> [God will surely agree to it all], since the entire essence of the
> desire *ratzon* [that motivates] the work of man is also from
> God's lovingkindness, for He wants the work of the righteous
> to shine the awareness of God in all the worlds. Therefore
> God will assuredly agree to their every action.

Once God indicates his desire for human activism—paradigmatically expressed by Lainer in this passage as מעשה צדיקים *ma'aseh tzadikim*, the deed
of the righteous—then God will certainly affirm all of human action as an
incarnation of divine will.

71

Source 19: *MHs vol. 1 Tzav s.v. hamakriv*

The final Two Hands passage revolves around uniqueness and radical individualism. The difference between this and the previous two-handed effluence passages is that in this case the effluence goes from human to God.

We begin our analysis here:

והוא כי ירצה לראות את מקומו ממי שהוא גדול וחפץ בהתנשאות, בזה
נאמר יביא את קרבנו ידיו תביאנה, היינו למסור כל בקשתו ותפלתו להש"י

[The purpose of the *shelamim* offering] is that [a person]
wants to see his place and whom he is greater than, and he
wants to be lifted up. Concerning this it says, 'He shall bring
his offering, his hands will bring it'. This means that he should
surrender all his supplication and prayer to God.

The context is the *shelamim*, the 'wholeness' offering sacrifice, which apparently hints to the human perfection that comes from fully accepting one's unique story. Specifically, a person can pray to know their unique story and their place in the world and to understand their place relative to their friends. The offering requires two hands, which indicates that one gives oneself totally over to God.

Lainer states further that individualism will not be effaced in the future. Rather, in the future, everyone[27] will embrace their own uniqueness:

כי באמת לעתיד יהי' מקום לכ"א מישראל ביחוד להתגדר בו ויהי' כ"א
מדוגל במעלתו נגד כל ישראל ולעתיד אף שהכל יהי' בד"ת, אך ימצא
ענינים גדולים מאוד שאין אחד דומה בהתנשאותו נגד חבירו

For in truth, in the future there will be a place defined
uniquely for everyone of Israel, and each and every individual
will be distinct in his achievement [level] in comparison with
all of Israel. And in the future, even though everything will
be as the words of Torah, even there one will find exceedingly
great matters, for no one will be similar to anyone else in their
unique elevation.

72

וע"ז מורה מה שנאמר ידיו תביאנה היינו בשני ידים כי באם האדם ירצה
לטעום מטובו בעוה"ז ומבקש מהש"י שיראהו מקומו צריך להיות נקי מצדו,
שאם יראה לו הש"י שהוא קטן במדריגה ממי שידמה לו בעוה"ז שהוא גדול
ממנו לא ירע לו... וזהו ידיו תביאנה כי הוא בשתי ידים בימין ובשמאל,
בימין היינו שיוכל להיות שיתנשא ובשמאל שיוכל להיות שישפל ע"י
התפלה הזאת

Thus the instruction, 'his hands will bring it'—meaning with
both hands. For if a person wants to taste His goodness in
this world and would seek for God to show him his place, he
must be clean from his side, so that if God shows him that
he is at a lesser level than someone else whom he thinks he is
greater than, it will not harm him...which is what is meant by
'his hands will bring it', since it is with both hands, with the
right and the left: the right means that he may be lifted up,
and the left that he may be brought down, by means of this
prayer.

As we saw above, the prayer represented by the *shelamim* sacrifice requires
complete surrender of one's desires to God. If one does not give oneself
totally over to God, then the revelation of their story is not part of divinity but serves merely to fulfill ego needs. Such a prayer would then be
dangerous, because the seeker can never know what they might learn. Rather,
their purpose must be to embrace in a clean and pure way their unique place
and their unique expression of divinity, whatever these might be. According
to Lainer, this is the meaning of offering prayer and sacrifice with two hands.

We will analyze one more Two Hands passage below, Source 34, in the
context of a related set of passages in Lainer, the *Tovat 'Ayin* sub-cluster.

The Face-to-Face Sub-Cluster

The final theme central to the David cluster of the Wisdom of Solomon texts is the desire for a 'face-to-face', unmediated relationship with the *Shekhinah*.[28] This theme ties Lainer's theology closely to Luria, who identifies the Wisdom of Solomon—and the full moon—with the process of *tikun ha-nukva*, the cosmic rectification of the feminine, whose goal is the realization of a 'face-to-face' relationship between *Ze'ir Anpin* and *nukva*.[29]

In the passage we already examined in volume 1, entering into a face-to-face relationship, symbolized by the *Shemitah* year, leads to Jubilee, 'when simple desire *ratzon pashut* will be awakened in the hearts of each soul of Israel [and] there could therefore be no subjugation over any soul of Israel'.[30] In this messianic state, one's own will and God's will, which is *Shekhinah*, are identical. Not being able to receive from God face-to-face is called by Lainer slavery, which is antithetical to redemption.

Source 20: *MHs vol. 2 Korah s.v. vayikah 1*

The essence of this desire for a 'face-to-face', unmediated relationship with the *Shekhinah* is expressed in David's yearning in the next passage. Lainer begins this passage with a discussion of prayer.

> כי כל התפלות שאנו מתפללין עפ״י סדר שסדרו אנשי כנסת הגדולה המה
> רק שיתגלה שהכל הוא מהשי״ת ואז נוכל להתפלל להשי״ת לבדו ולא יהיה
> שום מסך המבדיל שאז יהיה התפלה בלב ישר לא בקביעות, כמו שכתיב
> (תהלים קט) ואני תפלה, היינו שהוא עצמו הוא התפלה שהוא רואה
> תמיד נכחו את השי״ת שבלעדי ה׳ הוא חסר מכל ואין לו שום חיים בלתי
> כשיתחבר להשי״ת

For all the prayers that we pray according to the order determined by the men of the Great Assembly are only to reveal
that everything is from God. Then (i.e., once we realize that
everything is from God) we are able to pray to God *levado*
(alone), without any intervening screen *masah ha-mavdil*,
for prayer will be directly from the heart, not a fixed matter,

as it is written, 'And I am prayer' (Psalms 109:4)—meaning that the person himself is the prayer, for he always sees God *nokheho* facing him. For without God, he lacks everything, and he has no life other than when he connects to God.

Prayer in its fixed form, states Lainer, is but an exercise of consciousness, designed to remind us that all is from God. However, prayer in its fixed form is only for the time before *berur*. After *berur*, we will be able to pray to God *levado*, without any intervening barrier. At that time, prayer will be in the hearts of Israel, a permanent integrated expression of the person's deepest self. When this level is attained, he teaches, there is no *masah ha-mavdil*, no separating or intervening screen between God and the human being; the person no longer prays but literally becomes prayer. In this light, Lainer interprets the verse 'And I am prayer' literally:[31] Those who pray are themselves the prayer.

The clear implication is that the words of the formal prayer, important as they may be in the process of *berur*, at some point lose their efficacy, perhaps even becoming a hindrance, because they prevent unmediated access to the divine.

At the climax of the passage, Lainer illustrates with a powerful parable the notion of being face-to-face:

והענין הוא כמשל מלך שאמר לבנו שבל יראה פניו רק כל מה שיצטרך אליו ישלח דברו על ידי שליח, והיה משלח תמיד ע"י שליח בקשות רבות וכל הבקשות לא היו רק שיוכל לראות פניו ולא יצרך לדבר אליו עוד ע"י שליח

> This matter can be compared to a king who said to his son that he could not see his face, but that he should ask for anything he needs by means of a messenger. He would send many requests by means of a messenger, but all the requests were only that he should see his [father's] face, and not have to communicate with him by means of a messenger any longer.

In the parable, the king tells his son to send a messenger in order to ask of the king whatever he might need. However, the king's son refuses to ask for anything; instead, he always sends back the same message with the messenger: that there should be no messenger, but that instead he should merit seeing the king directly. True prayer, according to the parable, is not directed towards one's needs. Rather, the goal of prayer is to see God face-to-face, that is, without mediation.

Lainer then applies the parable to King David, whom Lainer depicts as the son, in contrast to the priests, who are servants and messengers:

וכן כל העבודות הם ע"י כהנים שהם נקראים עבדי ה', ואין לך גדול בישראל
כדוד המלך ע"ה שכתיב עליו (תהלים ב) בני אתה וגם איתא בגמ' (יומא
כה.) אין ישיבה בעזרה אלא למלכי בית דוד בלבד, וזה הוא מפני שנקראים
בנים מכל מקום אין רשאי לכנוס במקום שהכהן נכנס, מפני שהבן לא יבוא
כל כך במורא כמו העבד, ועל זה התפלל דוד המלך ע"ה (תהלים כז) שבתי
בבית ה' כל ימי חיי לחזות בנועם ה' ולבקר בהיכלו, שלא יצטרך לממוצע
רק לבקש מה' פנים בפנים

> Similarly, all the service is done by priests, who are called 'the
> servants of God'. And [we know that] there is none greater in
> Israel than King David, of blessed memory, concerning whom
> it is written, 'You are my son' (Psalms 2:7), and one finds in
> the Talmud, 'No one may sit in the [Temple] court other
> than kings of the Davidic line' (*bYoma* 25a)—because they
> are called 'sons'. Nevertheless, [the king] may not enter where
> the priest enters, for a son would not enter with fear like a
> servant. For this reason David prayed (Psalms 27:4): 'May I
> sit in the House of *Hashem* all the days of my life, to see the
> pleasantness of *Hashem* and to visit His palace'—[meaning he
> prayed] that he would have no need for a mediating agent, but
> would only ask God face-to-face.

In Lainer's reading, the priests are the messengers of the King. However, they prevent unmediated access to the king. Thus, says Lainer, the authentic desire of the king is to enter the Holy of Holies and be face-to-face with God, without the mediating presence of the priest. Not only David, writes Lainer, but all the kings of the house of David (i.e., the Judah archetype), yearn to be able to access the Holy of Holies unmediated by the priest. As implied here and made clearer in parallel texts,[32] this state is the essence and purpose of the Temple.

In a related passage whose entire theme is the *mikdash*,[33] being 'face-to-face' is also understood as being *beli masah ha-mavdil*, without an intervening screen. There, 'face-to-face' unmediated access to divinity is explicity linked

77

to the ability to access *retzon Hashem* beyond *kelalei divrei torah*, the general principles of law.

Source 21: *MHs vol.2 Likutim Pinhas s.v. bayom ha-shemini*

This Torah sets the stage for the next passage, where Lainer asserts, based on earlier Lurianic sources, that the goal of prayer is to move from 'behind the *Shekhinah*' to a state of being 'face-to-face' with the *Shekhinah*. Here Lainer, as restated by his grandson Gershon Henokh,[34] directly reformulates the Lurianic understanding of Shemini Atzeret in terms of achieving a face-to-face encounter with *Shekhinah*. During all prayer, as well as during the days of the Sukkot festival leading up to Shemini Atzeret, one is considered to be *mei'ahorei ha-Shekhinah*, behind the *Shekhinah*.

ביום השמיני עצרת תהיה לכם. אמר אדמו״ר הג׳ הק׳ זצ״לה מאיזביצא
שהארת הזווג משמיני עצרת אחר ימי החג הוא כעניין הארת הזווג של
ברכת שים שלום אחר תפלת שמונה עשרה. והעניין הוא שבכל התפלה
נחשב המתפלל כאילו עומד אחורי השכינה וכו׳

'On the eighth day you shall have an assembly'. The great and holy master of Izbica said that the light of the *zivug* of Shemini Atzeret, after the days of the holiday, is similar to the light coming from the *zivug* of the *sim shalom* blessing after the silent *amidah* prayer. This issue is that during the entire prayer service, the person praying is considered as if he is standing in back of the *Shekhinah* during the entire prayer.

Before the end of the prayer, the person sees *ahor ha-Shekhinah*, the back of the divine. However, when a person gets to the last blessing of the silent prayer, *Sim Shalom*, or to the last day of Sukkot, Shemini Atzeret, then one turns to be in *zivug*, in erotic embrace with God face-to-face.

וכשמגיע האדם לברכת שים שלום אזי צריך האדם ליתן שלום ברישא לצד
צפון שהוא שמאל דידיה, משום שהוא ימינו דקב״ה, כי כביכול ית׳ עומד
אז נוכח פניו של המתפלל וכו׳, הרי שעיקר הזווג פנים בפנים נעשה דוקא
בברכת שים שלום שהוא אחר הפירוד שמקודם שהיה בבחינת וראית את
אחורי וחזית ית בתרי, וכן הם כל שבעת ימי החג בבחינת אחורי וכו׳ עד
שמגיע שמיני עצרת אז מתחיל הזווג להנהיר פנים בפנים כמו הזווג של
ברכת שלום בברכת שים שלום

78

And when a person reaches the *Sim Shalom* blessing, the person should give greeting *shalom* to the north, which is his left side, but is the right side of God, for it is as if God is standing directly in front of the person praying. The essential face-to-face *zivug* is made specifically in the *Sim Shalom* blessing, which comes after the previous separation, which was the aspect of 'And you will see my back'. Similarly, all the seven days of the holiday are in the aspect of 'my back', until Shemini Atzeret comes. It is then that the *zivug* begins to give light face-to-face, just like the *zivug* of the blessing for peace (greeting) in the *Sim Shalom* blessing.

Here, in a twist on the face-to-face theme, an individual in true prayer is already facing God, but through his service, *Shekhinah* turns to face him. The resulting *zivug* is the same.

Source 22: *MHs vol 1* Kedoshim s.v. *kedoshim 1*

In the following passage, which is explicitly messianic, Lainer establishes that holiness, in and of itself, means to be be fully open to receive the influx of divine revelation at any moment in anticipation of imminent redemption.

קדושים תהיו קדושה לשון הזמנה היינו שהש״י מזהיר לבני ישראל שיהי'
תמיד מקודשים ומזומנים ויצפו תמיד לישועת הש״י שיושיע להם ויאיר
עיניהם בד״ת. כי קדוש אני. היינו שהש״י אומר כי הוא יתברך מזומן תמיד
להושיע לישראל ועי״ז גם ישראל צריכין להיות מזומנים ולצפות תמיד
להשם, ושלא יטרידו את עצמם בעסקי עוה״ז. כמ״ש חסד ואמת אל יעזבוך
(משלי ג) ולא אמר חסד ואמת אל תעזוב, ורצה בזה כי האדם צריך לעמוד
תמיד נגד הש״י ולצפה שיאיר עיניו בכדי שבעת שישפיע הקב״ה חסד של
אמת, והוא חסד הקיים לעד ואז החסד ישיג לאדם המצפה ולא יעזוב את
כל אדם המחכה שיכנסו ד״ת בלבו, וצריך האדם לראות שלא יפנה עורף רק
יעמוד נגד ה' פנים בפנים

'You shall be holy...'—holiness implies preparation, that is, God is warning Israel to always be made holy and prepared so that they will always be expecting God's deliverance, that He should deliver them and enlighten their eyes in Torah. '...for I am holy'—meaning that God is saying that He is always prepared to save Israel, and therefore Israel should be prepared and always expecting God, and should not trouble themselves with the matters of this world. As it says, 'Kindness and truth shall not forsake you' (Prov. 3:3)—it does not say, 'You shall not forsake kindness and truth'. This means that a person must always stand before God and expect that his eyes be enlightened so that in the moment when God emanates true kindness, which is the kindness that lasts forever, then the kindness will reach the person who is expecting it, and will not forsake the person who is waiting for the words of the Torah to enter his heart. The person must see to it that he does not turn his back, but stands face-to-face before God.

Not to be available to true kindness from God is called by Lainer the turning of the back, which is antithetical to redemption. Rather a person should always be facing God—even when his relationship with God is not immediate—in order to be able to come face-to-face when grace makes this possible. Here 'face-to-face' means anticipation of imminent redemption, the essential Judah stance.

Source 23: *MHs vol.2* Ki Tisa *s.v. vayedaber Hashem el Mosheh lekh reid*

In the last face-to-face passage, we see clearly the Wisdom of Solomon genre's emphasis on accessing the unmediated will of God, the valuation of incense over sacrifice—paralleling the valuation of incense over sacrifice[35] and the contrast between king and priest[36]—and the crucial role of the *mikdash* (symbolized in this passage as well by the Temple pilgrimage and by Bezalel). Two themes, however, are connected to the face-to-face motif for the first time in this passage. The first is the by now familiar idea that the unique metaphysical nature of Israel means that their actions are *nikra 'al shemo*, which we have seen is a byword for human participation in divinity and the ontological value of human activism—the core of acosmic humanism. The second is that Lainer connects the consciousness of acosmic humanism to the experience of *teshuvah*, repentance after sin.

כי כל הימים טובים נקראים פני ה׳ כמו שכתיב (שמות כג) ולא יראו פני
ריקם שהאדם צריך לעמוד אז פנים בפנים נגד השי״ת כי אז משפיע השי״ת
השפעה מרובה לישראל, ושבת היא תוך ופנימיות מכל המועדים והתוך
מקדושת כל ההשפעות

80

For all the holidays are termed 'God's face' as is written, 'And they shall not see my face empty handed' (Exod. 23:15). For a person must stand face-to-face with God, for then God sends great bounty to Israel. And Sabbath is the center and inner-most of all the holidays, and the center sanctifies all forms of bounty.

Here we see that the Lurianic trope of 'face-to-face' has been fully absorbed into the conceptual structure of Lainer's teachings, and particularly into the Wisdom of Solomon genre. The passage continues:

ונגד זה כתיב קשה עורף שהפנו עורף מהשפעת השי"ת, והנה כל זה היה
כדי להיטיב לישראל בהחזרת טובה, בהוספה מרובה, כי אחר החטא
נתעורר לב האדם בתשובתו ועל ידי זה נקרא כל סגולת קדושה שסיגל על
שמו

And opposite this is what is described 'stiff-necked', [meaning] that they turned their faces away from God's bounty. And here, all this was in order to benefit Israel, by returning the good, with great increase. For after sin, the heart of a person is awakened through his returning, and by this means, all the achievements of the holiness that he achieved are called by his name.

The connection made here between sin and *berur* is intimate and impor-tant. Lainer's conclusion in this passage fits a more conventional under-standing of sin and repentance as the path to holiness. As we know however from other passages, *teshuvah* means *berur*,[37] the clarification of the true nature of reality. What appears as sin may in fact be God's will. Moreover, the particular sin committed is often understood by Lainer to be the high-est spiritual act possible for the one who sins.[38] A person's achievements are called by his name precisely because of his engagement with sin, that is, with engagement with his unique *hisaron*. Ultimately, a person's sins are what bring him face-to-face with God.

Cluster 4: The Moon Sources

At this point we turn the fourth cluster within the Wisdom of Solomon genre, the Moon cluster. We have already seen some of these sources in the context of other Wisdom of Solomon clusters; for example, where Lainer sees Solomon asserting, 'I intend God's deepest will, even without my knowing, since my heart is bound to God'— this is defined by Lainer as 'the aspect of the moon'.[39] King David, of course, is explicitly identified with *yarei'ah*, *Shekhinah* and the *sefirah* of *Malkhut*, not just in Lainer but in all of Kabbalah.[40] Lainer's reliance on earlier sources will become clearer when we explore Lainer's Zoharic sources, many of which deal specifically with the moon.

Beyond the texts cited above, we will adduce a few more brief references here before we go in depth into two of our sources. The moon motif recurs in the Likutim on the *Zohar*,[41] where Lainer refers to the Kingdom of David as *sihara*, a manifestation of the moon symbol: כי מלכות בית דוד הוא מבחינת סיהרא 'For the royal house of David is the aspect of the moon'. In addition to Solomon, David, and the Kingdom of David, Lainer also identifies Judah with the moon:

כי שבט יהודה נמשל לירח שלית ליה מגרמיה כלום כדאיתא בזהר
הקדש...שׁשׁבט יהודה מכיר תמיד הכרה מפורשׁת שׁהכל מה'

> For the tribe of Judah is compared to the moon, which has
> nothing in and of itself, as is written in the holy *Zohar*....the
> tribe of Judah always has explicit awareness that everything
> derives from God. [42]

Lainer takes the moon theme one step further in his description of the moment of transition between night and day.[43] The sun and the moon— *kudsha berikh hu* and *Shekhinah*—are united when the morning star arises. This time of day, writes Lainer, is the time of David and Solomon. Here Lainer associates the *yihud* (the unification of the sun and the moon) with David and Solomon. As we shall see, this is a major theme in the Zoharic passages on the Wisdom of Solomon.

83

Further, the moon is directly associated in Izbica with the essential con-
struct of unmediated *retzon Hashem*, which is so central to Lainer's theology. Most importantly for our understanding of the Wisdom of Solomon,
in the passage we adduced above on Proverbs,[44] Solomon's unique wisdom,
termed *da'at kedoshim* 'knowledge of the holy', is equated with the moon
in its fullness. This kind of knowledge is identical with permanent and
unmediated access to *retzon Hashem*, beyond *seikhel*. It is the essence of
Solomon's wisdom and is at the core of the Judah archetype.

Source 24: *MHs vol. 1* Emor s.v. *vahaveitem*

Above we alluded briefly to a passage that explicitly links *yarei'ah* and
rei'ah.[45] This link allowed us to understand the *emet le'amito* passages within the broader matrix of the Goddess sources in Solomon's wisdom. We
need to fully analyze this passage here, because it is essential to the moon
genre. The passage explicitly roots the entire notion of unmediated *retzon
Hashem* in the matrix of moon-*Shekhinah*-consciousness:

> ובשבועות היינו מתן תורה היינו שהש״י קובע בינה בלב כל אדם שיבינו
> בנפשם רצון הש״י, וזה הבינה נקראת ירח וירח מורה על בינה בלב

> And on Shavuot, which is the giving of the Torah, *Hashem*
> fixes *binah balev* understanding in the heart of every person...
> This understanding is called *yarei'ah* moon, and moon indi-
> cates the understanding in the heart.

The context of the discussion is the nature of the holiday of Shavuot.[46] On
Shavuot, *retzon Hashem* is permanently internalized (*kavu'a balev*). *Binah
balev*, which is the source of unmediated *retzon Hashem*, is called *yarei'ah*.

The passage continues:

> כי שמש מורה על חכמה לעיני האדם והמה התרי״ג מצות שידע האדם על
> פי כללי המצות איך להתנהג בכל דבר אם הוא אסור או מותר, וירח מורה
> על בינה בלב האדם לקדש עצמו אף במותר לו, שיהי׳ לו גבול ותחום במיעיו
> להבדיל שעד כאן הוא ברצון הש״י ומכאן ואילך אינו ברצון הש״י

> For the sun indicates wisdom in the eyes of man. These are
> the 613 commandments with which a person may know,
> according to the principles of the commandments, how to act

84

in any instance, whether it is forbidden or permissible, and
the moon *yarei'ah* indicates the understanding of the heart,
whereby a man must sanctify himself also in that which is
permissible for him, so that he may have a boundary and a
limit in his innards, differentiating that up until here it is
God's will, and from here on, it is not God's will.

In contrast with the moon, the sun stands for the *kelalim*, which in Lainer
means the *mitzvot* commandments. These *kelalim* guide a person in the
normative decisions of prohibited and forbidden. It is the moon, however,
that is the source of *binah balev*. The moon is that which allows a person to
determine boundaries independently of the *kelalim*. This passage, like the
aforementioned Proverbs passage, is unique because unlike the usual understanding ascribed to Lainer—which in fact does appear in *MHs* texts—
in which expansion to *retzon Hashem* beyond *kelalim* involves breaking a
boundary, in these passages it involves creating a boundary. Lainer's point
is that the issue is not whether the boundary is expanded or contracted.
The issue is that a person's determination of boundaries is based not on
nomos[47] but on *mei'ayim*, innards or intestines, what my grandmother
called *kishkes*, and what is called in contemporary parlance 'your gut' in
the sense of a 'gut reaction'. What is of course essential for Lainer is that a
person's gut reaction is only considered sacred if they have first achieved
post-*berur* consciousness.

The passage continues:

וזה הבינה יצטרך לאדם בכל ענייניו, וזה מה דאיתא בגמ' או"ה מונין לחמה
וישראל מונין ללבנה כי שמש הוא חכמה שיש בכח האדם להשיגה, אבל
לבנה מורה על החיים שהיא למעלה מהשכל כי ירח היא מלשון ריח
שישראל יריחו בכל דבר את שורשו מחיי עולם הבא. אף שהירח הוא תחת
השמש אך כדאיתא בזו"הק אין לסיהרא עלאה קא מנינין, שהשמש היא
מקבלת אור מסיהרא עילאה

Such understanding is necessary for a person in all his affairs.
This is why the Talmud says that the nations of the world calculate according to the sun, while Israel calculates according
to the moon. For the sun is the wisdom that a person has the
potential to attain, while the *levanah* moon alludes to life that
is beyond *seikhel* intellectual knowledge. For *yarei'ach* (another
Hebrew word for moon) is similar to the word *rei'ach* smell,

85

for Israel can 'smell' in everything its root in the life of the world-to-come (eternity). Although the moon is lower than the sun, the holy *Zohar* says that 'we calculate by *sihara 'ila'ah* the supernal moon', whereas the sun receives light from the supernal moon.[48]

This moon quality, or what we have termed *Shekhinah*-consciousness, must guide people in all of their affairs, according to Lainer. לבנה *Levanah* moon, writes Lainer, is an expression of the suprarational life; ירח *yarei'ah* moon is an expression of the eternal life of the world-to-come. It is in this sense that the word *yarei'ah* is the conceptual source for the word *rei'ah*. This passage makes clear that *'olam ha-ba*, the world-to-come, is not limited to the distant eschaton, but is fully available in the present.[49] In fact, a person needs to be guided 'in all of his [worldly] affairs' using the suprarational 'moon' consciousness of *'olam ha-ba*.

Source 25: MHs vol. 2 Ki Teitzei s.v. ki teitzei 2

The final moon source we will present here links several important motifs we have already mentioned in our analysis of the Wisdom of Solomon. This text should also be considered the first source in the Idolatry cluster, which we will examine further below. We have already shown in our analysis of the Goddess passages[50] that a sympathetic relationship to the energy of paganism, when it is stripped of its externalities, is a vital strand in Lainer's concept of the Wisdom of Solomon. The intertwined motifs in this passage are *teshukah*[51] and paganism.

Recall that in the sources we saw in the Goddess section of the Solomon cluster, particularly in reference to Solomon's marrying foreign wives, Lainer suggested that Solomon's—and by extension Lainer's own—*Shekhinah* project involved the redemption of the unique *ko'ah* (spiritual energy) of every nation. In the sources we saw, this unique *ko'ah* was related directly to the pagan practices of the nation symbolized by the feminine and specifically the *bat melekh* (daughter of the king), which of course is a classic *Shekhinah* symbol.

The *Shekhinah* symbol of *yarei'ah* and the *Shekhinah* symbol of *bat melekh* are merely different names for the same *Shekhinah*-consciousness. Indeed, the Solomon project, simply stated, may be seen as an expression of Solomon's moon-consciousness. Solomon attempts to bring the many faces of the moon, including its pagan manifestations, under the realm of the holy. In Source 2 above, paganism is said to have powers in all of the following fields: sex, food and drink, finance, economy, physical prowess, and heroism. Lainer relates each of these qualities to a specific nation whose pagan practices engaged Solomon's attention and were possibly practiced by him.

In the following passage, Lainer brings together these themes, explaining the desire to redeem what Luria might have called the divine sparks of paganism as the essential goal not merely of Solomon but of the entire Jewish people. While the passage does not refer to paganism directly, when read in conjunction with the aforementioned Solomon passages, the intent is unmistakable.

כי תצא למלחמה על אויביך52...שכל אומה מעכו"ם יש לה כח מיוחד, לזו חכמה לזו עושר לזו גבורה, והכח הנמצא בהם אינו נקרא חיים כלל רק חיי שעה, כי הטובה שבהם הוא רק לפי שעה ובאחרית הימים יאספו, ורק מה שיש להם תשוקה לדבר שנחסר להם, כגון האומה מהעכו"ם שהיא משופעת בחכמה ומשתוקקת לעושר וכדומה זו התשוקה נקרא חיים, וזאת מקבלים ישראל מהם

> 'When you go to war against your enemies'...Each of the
> nations has a unique quality—one has wisdom, another has
> riches, another has power. However, these qualities are not
> called life at all, but only temporary life. For goodness in them
> is merely transitory, and in the end of days it will become
> as nothing. Only their desire for that which they lack—for
> example, the nation that is blessed with wisdom but longs for
> wealth, and so forth—this desire is called life, and this is what
> Israel receives from them.

The context of this passage is the *eishet yefat to'ar*, the beautiful captive woman taken by the Israelite warrior in battle. For Lainer, this is an obvious *Shekhinah* symbol. Lainer writes that the unique *ko'ah* which every nation has is ephemeral and limited. It is not called *hayyim* life, meaning it has no ultimate existence and value, no ontological reality.[53] However, among the nations, what does have *hayyim* is their *teshukah* for their *hisaron*. This *teshukah*, which <u>is</u> called *hayyim*, is what Israel must receive from them.

The passage continues:

כי ישראל מונין ללבנה שאין לה מגרמה כלום, רק תשוקה שמשתוקקת
שהחמה תאיר בה אורה

> For Israel calculates according to the moon, which has noth-
> ing in and of itself, only desire, for she desires that the sun will
> shine its light through her.

It is Israel's quality of *levanah* (moon) that allows it to absorb the unique *teshukah* of every nation for what they are missing. Moon-*Shekhinah* is consistently described in the *Zohar* as *leit leih megarmeh klum* (it has noth-ing, i.e., no light, of its own). Because of this quality, it is able to receive the powers of all of the *sefirot*. Lainer suggests that the essence of the moon's essential power is its *teshukah* to receive light from the sun:

The passage continues:

וזה ושבית שביו כח התשוקה שאצלם זה הכח הוא בשביה זה יקבלו מהם
ישראל אבל שאר כחם יאפסו

> This, then, is the meaning of 'and you take captives'—that
> among the nations this power is in captivity; this is what
> Israel will receive from them. The remainder of their powers
> will cease [to exist], however.[54]

With the above ideas in mind, Lainer can now explain the symbolism of the captive woman. The dimension of moon/Goddess-consciousness that is in exile is considered to be incarnate in the captive woman, and through her this consciousness is re-absorbed into Israel. She represents the pow-er of *teshukah* held captive among the nations that must be redeemed by Israel.[55] In effect, Lainer is saying that the captive woman is a symbol for the faces or powers of the feminine that must be redeemed. This is of course is precisely how Lainer defined the Solomon *Shekhinah* project in the Goddess sources we saw above. In this text, however, it has moved beyond being merely a Solomonic project and been transmuted into a project of the Jewish people.

The passage continues: וזה התשוקה נקראת שמושה של תורה שהיא גדולה מלמודה כי תשוקה אין בה גבול 'This desire is called "*shimushah* (service) of Torah", which is greater than [Torah] study, for desire has no limits.'

88

The preference for moon power over sun power or any other kind of power is expressed by Lainer as the interpretation of the classic Talmudic dictum 'Serving Torah is greater than learning Torah'. In this context, learning implies intellectual activity, while serving, which technically refers to serving the needs of Torah scholars, is more broadly viewed by Lainer as the erotic and primal connection of the scholar to Torah, something more basic than mere cognition.[56] This moon quality, expressed through *teshukah*, is the erotic, empowering acosmism of *MHs*, rooted in the Wisdom of Solomon. As we see, *teshukah* is synonymous with the power of acosmic humanism. *Teshukah* expresses the erotic dimension; *rei'ah* affirms human intuition as participating in the divine; and *ein bo gevul* indicates no-boundary consciousness.

Notes for Section Three

1 *MHs vol. 1* and *vol. 2* Devarim s.v. *ahad 'asar yom* (Source 12 above). Psalms 127:1–2 is cited in both passages. In the *vol. 2* passage, the verse in Psalms is placed in the mouth of Solomon. He is the ידיד *yedid* 'friend'. In the *vol. 1* passage, the *yedid* is David. The theme of both passages, adduced above, is that once Torah is *kavu'a balev*, it is manifested without *yegi'a* (effort and struggle). This is one defining characteristic of the Judah archetype.

2 Deut. 12:12.

3 See *MHs vol. 2* 2 Samuel s.v. *vayosef*, which deals in a complementary manner with the same Michal-David-Ark narrative and supports our reading of the *amhot* theme in this passage.

4 *Yashar* means 'straight', suggesting, for Lainer, unmediated, direct participation in the divine. According to Lainer, this quality is not accessed only by an elite; rather, it is the essence of Israel: ישראל is אל ישר *yashar El*. See *MHs vol. 1* Metzora s.v. *dabru*.

5 Further analysis of this passage can be found below, Source 40.

6 See the first section of Chapter Nine.

7 Though Lainer appears to merely repeat the *aggadah*, he leads us to a new interpretation of the *aggadah* by implicitly connecting it with David's words about himself through the term 'established', as well as through the explicit reference to hands. David is thus not only the progenitor of the Temple; he is its paradigmatic manifestation in the realm of human action. The implications of this connection are explored in the remainder of the passage.

8 See *MHs vol. 1* Vayikra s.v. *'al kol* (Source 19 below), where Lainer distinguishes between David and other kings of Israel, in that while the other kings struggle with *yir'ah*, David was born into and personifies love: 'All the kings struggled with *yir'ah*, except King David, who was born in the quality of love and was מדוגל בה מאד *medugal bah me'od* totally defined by it'. Both here and in the parallel passage in *MHs vol. 1* 2 Kings s.v. *ben sheteim*, David is contrasted with the idolatrous king Menasheh (Manasseh), who is defined by fear. On this general theme, see the discussion of love and acosmic humanism in volume 1, in the section 'Two: The Reality of Love in Lainer's Theology'.

9 In the 1973 edition of *MHs*, the closure of the paragraph is as I have placed it here, after the words Aaron the Priest. In the more recent edition, the one principally used for this work, the comma is placed after 'King David' (in the continuation of the passage below), which is apparently a mistake. However, even according to the first punctuation, the passage is ambiguous, because at the end of the passage, Lainer associates a different permutation of the divine name with Aaron.

10 See Chapter Eight, 'Empowering Acosmism and *Tekufot* (Personal Audacity and Determination)' in volume 1.

11 See Chapter Nine 'Models of Activism' in volume 1, where we discuss the terms מצידו *mitzido* and מצדינו *mitzideinu*. The term *mitzad ha-adam* in *MHs* has

the same meaning as *mitzideinu*.

12 See Ross, 'Shenei'.

13 See the section 'The Individual's Unique *Helek* (Portion) of Torah' in volume 1.

14 Schatz, *Hasidism*.

15 Weiss, 'Via Passiva'.

16 Elior, *The Paradoxical*.

17 This section appears under the heading *ule'atid* following the passage s.v. *Hashem YKHK*, although it is a continuation of the same teaching.

18 See the section 'No-Boundary Consciousness' in volume 1 (Chap. 8), esp. the discussion there of *MHs vol. 2 Re'eh s.v. ki yarhiv*.

19 See the section 'First Major Theme: Acosmism and Uniqueness' in volume 1 on the term *hitnas'ut* as it relates to uniqueness. See also the discussion of this passage in volume 1, 'All is in the Hands of Heaven: A Humanist Agenda'.

20 See our discussion of uniqueness and hierarchy in the section 'The Unique Individual, Dignity, and Redemption' in volume 1. This is, of course, also a description of the consciousness accessed by the Judah archetype (see Chapter 12 there). Note that Lainer's description of two ultimate *tzadikim* in one generation was a reflection on his establishment of a Hasidic court in the face of the Kotzker rebbe whom he left. See Faierstein, *Hands*.

21 See *mSukkah* 4:5.

22 On the terms *shorsho* and *helko*, see the section 'The Unique Individual, Dignity, and Redemption' in volume 1.

23 See our discussion of human activism and critique of Weiss in this regard in the section 'Third Major Theme: Affirmation of Human Activism and Critique of Scholarship'.

24 *Likutei Amarim* Ch. 4.

25 See, for example, *MHs vol. 2* Megilah 12b s.v. *bese'udato* and *MHs vol. 1* Likutim Megilah 12b s.v. *veha-karov* (Source 20).

26 See Chapter Ten and Chapter Twelve in volume 1.

27 Again, in Lainer's narrow view of acosmism, 'everyone' means all of Israel.

28 See the section 'The Face-to-Face Encounter' in volume 1, Chapter Fourteen; see also *MHs vol. 2* Likutim Pinhas s.v. *bayom ha-shemini* 2.

29 See the section '*Tikun Ha-nukva*' and Source 42 in volume 3. Though Luria's *tikun ha-nukva* is an intra-divine process, while the *MHs* texts are focused on a human-divine process, we will see there that the Lurianic project of *tikun ha-nukva* has profound resonances in Lainer and in his teacher Simcha Bunim. In that section we will further examine the important intertextual links between the David-Solomon and paganism motifs in *MHs* and this cornerstone of Lurianic theology. For a discussion of Lainer's reworking of other Lurianic themes, see Part Two in volume 1, 'Luria and Lainer: Provisional Conclusions'.

30 *MHs vol. 2* Mishpatim s.v. *sheish shanim*.

31 This seems to be related to the understanding of prayer found in Midrash Pinhas: 'People think that you pray to God, but that is not the case. Rather, prayer

itself is divinity' (Shapira, *Midrash Pinhas* 18, cf. Green, *Ehyeh* 155). The substantive similarities between the acosmism of Izbica to that of Pinhas of Koretz suggest that a comparative study is warranted.

32 See the sections 'Acosmism and Mikdash', 'Three: Shadows of Union and Activism' and 'The Paradox of Human Activism: Levels of Consciousness' in volume 1.

33 *MHs vol.* 2 Psalms s.v. *ahat she'alti.*

34 This passage originally comes from the book by Gershon Henekh, *Sod Yesharim* Shemini Atzeret 18 s.v. *uvei'ur.*

35 Lainer here contrasts *ketoret* incense, which unites all of creation, with *zevihah* sacrifice, which creates separation (e.g., between life and death). See the section 'Acosmism and *Mikdash* (The Jerusalem Temple)' in volume 1.

36 See *MHs vol.* 1 Proverbs s.v. *semamit*, discussed in volume 1 (Part One, 'Hisaron Meyuhad'), where Lainer interprets king Uziyahu going against the priests by entering the Holy of Holies to offer incense.

37 See *MHs vol.* 1 Vayigash s.v. *vayigash* 1; *vol.* 2 Berakhot s.v. *amar Raba.*

38 See, e.g., the sources of the Menutzah sub-cluster below, as well as *MHs vol.* 2 Berakhot s.v. *amar Raba.*

39 *MHs vol.* 2 Proverbs s.v. *ki va'ar* (Source 11 above).

40 See *MHs vol.* 2 Psalms s.v. *yadekha 'asuni* (Source 16).

41 See *MHs vol.* 2 Likutim Zohar Bereishit s.v. *veDavid malka.*

42 *MHs vol.* 2 Shemini s.v. *yayin* 2 (Source 31). We will read and analyze this passage in more detail below when we outline the Wine Cluster. This passage is one of the key wine passages. As we have seen and as will continue to be apparent, wine, David, Solomon, moon, idolatry, and *mikdash* are all closely linked themes.

43 *MHs vol.* 2 Likutim Berakhot 62b s.v. *sheinah.* The passage is originally from Tzadok Hakohen's *Tzidkat Hatzadik* 242; Tzadok uses the term *shama'ti* 'I heard', which indicates that he heard it from his teacher, Mordechai Lainer.

44 In the discussion of *MHs vol.* 2 Proverbs s.v. *ki va'ar* (Source 11).

45 Source 10.

46 The broader context is a clear statement of the essential threefold pattern that appears in many places in Hasidic thought. We saw another version of this pattern in Part Three of volume 1, in the section 'The Paradox of Human Activism: Levels of Consciousness'.

47 This description differs significantly from Shaul Magid's characterization of Izbica, which he bases on the important distinction suggested by Eliot Wolfson between antinomianism and hypernomianism (*Hasidism* 213–214). Our position is that the issue is not so much whether law expands or contracts (or in Magid's terms, whether it appears libertine or pious). It is rather that the boundary is determined by the unmediated divine will, rather than by the normative legal process. Wolfson's basic argument, adduced by Magid, is that most Jewish antinomianism is actually hypernomianism (Wolfson, 'Mystical Rationalization' 331–381, esp. 345–360). See Magid's helpful examples of hypernomianism (not cited in Wolfson) in *Hasidism* (352 n. 20).

48 See *Zohar* 1:236b (Source 27 in volume 3).

49 See our discussion on *'olam ha-ba* in the section 'Hisaron and Uniqueness'.

50 See Cluster 1 above.

51 See *MHs vol. 1* Toldot s.v. *vayeshev Yitzhak* (Source 3) for our discussion of *teshukah* in the context of Solomon's wisdom. On *teshukah* as a key feature in Lainer's acosmic humanism see esp. the section 'The Way of *Teshukah*' in Chapter Eleven of volume 1.

52 Note that the spelling in *Tanakh* is איביך.

53 For other sources and an explanation of the term *hayyim* in *MHs*, see the section 'Acosmism and Will' in Chapter Seven of volume 1.

54 See also *MHs vol. 1* Ki Teitzei s.v. *ki teitzei* (analyzed in 'The Way of Teshukah', Chapter Eleven of volume 1), where the same understanding is found.

55 See also *MHs vol. 1* Ki Teitzei s.v. *ki teitzei lamilhamah* on *teshukah* and the *eishet yefat to'ar*, discussed in volume 1, Chapter 11 'The Way of *Teshukah*'.

56 As we already noted in volume 1 on this passage, *shimush* can be a rabbinic euphemism for sexual relations.

Section Four

INTEGRATION AND ECSTASY

The next section deals with several inter-related clusters and sub-clusters that all point to ways in which one can be overcome by the divine presence.

Cluster 5: The Idolatry Sources

In Halbertal and Margalit's important work on idolatry within the Jewish tradition, the authors suggest that nothing positive can be found in Jewish sources regarding idolatry.[1] In fact, according to them, the negation of paganism becomes the essential component of Jewish identity. Clearly there is validity to this position. Yet, as we have already seen, Lainer of Izbica belies this overly sweeping generalization. Lainer has a nuanced and complex view of idolatry which derives from his essential understanding of the Wisdom of Solomon. In volume 3, we will highlight what we believe to be the conceptual textual matrix for Lainer within the *Zohar* and then Luria.

In this cluster, we will outline the three major strands in Lainer's relationship to the energy of paganism. Each of the strands derives in some way from the theology and ontology underlying Solomon's great project. All of them are directly related to his understanding of the Judah archetype.

The first strand is the ontology underlying Solomon's project, which is the ontology of acosmism. According to this ontology, all *kohot* (energies; plural of *ko'ah*), including pagan ones, are part of the One, as we saw in the previous source. In the future world, pagan expressions of divinity will also be worthy of service, at least as manifestations of the one God—one, not in the limited sense of the only god, but in the sense of the all-inclusive divine. In this way of thinking, the problem with paganism is not that it is essentially wrong; rather, it is 'too early', i.e., ahead of its time. Closely allied to this is the idea that paganism represents the great powers of ecstasy and *mesirut nefesh* (self-sacrifice), which, while not always appropriate, nonetheless have a role to play in the divine service. It is also worth noting that this assertion is somewhat at odds with Lainer's limited application of acosmism to Israel, which seems structurally to exclude non-Jews, as we have pointed out elsewhere. Acosmism does seem to assure idolatry a place at the table, even if only at the right time, for the right people, and in the right context.

The second strand is the concept that idolatry is connected specifically to the daughters of the king, the power of the *nukva*. Solomon—and by inference Lainer in his wake—viewed it as essential to re-integrate this power into the holy. *Nukva* includes *teva*[2] and manifestations of the world of *'igulim*.[3] In other words, the re-evaluation of idolatry is part of Solomon's *Shekhinah* project. This is Lainer's reading, as well as that of the important sources that preceded him.[4] Important in this reclaiming are the *kohot* (primary powers) that each pagan path incarnated, the most important among them being the *ko'ah* of *teshukah*.

The third strand we note is that for Lainer, paganism—like *mikdash*—represents an alternative to law and the garb (*levushim*) of *mitzvot* in the form of unmediated access to the divine. And yet the potential trap of paganism is precisely the opposite—getting caught in its own *maseikhah*,[5] its own mediated nature, which does not reach directly to the divine.

We will now examine the key sources for each of the strands.

Strand 1: Paganism as a Phenomenon
Whose Time Has Not Yet Come

Source 26: *MHs vol. 1* Vayikra s.v. *'al kol* and Gilyon Vayikra s.v. *'al kol*

The primary passage in which the suggestion is made that paganism represents a practice of the future is a relatively complex text followed by a *gilyon*;[6] both comments are based almost entirely on a radical *Zohar* text on sacrifice, *mikdash*, and idolatry.

> על כל קרבנך תקריב מלח הוא היפך הטוב כי לא ינוח להתפשט ולגדל
> הטוב כי ארץ מליחה אינה מגדלת, אך הוא דבר שיוכל להתערב עם הטוב
> ולהוסיף טעם לטוב...ועל ענין הזה נאמר וכל קרבן מנחתך במלח תמלח

> 'With all your sacrifices offer up salt' (Lev. 2:13). This [salt] is the opposite of good; it does not allow development and growth of goodness, for nothing can grow in salty ground. However, it can mix with something good and add a good taste...Concerning this it is written, 'and all your meal-offerings shall be salted'.

The context of Lainer's interpretation is an implicit comparison of idolatry to salt. The biblical verse asserts that the sacrifice must be made over salt. Salt is generally a damaging property, but in right proportion, it can be positive.

With this background in place, Lainer explains a strange story that appears in Chronicles:

ולענין הזה מתייחס גם ענין אמציה מלך יהודה כאשר הכה את אדום
עשרת אלף ועשרת אלף השליך מראש הסלע ויבקעו, ואח"כ עבד לאלקי
אדום (ד"ה ב' כ"ה), והענין בזה כי אדום הוא ראשית הקליפה החשובה
מכל האומות ואחר הקליפה הזאת מיד מתחיל שם ישראל, ולע"ע לא ניתן
לישראל רשות עליהם רק לעתיד כמו שנתבאר במקומו

> This matter also relates to the matter of Amatzyah the king
> of Judah, when he killed 10,000 Edomites, and threw 10,000
> from the top of a rock and they were split. Then he worshiped
> the gods of Edom (2 Chronicles 2:5)…The importance of this
> is that Edom is *reishit ha-kelipah* (the first or first fruit of the
> *kelipah*[7]), the most important of all the nations…Immediately af-
> ter this *kelipah* Israel begins, and at present, Israel does not have
> *reshut* (power) over them, but only in the future, as explained.

Amatzyah, king of Judah, wages a highly successful battle against Edom
and then, surprisingly, worships the idolatrous gods of Edom. Amazingly,
instead of the clear condemnation that Halbertal would have us expect
in Jewish sources, Lainer is definitely sympathetic to Amatzyah, even if
not wholly approving of him. Edom, explains Lainer, represents the *reishit
ha-kelipah*. Juxtaposed in immediate vicinity with this *kelipah* is the name
of Israel. At the present time Israel has no *reshut* over the *kelipah* but in
the future they will have *reshut*. *Reshut* here means both domination and a
sense of permission, in the sense of permission to recognize and possibly
even engage in their forms of service.

The passage continues:

והריגת אמציה את העשרים אלף כי בקליפה עשר מדרגות כי זה לעומת זה,
וע"ז רומז העשרים אלף היינו כל העשרה מדרגות מתתא לעילא ומעילא
לתתא והי' בדעתו מאחר שכ"כ גברה ידו עליהם בודאי כל מה שיעשה
מעתה לא יסור לבבו מה' ולא יהי' בכח שום דבר רע להתגבר עליו כמו
שיהי' לעתיד ע"כ ניסה לעבוד את אלקי אדום

> The killing of the 20,000 by Amatzyah was because there
> are ten levels in the *kelipah*, one parallel to the other (i.e., the
> profane parallels the sacred). This is what the 20,000 alludes

99

to, all ten levels, from below to above and from above to below. He thought that since he was so victorious, certainly in anything he did from now on, his heart would not stray from God, and no evil thing would have the strength to overpower him, as it will be in the future. This is why he attempted to serve the gods of Edom.

Amatzyah felt that his destruction of Edom—the 20,000 killed corresponding to the levels of *kelipah*—heralded a new age, a kind of initial eschaton in which he could trust his inclination not to stray from *retzon Hashem*. He therefore trusted his inner desire to worship the gods of Edom.

According to Lainer, Amatzyah then challenges Yoash to battle as a kind of theological duel:

ושלח ליואש מלך ישראל לך נתראה פנים, היינו אף שאני עשיתי דבר
שנראה רע אעפ״כ אני דבוק בהש״י יותר ממך

And he sent a message to Yoash, the king of Israel, saying, 'Come, let us meet'. That is, although I have done something that seems evil, nevertheless, I cling to God more than you.

Amatzyah challenges Yoash to show Yoash that although it appears that he committed a grave sin in worshipping idols, he is nonetheless more righteous than Yoash.

Already at this stage it is clear that Lainer is sympathetic to Amatzyah's inner logic—yet he writes, והנה לא הי׳ רצון הש״י בזה 'but this was not God's will'. This phrase is reminiscent of another fascinating *MHs* passage,[8] where the same words are used in regard to worship of the idol Baal. Lainer suggests that Joshua, in commanding that anyone who rebuilds Jericho would be cursed, prevented great good, for Jericho was the *reishit* beginning of the conquest—similar to Edom in this passage who is *reishit ha-kelipah*. As Lainer explicitly states, בכל ראשית הוא נכלל שורש כל הכוחות 'for in every *reishit* is included the root of all the *kohot*'—hence much good could have come to Israel through her rebuilding, that is to say, through accessing her spiritual energy. Hi'el, who went to rebuild Jericho and suffered the terrible curse of Joshua, was in no sense evil, writes Lainer. Quite the contrary, he was מוסר נפש *moser nefesh*, he offered himself up in sacrifice for the sake of the people.

Mesirut nefesh in part represents for Lainer a quality that is associated with the ecstasy and passion of paganism. Yet Hi'el's *mesirut nefesh* was not accepted because 'it was not God's will', because כל זמן שלא היה רצון ה' לזה נקרא פעולה כזאת עבודת בעל '[t]he whole time that it is not God's will, such an action is called serving the Baal'.

The problem in both passages is one of timing. Hi'el, like Amatzyah, is viewed with great sympathy and even seems somewhat heroic. Yet Hi'el and Amatzyah were nevertheless punished. And yet Lainer is not prepared to end there. He feels impelled to further vindicate Amatzyah:

לכן נענש ויואש מלך ישראל תפסו, ואעפ"כ נאמר שם כי חי חי אמציה אחר מות יואש חמש עשרה שנה לרמוז כי בכל החמשה עשר מעלות שנמצא בישראל הי' אמציה גדול מיואש, וחטאו לא הי' רק לפי ערך גבול תפיסת אדם

> Therefore he was punished, and Yoash the king of Israel captured him. Even so, it says there that Amatzyah lived fifteen years after the death of Yoash, to indicate that in all of the fifteen positive qualities that are to be found in Israel, Amatzyah was greater than Yoash, and his sin was only in relation to the limits of human perception.

Even though Amatzyah is defeated and captured by Yoash, he was greater than Yoash. His sin was 'only in relation to the limits of human perception'. This is a very significant phrase which relates directly to Lainer's distinction between *mitzido*, God's perspective, and *mitzideinu*, our perspective.[9] It is only from the human perspective of duality, *tefisat adam*, that Amatzyah's paganism is indeed a sin, but Lainer's specific language implies that from God's side, it is not.

Unlike a thinker such as Hayyim of Volozhin, who considers the realm of human service of God to be almost exclusively in the realm of *mitzideinu*,[10] Lainer suggests repeatedly that is both possible and desirable to proceed from *mitzideinu* to *mitzido*. It would not be inappropriate therefore to suggest that precisely this cornerstone underlies Lainer's interpretation of Solomon's project, which he quite clearly reads as an attempt to incorporate paganism into the holy. Solomon was unwilling to wait for the eschaton in order to access reality from God's side; he was determined to move to God's side, to redeem consciousness in his own time. Therefore, after *berur*, this level of pagan consciousness should be incorporated in the holy.

At this point, Lainer suggests that the Amatzyah model is not a unique idolatry story. Rather, Lainer chooses to include this story as a part of his Judah archetype.

כי המבין בעניני מלכות בית דוד, כל מלכי יהודה הם החביבים אצל הש"י
מאוד מאד וכל מעשיהם לא הי' כפשוטם, והמבין בישעי' נאמר צא נא
לקראת אחז נא הוא לשון בקשה, כמו אב שהרע לבנו ונתרחק ממנו ואח"כ
משתדל האב לפייסו, וזה שאמר אחז לא אשאל ולא אנסה את ה' כבן
המתחטא לפני אביו

> For whoever understands matters related to the Kingdom of
> the House of David knows that all the kings of Judah are very
> much beloved by God, and all their deeds are not what they
> seem to be. He who understands what is written in Isaiah, 'Go
> out, please, to meet Ahaz' (7:3) knows that 'please' signifies
> asking, like a father who was unkind to his son, who then
> grew distant from him. Then the father tries to appease him.
> This is why Ahaz said, 'I will neither ask nor test God' (7:12),
> like a son who sins to his father's face.

Lainer writes that one who understands the nature of the house of David, 'knows that all the kings of Judah are very much beloved by God, and all their deeds are not what they seem to be'. The implication is that there is a Judah tradition, carried forward by the kings of Judah, of intimacy with God. According to Lainer, they do not need the signs and wonders of a prophet. Rather, the relationship is like that of a child and a parent.

The final part of the passage is an attempt to justify Menasheh, the most infamous idolatrous king of the Bible:

וגם ענין מנשה הי' כי נולד ביראה מופלגת עד שאין כח אנושי יכול לסבלו,
ולכל מלך יש יראה גדולה אך לו הי' ביותר התגברות, וכל חטאו הי' כי רצה
להסיר היראה מאתו ובכל המקומות נתברר אליו יראת השם יתברך ביותר

> The matter of Menasheh was also that he was born with ex-
> traordinary *yir'ah* awe, beyond what a person is strong enough
> to bear. Every king has great awe, but his was more intensely

overpowering. The whole of his sin was that he wished to eliminate this fear from himself, so that everywhere, the fear of God would become extremely clarified for him.

Menasheh was born with great *yir'ah*, in the sense that he feels that everything he does is connected to God. According to Lainer, this omnipresence of God was oppressive for Menasheh. In other words, Lainer excuses Menasheh. Lainer states in a parallel passage that Menasheh wants the experience of freely choosing God.

Of course, this does not mean that Lainer thought that one should literally engage in pagan worship or advocated in any way activity that could even be vaguely labeled as idolatrous.[11] Rather, it suggests that the *ko'ah*, what we would call in contemporary parlance the energy of paganism, can ultimately be accessed as part of divine service.

While in the passage itself sacrifice seems at least a clear conceptual possibility[12] according to Lainer, in the Gilyon comment he is more vague; in his concluding lines, Lainer seems to say that anything that is *derekh 'avodah* (the way of worship) would be proscribed and the only way in which it would be appropriate to give honor to these pagan forces is as servants of the king. Yet, earlier in the *gilyon* (in the context of his explication of the *Zohar* text upon which his reading rests), Lainer seems to say that in a redeemed reality, formal service is also a possibility, in the form of sacrifice. It is not clear in this reading whether sacrifice is limited to relating to the pagan forces as servants of the king or whether is it possible to relate to them in a non-hierarchical manner as simply manifestations of the One. Obviously, they cannot be considered independent forces; that is precisely idolatry. It is important to note that a close reading of the *Zohar* itself reveals that it, in fact, speaks in terms of allowing actual sacrifice to the pagan forces—what the *Zohar* calls *elohim aheirim* (other gods).[13] Let us turn briefly to an analysis of the *gilyon* itself and the underlying *Zohar* upon which it rests.

First, Lainer cites the well-known passage[14] in which Maimonides suggests that idolatry is rooted in a 'slippery slope' error in which people began by giving homage to pagan God-forces as manifestations or servants of the one God, and then gradually began to ascribe to them independent ontological status. After citing Maimonides, Lainer asks:

והנה באמת מפני מה אסור לכבד לכל הכוחות הלא השי״ת גם כן כח
וגבורה נתן בהם, אכן בעולם הזה לפי שכח השי״ת נסתר...ידמה שחולקים
להם כבוד מצד עצמותם שהם בפני עצמם יש בהם כח חס ושלום זולת
כח השי״ת אשר חלק ונתן להם...אבל לעתיד כשיתרבה הדעת ויתגלה כח
השי״ת מפורש בעולם אז יהיה מותר לכבד לכל מלאכי מרום ומשמשיו

> And, in truth, why is it forbidden to give honor to these
> *kohot?* After all, God did invest them with *ko'ah* and *gevurah.*
> However, since in this world God's power is hidden...one
> might therefore come to think that they are being accorded
> honor as independent beings and not because they manifest
> the energy with which God invested them. Therefore, in the
> future, when *da'at* will increase and God's power (meaning,
> the knowledge that all is part of God) will be clearly revealed
> in the world, then it will be permitted to honor all the ser-
> vants of the king (i.e., the pagan manifestations of divinity).

According to Lainer, this was the impetus for Amatzyah, who thought that
his victory over Edom indicated a significant weakening or even destruction of the *kelipah.*

We will now read the *Zohar* text that Lainer cites extensively in the *gilyon.*
To understand the text, we must start earlier in the *Zohar* passage than
Lainer's quotation. The *Zohar* (2:108a–b) begins with a general distinction between the name *YHVH,* to which sacrifice can be offered, and the
name *Elohim,* to which sacrifice must not be offered. This is consistent
with a Zoharic position that the name *Elohim* may refer to *elohim aheirim.*
Elohim aheirim are the forces just beneath or adjacent to the forces of
holiness, particularly the lowest *sefirah, Malkhut,* and are therefore often
confused with the Godhead. Lainer was very familiar with such Zoharic
readings and in fact bases one of the most striking passages in *MHs* on
such a passage.[15]

Returning to this theme several lines later, the *Zohar* posits the following distinction between *mikdash,* which personifies the eschaton, and *'olam
ha-zeh* 'this world', i.e., the as-yet-unredeemed world. In this world, the
exterior is called *sitra ahra* (the other side), and the interior is called the
mo'ah, literally 'brain', but connoting in the *Zohar* a sense of interiority and
essence. Let us read this text.

104

הכא אית רזא...דהא כל קליפה מסטרא אחרא הוי ומוחא מן מוחא,
ותדיר סטרא אחרא אקדים ורבי ואגדיל ונטיר איבא, כיון דאתרבי זרקין ליה
לבר...וזרקין להההיא קליפה, ומברכין לצדיקא דעלמא. אבל הכא בבניינא
דבי מקדשא, דסטרא בישא יתעבר מעלמא, לא אצטריך, דהא מוחא
וקליפה דיליה הוי...ההיא חומה דלבר דאיהי קליפה, דיליה היא ממש,
דכתיב (זכריה ב ט) ואני אהיה לה נאם יהו״ה חומת אש סביב, אני ולא
סטרא בישא

Here there is a secret…All *kelipah* is from the other side,
[but] the brain is from the brain (i.e., not from the other side).
The other side always precedes [the fruit], and it grows, en-
larges, and protects the fruit. When it has grown sufficiently,
we throw it out…We throw away the *kelipah* and bless the
Righteous one of the world. Here, however, in the building of
the Sanctuary, where the side of evil is gone from the world,
it is not necessary [to throw away the *kelipah*], for that brain
and *kelipah* are His. The exterior wall, which is the *kelipah*, is
literally His, as is written, 'For her, says the Lord, I will be a
surrounding wall of fire' (Zech. 2:9)—I, Myself, and not the
side of evil.

Kelipah, the husk, represents *sitra ahra* and *elohim aheirim*. In the eschaton,
which for Lainer is symbolized both by *mikdash* and *'olam ha-ba*—which,
as we have already seen, is accessible in the present—this distinction falls
away. The *kelipah* itself, i.e., the name *Elohim*, which also represents the pagan energies, is folded into the Tetragrammaton. Clearly, then, the absolute
negative perception of paganism described by Halbertal and Margalit has
fallen away in this passage. According to the *Zohar*, sacrifices to *Elohim* are
fully possible, because ultimately there is no name *Elohim*; all is included
under the great *ani* 'I'—the great, all-inclusive I of the Tetragrammaton.
Now we come to the part of the passage cited by Lainer:

בההוא זמנא (תהלים נא כא) אז תחפץ זבחי צדק, בגין דהא כדין יתחבר
כלא בחבורא חדא, ויהא שמא שלים בכל תקוניה, וכדין קרבנא להוי שלים
ליהו״ה אלהי״ם, דהשתא אלהי״ם לא אתחבר לקרבנא, דאלמלא אתחבר
ביה, כמה אלהי״ם יסלקון אודנין לאתחברא תמן, אבל בההוא זמנא...אתה
אלהי״ם לבדך, ואין אלהי״ם אחרא. ובההוא זמנא כתיב, (דברים לב לח)
ראו עתה כי אני אני הוא ואין אלהי״ם עמדי... כי אני אני תרי זמני אמאי.
אלא לדייקא דהא לית תמן אלהי״ם אלא הוא...דהא כל סטרא אחרא
אתעבר, ודייקא אני אני

105

At that time, 'then, I will want sacrifices of justice' (Psalms 51:21), for then all will be bound together in one unity, and the Name will be complete in all of its expressions; then sacrifice will be complete, for *YHVH Elohim*. For now, *Elohim* cannot be connected to sacrifice, for if *Elohim* were connected, how many gods would then lift up their ears to become connected there... But in that time, 'You shall be *Elohim* alone' and there [will be] no other *elohim* (i.e., the other gods will be incorporated into God's exclusivity). Concerning that time it is written, 'See now that I, I am he, and there are no [other] gods with Me' (Deut. 32:38). 'I, I'—why two times? [To show that] that there are no other gods there (i.e. in that time), only Him...for the other side is removed and 'I' (God) is truly [alone].

In this passage, it is clear that sacrifice to *Elohim* (i.e., what in this passage are understood by Lainer as the pagan energies) is permitted in the eschaton (the era of *mikdash*). As Lainer himself writes in explanation of the passage:

והוא כי עתה כי אסור בקרבן לכוון לשום כינוי וכח, כי יש כחות שיאמרו שיש
להם בפני עצמם איזה כח חוץ ממה שהשי״ת חלק להם

It is only now that it is forbidden to intend in a sacrifice to any power or denotation of divinity, for [at the current time] there are energies that will claim that they have power independent of what was given to them by God.

Thus far we have seen an ontological justification of paganism, again not in the literal sense, but in the desire not to have any force left out of the field of the sacred. This is coupled with an active desire—on the part of Amatzyah, for example—to include all energies in the field of the holy as primary expressions of the redemptive project. As we have already alluded to above, for a thinker who holds the lines between the present reality and the eschaton in such an intentionally blurred fashion, this is indeed a powerful and radical reading of paganism.

It is in this context that several otherwise surprising *MHs* passages, which seem to display considerable sympathy to the pagan, are better understood. Whether it is the *Asheirah* tree, the idolatry of *ov*,[16] the Golden Calf,[17] or Baal idolatry,[18] paganism gets a consistently sympathetic reading in the writings of Mordechai Lainer of Izbica.[19]

Strand 2: Reclaiming the Energy of the Feminine: The Many Faces of the *Shekhinah*

The second strand of Lainer's understanding of paganism involves the reclaiming of the energy of the feminine, the *Shekhinah* project, the power of the moon, intuition, and *teshukah*. We have already seen this strand in our discussion of the Goddess sources above. We will now briefly recapitulate to set these ideas in the specific context of paganism as a vital strand in Lainer's understanding of the Wisdom of Solomon.

It is clear that in the context of Lainer's interpretation of the *Zohar* on paganism, the essential sacred energy of paganism has a place in a redeemed world. We also saw in the Goddess sources that Solomon was in effect attempting to usher in a new redemptive age of consciousness. These two ideas make perfect sense when merged. Solomon's great mistake was not at all dissimilar to that of Amatzyah; he was, as Lainer wrote, ahead of his time.[20] Solomon was not seduced to idolatry because his wives had swayed his heart; indeed, as Lainer implies, his heart was not swayed towards paganism, and the thousand songs of Pharaoh's daughter had no effect on him.

In Lainer's reading, it was not Solomon who was seduced, but the daughter of Pharaoh, with Solomon initiating the seduction. Solomon's great project was to entice all of paganism's vital energies, which were the dominant life energies of his era, into the realm of the sacred, 'to subject them under holiness'. He understands full well that there are great powers of the erotic feminine that need to be integrated into the sacred, and that the work of integration is the work of redemption. *Teshukah*, passion, great heroism, physical prowess, and the sensuality of economics all had to find their way back to the holy, back to the Temple. Solomon saw himself as engaged in this very work. We saw clearly in many texts that this work was not separate from the Temple but of its very essence. Indeed, in Lainer's view, this was an essential part of the Temple project. In fact, it would be fair to say that according to Lainer, the Temple project and the redemptive integration of the feminine were the same project.[21] It is thus not accidental that according to the book of Kings, the temples to the female goddesses were built by Solomon in the precincts of the Temple. Indeed, that was the whole point. Building a temple merely to please a wife does not seem like a wise investment of time for a king, particularly if you have 999 other wives. The implication that emerges from Lainer's understanding of Solomon is that this was not a whim or weakness of the flesh; rather, it was Solomon's great spiritual project. This project unfolded in a very different conceptual and spiritual matrix than Lainer's, and yet, as we have shown above, Lainer clearly viewed himself as continuing it.[22] All of Lainer's key ideas are rooted in the matrix of the Wisdom of Solomon, and these ideas play an essential role.

This is an appropriate point to add a wonderful symmetry in Lainer's interpretation that clearly links, once again, Lainer's personal project—which we have already shown to have messianic implications—with Solomon's redemptive project. One of the matrix passages in the Wisdom of Solomon, which we adduced above,[23] explicitly links the key themes of Solomon, idolatry, and *mikdash*.[24] Clearly, Lainer was intentional in his choice of text upon which to comment. He chose a text prohibiting idolatry in order to imply that Solomon was *not* worshipping idolatry. In Lainer's reading, Solomon was obeying the injunction of the text and was not ruled by passion; his heart was not swayed by his wives. Lainer goes on to explain that Solomon was engaged in a grand spiritual project to 'expand God's holiness in the world': a project he began with his marriage to the daughter of Pharaoh, and which he wanted to complete with the building of the Temple. In Lainer's provocative image, one function of the Temple was to 'contain the holiness of all the vessels'; the vessels in this passage refer to the host of unique pagan energies personified in the archetypes of his different wives.

Source 27: *MHs vol. 1 Ki Tisa s.v. elohei maseikhah*

In the parallel passage, Lainer tells us what he does consider idolatry. In this classic passage, which we adduced in the context of our discussion of *retzon Hashem*, Lainer tells us that the idolatrous life is the life lived only according to the general rules of Torah, i.e., *taryag mitzvot*.[25] He then writes that to move beyond idolatry is to access *binat ha-lev*; once one has accessed *binat ha-lev*, one no longer needs to look towards the *kelalim*; rather, through *binat ha-lev* one will know how to act in every unique situation.

Lainer then refers us to the classic passage in Hukat in which he presents clearly his distinction between *kelalim* and *retzon Hashem*, which is accessed through *binat ha-lev*:

אלהי מסכה לא תעשה לך, מסכה היינו כללים וע״ז אמר הכתוב בעת שיהי׳
לך בינת הלב מפורשת אז לא תביט על הכללים להתנהג על פיהם רק בבינת
לבך תדע בכל פרט דבר איך להתנהג כמו שמצינו באליהו בהר הכרמל,
ועיין בפ׳ חקת ע״פ ויסעו מאובות ויחנו כו׳, ושם נתפרש דבר זה באר היטב

108

'Do not make molded gods for yourself' (Exod. 34:17).
'Molded' means general principles. Therefore the verse says
that when you have explicit understanding of the heart, do
not heed the general principles...but know by the understanding of your heart how to behave in each instance, as did
Elijah on Mount Carmel. See also the portion of *Hukat* on
the verse 'They travelled from Ovot, and camped, etc.,' where
this matter is fully explicated.

The point of the passage is clear. Paganism is not the straw man of evil that
emerges from foreign cultures. Rather, paganism means to live one's life by the
general normative rules, even if they are from the Torah, and never to access
the unmediated energy of *retzon Hashem*.[26] It is just such a life, and not classic
paganism, that is understood by Lainer in this passage to be idolatry. As we
have seen, this pagan energy is erotic energy. One accesses *retzon Hashem* precisely through the energy of moon/*Shekhinah*-consciousness, connected in
Solomon's wisdom directly to paganism. In a deliberate interpretive revolution, Lainer interweaves the linked sets of ideas in a stunning and radical
flow of thought and spirit. Not to access the energy of paganism implicit in
Shekhinah-consciousness, in *rei'ah* (the higher intuition that derives from
yarei'ah) is to miss the very telos of the Jewish religious service, according to
Lainer. *Yarei'ah* is the defining quality of the David, Solomon, and Judah archetypes; Lainer views himself as being from the House of David, that is, of
the Judah archetype. But even if he did not view himself as being from the
House of David, this would be of little consequence, for it is clear throughout *MHs* that the Judah persona is the ideal religious type for Lainer. Of
course, Solomon and David are deeply intertwined with the *mikdash* project;
Solomon, in particular, merges the *mikdash* project with the spiritual redemption of the pagan, restoring it to ontological legitimacy even as he integrates
the many faces of the feminine into the holy. Not to access the energy of the
moon is a spiritual travesty according to Lainer.

But here is the most dramatic point: According to Lainer, to not access the
energy of the divine sparks of the sacred in paganism would be to serve idolatry and to violate the prohibition 'Do not make molded gods for yourself'.

The replacement for idolatry, which was typically expressed in terms of the
feminine divine, seems to be *binat ha-lev*. *Binat ha-lev* is, of course, related
to the sefirotic energy of *Malkhut*, known as the lower *Shekhinah*, while
binah herself—the great mother—is known as the higher *Shekhinah*. This

reading is affirmed again by the third passage in *MHs* to comment directly on the verse 'Do not make molded gods for yourself'.[27] In this text, Lainer suggests that what is idolatrous is the ephemeral tug of this world, the goals and desires that prevent one from accessing *binah*, which is true *hayyim*, implicitly not of this world but of the world-to-come. Here again, *binah* would seem to represent *Shekhinah* either in her lower or higher forms. In particular, *hayyim* generally refers in the *Zohar* to the *sefirah* of *binah*, as does the world-to-come, which is the theme of the entire passage.[28] *Binah* and *Shekhinah* are the very *nukva* energy—'the *nekeivot* of the pagans, especially the *bat melekh*'—that Lainer, and Solomon in Lainer's reading, are intent on bringing into the realm of the sacred.

Source 28: *MHs vol. 2* Vayeira s.v. *vayikra*

One more remarkable passage captures with great insight the interlocking nature of at least three of the core motifs we have been exploring: *nukva*, paganism, and acosmic humanism. The text that Lainer chooses as the matrix of his discussion is rife with pagan imagery. Ashur/*Asheirah*, the masked gods of Ephraim in the Hosea narrative, are all part of the slide into paganism that so angers God. In the concluding chapter of Hosea, a moment of hope is introduced. God promises redemption and comfort to His people. A striking verse at the end of Hosea (14:8) reads as follows:

אפרים מה-לי עוד לעצבים אני עניתי ואשורנו אני כברוש רענן ממני פריך
נמצא

Ephraim [says]: What more have I to do with idols? I (God) have answered him *va'ashurenu* (lit., 'and I have beheld him', from the root *Sh.V.R.*). I am like a leafy cypress tree, from Me is your fruit obtained.

It is has already been pointed out by scholars and is clear from the biblical record that *Asheirah* was an integral part of the spiritual life of the ancient Israelites. While the biblical authors considered this unequivocally bad, contemporary scholarship—led in this regard by the often iconoclastic and far-reaching Raphael Patai—has suggested a more nuanced and complex relationship to *Asheirah* and her pagan pantheon, which dominated the age of the monarchy.[29] Patai adds important information to contemporary scholarship on this verse, particularly in light of new archeological finds. These finds suggest the verse should be read: 'Ephraim—what have I to do anymore with idols? I am his Anat (another goddess name) and his *Asheirah*. I am like a leafy cypress tree, from Me thy fruit is found'.[30] That is to say, 'I, *YHVH*, am the source of his fertility'.

I cite this approach to the verse in full not because I am suggesting that Lainer had any knowledge of the above. Rather, his intuition about the verse is strikingly similar: he senses the pagan energy in the text and the erotic, embracing presence of the cosmic feminine.

Citing the *Zohar*, Lainer interprets this verse as speaking of the 'passion of the נוקבא *nukva* (feminine)'. He quotes a short passage in the *Zohar* almost in its entirety. Before the point at which Lainer's quotation begins, the *Zohar* passage begins to report a conversation between the cosmic masculine principle *kudsha berikh hu* and the cosmic feminine principle כנסת ישראל *keneset Yisrael*, the 'Community of Israel', a Zoharic synonym for the *Shekhinah*. Lainer's quote begins with the following question: Why does the verse in Hosea say, 'From Me is *your* fruit obtained'? It should say, 'From Me is *My* fruit obtained'. He answers in the following manner:

זש"ה אני כברוש רענן ממני פריך נמצא (הושע י"ד, ט') ובזוה"ק (לך
פ"ה:) פריי נמצא לא כתיב אלא פריך, ההיא תיאובתא דנוקבא דעביד נפש
ואתכליל בתוקפא דדכורא ואתכליל נפש בנפש ואתעבידו חד כליל דא בדא
כדאמרן. לבתר אשתכחו תרוויהו בעלמא ודא בחילא דדכורא אשתכח
איבא דנוקבא

> The verse says, 'I am like a leafy cypress tree, from Me is your fruit obtained' (Hosea 14:9). And the holy *Zohar* says, 'Not "My fruit" but rather "your fruit"—[this describes] the passion of the feminine, which creates a soul that is included in the *tokfa* (power) of the male. Each soul is included in each other, and they make one soul, which includes both, as we have already stated. Afterwards, both of them exist in the world. And this is [the meaning of] through the strength of the masculine the fruit of the feminine is obtained' (3:85b).

This describes the process whereby the cosmic feminine and masculine each provide part of a soul. After this process, the masculine and feminine sides 'exist in the world...through the strength of the masculine'.[31] Lainer uses this framework to explain the primal passion of the *nukva*, together with the biblical incident that occasioned the discussion, namely, the binding of Isaac. Lainer states that everything yearns for its root:

הענין בזה כי כל דבר שואף לשרשו, האבן שואף לירד, והאש לעלות, וכן
אברהם אבינו שאף לעשות רצון השי״ת

> The point is that everything yearns for its root. The rock wants to go down, the fire to rise, and likewise did Abraham yearn to do the will of God.

At this point, some background is necessary so that we can fully understand the subtlety of Lainer's next exegetical move, in which he uses another *Zohar* passage to radically interpret the biblical story of the binding of Isaac. Lainer's interpretation of the binding of Isaac is based on an exegetical principle of the *Zohar* to which we have referred,[32] namely, that when the biblical text uses the divine name *Elohim*, it may be referring to *elohim aheirim*. The *Zohar* passage mentioned by Lainer suggests that Abraham cannot access the clear energy of the *Shekhinah*. The problem is that the feminine *Shekhinah* principle of *dibur* (speech) is disconnected from the masculine *Tif'eret* principle of *kol* (voice), and therefore conveys to Abraham a *dibur* that is not *meforash* (explicit). The *Zohar* describes this *dibur* as being conveyed through an אספקלריא דלא נהרא *aspaklariya delo nahara* 'unclear prism'. This is what Lainer refers to in the continuation of the passage:

אבל אברהם אף שזה הנסיון היה באספקלריא דלא נהרא כדאיתא בזוה״ק
(וירא ק״כ) והיינו שנעלם ממנו הבהירות, ורק בשרשו כיון לרצון השי״ת אף
בעת שנסתר ממנו הסייעתא, ולכן כתיב פריך ששואף בטבעו לרצון השי״ת
אף למעלה מדעתו, וזה נקרא תיאובתא דנוקבא, שבשרשו מקושר באהבת
השי״ת

> Abraham, however, although his test was [in the realm of] the unclear prism, as one finds in the holy *Zohar* (1:120a), which means that clarity had gone from him, still, in his root, he sought *retzon Hashem* God's will, even when divine assistance was not apparent. Thus it is written, 'your fruit', for his nature is to aspire to God's will, even *lema'alah mida'ato* beyond his awareness. This is called 'the passion of the female'—that is, his root is bound to the love of God.

112

Abraham's job is to disambiguate the voice of unredeemed paganism. His job is not to advance beyond the feminine of the pagan to the masculine voice of the biblical God as we might have expected. On the contrary, Abraham in this passage must go deeper into the primal feminine of his nature and access the deepest erotic feminine voice, what the *Zohar* adduced by Lainer calls תיאובתא דנוקבא *tei'uvta denukva* 'the passion of the feminine'. In the context of Izbica, we might want to term this 'redeemed or purified pagan consciousness'. This means in effect that Abraham has to seek his *teva'* (deep nature), which is rooted in God. To put it more dramatically, according to this passage, Abraham's deep nature is God. This is the category of 'non-dual humanism', which radically affirms human dignity by claiming that if one can but see through one's superficial nature and access one's *teva'*, one will realize that just like the rock or fire, one can only do the will of God.

Lainer uses this understanding to explain the Hosea verse which initiated the Zoharic conversation. The verse is saying that it is not the fruit of *My* tree that I give you from me. Rather, I give you from me the fruit of *your* tree, for you and I are, in an ultimate sense, one. According to Lainer, this is the matrix of divine love: the desire of the human being to follow their nature back to its source. Actually, it has never left its source, other than in an epistemological sense. Therefore, the journey back is a journey of *berur*, which in this context means the clarification of consciousness and desire that allows one to see the true nature of reality.

Here again, the nonduality and acosmism that underlie Lainer's theology are apparent in their radically empowering form. This entire passage is directly linked to the Judah archetype, as we are reminded by Lainer in this passage. Abraham כיון לרצון השי״ת...אף למעלה מדעתו 'intended *retzon Hashem* God's will...even *lema'alah mida'ato* beyond his awareness'. These two phrases, as we have seen, are defining characteristics of the Judah archetype.

In light of all of the above, we can suggest what might be Lainer's reading of the Hosea text. Ephraim asks, 'What have I to do with idols?' and God answers, 'I will be your *Asheirah*'. In other words, you can access the primal erotic energy of the Goddess within the precincts of the sacred. God continues, 'I am your leafy cypress tree'—this is a Goddess-tree image—'from Me your fruit will come.'

Given this reading, which brings to the fore the engagement of pagan energy in the text, the otherwise virtually inexplicable final verse of Hosea makes perfect sense: מי חכם ויבן אלה, נבון וידעם. כי ישרים דרכי יהוה, וצדקים ילכו בם ופשעים יכשלו בם 'Who is the wise one who will understand this? Straight are the ways of the Lord; the righteous will walk in them, and the wicked will stumble in them.'[33]

What is the great secret that requires someone wise to understand it? What is the double-edged sword implicit in the verse that will guide the righteous but cause the wicked to fall? According to Lainer, it would be the power of the feminine that inheres in the pagan. The wicked will get lost in the realm of the *kelipah*—of *elohim aheirim*. Only the *tzadik* will find their way to the *tei'uvta denukva* that is their deepest nature, which is one with God.

The *Teva'-Nukva-'Igulim* Sub-Cluster

The concept of the *teva'* (deepest level of nature) being one with God is essential to *MHs* and is a leitmotif of the Wisdom of Solomon genre. This idea was one of the great attractions of paganism. A cluster of terms, including *nukva*, *teva'*, and *'igulim* serves to express this idea in Izbica. These terms are often related to *hitpashtut*. When used in this sense, *hitpashtut* is the natural expansion of *teva'* to its deepest and fullest expression. Of course, this in turn is related to *teshukah*—a core expression linked with *teva'* and *hitpashtut*, which, as we have seen, is radically affirmed in Lainer's thought.

We will point out very briefly some of the specific *MHs* sources[34] that allude to the *Teva'-Nukva-'Igulim* sub-cluster. The first passages are found in the Goddess sources adduced above, which told of the *nekeivot* that Solomon wants to bring into the realm of the holy. The second source concerning the *tei'uvta denukva*, which talks both about *nukva* and *teva'*, we have just analyzed.

The third term, *'igulim*, is a leitmotif in a number of *MHs* texts. *'Igulim*, circles, represent the natural order, which is nonhierarchal and inclusive which all have a place. The meaning of *'igulim* is best represented by the image of מחול *mehol*, the circle dance in which everyone has a unique place and in which there is no התעלות *hit'alut* (hierarchy).[35] Not surprisingly, *'igulim* are associated in *MHs* with a *nukva* image, specifically, with the matriarch Sarah.[36] The argument for the greater dignity of the *'igul* is put forth by Korah. This would seem to be a prima facie indication that Lainer—like much of Hebrew mystical thought—while granting *'igulim* an important place in the spiritual dynamic, affirms the spiritual supremacy of *yosher*.[37] In Izbica, however, the issue is far from clear. A closer reading reveals that in the eschaton,[38] the spiritual dignity and paradoxical validity of Korah will in fact be affirmed.[39]

'Igulim in kabbalistic literature is often synonymous with *teva'*.[40] It was precisely this natural order, *teva'*, that was affirmed, deified, and worshipped in the underlying energy of paganism.[41] *Teva'* in this sense, for Izbica, means not just nature in its superficial sense but deep nature as a principle

of spiritual organization in which competition, hierarchy, and angst give way to egalitarianism, cooperation, and the centeredness of knowing that everyone and everything has a place.[42]

Strand 3: Paganism in Relation to Unmediated *Shekhinah*

The final strand we will examine in the Idolatry cluster is the concept of idolatry as an unmediated approach to God. Lainer's attraction to the energy of paganism seems to lie in his desire to embrace the *Shekhinah* in her fullness, unmediated by the law. This desire is the impetus for Lainer's conflation of the Solomon project of integrating the feminine within the realm of the sacred by including the many faces of *Shekhinah* in the *mikdash*, along with the powers of the moon that allow one to transcend the normative *kelalei divrei Torah* and *taryag mitzvot*, in order to access, align with, and incarnate *rei'ah* and *retzon Hashem*.

With this understanding, we can analyze three passages whose reference to idolatry is not apparent upon first reading. The three passages, which we will cite in brief, share a feature in common—they connect access to the unmediated will of God/*Shekhinah* without her *levushim* with the *berur* clarification of the drive for idolatry (as well as of the drive for illicit sexuality[43]). While these idolatry texts might otherwise be inexplicable, they can be properly understood within the framework of the Wisdom of Solomon genre as an expression of the core Judah archetype idea of accessing the unmediated will of God.

Source 29: *MHs vol. 1 Megilah 12 s.v. veha-karov* and *vol. 2 Megilah 12b s.v. bise'udato*[44]

The context for the first two passages is the story of Vashti being ordered to appear before King Ahaseurus. According to the Talmud, it is the king's celebrants, who, when asked if they want to see Vashti, respond, 'Yes, but only if she is naked.' According to the Baal Shem 'naked' means they desired to see the *Shekhinah* without her *levushim*. Vashti's refusal to come indicates that the time for this has still 'not yet come.' In the passage from *MHs* volume 2, we read:

איתא בשם הבעש״ט שזה הענין ערומה ועדיין לא בא, ביאור הענין בזה
כמו שכתיב (ישעיה סא י) שוש אשיש בה׳ תגל נפשי באלהי כי הלבישני
בגדי ישע מעיל צדקה יעטני...שזה הענין הוא ערומה ולא בא שהיה קרוב
להתגלות מפורש האור בלי לבוש אך עדיין לא בא עד עת קץ

116

It was said in the name of the Baal Shem Tov that this is
the matter of 'naked and still not yet come'. The explanation
of this matter is found in the verse, 'I will greatly rejoice in
the Lord, my soul shall be joyful with my God; for He has
clothed me with garments of salvation, He has cloaked me
with the robe of righteousness' (Isa. 61:10)…This matter
refers to 'naked and still not yet come', for it was very close to
the explicit revelation of the light, without garments, but the
end-time had still not yet arrived.

In the volume 1 passage, Lainer explains that for the Besht, the desire to
see Vashti naked is a symbol of the desire to move beyond *mitzvah* and
embrace the *Shekhinah* without her garments.

הנה שייכות המאמר הזה למיתת ושתי, דהנה הבעש״ט ז״ל אמר על ערומה
ולא באה שזה הענין ערומה עדיין לא בא עכ״ל, הענין בזה כי הש״י נתן להם
לישראל תורה ומצות שהם לבושים שעל ידם יוכלו להשיג עצמותו ית׳, כי
בעו״הז אין בכח אנושי להשיג עצמותו ית׳ בלתי ע״י לבושים מתגשמים עד
שכל מה שאנו מקבלים הוא באמצעות הלבושים, ולע״ע כאשר ישופע שפע
מהש״י משפיע דרך הארבעה עולמות ע״י מדה של עשר ספירות שהעולם
צריך כעת עד שמגיע לעו״הז שיוכלו להשיג ההשפעה

This comment is related to the death of Vashti. For the Baal
Shem Tov said concerning 'naked, and still not yet come'
that this matter of 'naked' had not yet arrived. That is, God
gave Israel Torah and commandments, which are garments,
through which they may attain His essence. For in this world,
it is not within human power to achieve His essence other than
by means of physical garments, to the point where everything
we receive is through garments. At present, when the flow [of
blessing] flows from God, it flows through the four worlds by
means of the ten *sefirot*, which the world needs right now, until
it reaches this world, so that they all may attain to the flow.

In the second part of this passage, *mitzvot* serve a vital function—they
are the mediating presence between the person and God. Through the
mitzvot, one is able to even touch עצמותו *'atzmuto*, something of God's essence. *Mitzvot* serve the dialectical function of connecting human to God
while at the same time retaining the separation between human and God.

The *MHs* passage from volume 1 continues:

וגם האומות יוכלו להשיג כי בלבוש יש להם ג"כ איזה אחוזה, אך
בההשפעה הלזו הם עושים כל התועבות, ע"כ כאשר ראו אנכ"הג שצוה
אחשורוש שתבוא ושתי ערומה הבינו כי רוצה השי"ת להנחיל להם לישראל
התגלות האמיתי בלי שום לבוש כמו שיהי' לעתיד שיגלה הקב"ה אורו בלי
שום לבוש

> The nations would also be able to attain this, for they have some
> grasp of garments, but with this influx, they commit all kinds of
> abominations. Therefore, when the Men of the Great Assembly
> saw that Ahasuerus commanded Vashti to come to him naked,
> they understood that God wanted to bestow upon Israel the
> true revelation, without any garments, as it is to be in the future,
> when God reveals His light without any garments whatsoever.

Since God's essence is translated into more accessible cultural spiritual categories, *levushim*, it can be accessed even by the non-Jewish world.[45] When
the rabbis saw this great desire on the part of the nations to see Vashti
naked, they understood it to be but a lower physical manifestation of a
higher process. The nations were correctly attuned to a spiritual movement
in the higher worlds but were only able to experience it on a lower level.
Clearly, says Lainer, this was a new time, a time which partook of the *'atid*,
the redemptive eschaton, when the *Shekhinah* would be prepared to reveal
herself without her garments. Of course, the desire to access the redemptive eschaton in the present, which Lainer reads into this text, is the very
essence of Lainer's Wisdom of Solomon project.

Because this would be a time of unmediated *Shekhinah*, there was an
implicit danger that עריות *'arayot*, illicit sexuality, and *'avodah zarah*,
idolatry—which are both understood here as expressions of unmediated
divinity—would run rampant: ומזה יבא להם התאוה בהתגברות 'and as a result,
overwhelming passion will come upon them'. In effect, what Lainer is pointing to in these passages is the danger of the attempt to access the Judah
archetype—which belongs to the eschaton—before its time, or put another way, before there are appropriate vessels to hold the light.[46] According to
Lainer, this danger was the impetus for the great cultural spiritual project
of the Men of the Great Assembly who sought not to 'uproot', which is the
Talmudic idiom, but to—in Lainer's language— *mevarer* clarify the drive

to pagan idolatry and illicit sexuality (in other words, the *yetzer* for *'arayot* and the *yetzer* for *'avodah zarah*):

וכן ע״י שנתן לנו השי״ת תורה ומצות שהם לבושים לאור השי״ת, ע״י כן
אנו דבוקים בהשי״ת ומכירים שנמצא בורא עולם, וזה הוא מחמת שלבו של
אדם הוא מלא נגיעה לכן ע״י יגיעה ועבודה מברר את לבו בהלבושים האלו
וסבל מזה ההשתדלות ועבודה, אכן לעתיד כאשר יהיה לב האדם מנוקה
ומבורר בשלימות, אז יהיה התגלות אלהות מפורש בלי שום לבוש. והנה
בזמן ההוא היה היה אנשי כנסת הגדולה שנצחו יצרא דע״ז כדאיתא בגמ׳ (יומא
סט:) ויצרא דעריות גם כן

At that time were the Men of the Great Assembly, who vanquished the desire for idolatry, as brought in the Talmud (*b Yoma* 69b), as well as the desire for illicit sexuality (lit., 'nakedness').[47]

The *berur* of the drive to paganism refers to the classic passage in the Talmud when the rabbis pray to uproot the drive for paganism and then the drive for idolatry. Although in general we have deferred explicating Lainer's sources until volume 3, in this case we need to adduce the Talmudic text to which he refers in both passages in order to understand his intent.

ויצעקו אל ה׳ אלהים בקול גדול (נחמיה ט) מאי אמור אמר רב ואיתימא
ר׳ יוחנן בייא בייא היינו האי דאחרביה למקדשא וקליה להיכליה וקטלינהו
לכולהו צדיקי ואגלינהו לישראל מארעהון ועדיין מרקד בינן כלום יהבתיה
לן אלא לקבולי ביה אגרא לא איהו בעינן ולא אגריה בעינן נפל להו פיתקא
מרקיעא דהוה כתב בה אמת אמר רב חנינא שמע מינה חותמו של הקב״ה
אמת אותיבו בתעניתא תלתא יומין ותלתא לילוותא מסרוהו ניהליהו נפק
אתא כי גוריא דנורא מבית קדשי הקדשים אמר להו נביא לישראל היינו
יצרא דעבודה זרה שנאמר ויאמר זאת הרשעה (זכריה ה) בהדי דתפסוה
ליה אשתמיט ביניתא ממזייא ורמא קלא ואזל קליה ארבע מאה פרסי אמרו
היכי נעביד דילמא חס ושלום מרחמי עליה מן שמיא אמר להו נביא שדיוהו
בדודא דאברא וחפיוהו לפומיה באברא דאברא משאב שאיב קלא שנאמר
ויאמר זאת הרשעה וישלך אותה אל תוך האיפה וישלך את אבן העופרת
אל פיה אמרו הואיל ועת רצון הוא נבעי רחמי איצרא דעבירה בעו רחמי
ואמסר בידייהו אמר להו חזו דאי קטליתו ליה להההוא כליא עלמא חבשוהו
תלתא יומי ובעו ביעתא בת יומא בכל ארץ ישראל ולא אשתכח אמרי היכי
נעביד נקט ליה כליא עלמא ניבעי רחמי אפלגא פלגא ברקיעא לא יהבי
כחלינהו לעיניה ושבקוהו ואהני דלא מיגרי ביה לאיניש בקריבתה

119

'And they cried in a loud voice to the Lord their God' (Neh. 9:4). What did they cry?...Woe, woe, this is the one who has destroyed the Sanctuary, burnt the Temple, killed all the righteous, driven all Israel into exile, and he is still dancing around among us! You have surely given him to us so that we may receive reward through him. We want neither him, nor reward through him!...They ordered a fast of three days and three nights, whereupon he was surrendered to them. He came forth from the Holy of Holies like a young fiery lion. Thereupon the prophet said to Israel: This is the desire for idolatry, as it is said, 'And he said: This is wickedness...' (Zech. 5:8). As they took hold of him a hair of his beard fell out, and he raised his voice and it went (was audible) for four hundred parasangs (1000 miles). Thereupon they said: How shall we act? Perhaps, God forbid, they might have mercy upon him from heaven! The prophet said unto them: Cast him into a leaden pot, and close its opening with lead, because lead absorbs the voice, as it is said, 'And he said: This is wickedness. And he cast him down into the midst of the measure, and he cast the weight of lead upon the mouth thereof'. They said: Since this is a time of grace, let us pray for mercy concerning the desire for [sexual] sin. They prayed for mercy, and he [too] was handed over to them. [The prophet] said to them: Realize that if you kill him, the world is finished. They imprisoned him for three days, then looked in the whole land of Israel for a fresh egg and could not find it. Thereupon they said: What shall we do now? Shall we kill him? The world would be finished. Shall we beg for half-mercy? They do not grant 'halves' in heaven. They put out his eyes and let him go. It helped inasmuch as he no longer entices men to commit incest.[48]

A complex relationship to idolatry is evinced in the Talmudic text. First, note that the physical form in which the drive for idolatry is personified is a lion: a familiar form associated with both *mikdash* and idolatry in earlier sources.[49] Second, the drive for idolatry emerges from the Temple's epicenter in the Holy of Holies, indicating a profound relationship between paganism and the Temple.[50] The implication of the desire for idolatry being placed by the rabbis in a leaden pot is that even though the power of paganism is somewhat muffled, beneath the surface of reality, the lion's roar continues unabated.[51] The drive for idolatry lets out a great roar, causing the rabbis to realize that its potent force has divine sympathy. Therefore, instead of killing the lion they lock it in a leaden cauldron to muffle its roar. Similarly, upon attempting to entirely neutralize the power of the second lion, which personifies the sexual drive, they realize that neither the physical nor the spiritual world can continue without this vital power. So although they succeed in curbing a small measure of its destructive potential, its essential vitality and power remain.

It would seem that the impetus for the *berur* on the part of the Men of the Great Assembly was the desire to open themselves, without being spiritually undermined, to the great possibility of recovering Vashti: the *Shekhinah* without her *levushim*. What Lainer understands here, based on his careful and consistent use of this particular Talmudic text in the context of the drive to access the *Shekhinah* without mediation—symbolized in this passage by Vashti naked —is that one cannot engage in the Judah project without the implicit danger that is part and parcel of the passionate yearning for the unmediated embrace of the *Shekhinah*.

In the conclusion of the passage, our reading is confirmed as Lainer brings the whole discussion directly back to the Judah archetype. He employs King David imagery and verses that he has used before in one of the classic David passages[52] (analyzed above). Lainer views the project of the Men of the Great Assembly as just one episode in the ongoing spiritual project of the Judah archetype, namely, to access the unmediated *Shekhinah*:

ולכן מהראוי של עתיד יגלה להם הש״י את אורו בגילוי הגמור מבלי
אמצעית כמ״ש בשירי דוד מלך ישראל נכספה וגם כלתה נפשי לחצרות ה׳
לבי ובשרי ירננו לאל חי, היינו לע״ע כאשר נצרך ללבושים נכספה וגם כלתה
נפשי לחצרות ה׳ היינו לבושים לאורו, אבל לבי ובשרי ירננו אל אל חי היינו
היוחל והקווי שלי הוא להתגלות האור שיהי׳ לעתי׳ לבלי לבוש רק לחיים
פשוטים זהו לאל חי

> In the future, God will reveal His light, totally revealed,
> without any intermediary, as is written in the verses of David
> the King of Israel, 'My soul yearns and so longs for the court
> of the Lord; my heart and my flesh will sing to the living
> God' (Psalms 84:3). That is, at present, when garments are
> necessary, 'my soul yearns and so longs for the court of the
> Lord', this means garments for His light. However, 'My heart
> and my flesh will sing to the living God'—this means that

my hope and longing is for the revelation of the light of the future, without any garment, [through nothing] except simple life itself—that is 'the living God'.[53]

The point of the passage in its entirety is that both pagan ecstasy and illicit sexuality are tightly connected to the desire to see the *Shekhinah* without her *levushim*. They may perhaps be understood as shadow expressions of the higher drive to embrace unmediated *Shekhinah*.

It is worth noting in passing that the last part of the passage contains a sub-theme of the desire to move beyond *mitzvot*. This is the yearning for simplicity, which is referred to several times throughout *MHs*. It is a sophisticated and hard-won simplicity, but simplicity nonetheless.[54]

Source 30: *MHs vol. 1* Vayehi s.v. *uvedam*

Our interpretation of the *berur* of the *yetzer* of 'avodah zarah and of 'arayot as being fundamentally connected to the desire to touch the unmediated embrace of *Shekhinah*, that is to say, the Judah archetype, receives further support from the third mention in *MHs* of this same Talmudic passage (*bYoma* 69b). The context for the passage is the wine blessing given by Jacob to Judah, and given by Moses to the entire people. We will continue our analysis of the wine motif in this text below (Source 35). For now it is sufficient to know that wine is a consistent symbol for the Judah archetype.

רק משה מלגאו ויעקב מלבר, כי אצל יעקב נאמר ענבים היינו שני טעותים
יברר הש"י על שבט יהודה היינו יצרא דעריות ויצרא דע"ז, ובירר הש"י
שהוא נקי בשתיהן, ומשה מלגאו כי מרע"ה ראה כי אין ליהודה שום טעות
ביצרא דע"ז כי בזה כבר נתברר שהוא נקי מאז, רק יצרא דעריות צריך עוד
להתברר, כדאמר רב לא עבדו ישראל את העגל אלא להתיר להם עריות
בפרהסיה אבל ביצרא דע"ז כבר הם נקיים והבן

It is 'Moses from inside, and Jacob from outside'. For regarding Jacob it says, 'grapes', that is, God will clarify two errors related to the tribe of Judah: the desire for (illicit) sex and the desire for idolatry. And God ascertained that he was cleansed in relation to them both. Moses from inside—for Moses saw that Judah made no mistake with regard to idol worship, for it was already clarified that he was exceedingly clean. It was only the desire for sex that still needed to be clarified. As Rav said,

122

'Israel worshipped the golden calf in order to allow incest in public'. Regarding the inclination for idol worship, however, they were already cleansed. Understand this.

In this passage we see clearly that the *berur* of the *yetzer* for *'avodah zarah* is precisely the accomplishment of the Judah archetype, whose demarcating spiritual quality is the ability to embrace, without danger, the unmediated *Shekhinah*.

Cluster 6: The Wine Sources

The context for the previous passage is one of the wine passages—a cluster in *MHs* that we will analyze presently. The wine texts outline several major themes. The first is the association of wine with Judah and *Shekhinah*, and with the salient features of the Judah archetype. The sources dealing with this theme link all the distinctive motifs of the Judah complex to wine, including uniqueness, the move beyond *da'at* to a higher place where one participates in unmediated divinity, and the ability to access the unmediated *retzon Hashem*.

In this theme we come in full glory to the merging of the two paths of descending from the One and ascending to the One.[55] The first is the path from the many to the One, an ascending path of eros, and wisdom. The second is the descending path of agape and compassion; this is the flowing of the One into the many. Wine—associated in myth with Dionysus[56]—is the paradigmatic symbol of ascending to the One through eros. For Lainer, however, the descent and ascent merge into a seamless whole. One of the places this becomes most clear is in a series of passages on wine that are both provocative and completely unnoted—both in scholarship and more traditional writings on Izbica. Almost every mention of wine is seized on by Lainer to make a comment supporting the Judah archetype he develops throughout *MHs*.

Second, we will note the Izbica motif of wine as that which allows people to access levels of perception and vision beyond the normative. Third, we will explore a unique sub-cluster within the wine sources which we term the *menutzah* sub-cluster. The *menutzah* sources discuss the need to give up control to God and let God act 'through you'. In the language of these wine texts, one becomes '*menutzah*'—overpowered and overwhelmed by God.

These sources are best introduced with the following passage in which Lainer presents the core principles of the wine motif.

יין ושכר אל תשת אתה ובניך אתך וגו'. איתא בגמ' (כריתות י"ג:) אל
תשתהו כדרך שכרותו. כי ענין שיכור הוא שנדמה לו שאינו צריך להשי"ת
כי נטרד דעתו ואין לו בינה, ולכן הכהן אסור לשתות דרך שכרותו כי הכהן
צריך להיות תמיד ביראה ובדעת כדכתיב (מלאכי ב',ה') ואתנם לו מורא
וייראני וגו' כי שפתי כהן ישמרו דעת וגו'

'Do not drink wine and liquor, you and your sons with you,
etc.'. It is brought in the Talmud: Do not drink in a manner
that one becomes drunk (*bKer.* 13b). The meaning of being
drunk is that it seems to one that he has no need for God,
for his mind is confused and he has no understanding. This
is why it is forbidden for a priest to drink in a manner that
he becomes drunk, for a priest must always be in awe and
of a clear mind. As it is written, 'I will give him fear and he
will fear Me, etc…for the lips of the priest keep knowledge,
etc.'(Mal. 2:5).

The first passage discusses the prohibition of drinking wine by priests in
a way that would inebriate them. The priest is associated with the tribe of
Levi, which is defined by *yir'ah*.[57] Naturally, Levi cannot drink wine: it would
confuse his *da'at*, which would adversely affect his ability to remain in *yir'ah*.

However, this is true only for Levi. The tribe of Judah is connected to the
energy of *Shekhinah* and the moon, and Judah's blessings from Jacob are
extravagant blessings of wine.

אבל בשבט יהודה נאמרו כל ברכות ביין (בראשית מט) אסרי לגפן עירה
ולשרקה בני אתנו כבס ביין לבשו ובדם ענבים סותה חכלילי עינים מיין, כי
שבט יהודה נמשל לירח שלית ליה מגרמיה כלום כדאיתא בזה"ק (ויחי רלז.
רלח.) (ר"ה כה)

Concerning the tribe of Judah, however, all the blessings were
said about wine: 'He ties his foal to a vine and his donkey's
colt to the choice vine; he washes his clothes in wine and his
garments in the blood of grapes; his eyes are red from wine'
(Gen. 49:11). For the tribe of Judah is compared to the moon,
which has nothing in and of itself, as is written in the holy
Zohar (1:237a, 238a)[58] (*bRosh Hashanah* 25a).

Lainer's reading links the verses connecting Judah to wine with the connection between Judah and *Shekhinah*, through the symbolism of moon, which has 'nothing in and of itself' *leit leih megarmeih klum*, being totally transparent to divinity. In this manner, Lainer weaves the Judah, wine, *Shekhinah*, and moon sources into one strand. The natural conclusion is that Judah, unlike Levi, can drink wine. Moreover, Judah can drink in a way that induces inebriation.

The passage continues:

> ששבט יהודה מכיר תמיד הכרה מפורשת שהכל מה׳ לכן נאמרו אצלו
> ברכות ביין , כי במלך איתא בגמ׳ (ברכות לד:) כיון שכרע שוב אינו זוקף
> שכל הכורע זוקף בשם, אבל המלך אינו יכול לזקוף בעצמו עד שיזקפהו
> השי״ת, שעומד בהתבטלות עצום נגד השי״ת, ולכל אינו נקרא אצלו דרך
> שכרותו

> For the tribe of Judah always has explicit awareness that everything is from God. This is why his blessings are related to wine. For concerning a king it is brought in the Talmud: 'After [the king] kneels down, he does not stand up again [at the recitation of God's name, instead concluding the blessing while kneeling]' (*bBerakhot* 34b). Everyone [else] who kneels down, stands up for [God's] name, but the king cannot stand up until God stands him up, for he is in a state of *hitbatlut ʿatzum* tremendous effacement before God, which is why this is not characterized for him as 'the manner of becoming drunk' (which is forbidden to all others).

Judah is the archetype of the king. The king, as Lainer points out, is different from the priest and even the prophet in that he does not only access but actually incarnates the will of God. He is essentially infallible; as Lainer states, even his *divrei hulin* express the will of God. This is because the tribe of Judah incarnates what Lainer calls *hitbatlut ʿatzum* to God. Normally one would translate *hitbatlut* as nullification. However, in this case that is clearly not what it means. It is not an effacing term but an empowering part of Lainer's acosmic humanism. It means something closer to 'fully transparent to God', as we interpreted the image of the moon above. God flows through the king, lifting him up after he kneels in prayer, and speaking through his mouth. This is all expressed in terms of inebriation, which is fully appropriate to Judah.

Of course, the difference between Levi and Judah implied here and explicated in many other passages[59] is that while Levi is defined by *yir'ah* and thus holds his *da'at* at all times, the essence of the Judah archetype is that he meets God in the place beyond *da'at*.

Source 32: *MHs vol. 2* Shelah s.v. *vehikriv*

Despite Lainer's emphasis on the tribe of Judah, the ability to meet God beyond *da'at* is not limited to the king; the king is simply the pure form of the Judah archetype. This archetype is accessible to all, as we see in the next source.

ויין לנסך רביעית ההין וגו'. זה שאמר הכתוב (יואל ב כו) ואכלתם אכול
ושבוע והללתם את שם ה' אלהיכם, היינו שאף אחר שתאכלו ותשבעו
תהללו את שם ה'. שלזה רומז ענין נסכים שישראל מקדישים יין ומביאין
למזבח שאף שלא מדעתם יהיה מלא הלולים לה', היינו אף מתוך שכחה
וטרדה שלזה רומז יין מכל מקום הם דבוקים בה'

'And wine for a wine-offering: a quarter of a *hin*, etc.' (Num. 17:5). The verse says, 'And you shall eat well and be satisfied, and praise the name of *Hashem* your God' (Joel 2:26). This means that even after you eat and are satisfied, you will praise the name of God. This is alluded to by the wine offerings. Israel sanctifies wine and brings it to the altar so that even *shelo mida'atam* unconsciously they should be full of praise for God, that is, even out of forgetfulness and distraction. Wine alludes to this, that no matter what, they still cling to God.

Here again, Lainer suggests that wine is the symbol of moving beyond *da'at* and connecting to God from that higher place. Here, however, this applies not only to the king, but to all of Israel. Even—and indeed especially—after Israel is full of food, says Lainer, they praise God from that place of fullness beyond *da'at*. The description, Dionysian in character, is one of fullness and physicality. The connection with God is the essence of wine libations.

Source 33: *MHs vol. 1 Shabbat s.v. vehineih*[60]

In the next passage, clarified wine is the symbol of redeemed consciousness.

והנה זה הפרק טולין את המשמרת מרמז על כל הבּרורים שצריך להיות בין
ישראל שעתיד הקב״ה לברר ביום שכלו שבת עד שיהיה היין נקי בלי שום
סיג ופסולת, וזהו עתידה תורה שתשתכח מישראל היינו שיהי׳ רצון השי״י
נעלם בהסתר הפנים בלי שום דעת ועצה מד״ת שהם תרי״ג עיטין כדאיתא
בזוה״ק

This…hints at all the clarifications that must occur among the
people of Israel, which God is destined to clarify on 'the day
that is wholly Shabbat', until the wine is cleansed, without any
dregs or waste. This is [what it means to say] 'in the future the
Torah will be forgotten from Israel' (*bShab.* 138b)—it means
that the will of God will be hidden by 'the concealment of the
face', [meaning] without any knowledge or counsel from the
words of the Torah, which are the six hundred and thirteen
suggestions, as is written in the holy *Zohar*.

In Lainer's language, the goal of all *berur* is to produce clean wine 'without
any dregs'. This is a third wine image in *MHs* that, as we will see, Lainer
returns to in other wine sources. Pure wine is the image of the future redeemed stage of consciousness, 'the day that is wholly Shabbat'. In this way,
Lainer radically reinterprets as blessing the dire rabbinic warning that 'in
the future Torah will be forgotten from Israel'. According to Lainer, this is
a positive development, for in the future—the stage of pure wine without
any dregs at all—everyone will be so God-intoxicated that they will no
longer need the commandments, the *taryag mitzvot*, as the mediator of the
divine will. After all, teaches the *Zohar* cited by Lainer, the *mitzvot* are really עיטין *'itin*, guidelines, advice and suggestions for *deveikut*.

The passage continues:

ואז יהי׳ הבירור גמור שיכוונו ישראל לרצון הש״י רק ממעמקי לבם...
ומדביקותם האמיתי לא יטה לבם מרצון הקב״ה ויתברר שהם דבקים בהש״י
דאורייתא וקודב״ה וישראל חד

Then will there be complete clarification, for Israel will be
attuned to God's will from the depths of their hearts alone…

And because of their true devotion, their hearts will not stray
from God's will, and it will become clear that they cling to
God. For Torah, the Holy One and Israel are one.

After *berur*, people will be drunk with God and therefore will be able to
align with the will of God from the depths of their hearts. At this point,
the veil will be removed and the full divine acosmic nature of reality will
be revealed. This, says Lainer, is the intent of the dictum 'Torah, the Holy
One and Israel are one'.[61]

'God builds the heart of the human', to cite another passage,[62] so that it is
connected to God's will even when God is apparently hidden. The model
for the God-intoxicated state in that passage is also a Judah archetype figure,
Hezekiah, King of Judah. Lainer states that this is the deep intent of the biblical verse 'I will surely hide my face on that day' (Deut. 31:18). As in the current passage, this is not a negative development or a curse but rather a blessing. This is the time when the face of God will not be seen but internalized.

The implication of the passage is that the human face, drunk with divinity,
will merge with the divine face, which is hidden because it is not separate.
Of course, as we might have expected, Lainer interprets the inebriation of
Purim similarly as one of the primary ways through which we access future
messianic consciousness. To drink until 'one no longer knows' the difference between cursing Haman and blessing Mordecai is to move beyond
da'at, for that is the place in which one accesses *binat ha-lev*.[63]

The wine theme introduced in these sources adds an ecstatic Dionysian
dimension to Lainer's thought that is not readily apparent in the other
strands we have discussed. Though the clusters we have studied thus
far include erotic or Dionysian subtexts, we might have interpreted the
Wisdom of Solomon on a more theological and intellectual plane, as a
kind of conceptual inclusion of all of the powers of divinity under the
rubric of the one God. Even excluding the wine cluster, erotic motifs appear throughout the Wisdom of Solomon: *teshukah*, *tei'uvta denukva*,
moon, and paganism are all major themes limned with eros. It is the wine
sources, however, that underscore the erotic dimension of the Wisdom of
Solomon genre in *MHs* and make it impossible to ignore this dimension
by intellectualizing or theologizing it. In the wine texts, the primal erotic cast of Lainer's thought is clear.[64] The images of fermented wine, תהום
tehom (the depths), *tekufot*,[65] and the drunken intoxication of the Judah

figure, in which the deepest divine nature is revealed, all represent the way in which a person accesses their supra-rational messianic consciousness, towards which the entire people are striving through the process of *berur*.

The images are striking indeed. As we will see, similar Dionysian images appear throughout the next few passages.[66]

Source 34: *MHs vol. 2 Mishlei s.v. hokhmot bahutz*

In the fourth passage we see that uniqueness, another demarcating characteristic of the Judah archetype, is also connected to wine.

חכמות בחוץ תרנה. זה רומז על כל מה שהאדם לומד דברי תורה ולא
נתגלה לו עדיין העמוק הצפון ונסתר בהד״ת, כי לעומק ד״ת לא יכול לבוא
בלתי כששיך אלו הד״ת לשורש נפשו, וכמו שמצינו בגמ׳ (חגיגה יג.) שיש
ד״ת שאין מוסרים אותם לכל אדם, וזה נקרא חכמות בחוץ שהאדם הוא
עדיין חוץ מהם, אכן אחר כן כשיושיע לו השי״ת ויזדכך לבו אז יתעוררו
בלבו אלו הד״ת שעסק בהם קודם התבררו בשלימות והשי״ת יאיר לו גם
בהם, וזה לשון תרנה כענין גבור מתרונן מיין שהוא לשון התגברות

'Wisdoms sing out abroad' (Prov. 1:20)—This hints concerning all the words of Torah a person learns where the hidden and concealed depth is not still not revealed to him in these words of Torah. For one cannot come to the depth of Torah unless these words of Torah are connected to the root of his soul, as we found in the Talmud (*bHagigah* 13a), for there are words of Torah that do not give themselves over to every person. And this is called *hokhmot bahutz* 'external wisdoms', meaning a person is still outside them. Therefore after a person is saved by God and his heart merits, then in his heart are awakened the words of Torah which he engaged with before complete purification, for God illuminates them also, and this is why [the verse says] 'sing out'—'like a *gibor* hero who sings out because of wine' (Psalms 78:65), which is an expression of *hitgavrut* empowerment.

In this passage, the hero is the *gibor mit'ronein miyayin*, the hero so full of wine that he sings and is joyous. This is Lainer's grand image for one who has connected to and realized the unique Torah that is connected to his soul. This wisdom is no longer external to him, but has become part of him; it becomes the Torah of his story. All of the Judah characteristics are revealed in the fullness of the human being. It is in the depths of intoxication that one can claim oneself.

Source 35: MHs vol. 1 Vayehi s.v. uvedam

The Dionysian moment naturally can lead to sin as well. In the biblical passage describing Judah's wine blessing, which Lainer also employs in the first wine passage we adduced,[67] Lainer makes an explicit connection between wine and sin:

> ובדם ענבים סותה, סותה היינו לשון הסתה כי הסתה של שורש יהודה היא
> אחרי החטא ומכשול שאירע לו יתעורר עוז בנפשו, אין זאת רק שהש"י
> ירצה להושיעני ביתר שאת כי ענבים היינו טעות ושכחה

> 'And in the blood of grapes his clothes *sutoh*' (Gen. 49:11)—
> *sutoh* 'his clothes' is like the word for straying *hasatah*. For the
> straying of the root of Judah is that after the sin and failure
> that happened to him, he awakens strength in his soul, [say-
> ing] that it must be that God wants to deliver him all the
> more. For grapes allude to error and forgetfulness.

Though Lainer interprets *sutoh* as *hasatah*, the fall into sin, for Judah, the fall into sin is not a tragedy but an invitation from God. The essence of Judah is this capacity to view sin as an opportunity to be engaged by divinity with great power.

At this point in the passage Lainer adds a strange phrase:

> ומשה רבינו אמר ודם ענבים תשתה חמר, חמר מורה על עין לא ראתה
> אלקים זולתך

> And our teacher Moses said, 'And from the blood of grapes
> you will drink wine' (Deut. 32:14)—wine refers to, 'No eye
> has seen any god beside You' (Isa. 64:3).

After referring to Moses, who also makes wine a key feature of his blessing to Judah, Lainer connects wine to a verse from Isaiah. The purpose of this verse is to teach that wine expands the realm of perception and allows one to see divinity in a way not accessible in a non-Judah state.

Wine as a facilitator of heightened vision of God is a major theme in the *MHs* wine texts. This verse is also cited in the Talmud[68] in reference to the higher states of being and consciousness (specifically, to 'olam haba, the righteous, and ba'alei teshuvah penitents). In that passage, the Talmud also makes a connection between wine and perception. The Talmud asks, to what precisely does this state of 'No eye has seen any god beside You' refer? One Talmudic response is, 'Fermented wine in its grapes from the six days of creation', that is, properly aged wine in which the dregs have done their work.

This fermented wine, comments Lainer, refers to a level of perception that is not available in this world and that is beyond the reach of *seikhel* (intellect). This level of joy—like wine fermenting in its grapes—is not yet revealed; this is the joy that God will reveal in the future days. However, says Lainer, this level of perception is not completely hidden; it is available to those who yearn for God. Our next sub-cluster will further explore this perception.

The Tovat 'Ayin Sub-Cluster

As we have seen, for Lainer wine represents the highest level of human perception of the divine. The wine-perception theme appears in one more dramatic sub-cluster, the *tovat 'ayin* sources. In these sources, wine, perception, uniqueness, and the Judah archetype are all linked to *tovat 'ayin*, literally 'goodness of the eye', or (in one case below) *'ayin tovah* 'a good eye'. 'A good eye' appears in these sources as a level of messianic perception that can be accessed within the present reality. As in other cases we have seen, the full power of Lainer's intention is only discernible upon close reading of this passage within the context of related passages.

Source 36: *MHs vol.1* Rosh Hashanah s.v. *amar leih Rabi*

Our first passage establishes a solid and essential connection between a good eye and the Judah archetype of King David. Commenting on a Talmudic passage in which Rabbi Yehudah Hanasi gives instructions to Rav Hiyya, Lainer writes:

אמר ליה רבי לרבי חייא זיל לעין טב וקדשיה לירחא ושלח לי סימנא דוד
מלך חי וקים...ושלח לי סימנא דוד מלך כו' כי כאשר נפש מישראל יש לו
עין טובה אז נקרא דוד מלך ישראל חי וקים, כי מדת דהע"ה הי' עין טובה
כמ"ש אצלו יפה עינים וטוב רואי

> Rabbi [Yehudah Hanasi] said to R. Hiyya: Go to 'Ein Tav (lit., 'good spring', but also 'eye') and sanctify the moon, then send me the sign 'King David lives and endures'...—for when any person from Israel has a good eye (*'ayin tovah*, a play on Ein Tav), then King David is called 'living and enduring', for the [essential] quality of King David was a good eye, as it is said concering him, 'beautiful eyes and good vision (i.e., 'good-looking')' (1 Sam. 16:12).

Significantly, Rabbi's instructions, interpreted by Lainer as teachings about *'ayin tovah*, concern the sanctification of the moon. What is clear is that the quality of vision of King David exists in the present for any individual, and that this vision itself brings the possibility of messianic realization to life. Lainer does not explicitly discuss the connection between the moon and a good eye here, though the association with the Judah archetype is already so firmly established ('for the royal house of David is the aspect of the moon') that it is hardly necessary. Some of the deeper implications of this are drawn out in the sources below.

Source 37: *MHs vol. 2* Eruvin s.v. *amar Rabi*

In the next passage, Lainer comments on the seemingly strange statement by R. Hanin bar Papa that one for whom wine is not 'spilled in his house like water' is not included in blessing. In Lainer's interpretation of this passage, wine is synonymous with *tovat 'ayin*, which is contrasted with *tzarat 'ayin*, a bad or narrow eye.

רב חנין בר פפא ראה פעם אחת לאדם ששותה יין בלי צמצום עד שנדמה לו שהוא מסובאי יין והרע זאת בעיניו, אכן אחר כן עלה בלבו אולי אין החסרון מחבירו רק ממנו מחמת שיש לו צרת עין שאינו נקי בזה...ובאמת הוא רק ממה שאין לו טובת עין בשרשו, לזה אמר כל שאין יין נשפך בתוך ביתו כמים אינו בכלל ברכה והיינו שצריך להאדם טובת עין כל כך עד שאפילו אם יראה יין נשפך כמים ג"כ לא ירע בעיניו כי האדם נקרא בית והבית שנשפך בו יין כמים אין לו שום צרת עין ויש בו ברכה, ולכן אחר כן יכול לשאול על חבירו השותה בהתפשטות בלי צמצום, אבל כל זמן שאין בו זה הוותרנות ידע בברור שמה ששואל על חבירו הוא רק ממה שנמצא בו צרת עין

Rav Hanin bar Papa once saw a man drinking wine without constraint until he seemed drunk, and this was a bad thing in his eyes. But after this, it occurred to him that perhaps the *hisaron* lack was not in his friend but in himself, because he had *tzarat 'ayin* 'a narrow eye', which was not clean in this [matter]...And in truth, this came only from not possessing *tovat 'ayin* in its root...For a person is called a house, and 'a house in which wine is spilled like water' is one which has no *tzarat 'ayin* and does have blessing. Therefore after this [Rav Hanin] was able to inquire about his friend who drank with expansive consciousness *hitpashtut* and without constriction. But the whole time that he did not have this capacity, he knew clearly *be-verur* that his inquiry about his friend came only from the *tzarat 'ayin* found within himself.

Tovat 'ayin emerges from expanded consciousness, while *tzarat 'ayin* is an expression of narrow or restricted consciousness. If one sees a person acting expansively without limits and is greatly troubled by this, as Hanin bar Pappa was according to Lainer, then one must realize that one is troubled not because of what he has seen, but because of his own internal *tzarat 'ayin*. Only by connecting to the energy of flowing wine, 'wine which is spilled like water in the house', is one able to access the quality of *tovat 'ayin*. Lainer teaches that it is only from this expansive, higher level of perception that one can engage one's friend who is acting expansively, 'without limit', without one's vision being blurred by one's own *tzarat 'ayin*.

Source 38 *MHs vol. 2* Pesahim s.v. *tanu rabanan*

The themes of *tovat 'ayin* and the Judah archetype come to the fore in the next passage, which explicitly links this theme to messianic times and implicitly connects it to Lainer's theory that every person has a unique pathology which is the source of divine insight. Lainer is commenting on the Talmudic passage that teaches that 'seven things are hidden from a person'.[69] One of them is 'when the kingdom of David will return'.

ויום הנחמה. היינו שיתנחם כל נפש מישראל בהשלימו את חסרונו הנולד
בשרשו, ועומק הדין היינו צריך לירא תמיד בכל עניניו אולי אינו ממליך
עליהם את השי"ת בשלימות...ומלכות בית דוד מתי תחזור היינו מתי יקבע
בישראל מדת טובת עין

> 'And the day of consolation'—this refers to the consolation of
> every soul of Israel when it completes the lack that it was born
> with in its root. 'And the depth of the judgment'—this means
> he needs to see constantly whether *Hashem* is ruling over all
> of his affairs completely and wholly...'And when the kingdom
> of David will return'—this is when the quality of *tovat 'ayin*
> will be fixed (internalized) within Israel.

The Judah archetype is understood by Lainer to mean 'when the quality of *tovat 'ayin* will be internalized within Israel'. This quality of *tovat 'ayin* is the suprarational quality of the Judah archetype, which indicates not just a moment of *deveikut* or *unio mystica*, but rather a stable consciousness internalized by the redeemed person, who fulfills the Judah archetype.

137

A fourth passage in the *Tovat 'Ayin* sub-cluster is also linked to the Two Hands sub-cluster above. We have already noted that the wine theme of Purim is linked by Lainer with the higher perception that transcends *da'at*,[70] a core feature of the Judah archetype. The inception of the evil decree of the Purim story[71] is the Kingdom of Persia understood by Lainer to be *tzarat 'ayin*. Thus, explains Lainer,

אכן כאשר חקרו אנכה"ג על זאת הגזירה מהיכן צמחה בשורשה ועמדו על אמיתת בדבר שהיא משורש צרת עין ומיד נתגלה להם הדבר לאמיתו היתה הישועה ונתבטלה הגזירה, לכן תקנו אח"כ השתי מצות אלו אשר שורשם טובת עין, והמצוה נתחלק לשתים, משלוח מנות איש לרעהו היינו לאנשים צדיקים וכשרים שתי המתנות היינו שתתפשט בטובת עין ליתן בשתי ידך מפני שהבינו כי צמיחת הגזירה הי' לפי שהתחיל לבא הצרות עין ועמדו ע"ז ותיכף כאשר לפניהם נתבטל הגזירה

[W]hen the men of the Great Assembly realized from where the decree [of Haman] arose in its root, and established the truth of the matter, that its root was *tzarat 'ayin*…and the decree was nullified, they thereafter instituted these two commandments whose root is *tovat 'ayin*. The *mitzvah* [of Purim] was divided into two: [the first was] sending gifts from a person to his friend…two gifts [to each friend]—so that one will expand with *tovat 'ayin* to give with *shetei yadayim* two hands.

Here the human incarnation of divine hands is linked with the incarnation of divine eyes. For Lainer, the realized human being is both the hands and the eyes of God. To be realized is to act with the hands of God and to see with the eyes of God.

The Menutzah Sub-Cluster

A second component of the wine sources, the Menutzah sub-cluster, is both paradoxical and erotic in nature. Wine represents the wild and ecstatic side of the Judah persona.[72] Wine in these sources is expressive of the idea that one must allow oneself to be defeated, overpowered, and, in some texts, even seduced by God.

Of course, this is a radically different religious demand than the mainstream religious position, which defines the vast majority of Jewish writing on the subject of morals and behavior.[73] This general understanding is summarized aptly by the well-known maxim in *Ethics of the Fathers*, 'Who is a hero? The one who conquers his inclination'.[74] Self-control is of course a desideratum of religious life, and is not absent from the writings of Lainer. However, according to Lainer, the place for self-control is in the realm of *'avodah* and *mitzvot*, before *berur* is completed. In the post-*berur* stage, the quality and character of the religious act are almost inverted. Rather than maintaining control, the *homo religiosus* is called upon to relinquish control. This is not an anarchic act as suggested by Joseph Weiss.[75] Rather, it occurs in a relational context. One does not simply give up control, but gives it up to God. But even that is not quite accurate. One does not give up control to God in the sense of a servant giving up control to his master—this idiom appears only rarely in *MHs*—but rather, one trusts and gives up control to the God-force flowing through the self.

Source 40: *MHs vol. 2 Va'eira s.v. vayikah*

This quality is found in *MHs* in the figure of King David. In this classic David passage, David is presented as one who lets himself be taken by God:

ולישרי לב שמחה ישרי לב נקרא מי שלבו נמשך אחר רצון השי״ת, אף
שעל הגוון נתראה שלפעמים יסור מדרך התורה, גם זה הוא ברצון השי״ת

'And for those who are straight of heart *yishrei lev* there is joy' (Psalms 97:11)—'Straight of heart' is a term for one whose heart is drawn after God's will *shelibo nimshakh ahar retzon*

139

Hashem. Even though on the surface it appears at times that he strays from the path of the Torah, this also is the will of God.

The language used here and throughout *MHs* to describe the Judah figure, is, as we have pointed out, erotic in nature. A person who accesses *retzon Hashem* is described as *libo nimshakh ahar retzon Hashem* (one's heart is drawn after the will of God). The Hebrew word for drawn, נמשך *nimshakh*, has erotic connotations, in the sense of the phrase משכני אחריך נרוצה *mashkheini aharekha narutzah* 'Draw me after you, let us run' (Song of Songs 1:4). Lainer is saying in this passage, 'If I am erotically drawn to God, then even if on the outside it appears that what I am doing is straying from the path of the Torah, it is acceptable, because this act which is on the surface wrong is actually the will of God'. The clearly implied, albeit subtly understated, image in this text and throughout this Izbica genre is almost one of someone willing to suffer public humiliation for the sake of their beloved.

The passage continues:

> וכמו שאיתא בגמ' (שבת נו.) כל האומר דוד חטא אינו אלא טועה. יען
> כי לבו היה נמשך אחר רצון השי"ת, ותמיד מוסכם בלבו להיות מנוצח
> מהשי"ת

As one finds in the Talmud (*bShab.* 56a), 'Whoever says
David sinned is mistaken', for his heart was drawn after the
will of God, and he always agreed in his heart to be overcome
menutzah by God.

The paradigm of this model is King David. The Talmud suggests that anyone who says that David sinned—which basically means anyone who reads the story of David and Bathsheba in 2 Samuel—is mistaken.[76] In Lainer's interpretation, this means that David was seduced, as it were, not by Bathsheba, but by God. That is to say, his attraction for Bathsheba was understood by him on a profound level to be the voice of God expressed in the desire by which his heart was drawn. Lainer describes David as the classic manifestation of the Judah archetype, whose heart is always overcome by God. In the language of Solomon, his decisions come from the intuitive 'yearning of the innards':[77]

> וכמו שכתיב (תהלים נא) למען תצדק בדברך תזכה בשפטך וכדאיתא
> (סנהדרין קז,, ז"הק משפטים קז.) דלא לימרו עבדא זכי למריה וזה שאמר

140

שלמה המלך ע״ה (שיר ה) דודי שלח ידו מן החור ומעי המו עליו, מן החור
נקרא דברים שאינם מיופים על הגוון, גם בזה כוון לרצון השי״ת בעומק,
וזהו ומעי המו עליו

[A]s it is written, 'So that You may be justified in Your words
and made right in Your judgment' (Psalms 51:6)—as one
finds (*bSanh.* 107a; *Zohar* 2:107a), 'So that they should not
say that the servant was more correct than his master'. And
this is what King Solomon said, 'My beloved sent his hand
from the portal, and my innards longed for him' (Cant. 5:4).
'From the portal' refers to things that do not seem beautiful
on the surface. Even in such matters, he intended God's deepest will. This is what is meant by 'my innards longed for him'.

The identification of sin (or apparent sin) with the notion of being defeated by God is the key interpretive principle in Lainer's understanding
of the biblical sins of both the golden calf and the spies. The shared motif
of these passages is accessing some form of *retzon Hashem* beyond appear-
ances and the demands of normative law. As we have seen, *retzon Hashem*
represents the *Shekhinah*.

According to Lainer, in each of these incidents the people allowed the higher spirit of God to move through them, i.e., to defeat and overpower them,
until they expressed perfectly the will of God. Therefore they cannot be
held guilty. However, this is much more than an absolution from responsibility. The sign of the holiness and correctness of their divine abandon in
both incidents is understood by Lainer to be none other than wine.[78] Wine
implicitly represents the *Shekhinah* that overpowers, is victorious over, and
even seduces the human. Wine thus comes to represent a kind of divine
abandon, which, although it seems at times to spill over into sin, is indeed
the will of God.

Before we turn to an analysis of these 'sin' texts, we must recognize that the
interpretation of sin in *MHs* which we provide here is radically different
from the understanding of biblical sin generally offered in Izbica scholarship, i.e., since humans have no real power, they cannot sin.[79] This does
not accurately represent Lainer's thought. Rather, according to this textual
cluster in Lainer, one must actively abandon oneself to the divine force that
runs through oneself.

As we have mentioned elsewhere, it is often easy to read Lainer incorrectly as saying something much less radical than he is indeed saying. Three out of four of the *menutzah* passages that relate to the sins of the golden calf and spies explicitly associate wine with these sins. We will explore both the apparent and deeper meaning in the following passage about the spies:

אחר פרשת מרגלים כתיב פרשת נסכים. היינו אחר שראה השי״ת את גודל
מרירות לבם אחר מעשה המרגלים לכן נתן להם פרשת נסכים להחיות
את נפשם ולבם הנמרר כמו שכתיב (משלי לא) ויין למרי נפש וזה שכתיב
(קהלת ט) לך אכול בשמחה לחמך ושתה בלב טוב יינך, היינו מי שהוא
בעוצב ומרירות ושותה יין שעל ידי זה יתחזק לבו ויהיה לו לב טוב מותר
לשתות, אבל מי ששותה יין לרתוח דמו ולכעוס זה הוא מדה מגונה מאוד,
וזה שליכא מידי בנביאי דלא רמיזא באורייתא שמזה הפרשה אמר שלמה
המלך ע״ה ויין למרי נפש

After the section about the spies, the section about the wine libations is written. That is, after God saw the great bitterness of their hearts following the incident of the spies, He gave them the chapter on wine libations in order to revive their embittered hearts and their souls. As it is written, '[Give] wine to the bitter of soul' (Prov. 31:6). And this is [the meaning of] what is written, 'Go, eat your bread in gladness, and drink your wine with a happy heart' (Ecc. 9:7). That is, whoever is sad and bitter, and drinks wine so that his heart be strengthened and that he have a happy heart, is permitted to drink. However, one who drinks wine to make his blood boil and to become angry, this is a most repellant attribute. This is [an example of the saying], 'There is nothing in the prophets that is not alluded to in the Torah', for it was because of this chapter that Solomon said, 'Wine to the bitter of soul'.

At first glance, this passage can mean something like 'the people were so devastated and depressed at their sins that God took mercy and gave them a drink', in Lainer's phrase, 'to revive their souls'. Wine in this reading is a drink of comfort offered to the people by God. Wine would appear to have this meaning in Lainer's interpretation both in the biblical section concerning *nesakhim* (wine libations in the sacrificial services), which appears in Numbers following the story of the spies, as well as in the verse from

142

Proverbs: '[Give] wine to the bitter of soul'. In fact, that verse is taken by Lainer to be Solomon's reference to the story of the spies. However, a close reading of parallel passages makes it clear that Lainer intends something far more radical and profound than a divine drink of comfort.

The passage continues:

על ענין פרשת נסכים וחלה, איתא במדרש תנחומא (שלח יד) לך אכול
בשמחה לחמך, ושתה בלב טוב יינך, ואחר כן על העבר צריך האדם
להתחזק בתקופות...כי אחר מעשה המרגלים נתיאשו בדעתם יען שראו
שבעומק לבם לא יאהבו את הארץ ולא יטב בעינם, כמו שכתיב אחינו
המסו את לבבינו, ולכן נדמה להם שחלילה חייהם הוא היפך מרצון
השי"ת...ולכן נתן להם השי"ת פרשת נסכים שמורה על תקופות, ולכן
נאמר פרשת נסכים תחילה

> Concerning the sections about wine libations and separating
> the dough, it is written in *Midrash Tanhuma* (Shelah 14), 'Go,
> eat your bread in gladness, and drink your wine with a happy
> heart'...Then, regarding the past, a person must strengthen
> himself with *tekufot* audacity....For after the incident of the
> spies, they despaired, since they had seen in the depths of
> their hearts that they would not love the Land and it would
> not please them. As it is written, 'Our brothers caused our
> hearts to melt' (Deut. 1:28). It therefore seemed to them as
> if their lives were, God forbid, opposed to God's will...God
> therefore gave them the chapter on wine libations, which
> teaches about *tekufot*.

In both this passage and the following two passages, the key text is from Solomon's Ecclesiastes: 'Go, eat your bread in gladness, and drink your wine with a happy heart' (9:7). Even before Lainer's radical reading is brought to bear on this verse, it does not seem to relate to wine as a source of comfort. Rather, wine expresses a sense of self-assuredness and even serenity. The key is in the next part of the verse, which is not quoted directly in the passage: 'For God has already affirmed your actions' (Ecc. 9:7). For Lainer, this verse is as an affirmation of the ontological value and dignity of human action, even when not directly commanded by God. Lainer states that this verse expresses a sense of *tekufot*—the Judah term we analyzed above—i.e., the personal audacity one accesses when one experiences oneself participating in the will of God.[80] Lainer's introduction of *tekufot* as an

143

expression of 'wine-consciousness' indicates that we are dealing here not just with a comforting tonic but with a divine affirmation that what might appear to be sin is not, and that the people's actions indeed expressed the will of God.

Source 42: *MHs vol. 1* Shelah s.v. *beḥa-sidrah*

The interpretation we just suggested is spelled out in another passage on the portion of Shelah:

פ' הנכסים ניתן להם להחיות ולהשיב נפשם אחר מעשה המרגלים לפיכך ניתן להם פ' נסכים שרומז על שמחה כפתיחת רבי תנחומא לך אכול בשמחה לחמך ורמז להם כי שמחו את הש"י במעשה הזאת

> The section on wine libations was given to them to revive and revive their souls after the incident of the spies. The section on wine libations was therefore given to them, as it hints at joy, as in the opening sermon of Rabbi Tanhuma (i.e., the *Midrash Tanhuma* passage cited above): 'Go, eat your bread with joy'. He hinted to them that they pleased God with this deed (i.e., the incident of the spies).

The portion of libations is not just God's way of comforting the Israelites but an expression of joy: 'they pleased God with this deed'. Lainer uses the same Solomonic prooftext here as he does in the two parallel passages adduced above: 'Go, eat your bread with joy'.

The people however were afraid that they had sinned not only externally, superficially—what Lainer calls in other passages *'al gavan*—but internally, ontologically, i.e. in a way that undermined the divine root of their lives. For indeed, God had said that they would not return to the land until the fourth generation, and that time had not yet arrived.

וזה ניתן להם אחר שסברו שחטאו עד עומק חיותם וע"ז נאמר תורת ה' תמימה משיבת נפש היינו שהשיב את נפשם כי באמת כוונו לרצון הש"י כי מאמר הש"י ודור הרביעי ישובו הנה ובאמת הי' ביכולתם לשבת את הארץ רק שהי' להם בינה בלבם מאת ה' שבזה שגינו אותה כוונו לרצון הש"י וניתן להם פ' נסכים. וזה נקרא שתיתי ייני היינו ששמחו את ה' במה שהי' מניחים א"ע להיות מנוצחים מהש"י

This was given to them after they thought they had sinned against the deepest level of their life source. Concerning this it is written, 'God's Torah is perfect, it restores the soul,' that is, their souls were restored to them. For they truly intended God's will, for God said, 'The fourth generation will return here' (Gen. 15:16). Actually, it was within their ability to settle the Land. However, they had an understanding from God in their hearts that by defaming it, they intended God's will, and they were given the section on libations. This is what is meant by, 'I drank my wine' (Cant. 5:1). They pleased God by allowing themselves to be *menutzahim* overcome by God.

Had the people desired, they could have praised the land. But their disparagement of the land was a function of their letting go of their more limited human faculties of understanding that separated them from God, and giving up their voices to God. This is precisely what Lainer means when he states in this passage that they allowed themselves to be *menutzahim* by God. This is the intent of the wine—not an expression of comfort but of joy and ecstasy.

Finally, Lainer reaffirms that *menutzah*, wine, and *retzon Hashem* are all expressions of one core idea, namely, his acosmic humanism, which affirms that human intention fully participates in the ontology of divine intention.

וזה לא יוכל כי אם ישראל. כי אין גוי מביא נסכים בלא זבח רק ישראל
כדאיתא במנחות לפי שאין נכרי יכול להסכים להיות מנוצח מה׳ כמבואר

This could not happen, except through Israel. For there is no nation that brings libations without [other types of] sacrifices besides Israel. As one finds in *bMenahot*, [this is] because a non-Jew cannot acquiesce to being overcome by God, as has been explained.[81]

Lainer concludes this section of the passage by making explicit the erotic or relational undertones of the *menutzah* notion, in terms of Joshua and Moses. In particular, he identifies the unique *Shekhinah* quality of Joshua as Joshua's fully receiving Moses to the point of allowing himself to be, in Lainer's phrase, seduced by Moses.

עדות ה׳ נאמנה מחכימת פתי. עדות הוא דבר ברור וזה הוא נגד יהושע כי
בעוד שאין ברור לאדם טעמי המצות יוכל בקל להתפתות לכל דבר שיבא

נכחו. אך כאשר נגלו לו טעמי המצות לא יוכל עוד להתפתות. ולפי שיהושע
הי׳ לו מדות התמימות כמו שנתבאר ולכן קבע אותו הש״י באוהל משה כי
ממשה רבע״ה הי׳ מניח א״ע להתפתות כי לא נתפתה רק לטוב, וזה שנקרא
שמו יהושע

'The testimony of the Lord is faithful, enlightening the fool'
(Psalms 19:8). Testimony is something that is clear. This
refers to Joshua, for as long as the reasons for the commandments are not clear to a person, he may easily be seduced by
anything that comes before him. However, when the reasons
for the commandments are revealed to him, he can no longer
be seduced. Since Joshua had the attribute of innocence, as
explained, God installed him in the tent of Moses. For with
Moses, he would allow himself to be seduced, for he could
only be seduced by goodness. This is why he was named
Joshua.

A person who lacks the wisdom of *ta'amei hamitzvot*, reasons for the commandments, is in danger, according to Lainer, of being inappropriately
seduced. According to Lainer, the mark of wisdom is not to avoid seduction. Rather, wisdom is knowing whom you should allow to seduce you.
This passage follows the discussion of the spies, who, in Lainer's reading,
allowed themselves to be overpowered by God. Lainer's point is that this
experience of being overpowered is not one of force but of intimacy and
eros, leading to a certain merging of identity and ego between the seducer
and the seduced.

Source 43: MHs vol. 2 Ki Tavo s.v. *arur ha'ish*

In the next passage Lainer deals similarly with the sin of the golden calf,
understanding that the people were *menutzah*, overwhelmed by God.

ארור האיש אשר יעשה פסל ומסכה נאמר נגד שבט לוי כי שבט לוי שמרו
עצמם בלי לצאת מגדר כללי דברי תורה, ובאמת כל הד״ת הם נלבשים
בלבוש שיוכל האדם לקבלם ולהשיגם, אכן לפעמים יחפוץ השי״ת לנצח
האדם כמו שכתיב (תהלים נא) למען תצדק בדבריך וגו׳ וכמו שנתבאר
בחלק זה

'Cursed is the man who makes a graven image or a molten
image' (Deut. 27:15) was spoken against the tribe of Levi, for

146

the tribe of Levi protected themselves, without going beyond the borders of the *kelalim* of the words of the Torah. And in truth, all the words of the Torah are enrobed in garments, so that a person can receive them and attain them. However, occasionally God desires to overcome a person, as it is written, 'so that You may be justified in Your words', etc. (Psalms 51:6), and this is as we explained in this volume.[82]

Lainer refers to the verse from Psalms cited in the original *menutzah*-Judah passage. This verse lies at the heart of the Talmudic image of David surrendering to God; this image is transposed in the *Zohar* to David becoming the Jester of the King who gives himself up to God, so that God's words may be justified over his own.[83]

According to Lainer, the inability to allow oneself to be seduced and overpowered by God does not reflect just a lack of spiritual development, it is idolatry. As we saw earlier,[84] for Lainer, one who lives within the *kelalim* and does not access *retzon Hashem* is guilty of idolatry. Paradoxically, the *kelalim* can foster the illusion of independence and autonomy. This passage, which was interpreted by Rachel Elior, needs to be read carefully, both independently and in the context of the parallel passages that precede and follow it.[85] The essence of the passage is that one must let oneself be *menutzah*, overpowered by God.

The passage continues:

אבל הם לא יכלו לעבוד את העגל, כי להם היה מגיע החטא לשורש חיים
ולא היו יכולים לתקן את החטא, לכן שמרם השי״ת

> But [despite this, the tribe of Levi] could not serve the golden calf. For them the sin would have touched the root of [their] life, and they would not have been able to correct the sin. God therefore protected them.

The concept of being *menutzah* is seen here not as a path for the elite but as an essential part of all nonidolatrous spirituality, excepting the tribe of Levi, whose *shoresh hayyim* 'life root' is to personify the pole of *yir'ah*. In this light, Lainer understands that Levi could not serve the golden calf. But this is not because Levi is more righteous than those who did serve the calf, as is classically assumed. Rather, the people who made the calf were serving God in the way of *menutzah*—allowing themselves to be overpowered by God. Levi could not serve in that way because it violated his *shoresh hayyim*.

Source 44: *MHs vol. 1* Vayeishev s.v. *vayeishev* 1

In the final passage we will examine in the *menutzah* sub-cluster, it becomes clear that the idea of allowing oneself to be overpowered and seduced by God is in fact another expression of acosmic humanism. In fact, as Lainer already stated in the first passage of this section (Source 40), David did not sin but allowed himself to be *menutzah*—defeated and overpowered by God. This was not a one-time event in David's life; rather, it was his essential spiritual stance. David is described as one who is always in a stage of consciousness in which the God force flowing through him overpowers any sense of David's separateness or disconnection. In the language of Lainer from that passage (Source 40): ותמיד מוסכם בלבו להיות מנוצח מהשי״ת 'In his heart it was always agreeable to be overcome by God.'

This state is explored by Lainer in this classic Judah *menutzah* passage, using once more, albeit implicitly, the core set of sources we found in the first passage. These include the image of David as the Jester of the King, who according to the Talmud says to the King, 'It is more appropriate, God, that you be right than me. Therefore I sinned with Bathsheba as you predicted—against my promise, because it would have been spiritual hubris for me to be right and you wrong.' Once the Judah figure allows himself to be overpowered by God, the God force of *retzon Hashem* animates all his choices and decisions.

The ability to give up control and let oneself be overpowered by God is the essential trait of the Judah figure, who incarnates *Shekhinah*.[86] Judah is appropriately identified with wine in the passage, which includes one of the most comprehensive analyses of the Judah archetype found in *MHs*.

ויהודה הוא נגד שר המשקה כי דהע״ה נקרא בדחנא דמלכא ועל ניסך היין
נשמעין שירי דוד, ובאמת ליהודה במעשה דתמר וכן בכל המעשים משבט
יהודה הדומין לזה נתן בהם השי״י כח התאוה כ״כ עד שלא הי׳ באפשרותם
להתגבר וכמו שמבואר שמלאך הממונה על התאוה הכריחו, ולכן לא עליו
האשם במה שלא הי׳ יכול להתגבר על יצרו וזה פירוש בדחנא דמלכא היינו
שמניח את עצמו להנצח מהש״י

148

Judah corresponds to the wine steward, for King David is the Jester of the King, and at the wine libations, David's songs are heard. And truly for Judah in the story of Tamar, and likewise with all the deeds of the tribe of Judah that are similar to this, God placed in them such strong desire that it was not in their capacity to overcome it. As it is explained, the angel in charge of passion coerced him, and he is therefore not guilty of being unable to overcome his inclination. And this is the meaning of the Jester of the King: he allows himself to be overpowered by God.

The image of the wine steward, explains Lainer earlier in the same passage, is one who cannot control that which occurs to him: a fly fell in the wine, and it was totally beyond his control. This is the implicit image of wine. What 'overpowered by God' means in this passage, as in the rest of Lainer's Torah, is that one realizes that indeed all one's actions are really expression of one's divinity, and that the notion of choosing independently of God is a metaphysical absurdity, for the person at the deepest level actually participates in divinity. Here again, the wine theme expressed in the Judah genre is consistent with the core of non-dual acosmic humanism in *MHs*.

The identification of Judah with wine is immediately associated with David: 'At the wine libations, David's songs are heard'. Moreover, for Lainer, these are not anomalies. They are all part of what we have identified as the *menutzah* genre, which is a subset of the broader Solomon-*Shekhinah* motif. In fact, in all incidents involving figures of the tribe of Judah that were similar to the story of Judah and Tamar, they had no power to overcome their desire. Each was like the Jester of the King, who lets himself be overpowered by the King.

Conclusion

Now that we have analyzed the Wisdom of Solomon sources, we can present with clarity the central, radical, and highly original synthesis that lies at the core of Lainer's theology. We can group the Wisdom of Solomon sources and sub-clusters above into two major genres. The first includes the wine, Goddess, moon-*sihara*, paganism and *menutzah* sources, which are driven by eros and desire. The second includes the *rei'ah*, moon-*yarei'ah*, *emet le'amito*, and *retzon Hashem*, which describe a kind of perception.[87] The first focus uses the Goddess-language of eros, *teshukah* and *tei'uvta denukva*. The second focus uses the language of moving beyond law to access *retzon Hashem*.[88] According to Lainer, these sources merely use different language to discuss the same thing: the *Shekhinah* without her *levushim*.

Transcending the law does not mean leaving the law behind. Quite the contrary; in virtually every *MHs* passage that discusses *emet le'amito*, the higher level of perception accessed by the Judah figure, Lainer relates it back to the prosaic example of Rava's cane in small claims court.[89] The higher messianic intuition of smell is drafted in the service not of Dionysian ecstasy but of true judgment and justice within the court system. It is at this point in *MHs* that ethics and eros merge.

However, the mandate imposed by the unmediated *retzon Hashem* is neither limited to the court system nor to normative ethics. *Rei'ah-yarei'ah*, the intuition and inner guidance represented by smell and by the moon which leads one to *retzon Hashem*, is also the ability to act audaciously beyond the *kelalim*, the general principles of the law. In response to the highly personal experience of the whisper of the divine, one may be called to a path different than that laid out by the law.

These ostensibly different languages and frameworks are really addressing the same ultimate reality that is indicated by the *Shekhinah* without her *levushim*. Both the wine-*menutzah* sources and the *emet le'amito* sources discuss accessing God unmediated by law. By taking this step, Lainer gains two monumental advantages of the spirit. First he imbues the struggle with law—the desire for its transcendence for the sake of a higher truth, even if it is a higher legal truth as in the case of Rava's cane—with enormous erotic energy. Implicitly, he brings to bear all of the energy of paganism, the Goddess, and the moon in the quest to break out of what he calls the idolatries of law and to touch *retzon Hashem*. Repeatedly in *MHs*, all of the energy of the Judah archetype, of *yarei'ah* and *rei'ah*, is brought to bear in the details of small claims court. Lainer channels and focuses the potentially anarchic, often ecstatic energy of the pagan moon Goddess into the system of law. Though Lainer's focus on the case of Rava is unique, his suggestion that all of the erotic energy of the moon and the Goddess be accessed in service of a higher justice, even in the prosaic details of the monetary law, is characteristic of Jewish mysticism, which is grounded in its relationship with the law. Even if the value of the law for Lainer is on occasion found in its transcendence, an engagement with the law is primary.

At the same time, there is a clear affirmation of the legitimacy—and moreover, the desirability—of ecstasy, erotic energy, moon, and wine-consciousness, which can on occasion transcend law and touch the rawness of the Goddess (in one image, Vashti), without her *levushim*. However, this is accomplished not only through the ecstasy of inebriation—which, according to Lainer, can occasionally play a role[90]—but also through the dramatic embrace of one's story, i.e., one's 'soul print', which, according to Lainer, is one of the important portals allowing one to access *retzon Hashem*, the unmediated *Shekhinah*, which is beyond law.

Though the methods are various, the goal is always the same: the embrace of the Goddess, i.e., the unmediated *Shekhinah*.

Notes for Section Four

1 Halbertal and Margalit, *Idolatry* 7, 236.

2 On *teva*, see *MHs vol. 1* Lekh Lekha s.v. *'od bamidrash*; Vayikra s.v. *vayikra*. However, *MHs* is ambivalent with regard to *teva*; see, for example, *MHs vol. 1* Hayyei Sarah s.v. *eileh*.

3 On *'igulim*, see *MHs vol. 1* Hayyei Sarah s.v. *vayehi* 2; Korah s.v. *umadu'a*; Vezot Haberakhah s.v. *vayehiyu*.

4 See, e.g., Source 16 in volume 3.

5 See, for example, *MHs vol. 1* Kedoshim s.v. *veilohei maseikhah*, where *maseikhah* is viewed as a separation that masks the divine from direct access. Similarly, see *MHs vol. 1* Metzora' s.v. *dabru*, where Yisra'el Israel, in contrast to idolaters, is called *yashar El* ('straight to God'), in unmediated and direct relationship to God. See also *MHs vol. 1* Va'et'hanan s.v. *va'asitem*; Shoftim s.v. *lo tita'*; Shoftim s.v. *asimah 'alai melekh*, where idolatry and the אומות *umot* (non-Jewish nations) in general are understood as *gavan*. *Gavan* is the surface that separates one from the divine, which is *'omek*. For more on *'omek* and *gavan*, see Elior, 'Temurot'.

6 A later addition to *MHs* by Mordechai Joseph the grandson, which appears as a footnote to the main text. In earlier printings these additions are found at the end of *MHs vol. 2*.

7 *Kelipah* kabbalistically refers to the husk or shell, which represents *sitra ahra* and *elohim aheirim*.

8 *MHs vol. 2* Likutim Yehoshu'a s.v. *vayishba' Yehoshu'a*.

9 On *mitzido* and *mitzideinu* see 'Paradox in *Mei Hashiloah*' and 'Models of Activism' in volume 1.

10 See Ross, 'Shenei'.

11 Also, obviously, in mid-19th century Europe, *Asheirah* worship was less than rampant. What this meant for Lainer's time is that Lainer felt that the Judah archetype need not be so afraid of pagan energy. In the modern context, this would probably amount roughly to a lack of aversion to a Buddha or Mary statue. For those who have attained Judah consciousness, the Buddha or Mary statue could be viewed as representing one moment in the divine panoply. Of course, Lainer is more sympathetic to the energy of paganism than he is to pagans themselves or to non-Jews in general.

12 The exegetical matrix for Lainer's whole discussion of idolatry is the command to include salt in all sacrifices. Because salt is conceptually parallel to idolatry in the passage, what emerges is actually a command to engage in pagan sacrifice, in the sense of engaging the energy of paganism within the realm of the sacred. It is worth noting the analogy between salt and the crushed grapes that generate the wine yeast that serves to ferment the wine. Each of these by itself is an inedible or spoiled product, but they serve as catalysts for the end product. See the Wine Cluster below for a discussion of the wine imagery in *MHs*.

13 The concept of *elohim aheirim* is essential for understanding the *Zohar's*

relationship to paganism. See further discussion of this concept in volume 3, Source 16.

14 For a thorough discussion of Maimonides and idolatry, including an analysis of this text, see Halbertal and Margalit, *Idolatry* 42–45, 54–62.

15 See Lainer's interpretation of the binding of Isaac (*MHs vol. 1* Vayeira s.v. *veha-elohim*). See *Zohar* 1:119b, where this idea is alluded to.

16 On *ov* idolatry and Lainer's implicit attempt to reclaim its energy for the sacred, see *MHs*, see *vol. 1* Kedoshim s.v. *beha-sidrah*.

17 See, for example, *MHs vol. 1* Ki Tisa s.v. *vayomer* 3, where Lainer suggests that:

כי באמת מעשה העגל הי׳ כי רצו שהש״י יראה להם את הסדר המסודר אצלו לכל
מדותיו לדורות באיזה זמן ינהג את עולמו במדה זו ובאיזה זמן במדה אחרת ולא
יצטרכו בכל יום להתפלל להש״י שיראה להם באיזה דבר ובאיזה מדה יבחר עתה
רק יגלה להם הכל בפעם אחד וילכו בדרכיו לבטח תמיד, ולפי שלא הי׳ נוגע החטא
רק משפה ולחוץ לפיכך נשכח

> In fact, the story of the calf was that the people wanted God to
> show them the order of all His *midot* (providential attributes) for
> all generations, i.e., when He governs the world with one *midah* and
> when with another. Thus they would not have to pray every day that
> He show them which attribute and matter He chooses at any given
> moment. Rather He would reveal everything to them at one time, so
> that they should always walk in His ways confidently. Since the sin
> touched them only superficially, it was forgotten [by God].

When Gershom Henokh refers to this passage (in the parentheses at the end of *MHs vol. 2* Ki Tavo s.v. *arur*), he interprets it as meaning that the Israelites wanted a higher revelation of divine light before the appropriate time.

18 See *MHs vol. 2* Likutim Joshua s.v. *vayishba‘ Yehoshu'a* and our discussion of this passage above in this section.

19 See also *MHs vol. 1* Shoftim s.v. *asimah ‘alai melek* and s.v. *lo tita‘*, where idolatry is referenced as *gavan*, similar to the sense in which the people's request for a king in the book of Samuel is a request *‘al ha-gavan*. Idolatry is presented as an error of mistaking the outside for the depth, the servant for the king. In *MHs vol. 1* Shoftim s.v. *lo tita‘*, Lainer suggests that prayer must be direct, without any mediating force; any mediating force is referred to as *gavan*—what is *gavan* could be a גדול בתורה *gadol baTorah*, a great Torah master, or an *Asheirah* tree. Thus in the verse 'You shall not plant an *Asheirah* by the altar of the Lord your God', the altar represents the unmediated approach to God through prayer, while *Asheirah* represents all types of mediation. All that is *gavan*, be it an *Asheirah* tree or a spiritual master, is a violation of the altar. This must be read both as a downgrading of the *tzadik* and an upgrading of Asheirah.

20 Source 18.

21 See, for example, *MHs vol. 2* Ki Tisa s.v. *elohei maseikhah* 1 (Source 4); *MHs vol. 1* Vayikra s.v. *‘al kol* and Gilyon (Source 23); and *MHs vol. 2* Megilah 12b s.v.

bise'udato and *MHs vol. 1* Likutim Megilah 12b s.v. *veha-karov* (Source 20).

22 We have already commented in part on the direct link between the energy of paganism and accessing unmediated *retzon Hashem*; see our discussion of *rei'ah* and its relation to the moon symbolism in *MHs vol. 1* Vayeishev s.v. *vayeishev* (Source 9) and *MHs vol. 2* Proverbs s.v. *ki va'ar* (Source 11). On Lainer's self-perception as the Judah archetype, see below in this section and in the introduction to volume 1, 'Messianic Self-Understanding'.

23 *MHs vol. 2* Ki Tisa s.v. *elohei maseikhah* 1 (Source 4).

24 This is not an exegetical flourish on the part of Lainer but rather part of a clear set of ideas central to Izbica. For a parallel passage capturing the same core idea, see *MHs vol. 2* Ki Tavo s.v. *arur ha'ish* (Source 28). We interpret this passage in full in the Wine Cluster below. It is sufficient for now to state that, according to Lainer, except for the tribe of Levi, anyone who does not let themselves be overpowered by God incurs the pronounced punishment: 'Cursed is the man who makes a graven image or a mask' (Deut. 27:15).

The source of the tradition that the *mitzvot* can be idolatry is not Lainer. At the very least, it comes from his teacher Menaham Mendel of Kotzk, who was well-known for sayings of this nature, for example, 'The *mitzvot* themselves can be idolatry'; 'Where is God? Wherever you let Him in'—that is to say, even if you are full of *mitzvot*, they may all be idolatrous if there is no real room for God. On the sayings of Kotzk, see Levinger, 'Imrot'.

25 This is just one of two basic concepts of idolatry in *MHs*. The second expression of idolatry, which is also a thread running through *MHs*, involves being stuck in a particular habit or trait which traps a person (see e.g. *MHs vol. 1* Kedoshim s.v. *veilohei maseikhah*; vol. 2 Ki Teitzei s.v. *vayomer*; Ki Tisa s.v. *elohei maseikhah* 1, Source 4 above). The common denominator between the two types of idolatry is not being spontaneous and free to respond to *retzon Hashem*, the divine call.

26 This is a consistent understanding of idolatry in *MHs*. See, for example, *vol. 1* Yitro s.v. *anokhi* 1, where Lainer interprets the verse 'Do not make for yourself a graven image' (Exod. 20:4) to refer to any attempt to limit the Torah to a set of rules that is eternal and unchanging. Lainer suggests that built into the very nature of the law is the possibility of its change and not merely its suspension. Just as the suspension of Shabbat when there is a hazard to life is in fact not a violation of Shabbat but rather its displacement by a higher value, so too the principle of '*eit la'asot*, 'a time to act for the sake of God' (Psalms 119:126) by abrogating the law, is not a sin but rather a displacement of the old law for the new one.

והענין בזה כי מלת פסל הוא דבר מחותך במדה וקצב ובהשלמה בלי חסרון שום
דבר בעולם וזאת אינו נמצא רק בתורת מרע״ה...וזה שמפרש בזוה״ק על לא
תעשה לך פסל היינו במצות עשה, וכל תמונה הוא במצות ל״ת, כי לא נגלה לאדם
שום דבר עד תכליתו

The matter is that 'graven image' refers to something that has been forged with dimensions, measures and that is perfectly finished, lacking nothing. This can only be found in the Torah of Moses, our teacher. Human intelligence cannot create anything so perfect… This is why the holy *Zohar* interprets the command of 'You shall not make for yourself any graven image' as referring to positive commandments, and [the continuation of the verse] 'or any picture' as referring to negative commandments, for there is nothing that is revealed to any person in its entirety.

According to Lainer, citing the Zohar, if the possibility for complete displacement of an existing norm would not be built into the system, then the positive and negative commandments would both be idolatrous.

27 *MHs vol. 2 Ki Tisa s.v. elohei maseikhah 2.*

28 We have already taken issue with Weiss, who suggests that *hayyim* is related to Sabbatean themes. See the section 'The First Quality of Will: Will and Uniqueness'. However, Weiss is correct in feeling that the word *hayyim* contains a primal energy. This energy is, however, *binah-shekhinah*-pagan energy and not necessarily related to Sabbateanism, other than in the important possibility that Sabbateanism may have partaken of the same energy. On the use of the term *hayyim* in Izbica, see, for example, *MHs vol. 2 Ki Teitzei s.v. ki teitzei 2.* This passage, which expands on the notion introduced in *MHs vol. 1* Beshalah s.v. *nikheho tahanu*, states:

העניין בזה כמו שנתבאר בחלק ראשון (פרשת בשלח) על פסוק נכחו תחנו וגו'
שכל אומר מעכו"ם יש לה כח מיוחד, לזו חכמה לזו עושר לזו גבורה, והכח
הנמצא בהם אינו נקרא חיים כלל רק חיי שעה, כי הטובה שבהם הוא רק לפי שעה
ובאחרית הימים יאספו, ורק מה שיש להם תשוקה לדבר שנחסר להם, כגון האומה
מהעכו"ם שהיא משופעת בחכמה ומשתוקקת לעושר וכדומה זו התשוקה נקרא
חיים, וזאת מקבלים ישראל מהם כי ישראל מונין ללבנה שאין לה מגרמה כלום

The matter is as was explained in *vol. 1* Beshalah on the verse *nikheho tahanu*, that each nation has its own unique strength or characteristic. One has wisdom, another riches, yet another strength. The powers that they possess are not deemed to be 'living' at all; they are only temporary life. For any good they may possess is only temporal, and at the end of days they (i.e., their particular characteristics) will all be gathered in. Only that which they had passion for, that which they lacked, for example, the nation that was full of wisdom but desired wealth—that passion is called life. This is what Israel will receive from them, for Israel goes by the moon, which has no light of her own.

29 Patai, *The Hebrew Goddess* 34–54.

30 In the finds, several striking inscriptions from the period of the divided monarchy link *YHVH* and *Asheirah* as a divine pair. (See Day, 'Asheirah'). In particular, finds from Kuntillet Ajrud in the northeast Sinai read in part 'may you be blessed by *YHVH* and by his *Asheirah*'. This find, together with other similar inscrip-

tions, has led some biblical scholars to emend the masoretic text. The masoretic version of this text reads *ani 'aniti va'ashurenu*. Some scholars have suggested that the text in this form does not make sense. They use the form *va'asheirato* found in the inscriptions and read the text as אני ענתו ואשרתו *ani 'anato va'asherato*. Given this reading, what God says through Hosea is, 'Tell Ephraim that I will redeem him. He does not need to turn to paganism for I, God, am his Anat and his Asheirah'.

31 In the second interpretation of the verse suggested by the *Zohar* (which is not cited by Lainer) *nukva* is portrayed as taking the more active role:

דבר אחר, בתיאובתא דנוקבא אשתכח איבא דדכורא, דאי לאו תיאובתא דנוקבא
לגבי דכורא, לא אתעבידו פירין לעלמין, הה"ד ממני פריך נמצא רק משפה ולחוץ
לפיכך נשכח

Another reading: The fruit of the male is to be found in the passion of the female. For if not for the passion of the female for the male would never yield fruit. As it says, 'From Me is your fruit obtained'.

32 In Source 26.

33 This is strikingly similar in tone and context to Job 27:17, cited in *Zohar* Exodus 108b, which is the primary *Zohar* passage cited by Lainer on paganism. This verse states: יכין צדיק ילבש *yakhin vetzadik yilbash* 'He may prepare it, but the righteous shall wear it' which the Zohar implicitly reads as *yakhin rasha' vetzadik yilbash*. 'The wicked may prepare it, but the righteous shall wear it'. In the context of the Zohar, the *tzadik* will wear—that is to say, access—the sacred power of the pagan which until this point in history (or consciousness) was the province of the *rasha* 'wicked one'.

34 As we shall see, the idea of *tikun ha-nukva* in Luria is an important source for Lainer's Wisdom of Solomon genre. Undoubtedly, a more extensive study would reveal the direct links between *nukva* and *teva'* in the *Zohar* and other early sources, and between *nukva* and *tikun ha-nukva* in Luria. However, such a study is beyond the parameters of this work and will have to await a separate monograph.

35 See *MHs vol. 1* Vezot Haberakhah s.v. *vayehi*.

36 See *MHs vol. 1* Hayyei Sarah s.v. *vayehi* 2.

37 For a scholarly discussion of these sources, see Pechter, 'Igulim Veyosher'.

38 *MHs vol. 2* Vezot Haberakhah s.v. *vezot*. In both this text and in *MHs vol. 1* Vezot Haberakhah s.v. *vayehi*, the vision of the eschaton is not one of exclusive *'igul* but of dialectical harmony between *'igul* and *yosher*, i.e., uniqueness and distinction integrated with egalitarian and nonhierarchal stances. See also *MHs vol. 1* Shabbat s.v. *mai Hanukah*, which paints a picture of the *'atid* in which the king and the priest collapse into one. This represents the end of nondialectical hierarchy, because, in this passage, the king represents the Judah archetype, which is accessible to the broader population. On the relation of the priest to the kings, see also *MHs vol. 1* Shoftim s.v. *shoftim* 2 (Source 6). However, in *MHs vol. 1* Likutim Shabbat

157

s.v. *mai Hanukah*, Lainer goes a step further. Here he clearly refers not only to the king, but also to a popular audience that can manifest the Judah archetype and receive the שפע *shefa'* (direct effluence) from God without an intermediary. There will be a revelation for every איש פרטי *ish perati*, every specific individual. In effect, every *ish perati* will become the High Priest.

39 See *MHs vol. 1* Korah s.v. *umadu'a* where the *'igul* nature of Korah's position is detailed. Then see *vol. 1* Likutim Shabbat s.v. *mai Hanukah*, where Korah is implicitly vindicated by Lainer's teaching that after the *berur*, the special status of Levi will no longer be necessary.

40 See Pechter, 'Igulim Veyosher'.

41 Of course, we are not suggesting that the actual pagan cultures were necessarily defined by these values. Rather, the underlying energy of paganism and its iden-tification with *teva'* was taken by Lainer (and by other systems) to be associated with the values of *'igulim*.

42 Although there is more to say on *teva', 'igulim*, and *nukva* in Izbica, constraints of length require that these brief remarks suffice for the time being.

43 On the relationship between these two drives, see Gafni, *On Eros*.

44 Since these two passages are closely intertwined and the second makes refer-ence to the first, we will read them together as one source.

45 Consistent with Lainer's consistent metaphysical chauvinism, only Israel can access the divine even without translation into *levush*.

46 In volume 3 (Source 43), we cite one of Lainer's primary teachers, Simcha Bunim of Przysucha, as an immediate source for Lainer's theory. Simcha Bunim there understands the attempt to access a level of light for which there were not yet appropriate vessels, to be precisely the mistake of Solomon.

47 *MHs vol. 2* Megilah 12b s.v. *bise'udato*.

48 *b* Yoma 69b.

49 For an extensive discussion of this text and the complex relationship to idolatry which it suggests, as well as an analysis of the biblical and midrashic lion motif in relation to the Temple and idolatry, including the symbolism of the lion, see Eisen, 'Ye Shall Be'.

50 One would have intuitively cited this text as an important source for the rela-tionship between *mikdash* and paganism in *MHs* even if Lainer had not cited the text directly. The fact that he cites it in the context of two different Wisdom of Solomon-*Shekhinah* passages merely confirms its importance. See also *MHs vol. 1* Vayehi s.v. *uvedam*.

51 This interpretation of the text is found in Dessler, *Mikhtav MeiEliyahu vol. 4* 105, 225; see also *vol. 3* 227. Dessler, however, as he himself indicates, intention-ally moderates the radical and potentially dangerous implications of his teaching. See also the passages by Mordechai Lainer's student Tzadok Hakohen referred to by Dessler: *Resisei Laylah* 43 and 23. See also Hakohen, *Takanat Hashavin*, Chs. 6 and 10. For an explication of the radical content implicit in these sources, see Gafni, *Mystery* 210 and notes *ad loc.*, as well as Gafni, *On Eros*. See also the

important discussion in Eisen, 'Ye Shall Be', 56, 57 and notes *ad loc* and Ezrahi, *Shenei Keruvim* 6–9 and notes *ad loc.*

52 On David, the Judah figure who desperately yearns לבקר בהיכלו *levakeir beheikhalo* 'to visit His Temple' (Psalms 27:4) directly, without the mediation of the priest, see *MHs vol. 2 Korah s.v. vayikah* (Source 15).

53 *MHs vol. 1 Likutim Megilah 12b s.v. veha-karov.*

54 The simplicity discussed here is what we would term 'level three' simplicity, and not 'level one' simplicity. The confusion between these levels is discussed by Wilber in 'The Pre/Trans Fallacy'. Level three is simplicity reclaimed after doing the hard work of sophistication. See our discussions in the sections 'Levels of Consciousness' (in the introduction to volume 1) and 'The Paradox of Human Activism: Levels of Consciousness' (in Chapter Nine of volume 1).

55 On descending from the One and ascending to the One in relation to Lainer's theology, see 'Lainer and the Idealists' (Part Five of volume 1).

56 For a fine bibliography on Dionysus, see Eliade, *A History vol. 1* s.v. Dionysus.

57 See, for example, *MHs vol. 2 2 Samuel s.v. vayosef*. See also *MHs vol. 2 Ki Tavo s.v. arur ha'ish* (Source 28, volume 2); see also our discussion of Levi, *yir'ah,* and wine in the *Menutzah* sub-cluster below.

58 See Sources 28 and 31 in volume 3.

59 See Chapter Twelve in volume 1, 'The Judah Archetype'.

60 The passage appears under the sub-heading 'Perek B'mah Tomnin' (the fourth chapter of *Shabbat*), though the chapter referred to in the passage is chapter 20.

61 On this phrase, see Tishby, 'Kudsha'.

62 *MHs vol. 1 Likutim Shabbat s.v. amar Rav.*

63 See *MHs vol. 1 Megilah .s.v. amar Rabah,* discussed in volume 1 (Chapter Nine, 'Called By the Name of God'.

64 As we shall see, the wine dimension to Lainer's theology, like the rest of the Wisdom of Solomon genre, has deep roots in Zoharic and post-Zoharic kabbalistic thought.

65 On wine and *tekufot,* see below Sources 41 and 42 (*MHs vol. 2 Shelah s.v. ahar* and *vol. 1 Shelah s.v. beha-sidrah*), as well as *vol. 2 Shelah s.v. 'al 'inyan.*

66 In fact, in one of the passages that we analyzed above (Source 17), which involves King David, the Judah archetype, uniqueness, *hitnas'ut* and *retzon Hashem,* the name of God said to express these qualities, based on an internal kabbalistic system of permutations is, *DYMSYM.* Although we have not located solid evidence linking this permutation of the divine name to Dionysus, Moshe Hallamish commented when I showed him the passage, 'It is hard to believe that it is not related to Dionysus' (personal communication, 2002).

67 *MHs vol. 2 Shemini s.v. yayin* (Source 21).

68 *bBer.* 34b. See the *MHs* passages on this Talmudic text, *vol. 1* and *vol. 2 Berakhot s.v. kol ha-nevi'im.* The first passage in particular connects wine with higher consciousness.

69 *bPes.* 54b.

70 *MHs vol. 1* Megilah s.v. *amar Rabah.*

71 As described in the Book of Esther.

72 Here I would like to partially defend Weiss against recent criticism in Izbica scholarship by Don Seeman ('Martyrdom'). Seeman disagrees with Weiss's existential characterization of Lainer as anarchic. Based on the sources Weiss adduced, Seeman's critique is valid. However, within the Wisdom of Solomon tradition in Lainer, and in particular in the wine sources, which have a distinctly Dionysian cast, Weiss's description is not far off the mark.

73 Note however that the notion of being defeated by God finds echo in modern Jewish thought in the writings of Joseph Soloveitchik. It is a major theme in *Lonely Man of Faith* and is even more pronounced in 'The Community', particularly in the second and third essays, 'Majesty' and 'Catharsis, Redemption, Prayer, Talmud Torah'.

74 *Pirkei Avot* 4:1.

75 Weiss, 'Determinism' 454.

76 See also *MHs vol. 1* Vayeishev s.v. *vayeishev* 1 on this theme, analyzed here (Source 44) and in volume 1 (in 'Laughter and Paradox in *Mei Hashiloah* – An Excursus').

77 See *MHs vol. 1* Emor s.v. *vahaveitem* (Source 16).

78 See the following three sources.

79 E.g. Faierstein, *Hands* 41.

80 See the section in volume 1, 'Empowering Acosmism and *Tekufot*'.

81 As is always the case, Lainer's ontology is chauvinistic.

82 *MHs vol. 2* Va'eira s.v. *vayikah* (Source 40). In the previous edition of *MHs*, this passage falls under the preceding heading of s.v. *v'anu ha-levi'im.*

83 Both passages are discussed in volume 1 in the section, 'Laughter and Paradox in *Mei Hashiloah* – An Excursus'; see also above Source 40.

84 *MHs vol. 1* Ki Tisa s.v. *elohei maseikhah* (Source 4).

85 See Elior, 'Temurot'. Elior misinterprets the line regarding Levi to mean that Levi is cursed and an idolater for remaining within the *kelalim*. Actually, it means that everyone but Levi is cursed and an idolater for remaining within the *kelalim* (see our analysis below), whereas Levi would destroy the root of his soul if he were to go outside the *kelalim*. Each curse is applied by Lainer to a particular tribe, which is warned to be very careful in one particular area where they are uniquely challenged. Most importantly, according to Lainer's reading of the verse 'Cursed is he who is disrespectful to his father and mother' (Deut. 27:16), Judah must be disrespectful to his mother and father—that is to say, he must access *retzon Hashem* beyond *Hokhmah* and *Binah*, in order to fulfill his essence. The curse of each tribe relates to their unique *hisaron* and therefore also to their unique source of greatness. How one understands the essence of the passage is the same however, regardless of this point of contention.

86 The direct identification of wine with Judah and *shekhinah* is made by the *Zohar*; see Source 31 in volume 3.

87 One could also include the *tovat 'ayin* sources in this group, speaking broadly. David Seidenberg has noted that these *tovat 'ayin* sources form the only sub-cluster which is fully part of both the genre of eros and the genre perception (personal communication 2009).

88 Note that both genres employ the image of the moon, though the first emphasizes *sihara* and the second *yarei'ah*.

89 See our discussion of Sources 5 and 7 above.

90 See *MHs vol.* 2 Shemini s.v. *yayin vesheikhar* (Source 21), where Lainer teaches that the priest, representing Levi, who is parallel to the Joseph archetype of law, cannot serve through intoxication; however, the king, expressing the Judah archetype whose unconscious is divine, can serve through intoxication.

RADICAL KABBALAH

The Sources and Evolution of the Wisdom
of Solomon in Kabbalah and Hasidut

Volume 3

by Dr. Rabbi Marc (Mordechai) Gafni
and Avraham Leader

Introduction

In the first volume of this work we examined some of the older kabbalistic sources that provide the ground for the core theological constructs that form Lainer's acosmic humanism,[1] as well as for his concept of *hisaron* (personal pathology). In this volume, we shall demonstrate not only that Lainer's acosmic humanism is rooted in general structures of kabbalistic thought, but that Lainer understood his own thought to be to an intentional unfolding of a very specific body of esoteric wisdom, namely, the Wisdom of Solomon.

Faierstein has argued that 'the daring and radical nature of Mordechai Joseph's thought raises many questions that remain unanswered. The single most important question pertains to the influences which shaped his...teaching'.[2] Below we will analyze several dozen key passages from the *Zohar* that are at the core of the traditions which shaped Lainer's teachings about the Wisdom of Solomon. We will also see that Luria explicitly labeled a key part of the cosmic rectification process as *hokhmat Shelomoh*. Lainer was aware of Luria's reading of the Wisdom of Solomon, and the Lurianic understanding is reflected in his teachings as well. We will also look at a key Hasidic source preceding Lainer where the Wisdom of Solomon is an important theme. Most importantly, we will be able to see very specifically how Lainer's understanding of the Wisdom of Solomon advances beyond both the *Zohar* and post-Zoharic sources. Finally, in Part Two, we will show that the theme of *hokhmat Shelomoh* was further advanced by one of his key disciples, Tzadok Hakohen of Lublin. We will refer to Tzadok to confirm that this esoteric lore was indeed an essential part of Lainer's teaching. Tzadok explicitly calls key tenets of his acosmic humanism *hokhmat Shelomoh*, giving this theme the same basic interpretation as his teacher. Indeed, for Tzadok, as we noted in regard to Lainer above, the Wisdom of Solomon is essentially what in this thesis we have termed acosmic humanism.

Notes for Introduction

1 In Chapter Fourteen, 'Models for Acosmic Humanism Within the Tradition of Kabbalah'.
2 *Hands* 110.

Part One

ZOHARIC SOURCES FOR
THE WISDOM OF SOLOMON

ZOHARIC SOURCES FOR
THE WISDOM OF SOLOMON

In our analysis of the Wisdom of Solomon in *MHs*, we identified and closely read several distinct textual clusters organized by theme, including *mikdash*, Solomon, David, wine, *menutzah*, paganism, moon, *nukva*, *teva*, and *'igulim*. We suggested that the interlocking themes that appear repeatedly in all of the clusters were consciously understood by Lainer to be part of a specific esoteric tradition known as *hokhmat Shelomoh*, the Wisdom of Solomon. The Wisdom of Solomon clusters are different manifestations of the fundamental basis of Lainer's radical and original thought. The Judah archetype as expressed in these Wisdom of Solomon passages is at once erotic, ecstatic, and Dionysian. Judah is overpowered by God in a way that does not efface his essential persona, but allows God-energy to course through him, effacing any distinction between the self and the divine.

The ultimate expression of the Judah archetype lies, as we have seen, in seeking the embrace of the *Shekhinah* unmediated by *levushim*—in other words, seeking to access and incarnate *retzon Hashem*, the unmediated will of God, which is anomian and at times even radically antinomian. Judah is all of these and more. In the King David model of this archetype, the embrace of the divine happens by letting oneself be *menutzah 'al yedei Hashem*, overcome by God. In the Solomon model, the power of one's radical individuality—in Lainer's language, one's unique *helek* and *shoresh*, or one's *perat nefesh*—allows one to transcend the *kelalim* and embrace *retzon Hashem*, i.e., the *Shekhinah*. The underlying drive expressed in all the above-mentioned models is always the same: to touch the *Shekhinah* that waits to be embraced behind the veils of law.

In volume 2, we demonstrated that this highly provocative and radical set of ideas revolves around the Wisdom of Solomon. The question then becomes: from where does the concept of the Wisdom of Solomon originate?

Faierstein, like the rest of Izbica scholarship, does not address this essential and controlling genre in *MHs's* thought, asserting that there seems to be no previous source for the highly original and radical thought in *MHs*.[1] In this volume, we will argue that the opposite is true: even though *MHs* itself contains only very limited references to rabbinic literature on the Wisdom of Solomon, the Wisdom of Solomon genre is a strand of thought strongly grounded in earlier texts. It is highly developed in Zoharic literature, and picked up later by both Luria and by the Hasidic masters, in some cases implicitly and in others explicitly, including but not limited to Lainer's primary teacher, Simcha Bunim. It was from this lodestone that Lainer primarily drew.

In rabbinic literature, the Wisdom of Solomon is primarily understood as indicative of Solomon's psychological understanding, his deep knowledge of nature, and his ability to communicate and rule over the animal world, the realm of demons, and the like.[2] Yet there are several important exceptions in which the primary themes of the Judah archetype that are manifest in the Wisdom of Solomon genre throughout *MHs* are foreshadowed. These precise themes comprise the motifs of a major strand of Zoharic literature on the Wisdom of Solomon. This strand of Zoharic literature, which can be identified as the major set of sources for Lainer's thought, reverberates through Cordoveran, Lurianic, and Hasidic writings.[3]

The Zoharic genre of the Wisdom of Solomon has never been fully explored in scholarship, to the best of our knowledge. The present treatment is an initial foray, rather than an exhaustive compilation of the sources. Our goal is to broadly present sources that Lainer would have read, and to show how these sources form a plausible matrix for Lainer's thought.

In the course of our discussion, we will cite the few Zoharic passages that are cursorily referred to by Lainer—it is these references that have directed our attention to this genre. We will also cite additional Zoharic passages that, while not explicitly cited by Lainer, are clearly part of the same genre. All would have been known to Lainer, serving as a textual basis for his terminology and concepts as well as a source of inspiration.

We will then turn to several later sources in Cordovero, Luria, and Simcha Bunim. Our first sources from Cordovero and Luria do not directly address *hokhmat Shelomoh*, but they each mention both Solomon and the general *hokhmat Shelomoh* theme of redeeming *nukva*, or, as we termed this theme in volume 2, the reclaiming of 'Goddess energy'. Our third source from Luria makes the connection between these themes and *hokhmat*

Shelomoh explicit. We then turn to a critical passage about Solomon from Simcha Bunim, Lainer's teacher, and conclude Part One with several other Hasidic sources that touch on *hokhmat Shelomoh*.

In the course of our review of these sources, three points will become evident. Firstly, this matrix of sources is indeed the basis of the Solomon-Judah archetype in Lainer's thought. By extension, it is the foundation for his non –dual humanism , which hangs as it does upon the Judah archetype. Secondly, it will become clear that Lainer views his work as the continuation of Solomon's, in a very real messianic sense. Here we mean 'messianic' in the 'Solomonic' sense found in *MHs*, i.e., not a rupture of history, but enlightenment and redemption within the historical frame.[4] Thirdly, we will develop a clearer sense of the ways from which Lainer departs and evolves beyond from the Zoharic and Lurianic source material with which he is working.[5]

Solomon in Rabbinic Literature

We begin with a brief look at the relevant pre-Zoharic literature. The sources for the notion of the Wisdom of Solomon are biblical. The historian of the book of Kings (1 Kings 3:4–15) tells the story of Solomon's dream theophany at Gibeon, in which God grants Solomon's request for wisdom in order that he may judge the people wisely. Along with wisdom, God grants Solomon two other boons that he had foregone for the sake of wisdom: long life and prosperity. The theme of wisdom is then elaborated in the familiar biblical story of the two women who come before Solomon claiming the same infant, where Solomon uses his understanding of human nature to determine the true mother. Solomon's wisdom is extolled once more in the story of the visit of the Queen of Sheba (1 Kings 10).

While there are a number of references to Solomon's wisdom in ancient pre-rabbinic literature,[6] it is in the aggadic literature that Solomon's wisdom receives its first major elaboration. The rabbinic sources see Solomon's wisdom in terms of psychological insight and a deep knowledge of nature, magic, the language of the animals, and the occult. This stands in contrast with the *Zohar* and *MHs*, where Solomon's wisdom is related to a set of esoteric and radical spiritual ideas. However, while the rabbinic sources do not make the same radical claims as we find in Lainer and in the *Zohar*, we will see how they prefigure certain themes found in both. Not surprisingly, some of these same sources are adduced by Lainer and by the *Zohar* as foundations for their own views.

Source 1: *bRosh Hashanah* 21b

The first Talmudic passage we will examine introduces the comparison between Solomon and Moses, which becomes critical in the *Zohar* and in *MHs*.

רב ושמואל חד אמר חמשים שערי בינה נבראו בעולם וכולן ניתנו למשה
חסר אחד שנאמר ותחסרהו מעט מאלהים בקש קהלת למצוא דברי חפץ
בקש קהלת להיות כמשה יצתה בת קול ואמרה לו וכתוב יושר דברי אמת
ולא קם נביא עוד בישראל כמשה וחד אמר בנביאים לא קם במלכים קם

173

אלא מה אני מקיים בקש קהלת למצוא דברי חפץ בקש קהלת לדון דינין
שבלב שלא בעדים ושלא בהתראה יצתה בת קול ואמרה לו וכתוב יושר
דברי אמת על פי שנים עדים וגו׳

Rav and Samuel [gave different interpretations of a certain
text]. One said: Fifty gates of understanding were created in
the world, and all were given to Moses less one, as it says: 'You
hast made him little less than a god' (Psalms 8:6). 'Kohelet
(Solomon) sought to find *divrei heifetz* words of delight'. [That
is to say,] Kohelet sought to be like Moses, but a heavenly
voice went forth and said to him: True words have been justly
written, 'There never again arose a prophet in Israel like Moses'
(Deut. 34:10). The other said: Among the prophets there
arose not, but among the kings there did arise. How then do I
interpret the words, 'Kohelet sought to find words of delight'
[which implies that Solomon was ultimately unsuccessful in
his desire]? Kohelet thought to pronounce *dinin shebalev* judgments (or, verdicts) from [his own] heart, without witnesses
and without warning, whereupon a heavenly voice went forth
and said: True words have been justly written, 'At the mouth
of two witnesses, etc.' (Deut 17:6).

The Talmud introduces the idea of a comparison between Solomon and
Moses—a comparison that is echoed throughout Lainer's writing, as we
have seen.[7] As we will show below, this comparison finds clear expression
in the Zoharic sources as well.

While Rav's approach in this passage is clearly to set Solomon below Moses,
the second approach—that of Samuel—suggests that while Moses is superior as a prophet, Solomon's superiority is of an entirely different order—
that of kingship, which is in itself superior to prophecy. This approach is
clearly the source for a series of Lainer passages that distinguish explicitly
between Solomon and Moses, as well as those passages that distinguish
between the prophet and judge on one hand and the king on the other.
In these passages, the king is clearly superior because he is considered by
Lainer to be participating in divinity to such an extent that even his *divrei
hulin* (casual conversations) are considered the word of the living God.[8]

The particular expression of Solomon's desire to find *divrei heifetz* (words
of delight, a term suggestive of the erotic) is his desire to judge *dinin*

shebalev, i.e., intuitively. In this remarkable Talmudic passage Solomon is portrayed as having a deep desire not to follow accepted judicial procedure, but rather to rely on his intuitive understanding of human nature. The Talmud struggles with the validity of this approach because it would seem to undermine the Talmudic enterprise itself, which is based on the analysis of a corpus of judicial procedures and decisions thought to be implicit in the biblical texts. This Talmudic approach displaced other, more inspired forms of reaching legal decisions such as *bat kol* (heavenly voice).

We should note that the phrase *dinin shebalev* is evocative of an Ishbitzer *terminus technicus: binah shebalev* or *binat ha-lev*. This term expresses precisely the same idea, namely, the desire of the Judah archetype to move beyond *kelalei divrei Torah* and to touch the unmediated *retzon Hashem* we have already identified with the *Shekhinah*. Lainer's choice of the term *binah* 'understanding' rather than *dinin* 'judgments' is indicative of this very point. *Binah* is in the Zoharic matrix the sefirotic symbol of the Great Mother, the higher *Shekhinah*.[9] In many early kabbalistic passages the source of *dinin* is also in *Binah*. In Izbica, *dinin shebalev*, the *divrei heifetz* or object of desire that Solomon sought, is transmuted into *binat ha-lev*. In the Talmud, this desire of Solomon is rejected by the *bat kol*. In Lainer's radical teachings, however, the Talmud's conclusion is implicitly overturned; the desire of Solomon is not only legitimated, it is lionized as the major goal of the religious service of the sublime expression of *homo religiosus*—the Judah archetype.[10] For Lainer, this text became a primary source for Solomon as a manifestation of the Judah archetype.[11] He uses this Talmudic passage as a model for how Solomon bypasses normative judicial procedure to directly access God's will, *retzon Hashem*.

In his interpretation of this passage, Lainer explicitly identifies *retzon Hashem* with the Zoharic idea of the moon in its fullness, a trope which appears again and again in the sources we will read below. Moreover, Lainer chose this passage as an anchor for the major idea of directly accessing *retzon Hashem*, even though he clearly knew that his paradigm contradicts the explicit Talmudic conclusion.

Source 2: *bMakot* 23b

Several other rabbinic sources prefigure the notion of Solomon acting beyond the letter of the law, or even uprooting the letter of the law in order to access the unmediated will of God. The next Talmudic passage we will cite refers directly to the case of the two women and the baby:

א"ר אלעזר בג' מקומות הופיע רוח הקודש בבית דינו של שם ובבית דינו
של שמואל הרמתי ובבית דינו של שלמה...בבית דינו של שלמה דכתיב
ויען המלך ויאמר תנו לה את הילד החי והמת לא תמיתוהו כי היא אמו.
מנא ידע דלמא איערומא מיערמא יצאת בת קול ואמרה היא אמו אמר
רבא ממאי דלמא יהודה כיון דחשיב ירחי ויומי ואיתרמי דחזינן מחזקינן
דלא חזינן לא מחזקינן שמואל נמי כולהו ישראל קרי להו בלשון יחידי
דכתיב ישראל נושע בה' שלמה נמי מדהא קא מרחמתא והא לא קא
מרחמתא אלא גמרא

R. Elazar said: The Holy Spirit manifested itself in three places: at the court of Shem, at the court of Samuel of Ramah, and at the court of Solomon....At the court of Solomon, as it says, 'And the king answered and said, "Give her the living child, and do not slay it, for she is his mother"' (1 Kings 3:27). How did he know [that she was its mother]? Might she not have been tricking him? But a heavenly voice *bat kol* came forth and said, 'She is its mother'...Said Raba: From what [can we prove this]? Perhaps...Solomon [knew which one was the mother] because he saw this one was compassionate and the other was not compassionate (i.e., he knew by logical inference and observation, not by revelation). Rather, it is traditional lore (that Solomon knew this through divine revelation).

In this Talmudic passage, we find that in three cases, those of Judah, Samuel, and Solomon, the agency of a *bat kol* validates the judgment pronounced. For any student of Talmud, the invocation of a *bat kol* as a means of deciding a case of law is more than surprising; the famous story of Rabbi Yehoshua and Rabbi Eliezer, in which Rabbi Yehoshua rejects the *bat kol* that supports Rabbi Eliezer's ruling, is the general Talmudic paradigm.[12] In the greater picture, however, this Talmudic passage serves to emphasize that in no other cases could it be appropriate to determine a verdict based on a heavenly voice.

Source 3: *Shemot Rabbah* 6:1

In the next source we will examine, the letters of the Torah itself accuse Solomon of attempting to nullify law. The great fear of the Solomonic

approach to the laws of the rabbinic establishment is poignantly captured
in the plaintive cry of the letter *yod* to God:

הה"ד (קהלת ב) ופניתי אני לראות חכמה והוללות וסכלות כי מה האדם
שיבא אחרי המלך את אשר כבר עשוהו. הפסוק הזה נאמר על שלמה ועל
משה. על שלמה כיצד כשנתן הקב"ה תורה לישראל נתן בה מצות עשה
ומצות לא תעשה ונתן למלך מקצת מצות שנא' (דברים יז) לא ירבה לו
סוסים וכסף וזהב וגו' ולא ירבה לו נשים ולא יסור לבבו. עמד שלמה המלך
והחכים על גזירתו של הקב"ה ואמר למה אמר הקב"ה לא ירבה לו נשים
לא בשביל שלא יסור לבבו. אני ארבה ולבי לא יסור. אמרו רבותינו באותה
שעה עלתה יו"ד שבירבה ונשתטחה לפני הקב"ה ואמרה, רבון העולמים לא
כך אמרת אין אות בטלה מן התורה לעולם. הרי שלמה עומד ומבטל אותי
ושמא היום יבטל אחת ולמחר אחרת עד שתתבטל כל התורה כולה. אמר
לה הקב"ה שלמה ואלף כיוצא בו יהיו בטלין וקוצה ממך איני מבטל

'I turned to see wisdom and madness and folly, for what can
a person [do] who comes after the king? [Only] what has
already been done' (Eccl. 2:12). This verse was said about
Solomon…How? When God gave the Torah to Israel, He
placed positive and negative commandments in it, and He
gave the king several commandments, as it is written, 'He may
not have many horses, he shall not amass gold and silver, and
he may not *yarbeh* have many women, so that his heart not be
turned away' (Deut. 17:17). King Solomon rose and became
'wiser' than the divine decree. He said: Why did God say 'He
may not have many women'? Is it not so that 'his heart not
be turned away'? I will have many women, for my heart will
not be turned away. Our rabbis said: At that time, the letter
yod from the word *yarbeh* arose and prostrated itself before
God, saying, 'Master of the world! Have you not said that
even a single letter from the Torah shall never pass away?
Today Solomon is canceling me, and tomorrow another letter,
until he will have canceled the entire Torah'. God replied to
her: 'Solomon and a thousand like him will be cancelled out,
before the smallest jot of you would be cancelled.'

A few lines down, the same text describes how futile and spiritually
destructive to Solomon himself this was:

177

מה כתיב ביה (מ״א יא) ויהי לעת זקנת שלמה נשיו הטו את לבבו אמר
רשב״י נוח לו לשלמה שיהא גורף ביבין שלא נכתב... עליו המקרא הזה
ולכך אמר שלמה על עצמו (קהלת) ופניתי אני לראות חכמה ודעת הוללות
וסכלות אמר שלמה מה שהייתי מחכים על דברי תורה והייתי מראה לעצמי
שאני יודע דעת התורה ואותו הבינה ואותו הדעת של הוללות וסכלות היו

'And it came to pass that in Solomon's old age, his wives
turned his heart away, [and his heart was not whole before
YHVH his God like his father David's heart was]' (1 Kings
11:4). Rabbi Shimon bar Yohai said: Solomon would have
preferred to have cleaned sewers rather than to have this
verse written about him. Therefore did Solomon say about
himself, 'I turned to see wisdom' (Eccl. 2:12) 'and [to] knowing madness and folly' (Eccl. 1:17).[13] Said Solomon: I became
wiser than the words of Torah, and I saw myself possessing
complete knowledge of Torah, but this understanding and
knowledge was madness and folly.

Solomon's attempt to apprehend the will of God beyond the letter of the
law and even in contravention to it is seen by the *midrash* as disastrous. He
would rather have cleaned sewers than have had the text say that his wives
caused his heart to stray and that he did evil in the eyes of God. We will see
below how this very *midrash* is cited and radically re-interpreted by Simcha
Bunim of Przysucha[14] who, according to the Lainer family tradition, was
Mordechai Joseph's primary teacher.[15]

This second rabbinic foreshadowing of the Zoharic Wisdom of Solomon
genre revolves around what we have shown to be a linchpin of Lainer's understanding of the Judah archetype, which is part of his acosmic humanism.

We saw in the chapters on Judah and Acosmic Humanism in volume 1 that
acosmic humanism—the blurring of the line between God and man which
results when human consciousness expands to realize its divine self—is essential to understanding of the Judah archetype. The Judah persona is able
to access *retzon Hashem*, the unmediated will of God, beyond the general
principles of Torah, because the human being ontologically participates in
that very will.

178

Source 4: *Shemot Rabbah* 15:26

The state in which the divine will is most fully accessible, indeed the underlying consciousness that allows Solomon himself to access *retzon Hashem*, is referred to in Lainer, citing the *Zohar*, as *sihara be'ashleimuta*, the moon in its fullness.[16] We will analyze this all-important set of Zoharic sources shortly. At this point, we note that a foreshadowing of this juxtaposition already appears in a rabbinic source. This *midrash* is in fact interpreting a verse in which the moon is central:

הלבנה בראשון של ניסן מתחלת להאיר וכל שהיא הולכת מאירה עד...
ט"ו ימים ודסקוס שלה מתמלא ומט"ו עד שלשים אור שלה חסר, בל 'אינה
נראית. כך ישראל ט"ו דור מן אברהם ועד שלמה אברהם התחיל להאיר
שנאמר (ישעיה מא) מי העיר ממזרח צדק יקראהו לרגלו בא יצחק אף
הוא האיר שנאמר (תהלים צז) אור זרוע לצדיק בא יעקב והוסיף אור שנא'
(ישעיה י) והיה אור ישראל לאש ואח"כ יהודה פרץ חצרון רם עמינדב
נחשון שלמון בועז עובד ישי דוד כיון שבא שלמה נתמלא דיסקוס של לבנה
שנאמר (דה"א כט) וישב שלמה על כסא ה' למלך

On the first of Nissan the moon begins to shine, and she continues to shine until the fifteenth of Nissan, when her disk becomes filled. From the fifteenth until the thirtieth, her light wanes. On the thirtieth, she cannot be seen. So too, is Israel: from Abraham until Solomon there are fifteen generations. Abraham began to shine, as it is said, 'Who aroused one from the East...' (Isa. 41:2). When Solomon came [after thirteen intervening generations], the moon's disk became full, as it is said, 'And Solomon sat on the throne of the Lord as king' (1 Chron. 29:23).

The full moon is said to be an expression of Solomon and is indicative of a messianic period. This is associated by the rabbinic writers with Solomon sitting on God's throne. How can a human being sit on the throne of God, ask the writers? They respond by offering a series of striking parallels between the throne of God and the throne of Solomon.

וכי יוכל אדם לישב בכסאו של הקב"ה מי שנאמר בו (דניאל ז) כרסיה
שביבין די נור אלא מה הקב"ה שולט מסוף העולם ועד סופו ושולט בכל
המלכים שנאמר (תהלים קלח) יודוך ה' כל מלכי ארץ כן של שלמה מסוף
העולם ועד סופו שנאמר (דה"ב ט) וכל מלכי הארץ מבקשים את פני
שלמה וגו' והמה מביאים איש מנחתו לכך נאמר וישב שלמה על כסא ה'

179

למלך הקב״ה לבושו הוד והדר ונתן לשלמה הוד מלכות שנאמר (שם א
כט) ויתן עליו הוד מלכות בכסאו של הקב״ה כתיב (יחזקאל א) ודמות
פניהם פני אדם ופני אריה ובשלמה כתיב (מלכים א ז) ועל המסגרות אשר
בין השלבים אריות בקר וכתוב א׳ אומר (שם) כמעשה אופן המרכבה
בכסאו של הקב״ה אין דבר רע נוגע שנאמר (תהלים ה) לא יגורך רע
ובשלמה כתיב (מלכים א ה) אין שטן ואין פגע רע הקב״ה עשה ששה
רקיעים ובשביעי יושב ובכסאו של שלמה כתיב (שם י) שש מעלות לכסא
ויושב במעלה השביעית הרי נתמלא דיסקוס של לבנה

But is it possible for a man to sit on the throne of God, of
which it is said, 'His throne is sparks of fire' (Dan. 7:9)?
Rather, just as God rules from one end of the world to the
other and has dominion over all kings, as it is written, 'All
the kings of the earth shall give You thanks,' (Psalms 138:4),
so did Solomon reign over the whole world, as it is written,
'And all the kings of the earth sought Solomon…And every
man brought his gift' (2 Chron. 9:23–4). For this reason it
says, 'And Solomon sat upon the throne of the Lord as king'
(1 Chron. 28:23). God is cloaked in splendor and glory, and
He gave Solomon the splendor of royalty, as it is written, 'And
the Lord bestowed royal majesty upon him,' (1 Chron. 29:25).
Concerning God's throne it is written, 'And the likeness of
their faces was the face of a man and the face of a lion,' (Ezek.
1:10), and of Solomon it says, 'And on the frames of its steps
were lions, oxen, etc.' (1 Kings 7:29). Another verse adds, 'As
a chariot wheel is made' (1 Kings 7:33). No evil can touch the
throne of God, for it says, 'Evil shall not sojourn with You'
(Psalms 5:5), and also concerning Solomon it says, 'There is
neither adversary, nor adversity' (1 Kings 5:18). God made six
heavens and resides in the seventh, and concerning the throne
of Solomon we read, 'There were six steps to the throne'
(1 Kings 10:19), while he himself sat upon the seventh.
Thus was the disk of the moon full.

Even though this text implies a merging of the persona of God and the persona of Solomon, it explicitly deems itself to be limited to metaphorical or
symbolic interpretation. The *Zohar*, however, took this motif and invested it
with profound ontological and mystical meaning. In the Zoharic passages we
will look at, just as in Lainer, the fullness of the moon and the *Zohar*'s version
of what we call 'non-dual acosmic humanism' became virtually synonymous.[17]

'Solomon' means God

The most famous of the rabbinic Solomon teachings that prefigure acosmic humanism is a provocative reading of the first verse of Song of Songs: '"The song of songs, which belongs to *Shelomoh*"—[*Shelomoh* means] the King to whom peace *shalom* belongs'. There are many sources for this comment, and they all interpret Song of Songs as a parable for the relationship between God and Israel, using this interpretation as their anchor.[18] Here we will bring two specific examples of the genre which are especially relevant.

Source 5: *Shir Hashirim Rabbah* 3:24

The first midrashic source that is grounded in the merging of human and divine is based on the idea that the *melekh Shelomoh* is referring not to Solomon the King but to God, and is as follows:

צאינה וראינה בנות ציון במלך שלמה, במלך שברא בריותיו שלמות, ברא
חמה ולבנה על מלאתן כוכבים ומזלות על מלאתן.

> 'Go out and gaze, O daughters of Zion, at Solomon the king'—at the King who created His creatures *sheleimot*, whole (perfect), who created the sun and the moon at their fullness, the stars and the constellations at their fullness.

God and Solomon are once again blurred. *Melekh Shelomoh* is understood to be *melekh shebara' beriyotav shleimot*, the King who created His creatures in their full perfection *beriyotav sheleimot*. This is taken to refer to, among other creations, the full moon. Solomon is understood to be an expression or symbol for the aspect of the godhead whose divine characteristic is that He created everything whole or perfect, *sheleimot*, including, most importantly for our purposes, the full moon.

Source 6: *Bamidbar Rabbah* Naso 11:3

I have chosen the second source presented here because it will also ground our discussion, below, of the relationship between eros and *mikdash*, Solomon's Temple.

הנה מטתו זה בית המקדש כשם שהמטה אינה אלא לפריה ורביה כך כל
מה שהיה בביהמ"ק היה פרה ורבה שנאמר (מלכים א ח) ויאריכו הבדים
ואומר הזהב זהב פרוים מהו פרוים שהיה עושה פירות ואומר (שם א ז)
בית יער הלבנון למה נקראת בית המקדש יער הלבנון לומר לך מה יער
עושה פירות אף בית המקדש הצורות שהיו בקירותיו של זהב שהיו מצויירין
שם כל מיני אילנות היו עושים פירות. שלשלמה זה הקב"ה שהשלום שלו

'Behold his bed, that is Solomon's' (Cant. 3:7). 'Behold his
bed'—this alludes to the Temple; as the bed serves primarily
for the purpose of enabling one to be fruitful and multiply,
likewise, all that was in the Temple was fruitful and multiply-
ing, as it says, 'And the staves grew long' (1 Kings 8:8); it also
says, 'And the gold was the gold of *Parvayim*' (2 Chron. 3:6).
What is the meaning of *Parvayim* (*PRVYM*)? It means that
it yielded *peirot* fruit (*PRVT*). It also says, 'He built the house
of the forest of Lebanon,' (1 Kings 7:2). Why was the Temple
called 'the forest of Lebanon'? To tell you that just as a forest
yields fruit, so it was in the Temple; the figures on its walls,
which were of gold and fashioned with all kinds of trees, used
to bear fruit. *Shelishlomoh* 'Of Solomon' (Cant. 1:1)—this
is the Holy One, blessed be He, *sheha-shalom shelo* to whom
peace belongs.

Here Solomon's bed becomes the Temple of God. Again, although for the
rabbinic reader this reading the Song of Songs is a metaphor, the kabbalistic reader sees this as an ontological assertion that Solomon is indeed
on some profound level merged with God. One may say that this subtle
shift from metaphor to ontology is the entire difference between *Midrash*
and the *Zohar*. This source understands *mikdash*, the sanctuary, as a place
of teeming erotic fertility and creativity. The distinctions between person
and tree, between the sentient and the non-sentient, the animate and in-
animate, fall away, and the world is awash with the divine creative eros of
the *Shekhinah*, which as we have seen, is the very essence of *mikdash* for
Lainer. In the *Zohar* too, a fundamental aspect of the Wisdom of Solomon
is *zivug*, erotic merger.[19]

The merging of Solomon's identity with God, even on the metaphorical level expounded by the rabbis, leads us by its inner logic to the
expression of *mikdash* as an actual place of *zivug* and spontaneous manifestation of *Shekhinah* energy. Thus, while the *midrash* can be seen as a

metaphor, it also can be read as foreshadowing that which the *Zohar* will later unpack and interpret in its own terms. For most Hasidic masters,[20] who did not read notions of historical development into the texts, this aspect of foreshadowing immediately takes the *midrash* out of the realm of metaphor and into the realm of ontology. While Lainer himself uses primarily Zoharic sources, we will see below that his student Tzadok of Lublin was fully comfortable citing these midrashic sources to ground the concept of acosmic humanism.

Source 7: *bMegillah* 11b

We now examine a final Talmudic foreshadowing of acosmic humanism, as expressed in a text from Tractate Megillah, which suggests that Solomon should not be included in the listing of human kings, for his kingship is of an entirely different order; the order of the divine.

תנו רבנן שלשה מלכו בכיפה ואלו הן אחאב ואחשורוש ונבוכדנצר אחאב
דכתיב חי ה' אלהיך אם יש גוי וממלכה אשר לא שלח אדוני שם לבקשך וגו'
ואי לא דהוה מליך עלייהו היכי מצי משבע להו נבוכדנצר דכתיב והיה הגוי
והממלכה אשר לא יתן את צוארו בעול מלך בבל אחשורוש הא דאמרן ותו
ליכא והא איכא שלמה לא סליק מלכותיה הניחא למאן דאמר מלך והדיוט
אלא למאן דאמר מלך והדיוט ומלך מאי איכא למימר שלמה מילתא
אחריתי הוה ביה שמלך על העליונים ועל התחתונים שנאמר וישב שלמה
על כסא ה'

Three kings were said to have ruled the entire world, and they are Ahab, Ahasuerus, and Nebuchadnezzar…But was there not Solomon [who also ruled the entire world]? Yes, but his reign was not successful. This answer suffices [according to the opinion that Solomon was] first a king, then an undistinguished person. However, [according to the opinion that] he became a king again, how can one explain it? [One could say that] Solomon was entirely different, for he ruled over both the lower and higher worlds, as it is written, 'And Solomon sat on the throne of the Lord' (1 Chron. 28:23).

The text ends, as did the above-cited *midrash*,[21] with the image of Solomon sitting on the throne of God. Even though the *midrash* may have understood this metaphorically, the idea that Solomon rules over 'the lower and higher worlds' implies an ontology that goes far beyond metaphor. We will see in Part Two how Lainer's major student, Tzadok Hakohen of Lublin, read this text ontologically in terms of acosmic humanism, understanding Solomon to be merged with God.

Source 8: *bHulin* 60b

The subject of the last rabbinic text we will adduce is not Solomon but the moon. It figures in many of the Wisdom of Solomon passages in the *Zohar*. Specifically, the idea that 'the moon in its fullness', in Kabbalah '*sihara bisheleimuta*', represents an ideal state that can or must be restored, derives from the following *midrash*.

רבי שמעון בן פזי רמי כתיב ויעש אלהים את שני המאורות הגדולים וכתיב
את המאור הגדול ואת המאור הקטן אמרה ירח לפני הקב"ה רבש"ע אפשר
לשני מלכים שישתמשו בכתר אחד אמר לה לכי ומעטי את עצמך אמרה
לפניו רבש"ע הואיל ואמרתי לפניך דבר הגון אמעיט את עצמי אמר לה לכי
ומשול ביום ובלילה אמרה ליה מאי רבותיה דשרגא בטיהרא מאי אהני אמר
לה זיל לימנו בך ישראל ימים ושנים אמרה ליה יומא נמי אי אפשר דלא מנו
ביה תקופותא דכתיב והיו לאותות ולמועדים ולימים ושנים זיל ליקרו צדיקי
בשמיך יעקב הקטן שמואל הקטן דוד הקטן חזייה דלא קא מיתבא דעתה
אמר הקב"ה הביאו כפרה עלי שמיעטתי את הירח והיינו דאמר ר"ש בן
לקיש מה נשתנה שעיר של ראש חדש שנאמר בו לה' אמר הקב"ה שעיר זה
יהא כפרה על שמיעטתי את הירח

R. Simeon b. Pazzi pointed out a contradiction [between verses]. It is written, 'And God made the two great lights', and then it is written, 'The greater light . . . and the lesser light'. The moon said unto the Holy One, blessed be He: Master of the Universe, is it possible for two kings to wear one crown? He said: Go and make yourself smaller. She said: Master of the Universe, because I have suggested that which is proper, must I then make myself smaller? He said: Go, and you will rule by day and by night. She said: But what is the value of this? Of what use is a lamp in broad daylight? He said: Go. Israel will calculate the days and the years according to you. She said: But it is impossible to do without the sun for the reckoning of the seasons, as it is written, 'And let them be for signs, and for seasons, and for days and years'. He said: Go. The righteous shall be named after you, we find, Jacob the Small, Samuel the Small, David the Small. On seeing that she

184

would not be consoled, the Holy One, blessed be He, said: Bring an atonement for Me for making the moon smaller. This is what was meant by R. Simeon b. Lakish when he declared: How is the goat offered on the new moon different, that it is described, '[a sacrifice] for *Hashem*'? Because the Holy One, blessed be He, said: Let this goat be an atonement for Me for making the moon smaller.

We have already seen in Source 4 how the moon in its fullness represents an ideal state associated with Solomon and the throne of God. Here we see that the diminishment of the moon is connected to a kind of diminishing of God. This story calls God by the name *Hakadosh Barukh Hu*, which, though not significant in the Talmudic context, lends itself readily to the Kabbalistic interpretation of this whole text as a dialogue between the feminine moon symbol of *Shekhinah*, and the masculine godhead of *Tif'eret*; in simpler terms, this means that the conversation is taking place within divinity.

The text describes three stages of relationship between the sun and the moon. In the first stage, both are equal; both implicitly share one *keter*, one crown. In the second stage, as a result of the moon's complaint, she is diminished. This is called *mi'ut ha-yareïah*, the diminishment of the moon. In Luria's system, it indicates the diminishment of *nukva*, the *partzuf* which represents *Malkhut/Shekhinah*. (Her counterpart, *Ze'ir Anpin* or *Tif'eret*, is of course represented by the sun.) This is the fundamental flaw in the cosmos which must be both reversed and rectified.

The text ends at this stage with *Hakadosh Baruh Hu* seeking atonement through the sacrifice of the new moon festival for having diminished the moon, that is, for having diminished *nukva*. Based both on the prophetic verse 'The light of the moon will become as the light of the sun' (Isa. 30:26), and on its midrashic interpretation, Luria posits that in the eschaton the moon, that is, *nukva*, will return to her initial stature and even exceed it. In Lainer, these motifs are adapted to his unique perspective on the contrast between the law and *retzon Hashem*, God's will or *Shekhinah*, in which the sun represents the former and the moon and the night represent the latter.

A second midrashic text, based on the biblical story of the creation of the first human, is conflated with the moon text in Kabbalah.[22] According to this text, man and woman were initially created back-to-back as one

185

being, as described in the first chapter, then separated by God through the process of *nesirah*, surgical separation, at which point they were free to turn and face each other. Again, the figures of the *midrash* represent *Ze'ir Anpin* and *nukva*. Here, according to the Lurianic interpretation, the diminishment of the moon corresponds to the state of the woman immediately after *nesirah*, whereas the ultimate state of redemption is represented by an as yet unrealized equality between man and woman. The connection between the moon, 'goddess energy', women, especially Solomon's wives, and *hokhmat Shelomoh* which figures so prominently in *MHs* and in the texts below, is predicated on these *midrashim*.

Notes for Zoharic Sources for
the Wisdom of Solomon

1 *Hands* 110.

2 See *Legends* vol. 4.

3 Sources 38–47.

4 Lainer's belief in the ahistorical nature of redemption is, of course, part of a major chorus within the Hasidic tradition (see Scholem, 'The Neutralization'). However, when this tradition is conflated with the anomian and antinomian strains pervading the Judah archetype, the results are radical indeed.

5 Ways in which we have already explored (in volume 1) Lainer's advances beyond his sources include his radical assertion that the Judah archetype is accessible, at least to some extent, by every person in the community and in the historical present, and that the historical present contains the realized eschaton within it. See, e.g., the sections 'The Democratization of Enlightenment' in Chapter Eight and 'Hisaron Meyuhad' in Chapter Three.

6 A later Jewish apocryphal work using Solomon's name, the well-known *Wisdom of Solomon*, as well as the Christian Testament (Mat. 12:42, Luk. 11:31) also make reference to Solomon's wisdom.

7 See e.g. Sources 5–7 in volume 2.

8 Source 7 in volume 2.

9 The *sefirah* of *binah* is considered the root of *din*, or *gevurah*. Nevertheless, punishment, associated with *din*, does not exist at its exalted level.

10 Interestingly, the *Tzemah Tzedek*, a contemporary of Lainer who was the third master of Habad Hasidut, asserts in his gloss to this Talmudic passage that the conclusion of the Talmud is that Solomon was warned 'from that day and and onwards that he should not budge from the laws of the Torah'.

11 See *MHs vol. 2* Proverbs s.v. *ki va'ar* (Source 11 in volume 2).

12 *bBaba Metzia* 59a.

13 The original verse quoted was Eccl. 2:12, while here the *midrash* combines two verses from Ecclesiastes. Though both of which speak about experiencing 'wisdom, madness, and folly', the second half comes from Eccl. 1:17, which reads in full, 'I set my heart to knowing wisdom, and to knowing madness and folly'.

14 See below, Source 43.

15 See the introduction to volume 1, esp. the section 'Secular Influences'.

16 Source 11 in volume 2.

17 See more on the kabbalistic use of *midrashim* about the moon, below (Source 8).

18 See e.g. *Shir Hashirim Rabbah* 3. In a second rabbinic teaching that appears in many places, the bold assertion is made that, save for specific exceptions, every single reference to Solomon in the Song of Songs refers in fact to God (*bShavuot* 35b).

19 The themes of eros and *mikdash* are indeed intimately related. See Source 14

later in this volume. This eros, which was essential to the *mikdash*, is ultimately equivalent to 'acosmic humanism'.

20 There are however notable exceptions. For example, Kalonymus Kalman Shapiro of Piacezna, author of many important Hasidic works, is fully sensitive to the historical development of the tradition. See the first five chapters of his work *Mevo She'arim*.

21 Source 4.

22 See for example *bEruvin* 18a and *Bereishit Rabbah* 8:1. The *midrash* emerges from the need to reconcile the first chapter of Genesis, in which 'male and female' are created as equals, and the second chapter, in which the man is created first and the woman is created from one rib, or side, of the man.

THE TEXTS OF THE ZOHAR

The sources for Lainer's ideas, however, are not primarily rabbinic, but Zoharic and post-Zoharic. Although Lainer does not cite all or even most of the major Zoharic texts that we will adduce in this volume, he does cite key texts that represent the core of these ideas.

Our analysis will revolve around key Zoharic passages that address the theme of *hokhmat Shelomoh*, the Wisdom of Solomon. In the *Zohar*, this term had a specific mystical understanding attached to it. Among the Zoharic passages we will cite below, a significant cluster regard Solomon's unique wisdom as an expression of *sihara be'ashleimuta*, the moon in its fullness. According to Lainer, the wisdom represented by the moon refers to the characteristic ability of the Judah archetype to bypass the general rules of Torah and to access unmediated *retzon Hashem*, that is to say, *Shekhinah*. Lainer refers to this wisdom with the phrase *da'at kedoshim eida'*, meaning, 'I will know knowledge of the holy'.[1]

In each of the *Zohar's* major Wisdom of Solomon passages, there are subthemes that are interlocked and textually interrelated. These themes will be recognized from our previous chapter, for they all belong to the matrix of the Solomon clusters in *MHs*. They include moon, messianism, *nukva*, *Shekhinah*, *mikdash*, and David, as well as a complex relationship to the pagan and to Solomon's many wives. Our presentation will focus on the analysis of key core passages, which, although they are not exhaustive, are a fair representation of the *hokhmat Shelomoh* genre in the *Zohar* that Lainer drew upon. We will identify recurrent motifs with special emphasis on the messianic, the nature of Solomon's *Shekhinah* project, and Solomon's fascination with and desire to integrate darkness. We will pay special attention to those passages that deal directly with the Judah archetype as well as the ontological symbolism of wine.

Zivug

What is perhaps most important at the outset is that in all of these passages, the recurring themes are all different ways of manifesting the *Shekhinah* symbol. The entire set of texts is a great song of longing for the *Shekhinah*, expressing both yearning and the real possibility of fulfilling that yearning through *zivug*, erotic merging, with *Shekhinah*.

Source 9: *Zohar* 1:216a

Solomon of course is not the first person in the *Zohar* to initiate or participate in *zivug* with the *Shekhinah*. Since the notion of *zivug* with the *Shekhinah* is, as we shall see time and again, central to the *Zohar's* understanding of the Wisdom of Solomon, we will begin with general comments about Zoharic sources on this general topic.

Every *tzadik*, according the *Zohar*, can potentially participate both in arousing the *Shekhinah* to *zivug* with her partner *Tif'eret*, and even more dramatically as a partner in the actual *zivug*. The *tzadik* may incarnate the *sefirah* of *Tif'eret* or *Yesod* and erotically merge with the *Shekhinah*. When reading these sources, we must distinguish between the *tzadik* as a symbol of *Yesod*—often expressed as Joseph who is engaged in *zivug* with the *Shekhinah* directly or effecting *zivug* between *Tif'eret* and *Malkhut*—and the actual human *tzadik* who is engaged in *zivug* with the *Shekhinah* or is effecting *zivug* with the *Shekhinah*.

From the plenitude of sources that touch on these themes in the *Zohar*, we will give a single example which emphasizes that the actual human *tzadik* can merge with the *Shekhinah*, and that this merging has an erotic cast. This source defines *tzadik* as anyone who is circumcised and guards the covenant. The *Zohar* uses the term *yarit*, which is also used in conjunction with Solomon, making it clear that this word is associated with *zivug*. The pleasurable and erotic nature of *zivug* is highlighted by the use of the word *itbasma*, a sensual word that evokes a kind of suffusion of *eros* in the *Zohar*.

רבי יצחק פתח ואמר, ועמך כלם צדיקים לעולם יירשו ארץ, האי קרא רזא
עלאה איהו בין מחצדי חקלא, דהא ברזא דאגדתא תני רבי שמעון דאחסנת

ירותא עלאה דההיא ארץ, לית מאן דיירית לה בר ההוא דאקרי צדיק, (ס"א
דהאי ארץ, ולית מאן דיירית לה בר ההוא דאקרי צדיק, דהא צדיק ירית
למטרוניתא ודאי) דהא מטרוניתא ביה אתדבקת לאתבסמא, וצדיק ירית
למטרוניתא ודאי. אוף הכא בחביבותא דקב"ה לישראל, אמר ועמך כלם
צדיקים, ובגין כך לעולם יירשו ארץ, אתחזון לירית למטרוניתא, מאי טעמא
אקרון צדיקים, ומאי טעמא ירתין למטרוניתא, בגין דאתגזרו, כמה דתנינן
כל מאן דאתגזר ועייל בהאי (ס"א ברית קדישא, ועאל בהאי) אחסנא,
ונטיר להאי ברית, עאל ואתדבק בגופא דמלכא, ועאל בהאי צדיק, ובגיני כך
אקרון צדיקים, ועל דא לעולם יירשו ארץ

Rabbi Yitzhak began and said: 'Your people are all righteous
(*tzadikim*); they will inherit the earth forever' (Isa. 60:21)—
This verse conceals a sublime secret for the harvesters of
the field (the initiated). It is written in the mysteries of the
agadah: Rabbi Shimon taught that the receiving of the higher
inheritance of that earth (*Malkhut/Shekhinah*) cannot be
inherited except by one who is called *tzadik*. For the *matronita*
clings to him in order to become intoxicated *itbasma*, and the
tzadik certainly inherits the *matronita*. Here too, because of
God's great love for Israel, he says, 'And your people are all
righteous' which is why 'they will inherit the earth forever'. For
they are worthy of inheriting the *matronita* (i.e., the earth).
Why are they called righteous, and why do they inherit the
matronita? Because they are circumcised. As we were taught:
Whoever has been circumcised has come into that inheritance, safeguards the covenant, enters and becomes attached
to the body of the King, and enters that *tzadik*. This is why
they are called *tzadikim*, and this is why they shall inherit
the earth.

The erotic dimension of this *zivug* relates to the representation of Solomon
in both the *Zohar* and in *MHs*; in *MHs* it signals that dimension which
transcends and is ontologically independent of the law. One aspect of this
source which is significant for our understanding of Lainer is that the
Zohar extends the possibility of erotic merging with *Shekhinah* to a broad
category of people, e.g., in this case, the circumcised. Such *Zohar* sources
already prefigure the move beyond the elite towards what I have termed
the democratization of enlightenment. This quality is given a prominent
place in *MHs*, though Lainer's application of *zivug* to those who complete
berur is of course quite different.

Solomon and Moses

We now proceed to a set of Zoharic texts comparing Solomon and Moses. The Judah model in *MHs*, as we saw, is represented by Solomon, while the Joseph model is often represented by Levi, as well as by Moses. Several passages in the *Zohar* prefigure the recurrent tension in *MHs* between the Judah and Joseph models through the figures of Moses and Solomon. These passages imply that there is an almost limitless potential for merging with the *Shekhinah* in the model of Solomon, as opposed to that of Moses. They first stem from the Talmudic passage in tractate Rosh Hashanah that states that Solomon desired to be like Moses,[2] and there is a difference of opinion as to whether Solomon actually fulfilled this desire. In the Zoharic texts, there continues to be ambiguity on this point. As with *MHs*, the general sense of these *Zohar* texts is that Solomon indeed enjoys some sort of advantage, ill-defined though it may be, over Moses.[3] The arena in which they are compared is critical, for it is no less than their respective abilities to merge with the *Shekhinah*. Hence we may to some extent find in these sources a foreshadowing of Lainer's Solomonic preference for *retzon Hashem*, the unmediated *Shekhinah*, over the law. The intention of these traditions is not that Solomon had some superior technique for merging with the *Shekhinah*. Rather, Solomon attained a level of enlightenment and expanded consciousness that was not reached even by Moses.

Source 10: *Tikunei Zohar* 28a

In our first source, from *Tikunei Zohar*, the discussion is about two sets of 'sixty', those of Moses and those of Solomon. The 'sixty' of Moses are derived from the *shema'* and are said to be male, while the 'sixty' of Solomon are female in nature.

ושלמה עלייהו אמר הנה מטתו שלשלמה ששים גבורים סביב לה, ואינון
נטרין (נ"א נטלין) ערסיה, ולקבלייהו ששים המה מלכות, אלין דכורין ואלין
נוקבין. אלין דקריאת שמע דתקין משה דכורין, אלין דשלמה נוקבין, ואלין
בית קבול לאלין, דרגין דשלמה אינון בית קבול לדרגין משה, וכד מתחברין
כלא כאחד, שלמ"ה אתהפך למשה

193

Concerning Solomon, it was said, 'Behold the bed of Solomon is surrounded by sixty warriors', and they guard his bed. Parallel to them are 'Sixty are the queens' (Cant. 6:8), these being male, and these being female. Those of the *shema'* that were decreed by Moses are males, and those of Solomon are females. These are a receptacle for these. The levels of Solomon are a receptacle for the levels of Moses. When they all join as one, *Shelomoh* is turned into *leMosheh*.

Here, Solomon is the female who receives Moses. 'These are the receptacle for those', that is to say, the levels of Solomon are a receptacle for the levels of Moses. Ultimately, when they merge as one, שלמה (Solomon) becomes למשה (to Moses). There is no hierarchy between them. We should note, however, that the females represented by Solomon are absorbed and transformed into the males of Moses; similarly, Solomon belongs, as it were, 'to Moses'.

Source 11: *Zohar* 2:140b

In the following citation, Solomon is subject to a two-fold comparison, first to David and then to Moses. In both, he emerges as superior.

תו שיר המעלות, כמה דאת אמר (תהלים מו) על עלמות שיר, (שיר א) על
כן עלמות אהבוך, לדוד בגין דוד מלכא עלאה דאיהו משבח תדיר למלכא
עלאה. כיון דאתא שלמה מלכא, אמר שיר דאיהו עלאה לעילא, דרברבי
עלמא עלאין קאמרי לגבי מלכא עלאה דשלמא כלא דיליה, כלהו דאמרי
שירתא לא סליקו בההיא שירתא לומר, אלא ההוא שירתא דמלאכי עלאי
קאמרי, בר שלמה מלכא, דסליק בההיא שירתא למה דרברבין עלאין עמודי
עלמא קאמרי, כל בני עלמא ברתיכין תתאין, שלמה מלכא ברתיכין עלאין

'A song of ascent *ha-ma'alot*, as it is written, 'a song for *'alamot* the young maidens' (Psalms 46:1), 'Therefore *'alamot* young maidens loved you' (Cant. 1:3). '[A song of ascent] of David' —because of David. David, the high king, was constantly praising the High King. When King Solomon arrived, he sang a song that was high beyond high, that the great ones of the upper world sing to the High King, to whom all peace belongs. All who sing do not rise with their song, other than the song that is sung by the higher angels, except for King Solomon, who rises through his song to where the high great ones, the pillars of the world do sing. All the children of the

194

world [are in] the lower chariots, whereas King Solomon is in the higher chariots.

As regards the comparison to David, there appears to be a two-step process, which David begins and Solomon completes. David is responsible for adorning the *matronita* (*Shekhinah*) and her virgins, enabling her to meet her bride in full beauty. Solomon then builds on David's first step and brings the bride to the groom, accompanying them with his songs of love.

The David-Solomon comparison is a recurring theme in other passages we will cite below. Some of these passages are similar to what we find here in presenting Solomon as one who inherits David's accomplishments and builds on them.[4] In other passages in the *Zohar*, David and Solomon seem to be engaged in separate spiritual projects. These two approaches are not necessarily exclusive; what is common to both is that Solomon is virtually always described as being at a higher or more advanced stage than David.

The passage now turns to the comparison with Moses:

ואי תימא, משה דסליק בדרגא דנבואה, ובחביבו לגבי קודשא בריך הוא
על כל בני עלמא, ההיא שירתא דקאמר ברתיכין תתאין הוה, ולא סליק
יתיר. תא חזי, שירתא דקאמר משה סליק לעילא ולא לתתא, אבל לא אמר
שירתא כשלמה מלכא, ולא הוה בר נש דסליק בשירתא כשלמה

And if you ask, what of Moses, who ascended beyond all other men in prophecy and love of the Holy One, blessed be He? Did his song also reach no farther than the lower chariots? Come and see, the song that Moses uttered did indeed ascend on high, but in truth it was not on the level of the song of King Solomon, who was equaled in poetry by none.

Moses' achievements, we learn, were of an entirely different source than Solomon's. The next part of the passage begins to flesh out the spiritual mechanics of this difference:

משה סליק בתושבחתיה לעילא, ותושבחתא דיליה הוה למיהב תושבחן
והודאן למלכא עלאה דשזיב לון לישראל, ועביד לון נסין וגבוראן במצרים
ועל ימא. אבל דוד מלכא ושלמה בריה, אמרו שירתא בגוונא אחרא, דוד
אשתדל לאתקנא עולמתן, ולקשטא לון במטרוניתא, לאתחזאה מטרוניתא
ועולמתהא בשפירו, ועל דא אשתדל באינון שירין ותושבחן לגבייהו, עד

דאתקין וקשיט כלהו עולמתן ומטרוניתא. כיון דאתא שלמה, אשכח
למטרוניתא מתקשטא ועולמתהא בשפירו, אשתדל למיעל לה לגבי חתן,
ואעיל החתן לחופה במטרוניתא, ואעיל מלין דרחימו ביניהו, בגין לחברא
לון כחדא, ולמהוי תרווייהו בשלימו חדא, בחביבו שלים, ועל דא שלמה
סליק בתושבחתא עלאה על כל בני עלמא

Moses rose by his song of praise and thanksgiving to the
supernal King who redeemed Israel and wrought many signs
and wonders for them, both in Egypt and at the Red Sea, but
King David and his son Solomon sang songs of quite a different
sort. David endeavoured to prepare the maidens and to adorn
them for the *matronita*, so that she and her maidens might be
manifest in beauty and grace….When Solomon came he found
the *matronita* and the virgins thus adorned, he in turn aspired to
lead the Bride to the Bridegroom. He brought the Bridegroom
beneath the marriage canopy where the Bride awaited Him, and
drew them together with words of endearment, that they might
be united as one, in one perfection, in perfect love. Therefore
Solomon evoked a more sublime song than all other men.

Moses sang his songs to the supernal King, while Solomon's (and David's)
songs were directed to the *matronita*. The next part of the passage compares Moses and Solomon in terms of the nature of their respective erotic
couplings with the *Shekhinah*. Indeed, the passage concludes with a direct
reference to the moon—that is to say, the *Shekhinah*—who reaches her full
erotic merging only through Solomon.

משה זווג למטרוניתא בהאי עלמא לתתא, למהוי בהאי עלמא בזווגא שלים
בתתאי, שלמה זווג לה למטרוניתא בזווגא שלימא לעילא, ואעיל החתן
לחופה בקדמיתא, ולבתר עאל לתרווייהו בהאי עלמא, וזמין לון בחדוה
בבי מקדשא דאיהו בנה. ואי תימא, היך עייל משה למטרוניתא בלחודהא
בהאי עלמא, דהא אתחזי פרודא, תא חזי קודשא בריך הוא זווג לה במשה
בקדמיתא, ואיהו הוות כלת משה כמה דאתמר, כיון דאזדווגת ביה משה
נחתת בהאי עלמא בזווגא דהאי עלמא, ואתתקנת בהאי עלמא, מה דלא
הוות מקדמת דנא, ולעולם לא הוות בפרודא. אבל לא הוה בר נש בעלמא
מיומא דאתברי אדם, דיעול רחימו וחביבו ומלין דזווגא לעילא, בר שלמה
מלכא, דאיהו אתקין זווגא דלעילא בקדמיתא, ולבתר זמין לון כחדא בביתא
דאתקין לון. זכאין אינון דוד ושלמה בריה, דאינון אתקינו זווגא דלעילא,
מיומא דאמר לה הקודשא בריך הוא לסיהרא זילי ואזעירי גרמיך, לא אזדווגת
בזווגא שלים בשמשא, בר כד אתא שלמה מלכא

196

Moses brought about the union of the *matronita* in this world down below, to be in perfect union in this world with the lower ones. Solomon brought about the perfect union of the *matronita* on high: he first led the Bridegroom to the canopy, and then brought them both down to this world and welcomed them with great joy into the sanctuary which he built. You may then ask, how could Moses bring the *matronita* down to this world alone? Would this not be deemed a separation? Come and see: the Holy One first caused the *Shekhinah* to be united with Moses, and she became the bride of Moses, as has already been explained. As soon as she was united with Moses she descended to this world and became united with it. She became firmly established in this world, as never before, and was never in a state of separation. However, since Adam was first created, no man has ever affected love and union above except for King Solomon, who first prepared the union above and then welcomed the bridegroom and the bride as one to the House which he prepared for them. Blessed are David and his son Solomon who have brought about the supernal union. Since the day when the Holy One said to the moon go and make yourself small,[5] she was never again joined in perfect unity with the sun, until the advent of Solomon.

Unlike David and Solomon, who represent two stages of the same project, Solomon and Moses are engaged in two different spiritual projects. Moses brings about erotic union between the *Shekhinah* and the world below. In order to do so he must separate the *Shekhinah* from her celestial partner *Tif'eret*. Therefore, *Tif'eret* is replaced by Moses, as it were, initiating Moses into *zivug* with the *Shekhinah*. After this initial *zivug* has been accomplished, Solomon can effect *zivug* between the *Shekhinah* and *Tif'eret* on high. After they are in union, Solomon brings them down into the Temple. The passage then concludes with a flourish of praise for Solomon, who accomplished for the moon/*Shekhinah* a level of *zivug* that no one before him had been able to accomplish.

Source 12: *Zohar Hadash* Shir Hashirim 4b

In this next, fascinating text, where Solomon and Moses are once again brought face-to-face, we find a complete conflation of two important mystical themes with the history of Israel's sanctuaries: the evolution of male and female from original oneness, and the separating and re-uniting that happens within the divine process.

כיון דאתבני בי מקדשא לתתא, ואתתקן היכלא על בורייה, כדין אתגלי
שיר השירים, דאצטריך לאתחברא מקדשא במקדשא. כד הוה משה
במדברא, בגין חוביהון דישראל, זווגא דמשה הות מתחברא ביה, באחורא
הוו דכר ונוקבא מתחבראן כחדא. כדין, והבית ובהבנותו זעיר זעיר. כד
עברו ישראל ית ירדנא, ומשה אתכניש, נסר לה קב״ה, ואתקין לה במשכן
שילה עד דאשתלימת בבי עלמין ואתחברת במלך שלמה והוו עלמין אפין
באפין. כדין, אבן שלימה מסע נבנה. מסע, דלא הות באתר חד קביע,
אלא אתעקר ואשתיל, וכדין נבנה כדקא יאות. וכל זיינין בישין וכל רוחין
בישין, כדין אתעברו מעלמא ולא שליטו כלל, הה״ז, ומקבות והגרזן כל כלי
ברזל לא נשמע בבית בהבנותו. בההיא שעתא, כד אתעברו כולא מעלמא,
ואשתארת אתתא בבעלה אפין באפין, כדין אתגלי שיר השירים. ודא איהו
שיר השירים אשר לשלמה, בלא ערבוביא כלל. אשר לשלמה, אפין באפין.
אשר לשלמה, דאתעקר ואשתיל באתר דשלמה כולא דיליה

When the Temple was built below and the sanctuary was firmly established, then the Song of Songs could be revealed, as sanctuary needed to be joined with sanctuary. When Moses was in the wilderness, because of Israel's sins, the *zivug* that Moses was joined with was back-to-back, male and female united as one. Then, '[w]hen the house (Temple) was being built'(1 Kings 6:7) [the *zivug* was] little by little. When Israel crossed the Jordan River, and Moses died, The Holy One set her apart, and installed her in the tabernacle of Shiloh, until she could be perfected in the eternal house. Then she joined with King Solomon and the worlds were face-to-face. Accordingly, [it is written that from] 'a perfect (complete, uncut) *masa'* (quarried stone) was [the house] built...' (1 Kings 6:7)—*masa'* [literally means] journeying, since [until then] *Malkhut/Shekhinah* was not fixed in one place but was uprooted and transplanted. Only then was she built (made complete) as she should be. And all evil offspring, and all evil spirits, were then gone from the world, and had no dominion. As it is written, '...and neither hammer nor ax nor any tool of iron was heard in the house when it was constructed.' At that time, when they were all removed from the world, and the Woman and her Man were left face-to-face, it was then that the Song of Songs was revealed. This is 'the Song of Songs of

Solomon', with no admixture. [Literally] 'to Solomon', that is, face-to-face. 'To Solomon'—that it was uprooted and transplanted in the place where all perfection *shalamah* is His.

When Israel was in the wilderness, their sins caused the erotic coupling with the *Shekhinah* to be *ahor be'ahor*, back-to-back. When they crossed the River Jordan and entered the land, male and female were separated and a new process of gradual merging began. The building of the tabernacle in Shiloh was an important milestone in the process that climaxed with the completion of the Temple by Solomon.[6] When that happened, the *zivug* became face-to-face rather than back-to-back. This state is reflected in the revelation of the Song of Songs to Solomon. Finally, in the last two lines of the text, Solomon once again blurs with the Godhead, as it says, 'to Solomon' means *be'atar deshalamah kula dileih'* [brought to] the place where all perfection is his/His', that is, Solomon is identified with the ultimate whole.

Source 13: *Tikunei Zohar* 24b

As we have seen, in the *Zohar*—in contradistinction to the Talmud—there is a strong preference for Solomon over Moses, with the implication that Solomon achieved *zivug* with *Shekhinah*, that is, a level of consciousness, which Moses simply did not. Our final source suggests a very different model of *zivug*, one in which Moses and Solomon work in a kind of partnership in order to effect *zivug* with the *Shekhinah*. This is also the first passage in our examination that discusses Solomon's wisdom.

בראשית, שי"ר תא"ב, והאי איהו שיר משובח מכל השירים, תאב מכל
השירים, ועליה אתמר שיר השירים אשר לשלמה, למלך שהשלום שלו,
הכי אוקמוהו, והאי שיר מתי יתער, בזמנא דיתאבדון סמא"ל וממנן דיליה
חייביא מן עלמא, ובההוא זמנא (שיר) אז ישיר משה, אז שר לא כתיב אלא
ישיר, והא אוקמוהו. והאי שיר באז סליק בפומא, (באז סליק בפומא שיר
אל) אבל שיר איהו ודאי חכמת שלמה, בההוא זמנא ותרב חכמת שלמה,
(דבההוא זמנא ומלאה הארץ דעה את ה' וכו'). ומאן סליק לה לאתרה, דא
משה, ורזא דמלה אז ישיר משה

Bereishit—[its letters can be rearranged as] *shir ta'ev*, a song of desire. This song is most praiseworthy of all songs, most desired of all songs, concerning which it is written, 'the Song of Songs which is Solomon's', the King to whom peace belongs, as has already been stated. When will that song be awoken? When Samael and his functionaries, the wicked, will be destroyed from the face of the earth. In that future time that 'az (then) Moses will sing'. It is not written, 'And Moses sang', but rather 'will sing', as we have already stated. And that song rises in the mouth through [the word] az [which has a numerical value of eight, hinting at the unification of YHVH and ADNY, a total of eight letters]. This song is most certainly the Wisdom of Solomon, and at that time 'the Wisdom of Solomon waxed great' (1 Kings 5:10[7]). And who raises her to her place? Moses, and the secret of the word az Moses will sing'.

In Song of Songs, Solomon sings the perfect *Shekhinah* song, but it is only through the medium of Moses that *zivug* is accomplished. Solomon's participation in this *zivug* process is explicitly referred to by the *Zohar* as *hokhmat Shelomoh*, the Wisdom of Solomon. This is the first of many Zoharic texts which we will examine that directly references a specific body of wisdom belonging to Solomon.

The Wisdom of Solomon Texts

We now turn our attention to an analysis of select Zoharic texts focused on the Wisdom of Solomon.

We must make at the outset a distinction between *zivug 'im ha-Shekhinah* in the following set of sources, and a different set of sources that discuss the nightly divine incursion of *Tif'eret* into the lower Garden of Eden in order to unite with the *Shekhinah* and commune with the souls of the righteous.[8] In contrast with the latter, more general theme, the many of the sources we introduce below describe a unique level of consciousness that was achieved by Solomon at a particular point in history. While it is true that Solomon is not merely a historical figure—he is archetypal as well—these texts describe a unique breakthrough in spiritual consciousness that is not part of the regular order of things. It will remain for Lainer to suggest that Solomon's breakthrough in relation to *zivug 'im ha-Shekhinah* is available to 'every man in Israel from young to old',[9] thereby bridging the gap between these two seemingly different orders of *zivug*.

As is often the case in reading the *Zohar*, the flow of each passage, its frame and context, is as important as the formal theosophical or mystical ideas presented in any particular passage.

Source 14: *Zohar* 1:149b–150a

In our first passage, the goal of *zivug 'im ha-Shekhinah* is effected by Jacob, who as a symbol will eventually interchange with Solomon himself. Jacob as both a symbol and a person yearns to be united with the *Shekhinah* through the agency of *Yesod*. *Yesod* is in particular that which unites *'ila'ah* and *teta'ah*, the upper and lowers realms, a recurrent theme in several key *hokhmat Shelomoh* passages. *'Ila'ah* and *teta'ah*, upper and lower, represent *Tif'eret* and *Malkhut* respectively. In light of a number of passages that we will presently read, in which the Solomonic project is described as being engaged with the integration of the darkness, it is reasonable to assign to *teta'ah*, the lower realms, a second meaning as well: the realms of darkness, which *hokhmat Shelomoh* seeks to integrate into the holy. The *Shekhinah* borders the realms of the *sitra ahra* in the Zoharic reality map. It is for this reason that *Shekhinah* is both vulnerable to their seduction, and able to serve as the medium for their integration. As we shall see, this is a major sub-theme in the Zoharic genre, providing an essential part of the matrix for Lainer's teaching regarding *hisaron*.

בגיני כך יעקב בההוא זמנא כתיב, ויחלום והנה סלם מוצב ארצה (וראשו),
מהו סלם, דרגא דשאר דרגין ביה תליין והוא יסודא דעלמא וראשו מגיע
השמימה, הכי הוא לאתקשרא בהדיה וראשו מגיע השמימה, מאן ראשו,
ראשו דההוא סלם, ומאן איהות דא דכתיב ביה (בראשית מז) ראש המטה,
בגין דאיהו ראש להאי מטה ומנה נהיר, מגיע השמימה, בגין דאיהו סיומא
דגופא, וקאים בין עלאה ותתאה, כמה דברית איהו סיומא דגופא, וקאים
בין יריכין וגופא, ועל דא מגיע השמימה. והנה מלאכי אלהי״ם עולים
ויורדים בו, אלין ממנן דכל עמין, דאינון סלקין ונחתין בהאי סלם, כד ישראל
חטאן מאיך האי סלם וסלקין אינהו ממנן, וכד ישראל מתכשרן עובדייהו
אסתלק האי סלם וכלהו ממני נחתי לתתא, ואתעבר שולטנותא דלהון, כלא
בהאי סלם קיימא, וכד כלהו נחתין לתתא, אתעביד סלם קיימא, הכא חמא
יעקב בחלמיה שלטנותא דעשו ושלטנותא דשאר עמין.

Concerning Jacob at that time it is written, 'And he dreamed and behold, there was a ladder on the ground, and its head reached the heaven.' What is meant by ladder? That level in which all other levels are suspended, which is the foundation (*yesod*) of the world. 'And its head reached the heaven'—what is meant by 'its head'? The head of the ladder. And who is that? The one about whom it is written, 'at the head of the bed'(Gen. 47:31), for he is at the head of the bed (*Malkhut*), and she receives light from him. 'Reached the heaven'—for he (*Yesod*) is at the end of the body, and is suspended between the higher realms and the lower realms, just like the *brit* is the end of the body, and is suspended between thighs and torso, thus it 'reached the heaven'. 'And behold the angels of God were going up and down it'—these are the masters of all the nations, who ascend and descend on that ladder. When Israel sins, the ladder descends and these masters rise. However, when Israel's deeds are as they should be, the ladder rises and all those masters descend, and their rule ceases. Everything is in this ladder. This is where Jacob, in his dream, saw the dominion of Esau and the other nations.

The discussion is filled with erotic imagery. Its focus is the unification between *Tif'eret*, which is symbolized by Jacob and by *shamayim*, the heavens, and *aretz*, the earth, a symbol for *Malkhut* or *Shekhinah*. The ladder, a phallic symbol that is described as standing erect, reaches to the sky, connecting the earth and the heavens. *Malkhut* is also symbolized in this passage by the *mitah*, the bed of Jacob, which is a consistent *Shekhinah* symbol in the *Zohar*. Thus the verse describing Jacob bowing at the head of his bed is really a description of Jacob bowing through the agency of the head, which is the head of the ladder. The *yihud* (unification) between *Tif'eret* and *Malkhut* more generally takes place through *Yesod*, which is both *rosh ha-mitah* and *rosh ha-sulam—rosh* (head) is often used as a symbol for *Yesod*. The passage continues:

והנה מלאכי אלהי"ם עולים ויורדים בו, במאן, בההוא ראשו דההוא סלם,
דכד אסתלק ראשו מניה סלם אתכפיא, וסלקין כלהו ממנן, וכד אתחבר
ראשו בההוא סלם אסתלק, וכלהו ממנן נחתין, וכלא חד מלה

'Behold the angels of God were going up and down on it'. On
what? On the top *rosh* (lit., head) of this ladder. For when its
head is gone, the ladder is subjugated, and those masters rise,
but when the head is attached to the ladder, it rises and all the
masters descend. This is all one piece.

The ascending and descending of the ladder determine the course of history. When it is erect, *zivug* can be accomplished and the masters of the nations fall. When the sacred phallus is not aroused to *zivug*, the masters of the nations have the opportunity to rise. In other words, Israel's historical destiny depends on the state of this *zivug*.

After this introduction, the *Zohar* makes the transition to Solomon, citing the biblical verse that signals the Wisdom of Solomon genre.

כתיב (מ"א ג) בגבעון נראה יהו"ה אל שלמה בחלום הלילה, ויאמר אלהי"ם
שאל מה אתן...הכא אתכליל דרגא בדרגא, דרגא עלאה בדרגא תתאה,
בגין דעד כען שלמה לא הוה שלים, כיון דאשתלים, כתיב (שם ה) ויהו"ה
נתן חכמה לשלמה, וכתיב (שם ה) ותרב חכמת שלמה, דקיימא סיהרא
באשלמותא, ובי מקדשא אתבני, וכדין הוה חמי שלמה עינא בעינא חכמתא
ולא אצטריך לחלמא

It is written, 'In Gibeon God appeared to Solomon in a dream of the night. And God said: Whatever you ask for I will grant'… (1 Kings 3:5). Here level integrated with level, the higher level with the lower. For until now Solomon was incomplete. When he became complete, it is written, 'And God granted wisdom to Solomon' (1 Kings 5:26[10]), and it is written, 'And the wisdom of Solomon waxed great' (1 Kings 5:10). For *sihara b'ashleimuta* the moon was in its fullness, and the Temple was built, and then Solomon beheld wisdom eye-to-eye, and he did not need dreams.

The Wisdom of Solomon is about uniting the higher and lower. In this second reference to higher and lower, they refer to *Tif'eret* and *Malkhut*, indicating that the theme of *zivug* is being juxtapositioned with the Solomon part of the passage. At the same time, higher and lower also allude to Solomon's agenda of integrating the darkness, which as we shall see is an important motif of the Wisdom of Solomon genre in the *Zohar*. When this *zivug* transpires, Solomon becomes complete.

As we saw in the acosmic foreshadowing we identified in the rabbinic sources, the *Zohar* also blurs Solomon with God by extending the name *Shelomoh* to *melekh sheha-shalom shelo*, the king to whom peace, or completeness, belongs. The biblical expression *vateirev hokhmat Shelomoh* is cited repeatedly in the Zoharic passages as an indication both that Solomon became complete, and that the moon waxed great or full. In the *Zohar*, the moon waxing great and becoming full is a core *hokhmat Shelomoh* symbol. It parallels the building of the Temple and it is what allows Solomon to see wisdom.

Mikdash or Temple, Solomon, moon and eros all merge together in this passage, with the moon as the key symbol. In the *Zohar*[11] and in virtually all systems of symbolic thought,[12] the moon is the *Shekhinah*/goddess symbol. The fullness of the moon, the Wisdom of Solomon, represents not just the psychological or even occult knowledge used for governance and power, but rather a full, erotic and mystical consciousness in which Solomon is merged with the *Shekhinah* in her most expansive state.

לבתר דחטא אצטריך ליה לחלמא כקדמיתא, ועל דא כתיב (שם יא) הנראה אליו פעמים, וכי פעמים הוה ולא יתיר, אלא סטרא דחלמא הוה ליה פעמים, סטרא דחכמתא כל יומא הוה...בגין דאתכליל דרגא בדרגא, מרא״ה במרא״ה

204

After he sinned, he needed dreams again. Therefore it is written, 'which appeared to him twice' (1 Kings 11:9). Was it only
twice and no more? It was the aspect of dream that came to
him twice, although the aspect of wisdom was daily....for level
had been integrated with level, vision with vision.

The *Zohar* points out that Solomon has no more need to apprehend the
divine through the medium of dream for he is in constant participation in
divinity. This is the Solomonic *zivug* with the *Shekhinah* that is the underpinning of the entire Wisdom of Solomon motif. This of course leads us
to Lainer's description of *binah kavu'a balev*[13], the stage reached after *berur*
in which one is constantly able to access *retzon Hashem*. The symbol in
MHs for this stage of consciousness is the king, and the ultimate king is
none other than Solomon. The state of the moon in her fullness is brought
into being by *zivug* with the *Shekhinah*, expressed for the third time in this
passage as the integration of one level with another and the union of vision
with vision, that is, the union of *Shekhinah* with *Tif'eret*.

In the last part of the passage Solomon falls. Unlike the more radical readings we will see shortly, the *Zohar* echoes the biblical writer in attributing
Solomon's downfall to his marriage to foreign wives and to his not guard-
ing the *brit*, i.e., to sexual sin.

והא השתא בסוף יומי חשך יתיר, ודא בגין דחטא, וסיהרא קיימא
לאתפגמא, מאי טעמא, בגין דלא נטיר ברית קדישא, באשתדלותיה בנשים
נכריות, ודא הוא תנאי דעבד קב"ה עם דוד, דכתיב (תהלים קלב) אם ישמרו
בניך בריתי וגו', גם בניהם עדי עד ישבו לכסא לך, מאי עדי עז, היינו דכתיב
(דברים יא) כימי השמים על הארץ, ובגין דשלמה לא נטר האי ברית כדקא
יאות, שריא סיהרא לאתפגמא, ועל דא בסופא אצטריך חלמא, וכן יעקב
אצטריך ליה לחלמא כדאמרן

Then, at the end of his days, he darkened, for he had sinned,
and the moon was once again lacking. What was the reason?
Because he did not guard the holy covenant in his occupa-
tion with foreign women. This was the condition God had
made with David, as it is written, 'If your children safeguard
My covenant', etc., 'then their children will sit forever on your
throne' (Psalms 132:12). What is meant by 'forever'? It is written, 'As the days of the heavens upon the earth' (Deut. 11:21).
Since Solomon did not safeguard the covenant as he should

have, the moon began to wane. Thus he needed a dream again towards the end. Likewise, Jacob needed a dream, as we have already explained.

Solomon's sin caused the moon to wane and Solomon was no longer one with divinity. Like Jacob in the time that his ladder descended, Solomon once more required the agency of a dream to communicate with the divine.

Source 15: *Zohar* 1:223b

In the next passage, we find a repetition of the core themes of the previous passage, but with a far more dramatic and radical reading that is especially relevant to Lainer's thought. The piece opens with a relatively long exchange between Rabbi Abba and Rabbi Shimon, which indicates that the *Zohar* wants to highlight this passage and is using the dramatic story line to do so.

יומא חד הוה אתי רבי שמעון מקפוטקיא ללוד, והוה עמיה רבי אבא ורבי יהודה, רבי אבא הוה לאי והוה רהיט אבתריה דרבי שמעון דהוה רכיב, אמר רבי אבא ודאי (הושע יא) אחרי יהו״ה ילכו כאריה ישאג, נחת רבי שמעון, אמר ליה ודאי כתיב (דברים ט) ואשב בהר ארבעים יום וארבעים לילה, ודאי חכמתא לא מתיישבא אלא כד בר נש יתיב ולא אזיל אלא קאים בקיומיה, והא אוקימנא מלי על מה כתיב ואשב, השתא בנייחא תלייא מילתא. יתבו

One day Rabbi Shimon was going from Kapotkaya to Lod, and Rabbi Abba and Rabbi Yehudah were with him. Rabbi Abba was studying and running after Rabbi Shimon, who was riding. Rabbi Abba said: Certainly [this is what is meant by], 'They will follow the Lord like a lion roars' (Hos. 11:11). Rabbi Shimon dismounted *nahat* (also, 'rested'). He retorted: It is clearly written, 'And I sat (i.e., remained) on the mountain forty days and forty nights' (Deut. 9:9). Certainly wisdom cannot settle unless a person is settled (lit., 'sitting'). Instead of moving, he should stay in his place. We have already spoken of the fact that it is written 'and I sat'. Now [too], it all depends on [us] resting *beneiha talya milta*. They sat.

The phrase *beneiha talya milta* will immediately remind those familiar with the *Zohar* of Rabbi Shimon's declaration in *Idra Rabba*, *behavivuta talya*

206

milta, 'it all depends on love'.[14] *Neiha*, a difficult word to translate, means something like inner calm and tranquility.[15] The introduction to this passage mentions *neiha* since the underlying theme of the passage is indeed *neiha*, that is to say, *Shekhinah*. Once the participants have attained the spiritual status of *yatvu*, sitting, the discussion can proceed.

אמר רבי אבא, כתיב ותרב חכמת שלמה מחכמת כל בני קדם ומכל חכמת
מצרים, מאי היא חכמת שלמה, ומאי היא חכמת מצרים, ומאי היא חכמת
כל בני קדם, אמר ליה תא חזי, בכמה אתר אוקמוה בההוא שמא דסיהרא,
כד אתברכא מכלא כתיב ותרב, ביומוי דשלמה דאתרביאת ואתברכת
וקיימא באשלמותא

> Rabbi Abba said: It is written, 'And the Wisdom of Solomon waxed greater than the wisdom of all the sons of the East and all the wisdom of Egypt'. What is the Wisdom of Solomon, what is the wisdom of Egypt, and what is the wisdom of all the sons of the East? [Rabbi Shimon] said: Come and see: In many instances we have related this to the moon. When she is blessed by the All, it is written, 'and she waxed great'—[during] the days of Solomon, when she grew, was blessed and was present in her fullness.

The 'sitting session' begins with Rabbi Abba posing a clear and highly dramatic question to Rabbi Shimon. Abba's question concerns the verse *vateirev hokhmat Shelomoh*, 'Solomon's wisdom waxed greater than the wisdom of the sons of the East and all the wisdom of Egypt'. What, asks Rabbi Abba, is meant by 'the wisdom of Egypt and the wisdom of the sons of the East' and why should we be so impressed that the Wisdom of Solomon was greater? Rabbi Shimon explains that the verse refers to the moon, i.e., the *Shekhinah*. The nature of the moon, the *Shekhinah*, is that it receives blessing from 'the All' ('all' is a Zoharic code word for the *sefirah* of *Yesod*). 'She waxed greater' does not mean that this wisdom became greater than all other wisdoms, but rather that it included all other wisdoms. This is the meaning of the moon waxing great in the days of Solomon: it was blessed and in its fullness.

Before further elaboration on this subject, the *Zohar* appears to segue into an entirely different topic. A careful reading however, reveals that it is not a different topic at all. Rabbi Shimon has raised the full power of the *Shekhinah* archetype; the moon in her fullness. In the following passage, we see that he is fully aware of the dangers involved in engaging the fullness of *Shekhinah*.

תנינן אלף טורין מתרברבין קמה, וכלהו נשיבא חד הוו לקמה, אלף נהרין
סגיאין לה ובגמיעא חדא גמעא לון, טופרהא מאחדא לאלף ושבעין עיבר
ידהא אחידן לארבע ועשרין (וחמש) אלף עיבר, לית דנפיק מינה להאי סטר
ולית דנפיק מינה לסטר אחרא, כמה וכמה אלף תריסין מתאחדין בשערהא.
חד עולימא דאורכיה מרישא דעלמא לסייפי דעלמא נפיק בין רגלהא,
בשתין פולסי דנורא מתלבש בגוניי, דא אתמנא על תתאי (מתחות) מארבע
סטרהא, דא איהו נער דאחיד שית מאה ותלת עשר מפתחן עלאין מסטרא
דאימא, וכלהו מפתחן עלאין בשננא דחרבא דחגיר בחרציה תליין

We learned: A thousand mountains boast (grow) before her, and one breath of hers is sufficient to contain them. A thousand rivers suffice her, and she swallows them in one gulp. Her nails clutch in a thousand and seventy directions, her hands clutch twenty four thousand directions. None can free themselves of her grip in any direction, and none can free themselves from her in another direction. How many thousands of sprites are caught in her hair! One lad whose length is from one extreme of the world to the other goes out from between her feet. He wears the colors of sixty pulses of fire. He is appointed over the lower realms from her four directions. This is the lad who holds six hundred and thirteen high keys from the side of mother, and all these high keys are hung in the sharpness of the blade that he wears on his loins.

Here we have a vivid description of the *Shekhinah* archetype run amok which fully highlights the dangers of engaging it. The *Shekhinah* image blurs into that of Hanokh ben Yered who is born from between her legs.

ההוא נער קרון ליה חנוך בן ירד באינון ברייתי, דכתיב (משלי כב) חנוך
לנער על פי דרכו, ואי תימא מתניתין היא ולא ברייתא, במתניתא דילן
אוקימנא מילי והא אתמר, וכלא מלתא חדא אסתכלו (נ"א אשתכללו)
תחותיה תטלל חיות ברא, דתניא (נ"א דתא חזי) כמה דישראל קדישא
עלאה אקרי בן לאמיה, דכתיב (שם ד) כי בן הייתי לאבי רך ויחיד לפני אמי,
וכתיב (שמות ד) בני בכורי ישראל, הכי נמי לתתא דא אקרי נער לאמיה,
דכתיב (הושע יא) כי נער ישראל ואוהבהו. ובכמה גוונין אקרי בן ירד
והא אוקימנא, אבל תא חזי בן ירד ממש, דתנינן עשר ירידות ירדה שכינה
לארעא, וכלהו אוקמוה חברייא ואתמר, ותחות האי כמה חיותא קיימין

208

דאקרון חיות ברא ממש. תחות אינון חיוותא מתאחדן שערהא דסיהרא
דאקרון ככביא דשרביטא, דשרביט ממש. מארי דמארין, מארי דמתקלא,
מארי דקשיו, מארי דחוצפא, וכלהו אקרון מארי (נ"א שערי) דארגוונא,
ידהא ורגלהא אחידן בהאי, כאריה (קדישא) תקיפא דאחיד על טרפיה, ועל
דא כתיב (מיכה ה ז) וטרף ואין מציל

This lad *na'ar* is called Hanokh ben Yered in the *breitot*, as
it is written, 'Educate *hanokh* the lad *lana'ar*...' (Prov. 22:6)
(i.e., by reading the verb in this phrase as a proper noun, the
sentence reads, 'Hanokh became the *na'ar*'). You may say,
this is a *mishnah*, not a *beraita*, whereas in our *mishnah* we
explained the matter, as noted, and it is entirely one thing.
'Below him the wild animals shelter' (Daniel 4:9)[16]. As we
have learned: just as supernal Israel is called a son of his
mother, and it is written, 'For I was a son of my father, tender
and an only child to my mother' (Prov. 4:3), and also, 'Israel
is my firstborn son' (Exod. 4:22). Likewise below, this one is
called a son of his mother, as it is written, 'For Israel is a lad
and I love him' (Hos. 11:1). There are various reasons he is
called *ben Yered*, as already stated. But now, come and see: it
is literally *ben Yered*, one who descends, for we have learned,
the *Shekhinah* descended ten levels to the earth, as has been
noted by the companions. It has been said that beneath that
one, how many animals there are that are specifically called
chayot bara[17] wild animals. The hairs of the moon, which are
called falling stars, touch beneath these creatures. They are
masters of masters, masters of balance, masters of harshness,
masters of audacity, and all are called masters of purple. Her
hands and her feet hold it, like a powerful lion holds its prey.
Concerning this was it written, 'And it preys, and there is no
deliverer' (Mic. 5:7).

The name *Yered*, says the *Zohar*, is derived from *yeridat ha-Shekhinah*, the
descent of the *Shekhinah*. This is important for our context, as Hanokh
begins as a human being and metamorphoses into Metatron who in some
sources becomes a divine figure. As we explored in volume 1, the very possibility of such a notion supports the idea of acosmic humanism.[18]

The end of this introductory passage is highly relevant as well. It is a description of an unsuccessful *zivug* with the *Shekhinah*. Instead of achieving

oneness with *gufa demalka*, the 'body of the queen', which alludes to erotic merging with the *Shekhinah*, one becomes erotically merged with the side of impurity. This is the state that the *Zohar* refers to as *ḥatat Yehudah*, the sin of Judah. Later in our discussion we will see that this Judah reference is only one of a whole series of passages that constitute the Zoharic matrix for the Judah archetype in *MHs*. For now, let us note that when the Judah archetype is not in appropriate *zivug* with the *Shekhinah*, the natural result is *ḥatat Yehudah*:

כל אינון דאדכרין חובי בני נשא, וכתבין ורשמין חובייהו בתקיפו דדינא
קשיא, ועל דא כתיב (ירמיה יז) חטאת יהודה כתובה בעט ברזל בצפורן
שמיר, מהו שמיר, ההוא דרשים ונקיב אבנא ופסיק לה לכל סטרא.
זוהמא דטופרהא, כל אינון דלא מתדבקין בגופא דמלכא, וינקין מסטרא
דמסאבותא, כד שארי סיהרא בפגימו

> All who recall the faults of man, who write and register their failures with the force of harsh judgment, regarding them it has been written, 'The sin of Judah is inscribed with an iron pen, with a quill of *shamir*' (Jer. 17:1). What is *shamir*? It is what inscribes and pierces stone and cuts it on all sides. The filth of the nails [means] all these who do not cling to the body of the king, and who suckle from the side of impurity, when the moon wanes.

We are now introduced to the passage that addresses the moon and the Wisdom of Solomon: ובגין דשלמה ירתא לסיהרא בשלימותא, בעי לירתא לה בפגימותא 'And since Solomon inherited *sihara bisheleimuta* the moon in its fullness, he wished to inherit it *bipegimuta* in its incompleteness'.

Solomon inherits the moon in a state of fullness. As we will see in a later passage, it is his father David who has brought the moon to this stage by his having attained the level of mystical consciousness that is termed 'the moon in her fullness'. The passage can therefore be interpreted to mean that Solomon wished to merge with the *Shekhinah* in all her fullness. The moon in her fullness as an image for the Wisdom of Solomon means that at this stage, the *Shekhinah* integrates everything, including all that is *pagum*, imperfect and unrectified.

על דא אשתדל למידע בדעתא (ברעותא) דרוחין ושדין, למירת סיהרא
בכל סטרא, וביומוי דשלמה מלכא בכלא אתנהיר סיהרא, הדא הוא דכתיב

(מ״א ה) ותרב חכמת שלמה, ותרב דייקא. מחכמת כל בני קדם, רזא עלאה
הוא

Thus he strove to know the knowledge of spirits and demons,
in order to inherit the moon *bekhol sitra* in every aspect. During the days of King Solomon, the moon enlightened everything, as it is written, 'And the wisdom of Solomon waxed
great' (1 Kings 5:10)—specifically, 'she waxed great.' 'Greater
than (lit., 'from') the wisdom of all the children of the East'—
that is a loftier mystery.

In order to accomplish this, Solomon seeks to access all the powers of the
spirit, including the spirits and demon symbols of darkness. Solomon wants
to merge with the *Shekhinah*, what the *Zohar* calls 'to inherit the moon in
all aspects', including the dark side of the moon. In this project, according to
the *Zohar*, Solomon is successful. In the days of Solomon the moon shines;
this is what it means when it says, 'the wisdom of Solomon waxed greater
than all the wisdom of the children of the East and all the wisdom of Egypt'.
In a radical reading, as we will shortly see, the *Zohar* interprets this to mean
that the wisdom of Solomon waxed great through the wisdom of the East
and the wisdom of Egypt, that is to say, by incorporating these wisdoms.[19]

כמה דכתיב (בראשית לו) ואלה המלכים אשר מלכו בארץ אדום וגו', ואלין
אקרון בני קדם, דכלהו לא אתקיימו, בר מהאי דכלילא דכר ונוקבא דאקרי
הדר, דכתיב (שם לו) וימלוך תחתיו הדר וגו'

As it is written, 'And these are the kings that reigned in the
land of Edom, etc.' (Gen. 36:31), they are called the children
of the East *kedem*.[20] For none of them were sustained except
through he who integrated both male and female, who was
called Hadar, as it is written, 'And Hadar reigned in his stead
[and the name of his wife was Meheitavel]' (Gen. 36:39).

The Wisdom of Solomon is about attaining balance, and as a consequence
it has the potential to fix 'the death of the kings', referring to the Zoharic
myth of originary cosmic destruction.[21] The eighth king, the only one list-
ed in the Genesis text as having a wife, is the only one who is not said to
have died, which is taken to mean that the eighth mastered the balance of
male and female. For this reason he was called *Hadar*, 'beauty', indicating
the beauty of that balance.[22]

211

ותאנא דאף על גב דאתקיימת (נ״א דאתנהירת סיהרא) לא אתנהירת
באשלמותא עד דאתא שלמה דאתחזי לקבלהא כמה דאוקימנא דבגין כך
אמיה בת שבע הות. מכל חכמת מצרים, דא חכמה תתאה, דאקרי שפחה
דבתר ריחיא, וכלא אתכלילת בהאי חכמה דשלמה, חכמת בני קדם וחכמת
מצרים

And we learned that even though the moon was sustained
[i.e., waxed and waned], it did not shine in its entirety until
Solomon, who was worthy of receiving her, came, as we have
already noted, and because of this, Bathsheba (*bat sheva'* lit.
'daughter of seven', i.e. *Malkhut*/the moon) was his mother.
'[F]rom all the wisdom of Egypt'—this refers to Lower
Wisdom (*Shekhinah*, the seventh *sefirah* of the lower *sefirot*),
which is called the 'maidservant behind the millstone' and all
[of this] was included in the wisdom of Solomon—the wisdom of the children of the East and the wisdom of Egypt.

The wisdom of Egypt and the wisdom of the East refer to the paganism
that existed in the time of Solomon. It is the daughter of the Egyptian
Pharaoh and the idols of Kedem that infiltrate his court. According to this
Zoharic reading, Solomon's ability to integrate these forces is what made
his wisdom great![23] For the *Zohar*, the moon in her fullness means not only
being full, but also being inclusive.

In the *Zohar's* conclusion, all the themes have merged. Until the time of
Solomon the moon did not shine in all of her fullness; something was
always missing and the *Shekhinah* was therefore incomplete. When
Solomon came, he integrated all that was *pagum*, incorporating it into
the *Shekhinah*. Thus 'greater than the wisdom of Egypt' needs to be read
as 'greater *through* the wisdom of Egypt'. This is what is meant when we
say that Solomon's mother was called Bathsheba: she is of the seventh
sefirah, Malkhut/Shekhinah. Hokhmat Mitzrayim, the wisdom of Egypt, is
the 'handmaiden behind the millstone', a Zoharic term for the *Shekhinah* in
exile.[24] This is also synonymous with *hokhmah teta'ah*, lower wisdom, another term for *Malkhut/Shekhinah*.[25] Through the agency of Solomon, the
wisdom of Egypt becomes incorporated into the *Shekhinah*. In this source,
Solomon's sin is not referred to at all; and the ultimate integration that is
the *Shekhinah* in all of her fullness is the defining moment of Solomon.

One of the demarcating characteristics of the Wisdom of Solomon, as we will see validated in a number of key passages below,[26] is inclusiveness or integration. Everything is *itkalelet*, included in the moon. The *Shekhinah* embraces and integrates all the disparate forces of the spirit. Hence, Solomon's wisdom depends on the integration of the wisdom of Egypt and of Kedem, two seats of paganism. Indeed the simple reading of the biblical text itself seems to relate the Wisdom of Solomon to pagan practice. Solomon received his revelation in a dream at Gibeon, where he had gone to offer sacrifice on the high places or *bamot*. The verse immediately preceding suggests that Solomon followed God in everything, other than that he still offered sacrifices at the *bamot*. And yet, immediately after this practice, which is condemned, Solomon has his wisdom dream.

According to the *Zohar's* reading, '*vateirev hokhmat Shelomo*', the waxing of the Wisdom of Solomon, stems directly from its inclusiveness, which extends to making some sort of place for the pagan goddesses of his wives.

We saw in the previous volume that in Lainer's reading, this was a deliberate part of Solomon's *Shekhinah* project. He wanted to integrate into the holy, into the *mikdash*/Temple, the many faces of the *Shekhinah*, both conceptually and literally. We saw as well that *MHs* cited two key passages from the *Zohar* which supported Lainer's complex and nuanced relationship to paganism.[27] At this point we see that this drive to inclusiveness is rooted within the Wisdom of Solomon genre in the *Zohar* upon which Lainer based so much of his thought.

Of course the Temple itself, as the rabbinic writers[28] were well aware, was overladen with pagan motifs. Indeed, the rabbinic writers express this complex relationship between the Temple and the pagan through midrashic sources in diverse ways, e.g., in one passage, the conquerors of the Temple mistake the cherubs for pagan gods,[29] and in another passage, the seat of idolatrous energy is identified as being the Holy of Holies within the Temple.[30] Further rabbinic sources tell us that Solomon married the daughter of Pharaoh on the day of the consecration of the *mikdash*. The Talmud describes the thousand types of song that she played for Solomon on that very night, each song being an initiation into a differerent form of paganism.[31] At each song, the name of the pagan god to whom the song was connected was mentioned out loud, indicating that it was not merely a music festival that took place in Solomon's palace.[32]

We will cite one last source from the *Zohar* which places in bold relief this often radical engagement with the sacred energy of purified paganism. The *Zohar* makes the radical claim that the *mizbeiah*, the altar in the tabernacle and at the Temple in Jerusalem, was an *Asheirah* symbol itself. In an incredible reading, the *Zohar* suggests that *Asheirah* and *Asher* are the sefirotic pair of *Malkhut/Shekhinah* and *Tif'eret*.

כתיב (דברים טז כא) לא תטע לך אשרה כל עץ אצל מזבח יהו"ה אלהי"ך
אשר תעשה לך. אצל מזבח, וכי לעילא מניה או באתר אחרא מאן שרייה,
אלא הא אוקימנא, אשר דא בעלה דאתתא, (ד"א ה"א) אתקריאת על שום
בעלה אשרה, (נ"א הרי הם אשר ה"א), ועל דא כתיב (מלכים ב כג ד)
לבעל ולאשרה, בגין כך כתיב לא תטע לך אשרה כל עץ אצל מזבח יהו"ה
אלהי"ך, לקבל (נ"א אשרה) אתר דההוא מזבח יהו"ה, דהא מזבח יהו"ה
איהו קיימא על דא, ועל דא לקבלה לא תטע לך אשרה אחרא

It is written, 'You shall not plant for yourselves an *Asheirah* of any kind of tree beside the altar of the Lord thy God which (*asher*) you shall make for yourselves' (Deut. 16:21). Then is it permitted [to plant one] above it, or in another place? The truth is that *Asher* is the name of the woman's spouse; she is called *Asheirah* after [his] name (i.e., *Asher* plus the divine feminine represented by the letter *Heh*), hence it is written 'to *Baal* and *Asheirah*' (2 Kings 23:4). Therefore the meaning of the verse, 'You shall not plant an *Asheirah* alongside the altar of *YHVH* your God'...is 'You shall not plant *any other Asheirah*'.

According to this passage, the reason for the biblical proscription against planting an *Asheirah* tree near the altar is that it would be superfluous, for there is no need for two *Asheirah* symbols in the Temple. In this reading one could simply say that *Malkhut* is *Asheirah*, which is precisely what Cordovero says:

אשרה פי' בזהר בראשית (דף מט) כי מלכות נקראת אשרה בהיותה יונקת
מן התפארת שהוא בעלה בהיותו נק' בבחי' אשה. הוא אשר והיא אשרה. כי
כן דרך רוב כינוייהם במשקל צדיק צדק עופר עפר

Asheirah—In the *Zohar* on Genesis (49a) it is explained that *Malkhut* is called *Asheirah*, as it is nursed by *Tif'eret*, who is her husband, when he is called by his aspect of *Asher*. He is *Asher*, and she is *Asheirah*.[33]

What this suggests is that *Malkhut/Shekhinah* and the pagan *Asheirah* participate in the same primordial feminine Goddess energy. This energy is understood by the *Zohar* to be at the center of Solomon's temple in Jerusalem, the essence of the altar itself.[34]

תא חזי בכל אתר כל אינון פלחי שמשא אקרון עובדין לבעל, ואינון דפלחין
לסיהרא איקרון עובדי אשרה, ועל דא לבעל ולאשרה, ואשרה אתקרי על
שום בעלה אש"ר. אי הכי אמאי אתעבר שמא דא, אלא אשרה על שום
דכתיב (בראשית ל יג) באשרי כי אשרוני בנות, והוא (ד"א הא) דלא
אשרוה שאר עמין, וקיימא אחרא תחותה, ולא עוד אלא דכתיב (איכה
א ח) כל מכבדיה הזילוה, ובגין כך (נ"א אתעביד) אתעבר שמא דא בגין
דלא יתתקפון אינון דעבדי שאר עמין עעכו"ם, וקרינן מזבח דאיהו מאדמה,
דכתיב (שמות כ כב) ואם מזבח אדמה וגו', בגיני כך עפר מן האדמה

Come and see: throughout the Scriptures the worshippers of the sun are called servants of *Baal* and the worshippers of the moon servants of *Asheirah*. If this is so (i.e., that *Asheirah* is the name of the feminine aspect of God), why is this name not used [as a sacred name]? The reason is that '*Asheirah*' derives from [the words of Leah:] 'happy am I, for the daughters will call me happy (*ishruni*)', but the other nations do not call her 'happy', and another nation is set up in her place. More than this, it is written, 'all that honored her despise her' (Lam. 1:8). Therefore this name is not used, in order not to strengthen the other idolatrous nations, and she is called 'altar', which is made from earth, as it is written, 'An altar of earth *adamah* you shall make for me' (Exod. 2:22), and therefore [it says in Genesis, the human *adam* was made of] 'dirt from the earth'.

Here we see that the only reason the altar is not called *Asheirah* is that Israel does not occupy its rightful place among the nations. The ultimate reality is not yet made explicit, because to do so would give power to what is distorted in the world. *Adam/adamah* substitutes here for *Asher/Asheirah*.[35]

Of course this passage, coupled with the Zoharic passages on *elohim ahei-rim* (other gods) cited and interpreted by Lainer, together provide an important matrix for Lainer's relationship to paganism. As we proceed, we shall note that a similar position is also enunciated by Simcha Bunim, who preceded Lainer in viewing Solomon's marriage to many wives and his integration of their idolatry as a deliberate *Shekhinah* project, and that this position has roots in Luria as well.

Sihara – The Moon

In many of the sources we examine in this volume, both above and below, the moon is a prominent symbol for *hokhmat Shelomoh*.[36] In the next two sources, the moon's role is more complex and its significance is more detailed.

Source 17: *Zohar* 1:225b

רבי חייא פתח ואמר, (קהלת ז כג) כל זה נסיתי בחכמה אמרתי אחכמה
והיא רחוקה ממני, הא תנינן, שלמה מלכא ירית סיהרא מכל סטרוי, וביומוי
קיימא בשלמותא ההיא סיהרא דאתברכא מכלא, וכד בעא למיקם על
נמוסי אורייתא, אמר, אמרתי אחכמה וגו'

Rabbi Hiyya opened saying: 'For all I tried with wisdom, I said I would become wise, and it is far beyond me' (Ecc. 7:23). We learned, Solomon inherited the moon from all its sides, and during his time this moon stood in fullness, for it was blessed from the All. However, when he tried to understand the meanings of the Torah, he said, 'I said: I would become wise.'

At first glance, here are the same core themes that we encountered in Source 15: Solomon wants to merge with the moon in a way that integrates all of her sides or aspects, *kol sitroy*, that is, all the different faces of the *Shekhinah*. Here, however, the *Zohar* adds a new dimension: Solomon wanted to apply this expanded full-moon–consciousness to his interpretation of Torah, and in this venture, the *Zohar* says, he failed. Here Lainer clearly moves beyond the *Zohar*, for according to Lainer, the entire goal of this 'full moon exegesis' is to transform the way we interpret Torah, to move beyond the *kelalei divrei Torah*. This is the very foundation in *MHs* of the Judah archetype who is able to access unmediated *retzon Hashem*, which is *Shekhinah*; that is to say, the moon in her fullness.

Source 18: *Zohar* 1:248b–249a

The following text recapitulates some of the core themes and identifications that we have already noted. As in Source 14, we begin with Jacob, and as in that source, there is a natural transition from Jacob to Solomon. We find the same pattern in *MHs*: Solomon is the major figure, but Jacob is often portrayed in Solomonic terms as one who has constant and unmediated access to *retzon Hashem*.[37]

חמי מה כתיב, ויאסוף רגליו אל המטה, דאתכניש שמשא לגבי סיהרא,
שמשא לא מית, אלא אתכניש מעלמא ואזיל לגבי סיהרא. תא חזי, בשעתא
דאתכניש יעקב אתנהיר סיהרא, ותיאובתא דשמשא עלאה אתער לגבה
בגין דשמשא כד סליק אתער שמשא אחרא, ואתדבק דא בדא ואתנהיר
סיהרא

See what is written, 'And he gathered his legs into the bed'
(Gen. 49:33)—the sun entered into the moon. The sun did
not die; rather, it entered from the world and went to the
moon. Come and see, when Jacob was taken in, the moon
shone, and the desire of the higher sun awakened towards
her, for when the sun departed, another sun awoke, and they
clung to each other, and the moon shone.

This text introduces the following passage, which adds new dimensions to our understanding of *hokhmat Shelomoh* in the *Zohar* as the matrix for *hokhmat Shelomoh* in Lainer. Again we are telling the story of the erotic union between Jacob, who is *Tif'eret*, and *mitah*, which is a symbol, as it was above, for *Shekhinah*. The medium of union, *Yesod*, is this time symbolized by *shimsha 'ila'ah*, the higher sun. When union occurs, *sihara*—the moon/*Shekhinah*—shines in all her splendor.

אמר רבי שמעון, שפיר קא אמרת, אבל הא אתמר דעלאה עלמא דדכורא
אתקשר בתתאה דאיהו עלמא דנוקבא, ותתאה אתקשר בעלאה, וכלא דא
כגוונא דא

Rabbi Shimon said: You spoke well, but it has already been
said that the higher one, the male world, bonds with the lower
one, which is the female world, and the lower bonds with the
higher, and all of this one is like that one.

Rabbi Shimon unpacks the union one step farther to include the union of the higher with the lower and the lower with the higher. *Tita'ah* here can be understood, as in the previous texts, in two ways. Most simply it is *Malkhut/Shekhinah*. Alternatively it is a symbol for the lower realms that need to be integrated in the *Shekhinah*.

218

והא אתמר תרין עלמין נינהו, כדכתיב (דה״א טז לג) מן העולם ועד העולם,
ואף על גב דתרין נוקבי נינהו, חד מתתקן בדכורא, וחד בנוקבא

Moreover, it has already been said that there are two worlds,
as it is written, 'from the world and to the world' (1 Chron.
16:33). Although both are female, one is developed through
the male and one through the female.

The two worlds are the two feminine powers, *Binah* and *Malkhut*, otherwise known as higher and lower mother respectively. *Binah* finds *tikun*—
a word which means both *zivug* and expression—through the male, which
is her son *Tif'eret*, and *Malkhut* finds *tikun* by establishing a direct connection with *Binah*.[38]

דא שבע ודא בת שבע, דא אם ודא אם, דא אקרי אם הבנים, ודא אקרי אם
שלמה, כדכתיב (שיר ג) צאינה וראינה בנות ציון במלך שלמה וגו' במלך
שלמה, במלך דכל שלמא דיליה, דא אם שלמה כדכתיב (מ״א א יא) בת
שבע אם שלמה וכתיב (שם ה ל) ותרב חכמת שלמה, חכמת שלמה דא אם
שלמה

This one is seven, and that one is the daughter of seven, *bat
sheva'* (i.e., Bathsheba), this one is mother and that one is
mother, this one is called *eim ha-banim* 'the mother of children', and that one is called 'the mother of Solomon'; as it is
written, 'Go out and gaze, O daughters of Zion, at Solomon
the King [in the crown with which his mother crowned
him…]' (Cant. 3:11)—the King to whom peace belongs. That
one is 'the mother of Solomon', as it is written, 'Bathsheba
bat sheva', the mother of Solomon' (1 Kings 1:11). It is also
written, 'And the wisdom of Solomon waxed great' (1 Kings
5:10)—the Wisdom of Solomon is the mother of Solomon.

Here we find one of the clearest identifications of *hokhmat Shelomoh* with
Shekhinah that appear in the *Zohar. Sheva'* is *Binah* and Bathsheba is
Malkhut/Shekhinah. Both are called mother. *Binah* is 'the mother of children', while *Malkhut* is 'mother of Solomon'. The *Zohar* cites here the rabbinic dictum identifying King Solomon with God. The *Zohar* then turns
back to the basic *hokhmat Shelomoh* verse from 1 Kings 1:3, interpreting
it to mean that the mother of Solomon, *Malkhut/Shekhinah*, waxed great.

The *Zohar* next returns to Jacob and the original proof text:

תא חזי, יעקב אתכניש לגבי סיהרא, ועביד בה פירין לעלמא, ולית לך
דרא בעלמא דלא אית ביה איבא דיעקב, בגין דהא איהו אתער אתערותא
לעילא, בגין דכתיב ויאסוף רגליו אל המטה, דאיהו מטתיה דיעקב ודאי,
זכאה חולקיה דיעקב, דהא אשתלים לעילא ותתא, דכתיב (ירמיה ל י)
ואתה אל תירא עבדי יעקב נאם יהו"ה וגו', כי אתך אני, כי אתי אתה לא
אתמר, אלא כי אתך אני

> Come and see: Jacob was gathered into the moon, and in her,
> he made fruit for the world, and there is no generation in the
> world that does not have the produce of Jacob. For it is he
> who awoke the awakening on high, as it says, 'And he gathered
> his feet into the bed', for that was most certainly Jacob's bed.
> Happy is Jacob's portion, as he was complete both above and
> below, as is written (Jer. 30:10), 'And you, do not fear, Jacob,
> my servant, says the Lord, etc., for I am with you.' It does not
> say 'for you are with me' but rather 'for I am with you'.

The *Zohar* asks, why does the verse say 'I am with you', rather than 'you are
with Me'? The *Zohar's* answer is a precise allusion to acosmic humanism.
The more obvious phrasing would have suggested a classical theocentric
orientation. The actual phrasing however expresses the acosmic non-dual
humanist orientation: I, God, am manifest within you.

Solomon and David

The next several passages spell out in detail the spiritual relationship between David and Solomon, something which we have already learned about in Source 11. Our first passage takes up from the end of the previous source.

Source 19: *Zohar* 1:249b

We now continue further in the text. As in the previous pieces, the context is particularly important in deciphering the content, so we will unpack the introduction to the key passage in order to understand the flow of images and ideas. The verse from Isaiah being discussed reads, *Tzahali kolech bat galim hakshivi layashah* 'Let your voice ring out, daughter of the waves; listen, lioness' (Isa. 10:30). The *Zohar* understands 'lioness' as a *Shekhinah* symbol:

תא חזי האי קרא קשיא, בקדמיתא כתיב צהלי קולך, דהוא בגין לזמרא
ולארמא קלא, ולבתר כתיב הקשיבי, אי הכי אמאי צהלי קולך כיון דכתיב
הקשיבי, אלא צהלי, בגין לשבחא ולזמרא. תא חזי אי ישראל שראן לשבחא
ולזמרא לקב"ה, כדין כתיב הקשיבי, מאי טעמא, בגין דישראל אינון משבחן
ומזמרין בגינה לקב"ה, ועל דא כתיב צהלי קולך

> Come and see: this verse is difficult to understand. At first it
> says 'Let your voice ring out', that is, in order to sing and raise
> up the voice, and then it says, 'Listen'...Rather, it means, 'let it
> ring out' in order to praise and sing. Come and see: If Israel
> begins to praise and sing to the Holy One *kudsha berikh hu*
> when it is written 'listen', what is the reason? Because Israel
> praises and sings to God for her [and *Shekhinah* listens]. This
> is why it says 'Let your voice ring out'.

The cry of the lioness is the song of the *Shekhinah* for *kudsha berikh hu*. The *Zohar* of course moves seamlessly between the *Shekhinah* image and Israel, that is, the Jewish people, who also personify *Shekhinah* (the *Shekhinah* is called *keneset Yisrael*, the congregation of Israel) and can thus also fulfill the role of singing the song of the *Shekhinah* to God. As is characteristic throughout the *Zohar*, there is a deliberate blurring between the divine and the human being performing precisely the same function.

וכתיב הקשיבי לישה, בגין דאתיא מסטרא דגבורה, כמה דאת אמר (משלי
ל ל) ליש גבור בבהמה, והאי לישה גבורה לתברא חילין ותוקפין, עניה
ענתות, בגין דאיהי אספקלריא דלא נהרא (עלה) עניה ודאי, לית לה נהורא
לסיהרא מגרמה, אלא מה דיהיב לה שמשא...בגין כך סיהרא לית לה
נהורא מגרמה, אלא בשעתא דאתחבר עמה שמשא אתנהירת

> And it is written, 'Listen, lioness', because she comes from the side of *Gevurah*, as you said: 'The lion is the mightiest *gibor* of beasts' (Proverbs 30:30). And this lioness has power *giborah* to break armies and *tokfin* powers. 'Poor Anatot' (Isa. 10:30)—for she is the mirror that does not shine. She is certainly poor—the moon has no light of her own, only what the sun gives her...Only when the sun joins with her does she shine.

The *Zohar* now seeks to explain the use of the term *layisha*, lioness, as a *Shekhinah* image. Focusing on the ferocious aspect of the image, the *Zohar* explains that *Shekhinah*, which receives from the side of *Gevurah*[39], is filled with *dinim*—harsh judgments. These are the forces that break down and destroy powerful negative forces, *tokfin*.[40] In a parallel image of an imbalanced *Shekhinah*, she is also called Anatot, a name associated with Jeremiah and the destruction of the Temple, the vestibule for *Shekhinah*. Anatot is the name of the place where God sends Jeremiah to buy a field before the destruction of the first Temple, and stems from the word 'ani, the poor one—again an appellation of imbalanced *Shekhinah*.[41] Both Anatot and 'aniyah are referred to as *aspaklariya delo nahara*, an unclear prism, by the *Zohar*. As we have seen elsewhere, this Zoharic term is cited in two pivotal passages that convey Lainer's understanding of *retzon Hashem* and uncertainty.[42]

An 'unclear prism' is understood by the *Zohar* to mean *Shekhinah* that has been overpowered by the other side. The *Elohim* (God) who speaks to Abraham at the 'akeidah, commanding him to kill his son, is not the clear prism aspect of the divine but rather *elohim aheirim*, other gods, the *aspaklariya delo nahara*, i.e. the *Shekhinah* whose *zivug* has been breached and is thus temporarily overpowered by the Other Side. This is the

222

meaning of the last line of the quote that the moon/*Shekhinah* has no independent light that can shine when it is not in *zivug*.

In the next section of the passage the *Zohar* interchanges the various states of the *Shekhinah* with historical figures from the story of Solomon's ascent to power—including David, Evyatar the priest of David, who was initially loyal to Adoniyahu in his bid for the crown, and of course Solomon himself. The human and divine levels are both symbolically and ontologically enmeshed in the Zoharic web:

תא חזי, דכתיב (מ"א ב כו) ולאביתר הכהן אמר המלך ענתות לך על שדך,
כי איש מות אתה, וכי על דזמין ליה אדוניהו איש מות אקרי, אלא בגין
דהוה מאתר מסכנא, דאידבק ביה סיהרא, דאיהי עניה ענתות. ואי תימא
(שם) וכי התענית בכל אשר התענה אבי בגיני כך זכה דלא קטיל ליה אלא
אביתר בגין דהוה מאתר מסכנא זכה ביה דוד עד דלא סליק למלכו, כד הוה
מכמאן ליה שאול, והוי ארחוי כמסכנא, (לבתר) אביתר כגוונא דא, ולזמנא
דשלט שלמה, דסיהרא קיימא באשלמותא, והוה בחדוותא, דעתירו דכלא
הוה ליה, לא זכה ביה אביתר, ודאי שדה ענתות רזא דמלה הוה, וירמיה
דקני ליה כלא הוה בגין לאחסנא רזא עלאה.

> Come and see: It is written, 'And to Evyatar the priest the king said: Go to Anatot, to your fields, for you are deserving of death…' (1 Kings 2:26). Was it because he was invited by Adoniyahu that he is called deserving of death? It is rather because he was from a poor place, where the moon clings, which is 'Anatot/'aniya. And if you say that this was '…because you suffered *hit'anita* through everything my father suffered *hit'anah*', and this is why he was not killed, [there is a different explanation:] David merited Evyatar, who was from a poor place, until [David] emerged as king, when he was hiding from Saul and his ways were that of a poor man, as were those of Evyatar. Later on when Solomon reigned, when the moon stood in its fullness and was joyous—for she had the wealth of the *all*—Evyatar did not merit her. 'The field of Anatot' most certainly indicates the mystery of this matter, and Jeremiah acquired it in order to receive a lofty secret.

Anatot has already been identified as the *Shekhinah* which is not in her full *zivug*, and basing itself on this, the *Zohar* reinterprets a Solomon story in which Anatot plays a role. After Solomon puts his brother Adoniyahu to death,[43] Evyatar fears for his life. Indeed, his fear was far from groundless. Yoav, the other major supporter of Adoniyahu, is put to death in the following verse. Evyatar, however, is banished by Solomon from the priesthood and sent back to his fields in Anatot. The *Zohar* interprets the story not in political terms, but rather in mystical context as reflective of the very different *Shekhinah* projects of David and Solomon, which we have previously touched upon, and will shortly be examined in this passage. Solomon sends Evyatar away because in relation to *Shekhinah*-consciousness, his time has passed. He was connected to David, who embodied the *Shekhinah* in its incomplete state. David was often an outlaw, not in his fullness—especially during the time when he was constantly on the run from Saul. During this period of his life, Evyatar of Anatot was connected to David because they both were *miskena*, destitute and desperate.

This desperation, as we shall presently see, is not political at its core but rather stems from an unfulfilled yearning for the *Shekhinah*. When Solomon builds the *mikdash*—as will be described in rich detail in the continuation of the passage—*Shekhinah*-consciousness evolves and is expanded and enriched. Jeremiah, the prophet and witness to the temple's destruction, seeks out Anatot once more. He wants to learn the secret of how to live with the *Shekhinah* in a pre-Temple era; that is to say when the *Shekhinah* is not in *zivug* and the moon is not full. He therefore returns to the fields of Anatot, which is symbolic of the time of David and Evyatar.

Jeremiah stood at the brink of a post-Temple age and sought to reclaim the secret of engaging the *Shekhinah* when she would no longer be in her fullness. Lainer as the inheritor of Solomon seeks precisely the opposite; to engage the *Shekhinah* in her fullness, to return to the utopian moment when the Judah archetype was manifested in the world by Solomon and one could receive the moon in her fullness.

Source 20: *Zohar* 1:249b

The next passage from this block of text begins to unpack the difference between the Solomon and David *Shekhinah* projects:

תא חזי, כד שלטא סיהרא שדה תפוחים אקרי, כד איהו במסכנו שדה
ענתות, בגיני כך תושבחתא דלתתא עביד ליה עתירו ושלימותא, כמה דדוד
כל יומוי אשתדל למעבד שלימו לה, ולנגנא זמרי, לזמרא ולשבחא לתתא.
וכד דוד אסתליק מעלמא שביק לה בשלימו, ושלמה נטל לה בעותרא

בשלימותא, דהא סיהרא נפקא ממסכנו ועאלת לעותרא, דבהך עותרא שלט
על כל מלכי ארעא.

Come and see: when the moon has dominion, she is called
the Field of Apples; when she is impoverished, she is [called]
the Field of Anatot. It is praise from below that endows her
with riches and fullness. As one finds with David, who tried
all his days to make her complete and to play music, to sing
and praise below. And when David left the world, he left her
shalimu complete, and Solomon received her in wealth [and]
bisheleimuta in fullness, for the moon had left poverty and entered wealth, and with that wealth he ruled over all the kings
of the earth.

Unpacking the image for *Shekhinah* of *sedei tapuchim*, the apple field, apples are red and white, the colors of *Hesed* and *Din* (i..e. *Gevurah*), love
and judgment. The integration of *Hesed* and *Din* is essential in order to
attain a state of the dominion of the moon, or what the *Zohar* has called
sihara be'ashleimuta, the moon in its fullness—that is to say, fully integrated
Shekhinah-consciousness. Moreover, the word for *tapuah*, apple, can also be
read as *tafuah*—that is, swelled and therefore in fullness.

David, who receives the *Shekhinah* in her imperfect state, is *mishtadel
leme'bad*, that is to say, he has not arrived, and he is exerting great effort
trying to get there. David, like the lioness at the beginning of this passage, sings his song from below to the *Shekhinah*. Indeed, he succeeds to a
large degree in effecting *zivug* with the *Shekhinah*,[44] and thus leaves his son
Solomon a world in which expanded *Shekhinah*-consciousness already
exists, enabling his son to inherit the fullness of *Shekhinah*-consciousness.
It is on this theme that the next part of the passage elaborates.

The reign of Solomon is the time of *sihara bisheleimuta*, when the moon is
in its fullness. One could correlate these two states of the moon precisely
with the two states of *Shekhinah*-consciousness described in *MHs*: that
of Judah, the state of *'olam ha-ba*, after *berur*; and that of Joseph, the stage
before *berur*, in which the present state of consciousness has not yet been
pierced in order to reveal the expanded state of *'olam ha-ba'*. The *Zohar*
continues to delve into the Solomonic state:

225

ועל דא (דה״ב ט כ) אין כסף נחשב בימי שלמה אלא כלא דהב דאתרבי
דהב, ובההוא זמנא כתיב (איוב כח ו) ועפרות זהב לו, דהא עפר דלעילא
הוה מסתכל ביה שמשא, ובאסתכלותא דשמשא ותוקפיה עפרא עביד
ואסגי דהב. תא חזי מטורי דנהירו דתוקפא דשמשא תמן, עפרא דארעא
ביני טורי כלהו עבדי דהב, ואלמלא חיוון בישין דרביאו תמן, בני נשא לא
הוו מסכני בגין דתוקפא דשמשא אסגי דהב. בגין כך ביומוי דשלמה אין
כסף נחשב למאומה, דהא תקיפא דשמשא אסתכל בעפרא ואסגי ליה דהב,
ועוד דההוא עפרא סטרא דדינא איהו, כד אסתכל ביה שמשא נטל תוקפא
ואתרבי דהבא. כיון דאסתכל שלמה בה, שבח ואכריז ואמר (קהלת ג כ)
הכל היה מן העפר וגו.'

Therefore it is said, 'Silver had no value in the days of Solomon'
(2 Chron. 9:20), for everything was made of gold, gold had
abounded. And concerning that time it is written, 'And the
dust was of gold' (Job 28:6), for the gold of above, the sun
would gaze at it, and the gaze of the sun and its power would
cause the dust to be transformed into gold. Come and see: in
the mountains of light, where the power of the sun may be
found, the dirt of the earth of the mountains becomes gold.
And if not for the evil beasts who procreate there, people
would not be poor, for the power of the sun manifests gold.
This is why silver was worthless in the days of Solomon, for
the power of the sun would gaze upon the dirt and turn it
into gold. Moreover, dirt originates in the aspect of *din* judgment. When the sun gazes upon it, its strength is absorbed
and it becomes gold. When Solomon saw this, he praised and
declared, 'Everything has come from the dirt' (Ecc. 3:20).

This passage is almost alchemical in its tone. Silver, dust and the stones
mentioned further on in the text all seek transformation to gold. For the
Zohar, *kesef*, which is white, represents *Hesed*, while *zahav*, which is a
reddish yellow, represents *Din*. In this passage, *Din*, the left side, is not
the negative constricting force that we often associate it with. It is rather
the stage of fully realized and aflame love. Fulfillment and full realization are the characteristics of the type of love associated with the left side.
Solomon's fully realized *Shekhinah*-consciousness transforms *kesef*, which
may also be taken to mean yearning, into *zahav*, gold, the passionate love
whose origins are in the side of the left. It is in this sense that the future world
is often described as a time that will be governed by the attribute of *din*.

The present world, however, lacks the ability to sustain itself on the full level of *Shekhinah*-consciousness that is *din*, and it therefore requires the softer presence of *hesed*. It is this distinction that characterizes the difference between David and Solomon's *zivug ha-Shekhinah* that is described in the next part of the passage.

ועל דא שלמה לא אצטריך לנגנא כדוד, אלא שירתא דאיהו רחימו דעותרא,
דהוא נהירו ורחימו דכל תושבחן דעלמא ביה הוו, תושבחתא דמטרוניתא,
כד יתבא בכרסייא לקבליה דמלכא, קאמר. כתיב (מ"א י כז) ויתן המלך את
הכסף בירושלם כאבנים, בגין דכלא הוה דהב, ועפרא אתקשר בשמאלא
בסטרא דרחימו, כמה דאת אמר (שיר ב ו) שמאלו תחת לראשי, ושמשא
אתדבק בהדה, ולא אתעדי מינה.

This is why Solomon did not need to be a musician like
David, but rather wrote poetry, which is love that comes from
wealth. For he had the light and love of all the praises of the
world, [that is,] the praise of the *matronita*, when she sits
on the throne facing the King. As it is written, 'And the king
rendered the silver in Jerusalem as stones' (1 Kings 10:27), for
everything was of gold. For earth (i.e., dirt, dust) is associated
with the left side, with the side of love, as it is said, 'His left
[hand] is under my head' (Cant. 2:6), then the sun clings to
her and does not leave her.

Here the distinctions hinted at in the previous section of the passage begin to take on full form. David needs to play music because love has not yet been realized. He is by implication still in the state of *kesef*, of yearning. Solomon is the richness of fulfilled love, the radical fullness of light and love. Solomon has caused all of the *kesef* to become *zahav*; that is to say, he has ushered in a world of full realization. If so, asks the *Zohar*, where did Solomon go wrong? It is to this issue that the final section of this passage now turns.

שלמה טעה בהאי דהא חמא דאתקריב סיהרא בשמשא, וימינא מחבקא
ושמאלא תחות רישא. כיון דאתקריבו דא בדא, אמר הא אתקריבו כחדא,
ימינא למה הכא, דהא ימינא לאו איהו אלא בגין לקרבא, כיון דאתקריבו דא
בדא למאי אצטריך. מיד (דה"ב ט כ) אין כסף נחשב בימי שלמה, אמר ליה
קב"ה, אנת דחית ימינא, חייך אנת תצטרך לחסד בני נשא ולא תשכח. מיד
סטא שמשא מלקבל סיהרא וסיהרא שריא לאתחשכא, והוה שלמה מהדר
על פתחין ואמר (קהלת א יב) אני קהלת, ולא הוה מאן דיעביד עמיה חסד,

227

מאי טעמא בגין דדחה ימינא ולא חשיב ליה. הדא הוא דכתיב (דה"ב ט כ)
אין כסף נחשב בימי שלמה למאומה

> Solomon erred when he saw that the moon had become
> intimate with the sun, with the right embracing and the left
> under her head. Since they had become intimate with each
> other, he said: Now that they have become as one, what need
> have we here of the right? Whereas the purpose of the right is
> only to draw near, now that they are already close, who needs
> it? Immediately it then states, 'Silver had no value in the days
> of Solomon' (2 Chron. 9:20). [In response] God said to him:
> You have rejected the right, but I swear by your life that you
> will need the kindness of human beings and will not find
> it. The sun then immediately shifted from facing the moon,
> and the moon began to grow dim. And Solomon went from
> door to door and said, 'I am Kohelet' (Eccl. 1:12), and no one
> would be kind to him. What is the reason for this? Because
> he rejected the right and disregarded it, as it is written, 'Silver
> was not valued in the days of Solomon' (2 Chron. 9:20).

For Solomon, once the *zivug* had been accomplished, once left had merged
with *yamin* 'right', and they were so intimately embraced that they were
one, he thought there was no longer a need for the right side. If the purpose
of the right side were to get us to the place of union with the *Shekhinah*,
to the state of full eros and acosmic humanism, then once this was accomplished, Solomon thought that *yamin* was superfluous.

Two very solid understandings of the right seem to be implicit in our text. In
the first reading, the right represents yearning, that is, *Hesed* is *kesef*, which is
kisufim in the *Zohar*. Thus, Solomon's sin is characterized by the statement
that 'silver had no value'. In modern terms one could describe this yearning
as the dialogic moment when one feels the need to reach beyond oneself
towards union with another. This end goal is never realized, never wholly
fulfilled, for if it were, the dialogue would stop, becoming instead an autistic
monologue. In the second reading, which is not in any way exclusive of the
first, *yamin* is the sefirotic masculine, in which case the *yamin* that is rejected
is the masculine law. Bound up with law is ethics and the obligation to give.[45]

Solomon thinks he does not need *yamin*, says the divine voice. I will show
him, says God, that *yamin* is still critically necessary. Solomon loses his

kingship[46] and is reduced to begging. There is no one who is willing to help him. The need for *yamin*, for law, for ethics, as well as for yearning, then becomes clear to Solomon. All of the eros of *zivug* was insufficient to move people to help him.

This passage is very different than the first passage we saw, which more or less followed the simple reading of the biblical writers in attributing the sin of Solomon to his marriage to foreign wives. In this passage we find a far more nuanced reading of Solomon's sin as a misperception in the field of spiritual development and consciousness.

Source 21: *Zohar Hadash* Sitrei Otiyot Bereishit 13b[47]

The following passage amplifies two of the Zoharic themes we saw in the preceding text. First it talks about the need for Solomon to balance between *yamin* and *semol*, the energies of the right and the left. The right incarnates *hesed*, lovingkindess—the more dialogical, relational love of giving. *Semol* as *din*, judgment, exemplifies fiery love. In this passage, Solomon begins with a strong base in both right and left, integrating the two.

However, similar to what we just saw in Source 20, as Solomon progresses his *semol* becomes damaged, *pagum*. As a result of this imbalance, Solomon's project fails. So while in the previous passage Solomon is described as exceeding David, from this perspective David is spiritually the more successful figure.

ת״ח שלמה באמצעיתא איהו בין סטרא דימינא לסטרא דשמאלא
(ושכינתא) [וחכמתא] דילוה אסתלקת ברזא דימינא ברזא דמהימנותא על
כל בני עלמא, דהא אימיה אולפת ליה וביומוי קיימא סיהרא באשלמותא.
בג״ד כתיב (מ״א ד) ויחכם מכל האדם דאתבני בי מקדשא

> Come and see: Solomon is in the center, between the right
> side and the left side. And his *Shekhinah* arises through the
> mystery of the right, the mystery of faith, over all the inhabit-
> ants of the world, for his mother taught him, and in his days
> the moon was in her fullness. Because of this 'he became the
> wisest of men' (1 Kings 5:11), for he built the Temple.

Solomon's ability to balance between left and right is understood in this passage to be the essence of the Wisdom of Solomon. This is what is meant by the moon in her fullness: the integration in *Shekhinah* of both the right and left.

ובסוף יומוי שריא סיהרא לאתפגמא וכדין כתיב (שם יא) ויעש שלמה
הרע בעיני ה׳ ולא מלא אחרי ה׳ כדוד אביו. לא מלא דייקא לא אשלים מה
דאיהו הוי ליה לאשלמא כלא בתר דוד דאיהו מאינון שבעה סמכין ולא
מלייא סיהרא אלא דאיתפגים. בגין כך לא מנינן ליה לא עם אינון שבעה
זכאין סמכין דעלמא ולא עם אינון דמרדו במאריהון אלא איהו באמצעיתא
מסטרא דימינא שלים ומסטרא דשמאלא פגים

> And at the end of his days the moon began to be wounded,
> concerning which it states, 'And Solomon did evil in the eyes
> of God, and was not fully after God like David his father' (1
> Kings 11:6). 'Not full'—exactly! He did not complete that
> which he should have completed after David, who was one
> of the seven pillars. And the moon did not stay full, but was
> wounded. This is why we do not count him as one of the
> seven righteous pillars of the world, nor with those who re-
> belled against their Master. He is in the center, complete from
> the right side, but weakened from the left side.

At the end of his days, when Solomon married many wives and engaged with their goddesses, the moon became *itpagma*, wounded or diminished, and she lost her fullness. The essence of the evil that Solomon does is that the integrity of his left side is breached. His goddess attachments and many wives are all expressions of *semol*, of the left side, of eros and *rishfei eish*. They are imbalanced and therefore *pagum*, spiritually tainted. When Solomon begins his kingdom, he is *beraza diyemina*, in the secret of the right, that is, aligned with the spiritual power of the right side and fully intact. The *hesed* of the right rules and is taught by the mother, *Binah*, which is the higher *din* of the left side.

In the end of his days, however, the moon is *nifgam*. *Shelomoh* does *ra'* evil and is not *malei*, not full. The word *malei* of course refers both to the moon and to Solomon, *Shelomoh*, who is not *shalem*—unlike David, who fulfilled his mission and who is one of seven *samhin*, the seven pillars of the world. As in the beginning of the passage, Solomon is described as being in the middle, but this time its implication is negative. As a result, Solomon's kingdom is ripped away from him, as the continuation of the passage describes:

בג״כ כתיב (מלכים א) קרוע אקרע את הממלכה דא רזא דמלכא בזע
פורפירא דיליה דהא ממלכה עליה דשלמה היא ואמיה איקרי ודא בת שבע.
ונתתיה לעבדך. בג״כ כתיב (משלי ל) תחת עבד כי ימלוך ושפחה כי תירש
גבירתא. ת״ח האי עבד לא אתיהיב ליה מלכות אלא מהכא הה״ד ונתתיה
לעבדך וכדין שריא שפחה לשלטאה

This is why it is written, 'I will surely tear the kingdom [from
Solomon]' (1 Kings 11:11). This is the secret of 'the king
who tears his royal robe', for the kingdom was Solomon's, and
she is called his mother, and this is *bat sheva*' Bathsheba (lit.,
'daughter of seven', i.e., *Malkhut/Shekhinah*). '[A]nd I will give
it (lit., 'her') to your servant'. This is why it is written, 'Under
a servant who would reign…and a maidservant who would
inherit her mistress' (Prov. 30:22–23). Come and see: That
servant only acquired *Malkhut* from here. So it is written,
'and I will give her to your servant'. Then did the maidservant
begin to rule.

Solomon is torn and the kingdom is torn from him; his left side—his
feminine—is *pagum*. His kingship is torn, for *Malkhut* is from the side of
mother, *Binah*, and *Malkhut* is Solomon's mother, Bathsheba. In a classic
Zoharic description of exile, the kingdom is given to the other, to the servant, so that the maidservant will rule over her lady.

ת״ח בקדמיתא כתיב קרוע ולבתר אקרע. קרוע זעיר דאיתקרע ממילא בגין
דההוא שעתא שרייא סיהרא לאתפגמא ולבתר אקרע דאתכסיא בגלותא.
וזמין קב״ה לאתבא שכינתא לאתראה ולישראל לאתרייהו ולאתפרעא
מאינון דסטרא דשמאלא דעאקו לון הה״ד (עובדי' א) ועלו מושיעים בהר
ציון רזא דימינא לשפוט

Come and see: At first it says 'torn' and then after it says 'I will
tear' (*karo'a ekra'*). 'Torn'—a little bit, since it was being torn
at any rate, for at that time, the moon began to weaken, and
then 'I will tear', for [the moon] is covered in exile. And God
is prepared to return the *Shekhinah* to her place, and Israel
to its place, and to settle accounts with those on the left side
that oppressed them. As is written, 'And deliverers will go up
to Mount Zion' (Ovad. 1:21)—the mystery of the right, to
judge.

Since the moon is *pagum*, Solomon begins to lose his *malkhut*, meaning both his kingdom and the *Shekhinah*. However, God longs to return *Shekhinah* to her place. This redemption takes place through the reclamation of *yamin*, the right, which is identified here with *mishpat* or law, as we interpreted above in our reading of *yamin* in the previous passage.[48]

Mikdash

The next three sources pick up the theme of the *mikdash*, Solomon's Temple, which we have already seen in Source 12,[49] and which plays such a large role in the Wisdom of Solomon genre in *MHs*.

Source 22: *Zohar* 2:257b–258a

Lainer cites two sources from the *Zohar* in the passage where he describes Solomon as being able to bypass the normal logic of the law and to access *retzon Hashem* directly.[50] The major text is the one we cite presently, which alludes to the Solomonic state of *sihara be'ashleimuta*.[51] The connections made between the *mikdash*, the Oral Law, and bodily imagery in this source mark it as distinctive within the Zoharic Wisdom of Solomon genre.

דאיהו רזא מרזין עלאין, דקודשא בריך הוא אנהיג ביה עלמא. בית ראשון
קיימא בימי שלמה, לקבל עלמא עלאה, ואיהו אקרי בית ראשון, ואשתמש
כלא בבית קדשי הקדשים, אתר דאשתמש ביה שמשא בסיהרא, ורזין
עלאין כלהו בשלימו, וקיימא עלמא באשלמותא

> [T]his is a secret of the supreme mysteries by which God
> leads the world. The first Temple (*bayit rishon*) existed in
> the days of Solomon, to parallel (or, to receive) the higher
> world. It was called the first home, and all things coupled
> in the house of the Holy of Holies, the place where the sun
> coupled with the moon, and all higher secrets were in a state
> of completeness, and the world was established *be'ashleimuta*
> in completeness.

Here the *Zohar* is explicit. The *raza derazin*, the secret of the Temple in the days of Solomon, is the erotic union between sun and moon, *Malkhut/Shekhinah* and *Tif'eret*, which takes place in the Holy of Holies. At the time of this union the world is in its fullness; for Lainer, drawing on these sources, it means that one can access the will of God, the *Shekhinah*, unmediated by law. This unity, however, is broken by sin:

233

ולבתר גרמו חובין, ואתמשכו רזין ואתדחיין מבית קדש הקדשים לבר, כד
אתדחו לירכין, כדין קיימו לבר דאקרון בתי בראי, ואצטריכו לברייתי. בית
שני קיימו בבתי בראי בירכין, ומנייהו אהדרו ושארו בבית קדש הקדשים,
ואיהו בית שני, ואינון אחרנין אשתארו בברייתא לבר, ביני (נ"א בבי) ירכין
והוו אולפין ממתניתין, ואתנהיגו מינה, והיינו רזא דכתיב (ישעיה ב) כי
מציון תצא תורה

And later, the sins took effect, and the secrets were withdrawn
and pushed out of the house of the Holy of Holies, to the
outside. When they were pushed to the thighs, they were
then outside *lebar*, as [the thighs] are called 'outer houses', and
beraitei[52] were needed. The time of the second Temple (or,
house), they were in the outer houses, in the thighs, and from
them they return and dwell in the Holy of Holies, and that is
the second Temple. Others remain in the *beraita*, outside—
between (or, in) the thighs. And they would learn from the
Mishnah, and conduct themselves according to it. And this is
the secret meaning of what is written, 'Torah goes out from
Zion' (Isa. 2:3).

Being outside the Holy of Holies signifies a fall in consciousness. The
second Temple takes place on the level of consciousness that is the outer
chambers, in the thighs. Because they are on the outside 'in the thighs',
the Oral Law, signified by the *beraitot*, becomes a necessity. There are some
who are able, perhaps on a lower level, to return to the Holy of Holies.
Most, however, remain on the outside, in the place of the thighs, i.e. meaning outside of the place of *zivug* or sexual/mystical union. This is how the
continuation of the verse creatively and radically interpets the verse 'Torah
goes out from Zion'—the Torah is exiled from Zion which is the Holy
of Holies. That is to say, the necessity for law, identified in this passage as
Torah, stems from the initial exile from the Holy of Holies.

ולבתר כד גרמו חובין, אתעדי שולטנותא דהאי בית שני, (ואף על גב)
דשולטנא דיליה לא הוה כבית ראשון, דהוה ביה שלמא תדיר, בגין דמלכא
דשלמא דיליה תדיר הוה בגוויה, ועל דא הוה בשלם, בית שני לא הוה ביה
שלם הכי, בגין דערלה קטרגא ביה תדיר

And later, when sins took effect the rule of the second Temple
stopped. And its rule was not like that of the first Temple,
which was always complete, since the King to whom peace

234

belongs was always present in it, and therefore [the first Temple] was always complete. The second Temple was not complete in this manner...

The nature of the first Temple, unlike the second Temple, can be described in terms of acosmic humanism. There was a constant presence of 'the King to whom peace belongs', obviating the need for the Oral Law.[53] This dynamic is connected closely with the previous passage in which Solomon, having achieved *zivug* with *Shekhinah*, no longer felt he had a need for the *yamin*, which as we saw referred to the masculine law. Here the *Zohar* employs the same logic in the reverse. Once there has been an exile from the Holy of Holies and the *hieros-gamos*, the sacred union, is broken, then the need for law becomes manifest.

Source 23: *Zohar* 3:297a

שירותא וסיומא דכלא אתכליל בקדש (ס"א א') וחכמה עלאה קדש אקרי
וכד נהיר דא חכמה עלאה חכמה דשלמה נהיר כמה דכתיב ותרב חכמת
שלמה דקיימא באשלמותא והא אוקימנא. וכד אתברכא מיסוד הכי קרינן
לה קדש דאיהו אנהיר בשלימו. וכד לא אתנהרא מתעטרא באשלמותא,
קרינן לה רוח הקדש ולא אתקרי קדש כההוא דלעילא. וכד מתברכא מהאי
יסוד ויניקא לכל אינון דלתתא אתקרי אם כההיא דלעילא וקרינן ליה קדשים.
וכדין קרינן ליה קדש הקדשים דביה כלה כלה דכתיב אתי מלבנון כלה וגו'

The beginning and the end of everything are included in holiness, and higher *hokhmah* is called holiness. And when higher *hokhmah* would shine, the Wisdom of Solomon (lower *hokhmah* or *Malkhut*) would shine, as it is written, 'And the wisdom of Solomon waxed great' (1 Kings 5:10), for the moon stood in its fullness, and we have established this. And when she is blessed by *Yesod*, we call her holiness, because she shines in her fullness. But when she does not shine crowned in completeness, she is called the Holy Spirit *ruah ha-kodesh* (i.e., the spirit of holiness rather than fully embodied holiness), and she is not called holy like the one above. And when she is blessed by *Yesod* and she nourishes all the lower beings, she is called 'mother', like the one above, and called 'holies' *kodashim*, and then he (i.e., the Holy One, *Tif'eret*) is called Holy of Holies *kodesh ha-kodashim*, for through him [she is] a bride, as it is written, 'with me from Lebanon, my bride' (Cant. 4:8).

235

In this passage from *Idra Zuta* we see that there are really three spiritual stages associated with the evolution of the moon. When the light of the moon is not whole, then it is at the level of *ruah ha-kodesh*, an inferior level. When she is in the state of *zivug* with *Yesod*, she is called *kodesh*. When she has become pregnant and gives birth to the lower beings, she becomes mother and is *kodashim*—both mother and bride. These stages correspond with the stages of human consciousness in *MHs*.

Source 24: *Zohar* 2:235b

The next *Zohar* text talks about about the deeper identity between what seem to be two distinct and almost contradictory names of God, *Adnut* and *Havaya* (*YHVH*).

ה׳ איהו רזא דאת י׳ (נ״א י׳ איהו רזא דאת ה׳) בגין דהכא ה׳ (נ״א דה׳) דא
איהי חכמה זעירא, דאקרי חכמת שלמה. ואתכלילו אלין באלין, וכלא
איהו רזא חדא, כלילן אלין באלין, וכלא חז, וכלא איהו רזא חדא באתוון
קדישין. ועל דא משכנא דלתתא בארעא, קיימא ברזא דמשכנא עלאה,
וההוא משכנא עלאה קיימא ברזא דמשכנא אחרא עלאה על כלא, וכלא
איהו כליל דא בדא למהוי חז, ועל דא כתיב והיה המשכן אחד

[The letter] *heh* (of *YHVH*) is the secret of the letter *yod* (of *ADNY*), because this *heh* is the lesser *hokhmah*, which is called *hokhmat Shelomoh*. And these letters are included within each other, and it is all one secret; these are included with those, and all is one, and it is all one mystery of the sacred letters. For this reason, the *mishkan* tabernacle below, on earth, exists according to the secret of the higher tabernacle. And that higher tabernacle exists by the secret of another tabernacle, which is the highest of them all, and they are all included one in the other, to be as one, which is why it is written, 'The tabernacle will be one' (Exod. 26:6).

The *Zohar* is here explaining the *yihud*, unification, of the divine names *ADNY* and *YHVH*, creating י ה ו נ ד ה א י (*YAHDVNYH*). What the *Zohar* teaches is that the *yod* at the beginning is *Hokhmah*, and the *yod* at the end, the *yod* conjoined with the final *heh*, representing *Malkhut*, is also *Hokhmah*.[54] The *mishkan*—and likewise the Temple—weaves together these names, thus joining together upper and lower wisdom, and through this constitutes the universe itself. According to this Zoharic passage, this

236

unification is no less than the secret of the *mishkan,* which is the essence of *hokhmat Shelomoh.*

The original rabbinic source for this distinction between the names appears in a Talmudic passage we discussed in volume 1 (in the context of Lainer's commentary upon it).[55] Lainer's comments related the name of *Adnut* to this world, where it appears that human beings and their strivings are somehow separate from God. This is the world of human initiative and activism, where the split between God and man is real. The name *Havaya* (i.e., *YHVH*) according to the Talmud is related to the next world. For the *Zohar* this means a higher reality, while Lainer interprets this to mean a higher stage of human consciousness within this reality. We can see how this *yihud,* which lies at the center of this Zoharic passage about the Wisdom of Solomon, is developed by Lainer. At the level of *Havaya,* the place of a radical acosmism, all is in the hands of God. Everything including all human action is an expression of God's being and goodness. In the future world, both names, that of *Adnut* and of *Havaya,* will be read with the pronounciation of *Havaya.* For Lainer this means that in the place of deeper conciousness, we will realize that the name of man and the name of God are ultimately one, which is precisely acosmic humanism.

Integrating the Darkness

The essential topic of the next three passages is integration. An essential demarcating characteristic of the Wisdom of Solomon is the integration of *kola*—of everything—particularly the darkness.[56] The passages share something with modern Jungian passages which talk about integrating the shadow. The shadow in Jung means of course not only the darkness but all that is un-integrated.[57] Indeed Jung himself associates that integration with what he refers to as 'the kabbalistic marriage of *Malkhut* and *Tif'eret*' which is indeed a unifying motif in virtually all the Wisdom of Solomon passages.

In a number of the passages we have seen thus far[58] the theme of integration of the lower—that is, of the *Shekhinah*, which includes all that is un-integrated—has been central. In the next three sources the theme of integrating the darkness as an essential expression of *hokhmat Shelomoh* and a primary manifestation of *sihara bisheleimuta* will be sharply crystallized.

Of course, these passages are part of the matrix of sources from which Lainer developed his notion of *hisaron*. We have already suggested that Lainer's radical emphasis on *hisaron* is the continuation of a long tradition of Zoharic and kabbalistic fascination and desire for engagement with evil. What becomes clear in the sources, both in Lainer and his contemparies and predecessors, is that *hisaron* refers to none other than the *hisaron* of the moon, the moon in her lack. As we have shown, it is through the healing of *hisaron* that, according to Lainer, one does *berur*.[59] *Berur* is precisely what activates the Judah archetype and enables one to access the unmediated *retzon Hashem*, i.e., the moon in her fullness. Solomon's desire to incorporate all of the dimensions of the moon, to accomplish a union which is capable of integrating the moon in her *hisaron*—*leyarta lah sihara bepigumata*[60]—is precisely the Zoharic underpinning for the Torah of *hisaron* in Izbica. The healing of *hisaron* elicits the conciousness indicated by *sihara bisheleimuta*.

Source 25: Zohar 3:46b

This desire for the integration of everything, including the darkness, to *yarit mikol sitroy* 'inherit from all sides', is the core need of *zivug*,[61]; this is the topic of the following passage. The verse which the *Zohar* interprets comes from Ecclesiastes, attributed by the tradition to Solomon. The verse begins 'I saw everything *ha-kol*'.

האי קרא אוליפנא בי רבי דוסתאי סבא, דהוה אמר משמיה דרבי ייסא
סבא, את הכל ראיתי בימי הבלי וכי שלמה מלכא דהוה חכים על כלא, איך
אמר דאיהו חמא כלא בזמנא דאיהו אזיל בחשוכי עלמא, דהא כל מאן
דאשתדל בחשוכי עלמא, לא חמי מידי ולא ידע מידי

> This verse was studied in the houses of Rabbi Dostai Saba, who would say in the name of Rabbi Yaisa Saba: [Solomon wrote], 'I saw everything during the time of my vanity' (Eccl. 7:15). How could King Solomon, who was wisest of all, say that he saw everything when he was walking in the darkness of the world? For he who occupies himself with the darkness of the world, sees nothing and knows nothing.

The *Zohar* intimates that Solomon chose to 'walk on the dark side'; what the *Zohar* calls *hashukhei 'alma*. Given this reading of Solomon, the *Zohar* wants to know how Solomon was able to see in the darkness.

אלא הכי אתמר, ביומוי דשלמה מלכא קיימא סיהרא באשלמותא, ואתחכם
שלמה על כל בני עלמא, וכדין חמא כלא וידע כלא. ומאי חמא, חמא כ"ל
(דלא אעדי מן סיהרא, והוה נהיר לה שמשא (ס"א ליה כשמשא

> But this is the meaning: At the time of King Solomon, the moon was in its fullness, and Solomon was the wisest of all the people of the earth, and then he saw all and knew all. And what did he see? He saw 'all', (*Yesod*), which never leaves the moon, and which shone in her like the sun.

The basic answer of the *Zohar* is that since for Solomon the moon was always full, he was able to see. Solomon can see by the moonlight, as it were. This is the symbol for integration. The darkness was not a place in which Solomon was lost; rather because he integrated all, he was able to see as a result of the darkness instead of it being the object of his downfall. This notion of integration, alluded to up to this point, becomes clearer in the following lines.

הדא הוא דכתיב את הכל ראיתי בימי הבלי, מאן הבלי, דא סיהרא
דאתכלילת מן כלא, מן מייא ואשא ורוחא כחדא, כהבל דנפיק מן פומא,
דכליל מכלא, והוא חמא כ״ל בההוא הבל דיליה, דאחיד ביה

This is why it is written, 'I saw everything during the time of my
hevel (usu. translated, 'vanity')'. What is meant by *hevel* breath?
This is the moon, which integrates everything, water and fire and
air as one, like breath that comes out of the mouth, that includes
all, and he saw *kol* in this breath of his, in which he was united.

Kol in the *Zohar* is virtually always *Yesod*, the phallic interlocutor which ef-
fects *zivug* between the heaven and earth, between *Shekhinah* and *Tif'eret*.[62]
'I was able to see *kol* in my breath' is the *Zohar*'s translation. Breath for the
Zohar is a symbol of integration; it is grounded in the moon, that is to say,
the *Shekhinah*, in which all is integrated as one. In the second part of the
Zohar passage this process of integration is given erotic character.

יש צדיק אובד בצדקו, תא חזי, בזמנא דאסגיאו זכאין בעלמא, האי כ״ל לא
אעדי מן סיהרא לעלמין והאי כ״ל נטל כל משח ורבו וחידו דלעילא, ואתמלי
(ס״א ידוי ורוי) וחדי ורבי, בגין לאזדווגא בסיהרא, והוא רווח בגינה. ובזמנא
דאסגיאו חייבין בעלמא, וסיהרא אתחשכת, כדין צדיק אובד בצדקו, צדיק
נאבד לא כתיב, אלא צדיק אובד, דהא לא אתחזי (נ״א אתחבר) בסיהרא,
ולא נטיל משח ורבו וחידו למלייא לה ולאזדווגא עמה, ועל דא צדיק אובד,
בצדקו דא סיהרא, דבגין סיהרא דלא אשתכחת לאזדווגא עמיה, הוא אביד,
דלא שאיב מחידו כמה דהוה עביד

'There is a righteous man who is destroyed while he is righteous'. Come and see: When there are many righteous preople
in the world, that *kol* never leaves the moon. And that *kol*
takes all the oil and seed and joy from above, and is filled and
rejoices and grows, in order to couple with the moon, and
he receives abundance thanks to her. But when the wicked
proliferate in the world, and the moon waxes dark, then
'the righteous *oved* loses in his righteousness'. It does not say
ne'evad 'is lost', but the *tzadik oved* loses. For he is not seen/
connected with the moon, and he does not bring oil and seed
and joy to her to fill her with and to couple with her, which is
why 'the *tzadik* loses'. '[He loses] his *tzedek*'—that is the moon;
for since the moon is not present for him to couple with, he is
destroyed, for he does not draw from joy as he used to.

In the stage of *zivug*, when *kol* is integrated, then *itmalei* 'he is filled'; when the righteous are not in ascendancy; at the time of the wicked, so to speak, then joy and fullness recede, the moon is darkened and the *tzadik, Yesod*, is *oved betzidko* and loses his fullness. The *zivug* has been broken and the joy and fullness that is the expression of *kol* and of total integration is no longer manifest.

Source 26: *Tikunei Zohar* 95b

In other sources both midrashic and Zoharic we have seen Solomon described as sitting on the throne of God.[63] We have understood this, as did Tzadok Hakohen, in congruence with Lainer, as being an expression of the merging of divine and human that characterizes acosmic humanism. In the following passage, the *Zohar* deals with the shadows of acosmic humanism, which are projected onto Hiram, who declares 'on the seat of God I sat'. Solomon, who has integrated all of the sides of the moon, is able to help Hiram to hold his humanity and his divinity together.

> פתח רבי ייסא ואמר ויי׳ נתן חכמה לשלמה כאשר דבר לו ויהי שלום בין
> חירם ובין שלמה וגו׳. ויי׳ נתן חכמה לשלמה דא הוא דתנינן ביומוי דשלמה
> מלכא קיימא סיהרא באשלמותא. ויהי שלום בין חירם ובין שלמה. וכי מה
> (בין) האי להאי

> Rabbi Yeisa opened and said: 'And God granted wisdom to Solomon as He had promised him, and there was peace between Hiram and Solomon' (1 Kings 5:26). 'And God granted wisdom to Solomon'—this is as we have learned, that in the time of King Solomon, the moon was in her fullness. '[A]nd there was peace between Hiram and Solomon'—what does one have to do with the other?

The *Zohar* queries: what is the relationship between the two clauses of the verse? Is there some deep linkage between the Wisdom of Solomon and Solomon's ability to make peace with Hiram?

> אלא הכי תנינן ויי׳ נתן חכמה לשלמה והאי חכמה במאי אוקים לה א״ר יוסי
> אוקים לה בהאי בקדמיתא דשלמה עבד דנחית לחירם מההוא דרגא דהוה
> אמר מושב אלקים ישבתי וגו׳ דתניא חירם מלך צור עבד גרמיה אלוה. בתר
> דשלמה אתא עבר ליה בחכמתיה דנחית מההוא עיטא ואודי ליה לשלמה.
> ובגין כך ויהי שלום בין חירם ובין שלמה. ותנינן א״ר יצחק א״ר יהודה דשדר

242

ליה חד שידא ונחית ליה שבעה ליה מדורין דגיהנם וסלקיה ושדר ליה פתקין
בכל יומא ויומא בידיה עד דאהדר ואודי ליה לשלמה. ותנינן שלמה ירית לה
לסיהרא בכל סטרוי. בג״כ בכלא שליט בחכמתיה

But this is what we learned: 'And God granted wisdom to
Solomon'. In what was that wisdom expressed? Rabbi Yosi
said: It was expressed thus: At first, Solomon caused Hiram
to descend from that rung, for [Hiram] said, '[O]n the seat
of God I sat' (Ezek. 28:2),[64] as we learned: Hiram the king of
Tyre made himself into a god. After Solomon came, he caused
[Hiram] to abandon such counsel through his wisdom, and
he gave thanks (or 'submitted') to Solomon. This is why 'there
was peace between Hiram and Solomon'. And we learned:
Rabbi Yitzhak said in the name of Rabbi Yehudah that he
sent him a demon that took him down to the seven levels of
hell and took him back up, and he sent him letters everyday,
until he submitted to Solomon. And we learned: Solomon
yarit inherited the moon in all of its aspects. This is why he
ruled over everything in his wisdom.

Again, the full moon as a manifestation of the Wisdom of Solomon means
the integration of darkness. As we have seen, *yarit* indicates both *zivug*
and integration. Because Solomon *yarit* 'inherited' the moon in all of its
aspects, literally, 'from all of her sides', he is able to help Hiram reclaim his
appropriate place.

Several steps are necessary to accomplish this. Through the agency of a
spirit demon, Solomon takes Hiram down and back up through seven
levels of hell. Following this dramatic intervention, Solomon follows up
and sends letters every day to Hiram, which help sustain whatever breakthrough of insight Hiram had made after ascending from hell. In this
sense, Hiram may represent an externalized dimension of Solomon that
must be re-integrated. Hence, in our reading, Hiram is an allusion to
Solomon himself, who began to consider himself a god. Hiram would
represent what we moderns might call 'shadow' material, i.e., a part of
Solomon himself that was in *herem*, removed or excommunicated, which
therefore is projected onto Hiram.

What is new in this passage is the dynamic element that the *Tikunei
Zohar* introduces into our understanding of *hokhmat Shelomoh*. Solomon

falls and rises again. This ability is the essence of the Wisdom of Solomon. According to the continuation of the passage, this is what it means when it says Solomon's wisdom waxed great:

דאדם ואתתיה אתברייאו בדיוקנא דקודשא בריך הוא ושכינתיה, ובגין דא חובא דאדם הוה תליא בעמודא דאמצעיתא, וחובא דחוה בשכינתא, ובגין דא מה זאת עשית, לזאת עשית ודאי, וחובא דא גרם דנחתת שכינתא בגלותא, והאי איהו חכמת שלמה, ועלה אתמר וחכמת המסכן בזויה, ועלה אתמר כי מכבדי אכבד ובוזי יקלו, כד נחית שלמה ממלכותיה הוה חכמה דיליה בזויה בעיני שטיין, וכד אסתלק במלכותיה אתמר ביה ותרב חכמת שלמה, דאתרביאת עד דמטאת להאי אתר דאתנטילת מתמן, לאתר דחכמה עלאה, דאיהי חכמה ברישא, ואיהי חכמה בסוף, לעילא תורת חכם, לתתא חכמת שלמה, ובגין דא מסטרא דשלמה אתמר וחכמת המסכן בזויה, דנחיתת ביה, וסליקת ביה, כמה דאתמר ביה ותרב חכמת שלמה מחכמת כל בני קדם

For Adam and his wife were created in the image of *kudsha berikh hu* and the *Shekhinah*, which is why Adam's sin is related to the central pillar (*Tif'eret*), and Eve's sin to the *Shekhinah*. This is why it says, 'What is *zot* this that you have done?' (Gen. 3:13). Certainly it means, 'To *zot* (i.e., to the *Shekhinah*) you have done it'. And this sin caused the *Shekhinah* to descend into exile. And that is *hokhmat Shelomoh*, and concerning her it says, 'And the wisdom of the poor is disregarded', and concerning her it says, 'For I will honor those who honor me, and those who dishonor me will become worthless'. When Solomon descended from his kingdom, his wisdom was disregarded in the eyes of fools, and when he ascended [again] to his kingdom it says, 'And Solomon's wisdom waxed great', for it grew until it reached the place it had been taken from, to the place of supernal wisdom. For she is *Hokhmah* at the beginning, and she is *Hokhmah* at the end.

Solomon's wisdom waxed great like the moon, returning to its former heralded state. This capacity is what makes Solomon greater than all the children of Kedem. As *Tikunei Zohar* teaches in the conclusion of the passage, they lacked precisely this ability to fall and then integrate their fall into their ascent. Rather, the wicked, only ride this roller coaster down, taking the holy *Shekhinah* down with them. God then intervenes, pulling her up from her pit, where she was dry, that is, void of eroticism and disconnected from her lover.

אבל בחייביא מה כתיב בהו (איכה א) נתנני ה' בידי לא אוכל קום (עמוס
ה) נפלה ולא תוסיף קום, ואף על פי דלית לה רשו למיקם מגרמה, קודשא
בריך הוא יוקים לה, כמה דאת אמר ביום ההוא אקים את סכת דוד הנפלת.
ומאן גרים דנחתת לה מאתרה דא נחש, כמה דאת אמר ויאמר ה' אלקי״ם
אל הנחש כי עשית זאת, דאיהי שכינתא, דגרמת דאשתכחת יבשה ונפלת
מאתרה, ארור אתה מכל הבהמה וגומר

But concerning the wicked, what is written concerning them?
'God has given me over to the hands of one so that I cannot
rise'(Lam. 1:14); 'She has fallen, she can no longer rise' (Amos
5:2). And even though she does not have permission to get up
on her own, *kudsha berikh hu* the Holy One (*Tif'eret*) will pick
her up, as it says, 'On that day I will raise the fallen sukkah of
David up' (Amos 9:11). And who caused her to descend from
her place? It was the snake, as it says, 'And God said to the
snake: Since you did *zot* this…' (Gen. 3:14)—[*zot*] means the
Shekhinah. Since you caused her to be dry and to fall from her
place, '[c]ursed are you of all the beasts', etc.

At the end of the passage the *Zohar* introduces a major messianic
motif. The *nahash* sought to bring down *zot*, that is, the *Shekhinah*. Hence
Solomon, by raising the *Shekhinah*, affects the *tikun* of what the snake set
wrong in Eden. So it is Solomon alone who can go all the way down and all
the way up. This is *hokhmat Shelomoh* and the function of Solomon. This
is the *Shekhinah* falling and rising, whereas in the case of the wicked, when
the *Shekhinah* falls only *kudsha berikh hu* can raise her up

This restitution of the *Shekhinah* to her place, which is messianic, is intertwined with the redemption of evil itself, as we will see again below in
Source 36.

The Judah Archetype

At this juncture we will turn our attention to another set of sources, interlocked and often interlinked with the Solomon sources—the Judah sources. Lainer's mystical weaving together of the Judah and Solomon genres as one set of sources whose major topic is *Shekhinah* is a direct outgrowth of the *Zohar*. Judah of course is the literal source for Solomon and the spiritual source of the kingship he personified in most of rabbinic tradition and in the *Zohar*.

For the *Zohar*, however, Judah is more than just the progenitor of David and Solomon; both David and Solomon ultimately participate in the Judah archetype. In the *Zohar*, Judah is primarily *Shekhinah*. He is the ultimate king, a fully messianic figure and the personification of acosmic humanism. He is a manifestation and symbol of the moon and her energy. The entire Judah archetype so carefully elaborated in *MHs* and viewed by scholarship as his creation is in fact fully grounded in the Zoharic texts we will presently unfold. Every major theme in the Judah archetype that we have encountered in *MHs*—both within the Judah sources and in the related Wisdom of Solomon of sources—can be found in the *Zohar*. In these passages and in the Zoharic Wisdom of Solomon texts we have already examined, we find all of the major matrices for Lainer's thought.

The first set of passages in the Judah genre below is related directly to Judah, his *Shekhinah* nature, his kingship, which is a function of his *Shekhinah* quality, and of course his messianic implications. The second set of passages is related to another major Judah/Solomon theme which we saw expanded in *MHs*, the theme of wine. Wine, like Judah himself, is a central *Shekhinah* symbol. Let us turn to the texts.

Source 27: *Zohar* 1:236b–237a

This first passage, cited by Lainer,[65] lays out most of the major Judah themes.

יהודה אתה יודוך אחיך ידך בערף אויביך וגו', רבי יוסי פתח (תהלים קד)
עשה ירח למועדים וגו'

'Judah, you will be praised by your brothers, your hand is on the neck of
your enemies, etc.' (Gen. 49:8) Rabbi Yossi opened: 'He made the moon for
holidays, etc.' (Psalms 104:19).

The theme is immediately clear. Judah is connected to the moon, the classic symbol of *Shekhinah*. The passage begins with a classic statement of
the spiritual power of the moon and the sun. However, in this reading the
sun is related to the nations, while the primary spiritual power, the moon,
incarnates the Jewish people. Rabbi Elazer builds on this distinction, emphasizing the complete identification of the Jewish people with the moon.

כי הא דאמר רבי אלעזר, כתיב (ישעיה ט) הרבית הגוי לו הגדלת...
השמחה, הרבית הגוי אלין ישראל, דכתיב בהו (דברים ד) כי מי גוי גדול,
וכתיב (ד"ה א יז) גוי אחד דישראל בארץ לו בגיניה הגדלת השמחה דא
סיהרא דאתרביאת בנהורא בגיניהון

> As Rabbi Elazar said: It is written, 'You have multiplied the
> nation, increased its joy' (Isa. 9:2). 'You have multiplied the
> nation'—that is Israel, concerning whom it is written, 'For who
> is a great nation' (Deut. 4:7), and it is also written, 'One nation
> on earth' (1 Chron. 17:21). For [Israel's] sake you increased
> joy—this is the moon, whose light increased because of them.

The characteristic of the moon is joy, the same nature we associate with the
inclusiveness and expansiveness of the Wisdom of Solomon. The *Zohar*
then goes on to assert the superiority of the moon.

הי מנייהו עדיף ודאי סיהרא לעילא, ושמשא דאומות העולם תחות האי
סיהרא הוא, וההוא שמשא מהאי (ס"א סיטרא) סיהרא נהיר. חמי מה בין
ישראל להן, ישראל אחידו בסיהרא, ואשתלשלו בשמשא עלאה, ואתאחדו
באתר (ביה) (ס"א דנהיר לשמשא) דנהירא משמשא עלאה, ומתדבקן ביה,
דכתיב (דברים ד) ואתם הדבקים ביהו"ה אלהיכ"ם חיים כלכם היום

> Which of them is superior? Certainly the moon that is above,
> for the sun of the nations is beneath that moon, and that sun
> shines from the light of that moon. See what is the difference
> between Israel and them: Israel is one with the moon, and

248

unfolds from the higher sun,[66] and is united with the place that shines from the higher sun, and they cling to Him, as is written, 'And you that are cleaving to the Lord your God are all living today' (Deut. 4:4).

Israel is fully identified with the moon, and they cleave to it. In this light the *Zohar* interprets the well-known biblical text, 'you who are cleaving to the Lord, all of you are alive today' to mean cleaved to the moon, which is the *Shekhinah*. At this point the *Zohar* brings the discussion explicitly back to Judah:

יהודה אתה וגו', רבי שמעון אמר, מלכו ליהודה אתקיים, והיינו דאמרינן
מאי דכתיב (בראשית כט לה) הפעם אודה את יהו"ה, בגין דאיהי רביעאה,
אודה את יהו"ה בגין דאיהו רגלא רביעאה לכרסיא, יה"ו דא רשימא דשמא
עלאה, ובמה אשתלים בה"א (ס"א בדל"ת), והיינו ה"א בתראה דשמא
קדישא, שמא קדישא שלים באתווי, וקשר דאחיד לון, על דא יודוך אחיך,
דמלכו לך אתחזיא לאתקיימא

'Judah, you, etc.'. Rabbi Shimon said: The kingdom is sustained by Judah, as we have said: Why is it written, 'This time I will thank God' (Gen. 29:35)? [Said Leah:] Since [Judah] was the fourth, I will thank God, for he is the fourth leg of the throne. *YHV* is the imprint of the higher name, and how is it completed? With the *heh*, which is the final *heh* of holy name. The holy name is complete with its letters, and the knot that binds them. This is why 'your brothers will praise you', for its kingdom is fit to be sustained by you.

The source of the radical kingship motif in *MHs* is virtually identical with acosmic humanism. The essence of kingship is identified with Judah from birth, as exclaimed by Leah in her naming of Judah. Judah is the fourth leg of the throne, the fourth letter of the name of God. This is the *heh*, which in Zoharic symbolism of the name of God stands for *Shekhinah*.

The *Zohar* then cites a verse from Hosea from a group of verses which describe God as rejecting Ephraim while being loyal to Judah. Of course this is a major motif which runs all through *MHs*.

ודאי (הושע יב) ויהודה עוד רד עם אל, ועם קדושים נאמן, מאן קדושים,
אלין קדושים עליונין, דכלהו אודן לגביה, ושויוה נאמן, בגין כך הוא קדמאה

249

בכלא, הוא מלכא על כלא. רבי שמעון פתח ואמר, (תהלים מה יד) כל
כבודה בת מלך פנימה, כל כבודה דא כנסת ישראל, כבודה בגין דאיהו
כבוד, דא על דא, דא דכר ודא נוקבא, (ס"א דא
נוקבא)

Certainly, 'And Judah will rule with God, and with the faithful
holy ones' (Hos. 12:1). And who are 'the holy ones'? These are
the supernal holy ones, who all acknowledge him and make
him faithful. Because of this he is first in all *kola* and king over
all. Rabbi Shimon opened and said: '*Kol kevudah bat melekh
penimah* All glory of the king's daughter is within' (Psalms
45:14).[67] *Kol kevudah* means congregation of Israel, because
He is *kavod*, one upon the other, one a male, and the other a
female.

Judah is king over all as the archetype of the Messiah king. The *Zohar*
continues by identifying Judah with the *bat melekh* and with קול בת *bat
kol* (divine voice or echo), another well-known Zoharic appellation for
Shekhinah, which merges in *zivug* with *kol*, an appellation for *Tif'eret*.[68]
This is standard imagery in Zoharic *hokhmat Shelomoh* texts.[69]

ואתקרי כבודה בת מלך, היינו בת שבע, בת קול, דאיהו קול גדול, והאי מלך
עלאה הוא פנימה, בגין דאית מלך דלאו איהו לגו כוותיה. והאי כבודה בת
מלך ממשבצות זהב לבושה, בגין דאתלבשת ואתאחדת בגבורתא עלאה,
והאי אוף נמי מלך אקרי

[A]nd she is called 'glory of the king's daughter', which is
Bathsheba, *bat kol* 'daughter of a voice', meaning, a great voice
(*Tif'eret*), and this supernal high King is within, for there is a
king who is not as inner as he is. And that glory of the king's
daughter, her garments are interwoven of gold (paralleling the
High Priest's garments), for she is enrobed and united with
the higher *gevurah*, which is also called king.

After the description of *zivug* between Judah/*Malkhut* and *Shekhinah*, the
Zohar introduces a theme that we are familiar with from a number of the
Wisdom of Solomon *Zohar* sources. It is through Judah/*Malkhut* that
the land is sustained; not through *Shekhinah* alone, but rather through the
zivug, the erotic merger with *Tif'eret*, which in this passage is represented
as *mishpat*.

ובגינה קיימא ארעא. אימתי, בשעתא דאתאחדת במשפט, כמה דאת אמר
(משלי כט ד) מלך במשפט יעמיד ארץ, ודא קרינן מלכו דשמיא, ויהודה
אתאחיד בה ובירית מלכותא דבארעא

And for her sake the earth exists. When? When she is one
with *mishpat* justice, as it says, 'The king through justice will
cause the earth to stand' (Prov. 29:4). This we call the kingdom of heaven, and Judah united with her, and he inherits the
kingdom that is of the earth.

Finally, Judah is the personification of *Malkhut*, of *Shekhinah*, of kingship
on the earth. The need for *Shekhinah* to be in balance with *mishpat* is, as we
have seen, an important strand in the Solomon-moon-*Shekhinah* sources.
Judah and Solomon are two very closely identified symbols of *Shekhinah*.

Source 28: *Zohar* 1:237a

In the next Zoharic passage we see the same set of identities between
Judah, *Malkhut/Shekhinah* and moon. The description is of *galut ha-
Shekhinah*, the exile of the *Shekhinah*.

פתח רבי יצחק ואמר (בראשית ג כד) ויגרש את האדם וישכן מקדם לג"ע
וגו', האי קרא אוקמוה חברייא, אבל ויגרש, כבר נש דגריש לאנתתיה, את
האדם דייקא, תא חזי רזא דמלה, אדם במה דחטא אתפס, וגרים מותא
ליה ולכל עלמא, וגרים לההוא אילנא דחטא ביה תירוכין, לאתרכא ביה,
ולאתתרכא בבני לעלמין, הדא הוא דכתיב ויגרש את האדם, את דייקא,
כמה דכתיב (ישעיה ו א) ואראה את יהו"ה, אוף הכי את האדם

Rabbi Yitzhak opened and said: 'And he banished the man,
and east of Eden placed [the cherubs]', etc. (Gen. 3:24). The
companions have already discussed this verse. But 'and he
banished'—like a man who divorces his wife—'*et* the man',
exactly. Come and see the secret meaning of this matter. Man
was caught on what he sinned, and brought death to himself and all the world, and he caused the tree through which
he sinned to be banished, to wander with him, and to be
banished with his children forever. As it is written, 'And he
banished *et* the man'—*et* specifically, as is written, 'And I saw
et' (Isa. 6:1), so too here *et ha-adam*.

The *Zohar* then goes on to describe the Garden of Eden as the place of *zivug ʿim ha-Shekhinah*; the *zivug* being dependent on the ability to hold in their proper place the male and female energies; the revolving flaming sword is the sword that moves back and forth between male and female, as necessary and appropriate. In the continuation the *Zohar*:

וישכן מקדם לג"ע וגו', האי לתתא, וכמה דאית כרובים לעילא, אית כרובים
לתתא, והאי אילנא אשרי עלייהו. ואת להט החרב המתהפכת, אינון טפסי
דשלהובי דאשא, מההוא חרבא דמתלהטא, המתהפכת, דא האי חרבא
דינקא בתרין סטרין, ואתהפכא מסטרא דא לסטרא אחרא. דבר אחר,
המתהפכת, דא להט, אינון טפסי דשלהובא (ס"א דמלכותא), דקאמרן
דמתהפכן לזמנין גוברין ולזמנין נשין, ומתהפכן מדוכתייהו לכלא, וכל דא
לשמור את דרך עץ החיים, מאן דרך, כמה דאת אמר (שם מג טז) הנותן
בים דרך

'And he placed east of Eden'—This was below. Just as there are cherubs above, there are cherubs below, and that tree rests on them. 'And the flame of the revolving sword'—these are the tongues of flames of fire from that fiery sword; 'revolving'—this is that sword which suckles from two sides, and changes from this side to that side. Another interpretation: 'revolving'—this is flame, these are the tongues of the flame that change (revolve): sometimes they are men, sometimes they are women. And they change from all their places, and all this [is] in order 'to guard the way to the Tree of Life'. What is meant by 'way'? As it says, 'He who creates a way in the sea' (Isa. 43:16).

At this point the *Zohar* is building on its identification of 'et' as referring to the *Shekhinah*, hence the *Zohar's* almost cryptic comment that 'da shalimo de'adam', implying that the *Shekhinah* is actually the fullness of man.

משמע, דכתיב ויגרש את האדם, בגין דדא שלימו דאדם הוא ומההוא יומא
אתפגים סיהרא עד דאתא נח ועאל בתיבותא, אתו חייביא ואתפגים, עד
דאתא אברהם (ואתקיימו), וקיימא בשלימו דיעקב ובנוי

This is implied from what is written, 'And He banished man', for this is the completeness of man. And since that day, the moon was weakened, until Noah came and entered the ark. Then the wicked came and she was weakened [again], until

252

Abraham came, and she existed in the completeness of Jacob and his sons.

The repair of the moon is dependent on human beings: first Noah fixes the moon and then sin causes it to wane again; Abraham and then Jacob and his sons repair the moon. But it is Judah who comes and makes *Malkhut/* moon his exclusive and eternal territory, for Judah and all of his descendants.

ואתא יהודה ואחיד ביה, ואתקף במלכותא, ואחסין ליה אחסנת עלמין הוא וכל בנוי בתרוי, הדא הוא דכתיב יהודה אתה יודוך אחיך (ס״א בגין דדיליה מלכותא עלייהו, כמה דאת אמר (דה״א ה ב) כי יהודה גבר באחיו יודוך אחיך

Then Judah came and was united with her, and was empowered through kingdom, and inherited it as an eternal inheritance, he and all his children after him. As it is written, 'Judah, you will be acknowledged (above trans. 'praised') by your brothers'…as it says, 'For Judah was triumphant over his brothers' (1 Chron. 5:2).

Here again the roots of *MHs* in the Solomon/Judah genre in *Zohar* are clear.

Source 29: *Zohar* 1:237

The next *Zohar* passage again revolves around the Judah-*Shekhinah* identity. Three new themes which we have not yet seen in the Judah texts are added here. The first is the relation of Judah to smell, a central theme in the Judah/Solomon genre in *MHs*. Judah's sense of smell allows him to intuit beyond the general principles of law. The second theme is Judah and sin. Sin, or falling/crouching, as it is expressed in this passage, is part of Judah's unique strength.[70] The third theme is that Judah, like Solomon, includes the darkness within himself.

גור אריה יהודה בקדמיתא גור, ולבתר אריה, ורזא דמלה, בקדמיתא נער, ולבתר איש

'Judah is a lion cub, [from the prey, my son, you rose up; he stooped down, he crouched like a lion, like a lioness, who can

253

raise him up?]' (Gen. 49:9). At first he is a cub, and then a
lion. The secret of this matter—first a boy, then a man.

The image is clear: the way of the lion is to first crouch and then rise up.
As we shall see, this is the way of Judah, the lion of Judah, the *Shekhinah*.

מטרף בני עלית, מאי מטרף, לאכללא מלאך המות דאיהו קיימא על טרף
לשיצאה בני עלמא ולא משזיב, כמה דאת אמר (מיכה ה ז) וטרף ואין
מציל, (ומהו) ומההוא טרף אסתלקת שכינתא

'From the prey, my son, you rose up'. What is [meant by] 'from
the prey'? To include the angel of death, who is standing over
the prey to destroy the people of the earth, and from whom
there is no deliverance, as it says, 'And he will prey, and none
will come to save' (Mic. 5:7). And the *Shekhinah* rises from
that prey.

The verse cited describes Judah as rising from the 'teref of my son', an allusion in Genesis to the story of Joseph about whom the brothers said *tarof
toraf*, 'He is surely torn' (Gen. 37:33). In the deep structure of the Genesis
story, Judah goes down, *vayered*, after the sale of Joseph. Yet he is able to
rise from that fall in a kind of proto–'yeridah tzorekh 'aliyah', going down
for the sake of rising,[71] in the structure of the biblical text itself. *Miteref
beni*—from the fall, the ripped-apartness, 'the *teref* of my son', you rise.

It is from the very sin that Judah the person and Judah the *Shekhinah* will
rise. The passage continues. *Teref* includes the dark side, integrating even
death.

כך שכינתא, דאף על גב דכתיב (עמוס ה ב) נפלה ולא תוסיף קום
בתולת ישראל, היא תקיפא כאריה וכלביא בהאי נפילה, מה אריה ולביא
לא נפלין אלא בגין למטרף טרפא ולשלטאה, דהא מרחיק ארח טרפיה,
ומשעתא דארח נפל ולא קם עד דדליג על טרפיה ואכיל לה, כך שכינתא לא
נפלה אלא כאריה וכלביא, בגין לנקמא מעמין עובדי ע"ז ולדלגא עלייהו

…so too the *Shekhinah*, even though it is written concerning
her, 'The virgin of Israel has fallen, and she will no longer arise'
(Amos 5:2), she is as strong as a lion and a cub in that fall.
Just as a lion or cub does not fall other than in order to prey
upon prey and conquer, for he smells his prey from afar, and

from the moment he smells his prey, he falls and will not rise, until he pounces upon his prey and consumes it. So too the *Shekhinah* falls only like a lion, in order to take revenge on the idol-worshipping nations, and to pounce upon them.

The *Shekhinah*'s crouching down is like that of a lion, a sign of strength, in order to redeem that which has fallen. The *Zohar* then introduces a new theme, the faculty of smell, which is critical to the *Shekhinah*'s endeavor. She smells her prey from afar and then pounces. All of this the *Zohar* then relates to idolatry, although here there is no ambivalence—the *Shekhinah* is avenging herself. In the concluding paragraph below, the subject is *mi* 'who'—a standard reference to the higher *Shekhinah*, *Binah*.

כמה דאת אמר (ישעיה סג א) צועה ברוב כחו. מי יקימנו, הוא לא יקום
לנקמא מנייהו נוקמא זעירא, אלא מי יקימנו, מי, כמה דאת אמר (איכה ב
יג) מי ירפא לך, והוא איהו עלמא עלאה, דביה שלטנותא לאתקפא לכלא,
וכתיב (איוב לח כט) מבטן מי יצא הקרח ואוקמוה

...as it says: 'Striding in the greatness of his strength' (Isa. 63:1). Who will raise him up? He will not rise to take a small revenge on them. But 'who' *mi* will cause him to rise up? *Mi*, as it says, 'Who *mi* will heal you?' (Lam. 2:13). And this one is the higher world, where there is the authority to empower all things, and it is written, 'From whose belly did the forest emerge?' (Job 38:29). And we already interpreted this.

Source 30: *Zohar* 2:85a

The three previous passages we have cited in this section all come from one block of pages within *Zohar* Bereishit. The next passage, which comes from an entirely different section of the *Zohar*, explicitly points out the identity between the Judah and Solomon sources. Here Judah's *Shekhinah* nature is tied not only to a word or verse involving *yarei'ach* and even to *sihara*; Judah is himself directly identified with our core *terminus technicus* of *sihara bisheleimuta* or *be'ashleimuta*. This is found together with the *Zohar*'s adoption of the midrashic motif of Solomon sitting on the throne of God in terms of acosmic humanism. It is with this theme that the passage begins. The first half of the passage is a virtual repetition in Zoharic terms of the *midrash* we cited earlier as a precursor to acosmic humanism.[72]

תאנא כתיב (דה"א כט) וישב שלמה על כסא יהו"ה למלך, כמה דכתיב
(מ"א י) שש מעלות לכסא, רבי אבא אמר, דקיימא סיהרא באשלמותא
דתנינן ביומוי דשלמה קיימא סיהרא באשלמותא. אימתי באשלמותא (נ"א
תנא כתיב (שם ה) ותרב חכמת שלמה וגו' מאי ותרב, אמר רבי אבא,
(דקיימא סיהרא באשלמותא)

We learned: it is written, 'And Solomon sat on the throne of
God as king' (1 Chron. 29:23), as it is written, 'six steps [lead-
ing up] to the throne' (1 Kings 10:19). Rabbi Abba said: [It
means that] that the moon was existing in its fullness. As we
already learned, in the days of Solomon, the moon was in its
fullness. When was it in its fullness? We learned, it is written,
'And the wisdom of Solomon waxed great' (1 Kings 5:10).
What is meant by 'and it waxed'? Rabbi Abba said: That the
moon was in its fullness.

As in the midrashic source, the *Zohar* charts the path of the moon waxing until it achieves completeness with Solomon. The *Zohar* assumes that
when a biblical text talks about *yareiah* (as in the verse in Isaiah which the
text cites), it is describing the *Shekhinah*, and in the case of the waning of
the moon, *galut ha-Shekhinah*, the exile of *Shekhinah*.

מאי באשלמותא. דקיימא בחמשה עשר, כמה דתנינן, אברהם, יצחק, יעקב,
יהודה, פרץ, חצרון, רם, עמינדב, נחשון, שלמון, בועז, עובד, ישי, דוד,
שלמה, כד אתא שלמה קיימא סיהרא באשלמותא, הדא הוא דכתיב וישב
שלמה על כסא יהו"ה למלך, וכתיב שש מעלות לכסא, כלא כגוונא דלעילא.
ביומוי דצדקיה קיימא סיהרא בפגימותא ואתפגים, כמה דאת אמר (ישעיה
יג) וירח לא יגיה אורו, דתנינן ביומוי דצדקיה אתפגים סיהרא, ואתחשכו
אנפייהו דישראל, פוק וחשוב, רחבעם, אביה, אסא, יהושפט, יהורם,
אחזיה, יואש, אמציהו, עוזיה, יותם, אחז, יחזקיהו, מנשה, אמון, יאשיהו,
צדקיהו, וכד אתא צדקיהו אתפגים סיהרא וקיימא על פגימותא, דכתיב
(ירמיה נב) ואת עיני צדקיהו עור

What is meant by its fullness? As it is on the fifteenth, as
we learned: Abraham, Isaac, Jacob, Judah, Peretz, Hetzron,
Ram, Aminadav, Nahshon, Salmon, Boaz, Ovad, Jesse, David,
Solomon. When Solomon came, the moon was in its fullness,
and so it is written, 'And Solomon sat on the throne of God
as king', and it is written, 'Six steps to the throne', all similar
to [what was learned] above. In the days of Zidkiyah, the

moon was in its waning state and was lacking, as it says (Isa. 13:10): 'And the moon's light will not shine'. As we learned: In the days of Zidkiyah, the moon was lacking, and the faces of Israel were darkened. Go and count: Rehobam, Avya, Asa, Yehoshafat, Yehoram, Ahazayhu, Yoash, Amatzyahu, Uzziya, Yotam, Ahaz, Yehizkiyahu, Menashe, Amon, Yoshiyahu, Zidkiyahu. When Zidkiyahu came, the moon was lacking and remained in its wounded state, as is written, 'And the eyes of Zidkiyahu were blinded' (Jer. 52:1).

At this point we are approaching the key part of the passage. The earth being thrown down by the sky is the rupturing of the *zivug* between *Tif'eret* and *Malkhut/Shekhinah*.

ביה זמנא (איכה ב) השליך משמים ארץ, האי ארץ אתעברא מקמי שמים
(ואתרחקת מניה, ואתחשכא האי ארץ, (כלומר דקיימא סיהרא פגימותא

At that time 'earth was cast out from the heavens' (Lam. 2:1). The earth (*Malkhut*) was taken away from before the heavens and distanced from it, and that earth was darkened—meaning, the moon remained *pegimuta* lacking.

The question in the *Zohar* is: how can that broken coupling be mended? How can *Tif'eret* and *Malkhut* become erotically coupled once more, restoring the primary *zivug* of the cosmos? It is to this question that the *Zohar* now turns. The answer is: 'Judah and Sinai'. The biblical theophany at Sinai is re-read as the time when Judah is somehow appointed the *Shekhinah* figure. The moon is recovered by, and in, the Judah figure. This is the flag of the encampment of Judah. It is the realization of divine consciousness, which is the channel through which the word of God is realized in the people. Judah who is the moon in her fullness heals the moon, which according to the verse cited earlier from Isaiah, is waning.

תאנא בשעתא דקיימו ישראל על טורא דסיני, שארי סיהרא לאנהרא,
דכתיב (תהלים יח) ויט שמים וירד, מהו וירד, דקריב שמשא לגבי סיהרא,
ושרי לאנהרא סיהרא, דכתיב (במדבר ב) דגל מחנה יהודה מזרחה, בטורא
דסיני אתמנא יהודה רופינוס במלכותא דכתיב (הושע יב) ויהודה עוד רד
עם אל ועם קדושים נאמן

257

We learned: When Israel stood at Mt. Sinai, the moon began to shine, as it is written, 'And he turned the heavens and descended' (Psalms 18:10). What is meant by 'He descended'? That he brought the sun close to the moon, and the moon began to shine, as it is written, 'The flag of the camp of Judah to the east' (Num. 2:3). At Mount Sinai, Judah was appointed to be in charge of the kingdom. As it is written, 'And Judah still rules with God, and is faithful with the holy ones' (Hos. 12:1).

The proof text for Judah's nature is the text from Hosea which expresses the divine preference for Judah over Efraim, a highly significant source for *MHs*, as noted above. For the *Zohar*, followed by Lainer, that significance is of course not political but ontological; Judah personifies moon/*Malkhut/Shekhinah*. The *Zohar* concludes with a dramatic reading in which the trust of God in the Jewish people and the loyalty of the people to God are expressed by Judah receiving *Malkhut*, meaning both Kingship and *Shekhinah*, and causing the moon to shine!

נ"א רבי יצחק אמר מהכא, ויהודה עוד רד עם אל, הוה שולטניה בשעתא (
דהאי אל שליט מלכותיה על טורא דסיני, בהאי שעתא שליט מלכותיה
דיהודה) מהו ועם קדושים נאמן, כד אמר קודשא בריך הוא לישראל ואתם
תהיו לי ממלכת כהנים וגוי קדוש, נאמן הוה יהודה לקבלא מלכותא, ושארי
סיהרא לאנהרא

Rabbi Yitzhak deduced it from here: 'and Judah still rules with God' (Hos. 12:1)—His rule began when that God caused his kingdom to rule at Mount Sinai—at that time the kingdom of Judah ruled. What is meant by 'and he is faithful with the holy ones'? So said God to Israel: 'And you will be unto me a kingdom of priests and a holy nation' (Exod. 19:6). Judah was trustworthy to receive the kingdom, and the moon began to shine.

All of this relates to the second Zoharic passage on the Wisdom of Solomon that we discussed above (Source 15) which suggested that the rupture of the *zivug* between *Tif'eret* and *Shekhinah* is *hatat Yehudah*. Judah and Solomon once again participate in the same *Shekhinah* archetype in these passages.

The Wine Sources

The second part of the Judah genre relates to the other major theme in Lainer's Judah archetype, that of wine. Lainer's theme emerges from this cluster of Zoharic texts, to which he refers to directly at least once, although cryptically.

The *Zohar* is guided to the association between wine and Judah by Jacob's blessing to Judah, in which wine is a major motif: 'He ties up his young ass to the vine, to its stock (of the vine) the foal of his she-ass; he washes his coat in wine, his cloak in the blood of grapes; his eyes are cloudy with wine, his teeth are white with milk' (Gen. 49:11–12). The mystical exegesis of these verses, as we have seen, is an organizing thread of many of the Judah texts.

Before we turn to the Zoharic sources, note that wine appears as a motif in the Solomon sources already within midrashic literature. It is told that Solomon married the daughter of Pharaoh and listened to her pagan songs, witnessing and possibly even engaging in pagan practice on the night of the Temple's consecration.[73] These two events become integrally related, an important allusion to the proximate nature of pagan and Temple energies. Solomon sleeps late the next day, overwhelmed it would seem by the intoxication of the daughter of Pharaoh. The daily sacrifice could not be offered, for the keys were under Solomon's pillow. The people are overcome with grief and word is sent to Bathsheba to rouse her son. She does so with a series of stern admonitions, the last of which is, 'it is not fit that you should do like kings who drink wine and live in lewdness; be not like them. He to whom the secrets of the world are revealed should not intoxicate himself with wine!'

In the Zoharic sources, however, there is a recognition of more than one kind of wine—*it gefen ve'it gefen* in the language of the *Zohar*. While there is certainly the kind of wine described by Bathsheba, not suitable to a king, there is also the wine of *Shekhinah*, of Judah and ecstasy, the wine that Lainer will suggest is the essence of a king, and a central manifestation of the Judah archetype.

259

In the first passage, we see a number of major Judah/Solomon motifs unfolded alongside the connection between Judah and wine: the Judah messianic motif, the darkness and its role in catalyzing redemption, and the related theme of the paradoxical relationship between Judah's greatness and his imperfection.

אסרי לגפן עירה, מאי גפן דא כנסת ישראל, כמה דאת אמר (תהלים פ ט)
גפן ממצרים תסיע, וכתיב (שם קכח ג) אשתך כגפן פוריה, אשתך כהאי גפן
קדישא. אמר רבי יוסי, האי גפן דמברכינן ביה בורא פרי הגפן, בורא, היינו
דכתיב עץ עושה פרי, פרי הגפן, דא עץ פרי, עושה פרי דכר, עץ פרי דא
נוקבא, בגיני כך בורא פרי הגפן, דא דכר ונוקבא כחדא

'He ties his ass to the vine'—what is 'vine'? *Keneset Yisra'el*, as it says (Psalms 90:9): 'bring a vine from Egypt', and it is written (Psalms 128:3): 'Your wife should be like a fruitful vine'—[meaning] your wife should be like that sacred vine. Rabbi Yosi said: That is the vine for which they bless 'who creates the fruit of the vine'. 'Who creates', this means what is written, *'eitz 'oseh peri* 'the tree that makes fruit'. 'The fruit of the vine'—this is *'eitz peri* 'fruit tree'. *'Oseh peri* [the tree] that makes fruit'—this is male. *'Eitz peri* 'fruit tree'—this is female. This is why we say 'who creates the fruit of the vine': this is male and female as one.

Here the *Zohar* immediately establishes the identity between wine and *Shekhinah*. Based on this identity the *Zohar* suggests that the blessing of *borei peri ha-gafen* is in effect a *yihud* of *Shekhinah* and *Tif'eret*. The word *borei* parallels the biblical phrase *'eitz 'oseh peri*, which is the masculine side, and *peri ha-gafen* parallels *'eitz peri*, which is the feminine. In the *yihud* of *Shekhinah* and *Tif'eret*, the unity of *'eitz peri* and *'eitz 'oseh peri* is accomplished.

One cannot read this passage without associating it with the rabbinic passage that was core to the consciousness of the Zoharic writers.[74] In that passage a textual anomaly in the Genesis verses describing the creation of trees is interpreted to mean that at their creation, trees were meant to be both *'oseh peri*, fruit-bearing, and *'eitz peri*, tree that is itself fruit, that is, each tree itself would taste like its fruit. The symbol of the fallen world, suggests the *midrash*, is that the tree itself lost its fruit nature. The sign of the eschaton is therefore that both the tree and fruit should once again partake in fruit nature.

In effect what the *Zohar* is suggesting that the *yihud* or *zivug* between *Shekhinah* and *Tif'eret* restores the original eroticization of reality. *Shekhinah* is often—like the term *zohar* itself—quite close in content to the Greek idea of eros.[75] The image of *zivug* in the *Zohar* takes on profound conceptual depth in this light that goes far beyond its overt sexual significance.

The *Zohar* continues by introducing the core identification between Judah, wine, and the Messiah. The characteristic that is most apparent in Judah is *tokfa*, which later appears in Lainer as the word *tekufot*—a demarcating characteristic of Judah. *Tokfa* and *tekufot*, as we have seen, mean personal audacity, courage, power, a king filled with holy confidence that whatever he does is the will of God—the essence of acosmic humanism. Judah, who is *Shekhinah* and wine, possesses *tokfa*.

אסרי לגפן עירה, דא מלכא משיחא, דזמין לשלטאה על כל חילי עממיא, חילין די ממנן על עמין עעכו״ם, ואינון תוקפא דלהון לאתתקפא, וזמין מלכא משיחא לאתגברא עלייהו, בגין דהאי גפן שליט על כל אלין כתרין תתאין, דשלטי בהו עממיא עעכו״ם, האי נצח לעילא, ישראל דאינון שרקה ישיצון וינצחון חילין אחרנין לתתא, ועל כלהו יתגבר מלכא משיחא

'Ties his ass to the vine'—this is the Messiah king, who is ready to rule over all of the armies of the nations, armies of hosts appointed over the pagan nations—these are their *tokfa* strength which makes them strong…—because that vine rules over all the lower crowns through which the pagan nations rule that [vine] is *netzah* victory above. Israel, who is the grapevine branch, will destroy and vanquish the other armies below, and the Messiah king will triumph over them all.

We also see that it is the Messiah's function to deal with the lower crowns, whether by means of revenge as we saw in an earlier Judah passage or by integration—it is not entirely clear from this text. This messianic consciousness, as the *Zohar* will now observe, is from the side of *semol*, which is the side of fiery love whose source is *din*. On the side of *semol*, as we have seen elsewhere, there is a great capacity for corruption, for the side of *semol* is also *sitra demas'ava*, the side of impurity.

261

הדא הוא דכתיב (זכריה ט ט) עני ורוכב על חמור ועל עיר, עיר וחמור,
תרין כתרין אינון דשלטי בהו עממיא עעכו״ם, ואינון מסטר שמאלא סטרא
דמסאבא

This is what is written, 'Poor and riding on a donkey and a
mule' (Zech. 9:9)—a mule and a donkey, two crowns through
which the pagan nations rule. They are from the left side, the
side of impurity.

At this point we turn the last major theme in this text: the highly paradoxical nature of the messianic archetype. On the one hand, he is poor
and lacking, an *aspaklariya delo nahara*, an unclear prism which sometimes
might distort the light, the word of God.[76] On the other hand, he is capable of triumph over the mule and donkey, the lower crowns. It seems
that it is from this very weakness that he derives his strength; as the *Zohar*
implies, his emptiness allows him to fill with strength from above. It may
also be saying that he is close to these lower crowns, coming from the same
source as they do, namely, *din*, *Gevurah*, and *elohim aheirim*, all expressions
of *semol* and *aspaklariya delo nahara*, which is the source or sustenance of
both the Messiah and *Shekhinah*. The fact that Judah shares a common
source with the lower dark side would seem to be a major piece of the
Judah-Messiah puzzle. The *Zohar* in the whole second half of this passage
is also playing with the similarity of *hamor* donkey, and *hamra* wine, drawing out the connections between wine, Judah, and the Messiah.

ומה דאמר עני, וכי מלכא משיחא עני אקרי, אלא הכי אמר רבי שמעון, בגין
דלית ליה מדיליה וקרינן ליה מלך המשיח, דא הוא סיהרא קדישא לעילא
דלית לה נהורא אלא משמשא. מלכא משיחא דא ישלוט בשלטניה, יתייחד
בדוכתיה, וכדין (שם) הנה מלכך יבא לך סתם, אי לתתא עני הוא, דהא
בסטרא דסיהרא הוא, אי לעילא עני אספקלריא דלא נהרא, לחם עני. ועם
כל דא רוכב על חמור ועל עיר, תוקפא דעמין עעכו״ם לאכפייא תחותיה,
ויתתקף קב״ה בדוכתיה.

And how could it say 'poor'? Is the Messiah king called poor?
But this is what Rabbi Shimon said: Since he has nothing
of his own, and he is called the Messiah king, this is the holy
moon above, who has light only from the sun. The Messiah
king will rule in his reign, will unite in his place, and then, 'behold your king will come to you'—stated generally, [without
specifics. That is because] if it is from below, he is poor, for he

is from the side of the moon. If it is from above, poor [means] the prism that does not shine, the bread of poverty. And with all of this (despite this), he is 'riding upon a donkey and a mule', [representing] the *tokfa* strength of the pagan nations, to subdue them beneath him, and the Holy One will become strengthened in His place.

Messianism is a major motif here as in other moon passages. The moon's fullness heralds a messianic age in both the restorative and utopian sense, since the moon is not only destined to return to its former glory but also to far transcend what it could have achieved without this fall.[77]

Source 32: *Zohar* 1:238a–b

The major scriptural text being interpreted in the following passage is the Genesis story of Pharaoh's dreams. This segment of the passage focuses on analyzing the dream of the wine steward, in which grapes play a major role.

רבי יוסי פתח ואמר, אסרי לגפן עירה, וכתיב (בראשית מ) ובגפן שלשה שריגים, והיא כפורחת עלתה נצה...והיא כפרחת עלתה נצה הבשילו אשכלתיה ענבים...והיא כפרחת, דכתיב (מ"א ה) ותרב חכמת שלמה, דאתנהיר סיהרא, עלתה נצה, דא ירושלם דלתתא...הבשילו אשכלותיה ענבים, לנטרא בהו יין דמנטרא

Rabbi Yosi opened and said: 'Ties his ass to the vine'—it is written, 'And on the vine there were three branches, and it was as if she were flowering, and her blossom came out' (Gen. 40:10)...'and it was as if she were flowering'—for it is written 'And the wisdom of Solomon waxed great' (1 Kings 5:10), [meaning] that the moon was shining, 'and her blossom came out'—this is the lower Jerusalem...'her clusters ripened with grapes'—in order to guard within them the protected wine.

The swelling grapes of the wine steward's dream are an expression of the Wisdom of Solomon. The classic Wisdom of Solomon text is invoked, along with the classic Zoharic symbol, the moon in her fullness, i.e. *Shekhinah*. In this text Judah, the Wisdom of Solomon, the Temple and wine themes all conflate. The protected wine is a symbol of messianic redemption, a common theme in the *Zohar*, referring to wine which has fermented long enough to be purified of its dregs. It indicates the transformation of evil, as well as the *sefirah* of the *Binah*, the great mother who is also known as *Shekhinah 'ila'ah*, the higher *Shekhinah*.

This brief allusion to the Wisdom of Solomon is actually critical in terms of *MHs*. For it is only once one notices the wine genre in *MHs* that one notices that the wine steward is a key symbol of the Wisdom of Solomon in one of the classical Judah passages, by virtue of being *menutzah*, overpowered by God.[78] In the *Zohar* the valence of this association is quite different, as we will see presently.

חמי כמה חמא ההוא רשע. מה כתיב (שם מ יא) וכוס פרעה בידי ואקח
את הענבים ואשחט אותם, הכא חמא ההוא כוס תרעלה יניקא דבי דינא
דנפיק מאינון ענבים, דאתייהיב לפרעה ושתי ליה, כמה דהוה בגיניהון
דישראל, כיון דשמע יוסף דא חדי,וידע מלה דקשוט בהאי חלמא, בגיני כך
פשר ליה חלמא לטב, על דבשר ליה ליוסף בהאי

See how much that wicked person saw. What is written (Gen. 40:11)? 'And the cup of Pharoah was in my hand, and I took the grapes, and I squeezed them.' Here he saw that cup of poison, the nursing source of the house of judgment that comes out of those grapes, which he gave to Pharoah, who drank it. Since it was for the sake of Israel, when Joseph heard this, he rejoiced, and he knew the true essence of that dream. Because of that, he interpreted [the dream] positively, for through this was the news announced to Joseph.

The first part of this passage explains how Joseph was able to correctly interpret the dream of the wine steward through his recognition that wine symbolized the ascendancy of Israel. The *Zohar* continues by distinguishing between two types of wine, that of Israel and that of the nations. Wine, depending on which kind it is, can either drown Israel or express her divine glory. Israel as wine is *Shekhinah*, which is able to subjugate as well as integrate the nations under it. In an allusion to the identification of Israel with the divine, Israel is viewed as literally coming out of the *gefen*, the vine.

תא חזי, אסרי לגפן עירה דאתכפיין תחות האי גפן כל אינון חילין תקיפין
דעמין עע"ז כדאמרן, בגין האי גפן אתקשר ואתכפייא ההוא חילא דלהון
ואתמר. רבי שמעון אמר, אית גפן ואית גפן, אית גפן קדישא עלאה, ואית
גפן דאקרי (דברים ל לב) גפן סדום, ואית (ירמיה ב כא) גפן נכריה, בת אל
נכר. בגין כך כתיב גפן זאת, ההיא דאקרי (שם) כלה זרע אמת, שורק אלו

264

ישראל דנפקי מהאי גפן, כד חבו ישראל ושבקו להאי גפן, מה כתיב כי מגפן
סדום גפנם וגו׳, ובגין כך אית גפן ואית גפן

Come and see: 'Ties his mule to the vine'. All the powerful
armies of the pagan nations are subjugated to that vine as
we have previously said, since that vine ties and subdues that
strength of theirs, as we have already commented. Rabbi
Shimon said: There is a vine, and there is a vine. There is a
holy vine above, and there is a vine called 'the vine of Sodom'
(Deut. 32:32), and there is 'the foreign vine' (Jer. 2:21), the
daughter of a pagan god. This is why it is written *gefen zot* 'this
vine' (Psalms 80:14), she who is called 'the bride of the seed
of truth' (Jer. 2:21). *Soreik* 'vine branch', this is Israel, which
emerges from that vine. When Israel sins and forsakes that
vine, what is written? 'Their vine is from the vine of Sodom,
etc.' This is why there is a vine and there is a vine.

All of this is part of the general Zoharic theme about the aged wine of
gladness, which brings freedom, in contrast with the wine of drunkenness,
which causes lack of energy and addiction. Characteristically, in Lainer's
appropriation of the image of the wine steward, the distinction between
the wine of the nations and Israel's wine is lost, and the wine steward simply becomes a symbol of Judah.

Source 33: *Zohar* 1:240a

The next passage expresses the identity of wine and the Messiah in terms
of their shared qualities and trajectories. Both express ecstatic Dionysian
qualities of joy even as both are rooted in *din*. Wine in the *Zohar* is usually
rooted in *Binah* which is both the source of joy and the source of *din*. The
din in this text is related to the nations of the world, a kind of Judgment
Day image. The Messiah is described as being 'adorned in the higher wine'
from the day the world was created. Again the link between wine, messianism and Judah, who is the topic of the passage, is reaffirmed.

The text begins by continuing the interpretation of Judah's blessing in the
book of Genesis.

דבר אחר, כבס ביין לבושו, כגוונא דהאי חמרא אחזי חידו וכוליה דינא,
(עמין עכו״ם), הכי נמי מלכא משיחא יחזי חידו לישראל וכוליה דינא

265

לעמין עכו״ם. כתיב (בראשית א ג) ורוח אלהי״ם מרחפת על פני המים,
דא רוחא דמלכא משיחא, ומן יומא דאתברי עלמא אסחי לבושיה בחמרא
עלאה. חמי מה כתיב בתריה, חכלילי עינים מיין ולבן שנים מחלב, דא
חמרא עלאה דמרוי דאורייתא מניה שתי, ולבן שנים מחלב, דהא אורייתא
יין וחלב, תורה שבכתב ותורה שבעל פה. כתיב (תהלים קד טו) ויין ישמח
לבב אנוש, (ס״א אמאי), בגין דמאתר דחדוה קאתי מאמר למנצח על
שושנים

Another interpretation: 'He washes his garment in wine'—just
as wine shows joy, and is entirely *din*, so too the Messiah king
will show joy to Israel, and he is all *din* for the pagan nations.
It is written, 'And the spirit of God hovered above the water'
(Gen. 1:3)—this is the spirit of the Messiah king. Since the
day the world was created he has been washing his clothes in
the higher wine. See what it says immediately afterwards: 'His
eyes are red from wine and his teeth are white from milk' (Gen.
49:12). This is the higher wine that satisfies, that the Torah
drinks from.'And teeth white from milk'—this is the Torah,
wine and milk, written Torah and oral Torah. And it is written,
'And wine makes the human heart rejoice' (Psalms 104:15).

The text continues by introducing a new identification, that of higher wine
and Torah, suggesting that built into Torah is a wine-Judah-*Shekhinah*
quality. This is understood by Lainer to mean that there is a quality to
Torah which is beyond the general principles of Torah and even beyond
da'at. It is by accessing this dimension of Torah that one can apprehend
unmediated *retzon Hashem*, that is to say, *Shekhinah*.

The passage continues by affirming the ecstatic quality of joy in wine.

כתיב יין ישמח לבב אנוש להצהיל פנים משמן, ודאי מאתר דאתקרי שמן,
תא חזי שירותא דחמרא חדוה הוא, אתר דכל חידו מניה נפקא, וסופיה
דינא, מאי טעמא, בגין דסופא דיליה אתר כנישו דכלא דינא הוא, וביה
אתדן עלמא, ועל דא שירותא חדו וסופא דינא, בגיני כך להצהיל פנים
משמן, מאתר דכל חדו מניה נפקא

It is written, 'And wine that makes glad the heart of man; to
brighten the face *mishemen* with oil (lit.,'from oil')' (Psalms
104:15). Indeed [wine] is from the place called oil. Come
and see: The beginning of wine is [from the place of] joy, the

266

place that all joy emerges from, and the end is *din*. What is the reason for this? Because its end is the place where all *din* is gathered in, and through it the world is judged. For this reason, the beginning is joy and the end is *din*. This is why it says 'to brighten the face from oil'—from the place that all joy comes from.

Oil and wine both begin with joy, and end with *din*. Since 'its end' implies the end-times, there the world is judged. However, I think that this is not just a question of judgment day, but of the fact that all *din* is gathered there, i.e the dark side is present and therefore either redeemed, or judged and 'revenged' (in the language of a previous passage). All this happens through wine which has the unique ability to enlarge consciousness to see possibilities that are otherwise invisible.

Din in this passage implies more than judgment. *Din*, as the *Zohar* points out in the preceding paragraph, comes from the side of *semol. Semol* includes burning, passionate love. The passage should not be read as moralistic, e.g., one begins in joy but in the end *din* is triumphant. Rather, *din* in this passage is not the opposite of joy but the fullfillment or the next stage after joy. It is the purifed burning love that allows for no inauthenticity, the *din* that according to the *Zohar* in the future world will become the spiritual fabric of the cosmos.

Source 34: *Zohar Hadash* Hukat *Maamar Lamenatze'ah 'Al Shoshanim*

Wine as the *sefirah* of *Binah*, the *zivug* of *Shekhinah* and *Tif'eret*, the Wisdom of Solomon, the Temple, and the correlation between Solomon and the full moon, are the interwoven themes and symbols that run through the next passage. All these congruent themes appear here together and help fill out our interpretation and understanding of each of them.

ד"א, מ"ט רחש לבי. בגין דדבור בלא קול, לא יכיל למללא. והאי לב"י דאקרי דבור, עד השתא לא אשתלימת, עד דאתא שלמה מלכא, ובנא לה ביתא, ואשתלימת סיהרא ברבו יתיר על כולא. בגין דקול אתחבר עמה

Why does it say 'my heart whispers' (Psalms 45:1)? Because speech without voice cannot talk. And that 'my heart', which is called speech, was not complete until King Solomon came, and built her a house, and the moon was completed in full- ness beyond all, because voice was joined with her.

267

In classical *Zohar* symbolism, דבור *dibur* signifies *Shekhinah* while קול *kol* signifies *Tif'eret*. When there is no *zivug* between them then one cannot speak; in modern terms one cannot find voice. When they are erotically merged, the moon waxes full. The moon becomes full because *Tif'eret, kol*, is coupled with it.

> וההיא שעתא, אתייהיב רשות למללא, דהא אשתלימת בקלא. ויתבא
> בשלימו עם מלכא בגין דאפיקת ברא חכימא לעלמא, ואתקינת ביתא
> למלכא. כדין מלכא שוי מדוריה עמה, ושראת למללא, ואמרת ישקני
> מנשיקות פיהו

[A]nd at that time, she was given permission to talk, for she was made complete by the voice. She sits at peace with the king, in order that a wise son should go out into the world, and she prepares a house for the king. Then the king makes his dwelling with her, and she begins to speak, and she says, 'Kiss me with the kisses of your mouth' (Cant. 1:2).

The *Shekhinah* is in exile until Solomon comes and and builds a house. Permission is then given to her speak; the King, *Tif'eret*, dwells with her, and she says *yishakheini mineshikot pihu*, 'kiss me with the kisses of your mouth'. Now the *Zohar* turns to David. This passage now expresses the dominant view in the *Zohar* which sees Solomon as being more spiritually advanced than David.

> אבל השתא ביומי דדוד, עד כדין לא יתבא באשתלמותא. בג"כ רחש לבי
> ודאי ההוא דבר טוב. השתא טוב, ולא טובים. כיון דאתחבר קול עמה, כדין
> טובים ודאי בכולא. צדיק טוב אקרי, דכתיב, אמרו צדיק כי טוב. אוף איהי
> אתקריאת טובה, טובה חכמה. וכד איתקריבו אתחברו כחדא באינון נשיקין,
> כדין כי טובים דודיך מיין, אינון דודים תרווייהו כחדא

But now, in the time of David, until then, she had not sat in completeness. This is why it says, 'My heart whispers', certainly, '...something *tov* good' (Psalms 45:2). Now [it is] '*tov* good' (in the singular), not 'they are *tovim* good'. [However,] when voice joins with her, then 'they are good', certainly, in everything. *Tzadik* (*Yesod*) is called 'good', as it is written, 'Say, it is good for the *tzadik*' (Isa. 3:10). She, too, is called good, [as it says,] 'Wisdom (*Shekhinah*) is good' (Eccl. 9:18). And when they are intimate, they unite as one through their kisses.

268

Concerning [this moment] it is written, 'For your caresses *dodekha* are *tovim* better than wine' (Cant. 1:2)—these are *dodim* lovers (in the plural), when both are as one.

In the days of David, actual union was not accomplished as it was in the days of Solomon. This is because conciousness did not get to the level of *tovim*—as in *tovim dodekha* 'your caresses are good'—for that level express-es *zivug* and David did not get to *zivug*.[79] This is the difference, says the *Zohar*, between *dodim*, which is *zivug*, and *yedidut*, which is when *zivug* has not yet been accomplished:

הכא דודים, והכא ידידות. ואימת אינון טובים מיין. כד אשתקיין מניה
דההוא יין דמנטרא. וע״ד כתיב, שתו ושכרו דודים. דהא נטיען שקיו בעיין
מנהרא עמיקא, אימא עילאה, דאיהי אשקיאת לון בקדמיתא מההוא יין

Here lovers, and here *yedidut* friendship. And when are they 'better than wine'? When they are given to drink of that protected wine. This is why it is written, 'Drink and become drunk, *dodim* lovers' (Cant. 5:1). For seedlings need to be watered from the deepest river, the supernal mother, for she first gives them to drink from that wine.

The achievement of union is naturally associated with wine, based on the verse from the Song of Songs. Hence wine represents the time of Solomon when the moon was always full, the time of *zivug* between *Malkhut* and *Tif'eret*. The wine at the end of this passage symbolizes *Binah*. She is the river of properly aged wine, *yayin demantera* or *yayin meshumar*, the higher mother which waters the plants from her wine.

Source 35: *Zohar* 3:40b

The final source we will cite in the wine genre brings together the wine theme with the Wisdom of Solomon and some of the recurrent motifs we saw in those passages. In particular, we saw that one of the primary weak-nesses of Solomon in the Zoharic view was his inability to balance the right and the left sides, representing masculine and feminine, eros and law, *hesed* and *din*. This same theme will be implicit in the following passage; this time however it is related to the wine which flows from its source in *Binah*.

269

תא חזי, כל יומוי דדוד מלכא הוה משתדל, (בגין) דהאי תרומה יתקשר
במשפט, ויזדווגון כחדא, (בגין דיתקיים בארעא), אתא שלמה וזוג לון
כחדא, וקיימא סיהרא באשלמותא, וקיימא ארעא בקיומא. אתא צדקיהו
ואפריש לון ואשתארת ארעא בלא משפט ואתפגימת סיהרא ואתחריבת
ארעא, כדין ואיש תרומת יהרסנה.

Come and see: All the days of King David he was making an
effort to tie *terumah* tithing to *mishpat* justice, so that they
should couple as one. Solomon came, and he united them as
one, and the moon was in her fullness, and the earth was fully
present. Then Zidkiyahu came and separated them, and the
earth was left without *mishpat*, and the moon waned, and the
earth was destroyed. [Concerning such a moment it is writ-
ten], 'And a man of *terumot* will destroy it' (Prov. 29:4).

Terumah here is *Malkhut/Shekhinah* and *mishpat* is *Tif'eret*. The *Zohar*
is insisting on the merger between the erotic (*terumah*) and the ethical
(*mishpat*).[80] When the moon is not full, when there is no *zivug* between
terumah and *mishpat*, the world becomes unjust.

Here again we see the comparison between David and Solomon.[81] David,
attempted to erotically merge *terumah* with *mishpat*; Solomon however
succeeded in achieving the *zivug*. This is the moon in her fullness.

ותא חזי, שמן לכהני ויין ללויאי, לא בגין דבעיין יין, אלא מיין דמנטרא
אתי לסטרא דלהון, לחברא כלא כחדא, ולמחדי עלמין כלהו, לאשתכחא
בהו כלא ימינא ושמאלא כליל דא בדא, לאשתכחא בהו חביבותא דכלא
ורחימותא דבני מהימנותא. מאן דאתדבק רעותיה בהאי, הוא שלים בהאי
עלמא ובעלמא דאתי, וישתכח כל יומוי דאתדבק בתשובה, אתר דיין ושמן
משתכחי, כדין לא יתדבק בתר עלמא דא, לא לעותרא ולא לכסופא דיליה.
ושלמה מלכא צוח על דא ואמר, (משלי כא יז) אוהב יין ושמן לא יעשיר,
דהא עותרא אחרא יזדמן ליה, למהוי ליה חולקא ביה, ולמהוי ביה חולקא
בעלמא דאתי, אתר דיין ושמן שריין, בעלמא דא ובעלמא דאתי, ומאן
דרחים ליה להאי אתר, לא בעי עותרא, ולא רדיף אבתריה

Come and see: 'Oil for the *kohanim*, and wine for the
levi'im'— not because they need [any] wine, but [they receive]
from protected wine [that] comes to their side, to connect all
as one, and to cause all the worlds to rejoice, to find all, right
and left, in them, one included within the other, to have the

love of all things present in them, and the adoration of the children of the faith. Whosoever causes his passion to cling to this place is complete in this world and in the world-to-come. For all his days, he will cling to *teshuvah*, the place where oil and wine can be found. Then he will not cling to this world, neither to its riches nor to its desires. Solomon the king protested against this and said, 'He who loves wine and oil will not become rich' (Prov. 21:17), for a different sort of riches awaits him for him to have a portion of it, and to have a share in the world-to-come, the place where wine and oil dwell, in this world and in the world-to-come. And whosoever loves this place, does not need riches, and does not pursue them.

Oil is *hesed* and wine is *din*. *Din*, as we discussed in the parallel passage above,[82] is love, but a very specific kind of love, from the left side, a passionate love which needs to be balanced by the love of *yamin*, which is dialogical, interpersonal, and ethical.[83] When healthy *zivug*, that is, eros, is not achieved, then one needs to fill the emptiness with the wealth and desires of this world. If however *terumah* and *mishpat* are in *zivug*, which is the time of *sihara besheleimuta*, then one can move from emptiness to fullness.

In this light, we can read our passage as follows: Levi not only needs *yayin*, he needs *yayin demantera*, properly aged wine, which is *Binah*, symbolized by *alma de'ati*, the world-to-come. What this means is that the *din* and *gevurah* of Levi needs to be connected through its source in *Binah* in order for the *zivug* between *Hesed* and *Din*, priest and Levite, *Malkhut* and *Tif'eret*, to be effective. Apppropriate *zivug*, where *yamin* and *semol* are *kalil da beda* 'integrated with each other', must draw from *Binah*, which is called *alma de'ati* and *teshuvah*. *Teshuvah* then is the stage of *zivug* of *hokhmat Shelomoh*.

Sitra Ahra

Source 36: *Zohar* 2:103

We saw above (Source 34) that the wine theme which is so central to the Judah genre is equally interwoven with the Wisdom of Solomon. Judah and Solomon are part of an overarching unified genre of *Zohar* texts. Indeed, in the following complex and daring passage, the *Zohar* very explicitly understands Judah in terms that we have already seen in the Solomon passages, that is, in terms of his deep relationship to darkness and to the other side.

This passage highlights two themes: first, the by now familiar identification of Judah with *Malkhut/Shekhinah*, and second, the relationship between Judah and *sitra ahra* and *hakal bishin*, that is, the side of evil. Indeed as the *Zohar* will teach here, the very name Judah invokes *sitra ahra*. Name, as we have seen, is a critical concept both in *Zohar* and in Lainer. Here the suggestion is that Judah participates in that dimension of divinity to which *sitra ahra* is most proximate. The passage both highlights this affinity, and understands it in a particular way; namely that Judah's affinity for *ra'* (evil) is precisely what allows him to transform the *ra'* into good. This is the integration of the *sitra ahra*, which in Lainer is represented by Judah, who does *berur* and thereby crosses over into God's side through the door of his unique *hisaron*, the *MHs* equivalent of *ra'*.

The discussion is led by the *Saba demishpatim*. The passage assumes that Ovad, David's grandfather, is a *gilgul* (reincarnation) of Mahlon (Ruth's frst husband). According to the Saba, the souls of people who die childless are essentially imperfect; for this reason, the Saba is troubled by the fact that the soul of Ovad, who was a progenitor of David, could come from the root of such a person as Mahlon, who left the world without children.

השתא אית לאהדרא ולעיינא, על אתר (נ"א אילנא) חד רב ועלאה דהוה
בעלמא, וגזעא ושרשא דקשוט, ואיהו עובד אבי ישי אבי דוד, דהא אתמר
דאחרון הוהת היך נפק שרשא דקשוט מגו אתר דא

Now we must go back and examine this, concerning one great and high tree that there was in the world, with a trunk and roots of truth, which is Ovad the father of Jesse the father of David, who is said to be the last. How could a root of truth emerge from this place?

The result of this question will be a discussion of the nature of David's soul, which is seen to be rooted in the soul of his progenitor Judah and is implicitly and explicitly the root of the soul of the Messiah.

אלא עובד אתתקן בתקונא עלאה, ואהדר שרשא דאילנא דקא אתהפך על
תקוניה, ואסתלק ביה ואתתקן כדקא יאות, ועל דא אקרי עובד, מה דלא זכו
הכי שאר בני עלמא, אתא איהו פלח ואעדר עקרא ושרשא דאילנא, ונפק
מענפין מרירן, ואהדר (נ"א: ואעדר) ואתקן בגופא דאילנא

But Ovad was restored in the highest pattern, and the root of the tree that was reversed went back to its right pattern, and rose into it and was rectified, as is fitting. This is why he is called Ovad (like *avodah* 'work'), which was not the case with other people. He came and cultivated and tilled the main part and the roots of the tree, and emerged from bitter branches, and effected a fixing in the body of the tree.

The answer is that Ovad 'worked', effecting a *tikun*, fixing the tree, giving birth to children and good deeds (the children of *tzadikim*), and therefore enabled a transformation in the body of the tree.

אתא ישי בריה ואחסין ליה ותקין ליה, ואתאחד בענפוי דאילנא אחרא
עלאה, וחבר אילנא באילנא, ואסתבכו דא בדא, כיון דאתא דוד, אשכח
אילנין מסתבכן ומתאחדן דא בדא, כדין ירית שלטנו בארעא, ועובד גרים דא

Jesse his son came and inherited him and rectified him, and bonded him with the branches of another high tree, and he connected tree to tree, and they intertwined one with the other. When David came, he found trees that were intertwined and unified with each other. He then inherited rulership on earth, and Ovad was the cause of this.

His son Yishai continued the work of *tikun*, so that when David came, he found the two trees, *Malkhut* and *Tif'eret*, engaged and entwined in each

274

other, in *zivug*, as a result of which so he inherited the kingdom of the Earth. The Aramaic word for inherit is *yarit*, which we have already seen in the Solomon passages[84] has implications of *zivug*. David himself participates in this *zivug*.

At this point, perhaps in order to highlight the full drama of the revelation which is about to take place, the *Zohar* has the Saba cry out over the turbulent and deep waters of the spirit that he has plunged himself into. The Saba, as one finds elsewhere in the *Zohar*, admonishes himself for revealing secrets which were never before revealed, then encourages himself to continue. The revelation will involve David and his relationship to the side of evil.

עובד דא אתתקן, ונפק מגו חקל בישא דגובין בישין, אתא ישי בריה ואתקין
ואעדר אילנא, ועם כל דא (ועובד) דא רזא דרזין, ולא ידענא אי אימא
אי לא אימא, אימא מילך סבא, ודאי אימא, בדא ידיעאן כל שאר בני
גלגולא. (נ"א עובד אילנא אתקין, ועם כל דא דאילנא אתקין), עובד עם
כל דא אילנא אתקין, כד אתא דוד מלכא, באילנא תתאה דנוקבא אשתאר,
ואצטריך לקבלא חיין מאחרא

Ovad was healed, and left the evil field of the evil lions. Jesse his son came and fixed and plowed the tree. Even so, these are the secrets of the secrets, and I do not know whether to say them or not to say them. [They said to him:] Say your peace, Saba, certainly you must speak, through this all the other children of the *gilgul* will become aware. [He continued:] Ovad fixed the tree, but even though the tree was fixed, when King David came, he remained in the lower tree of *nukva*, the feminine, and had to receive life from another one.

The lower tree of the feminine which the *Zohar* describes is so close to the 'Other Side', the side of evil, that it cannot sustain itself from the side of the sacred alone without being connected and receiving nourishment from that other tree.[85] David therefore had no life of his own, as he comes from such a low place, bordering on the side of evil, the abode of death.

ומה אי האי דאתתקן ואתקין כלא, הכי, שאר בני עלמא דאתיין בגלגולא,
דלא יכלין לאתתקנא הכי, על אחת כמה וכמה, דבכל סטרין אתהפך
בגלגולא, פרץ הכי הוה, בעז הכי הוה, עובד הכי הוה, (נ"א ועם כל דא
אילנא אתתקן), ובכלא נפק אילנא מסטרא דרע, ואתדבק לבתר בסטרא

275

דטוב, בקדמיתא (בראשית לח) ויהי ער בכור יהודה רע, (נ״א אונן אוף
הכי) מחלון אוף הכי, ולאו כל כך, אבל בהני אתעכל רע ונפק טוב טוב לבתר,
נפק ההוא דכתיב ביה (ש״א טז) וטוב ראי, (שם) ויהו״ה עמו, הכא קיימא
אילנא תתאה על תקוניה, ומלך אלהי״ם על גוים

And if this is so concerning one who was fixed, and who fixed
everything, then all other people of the world who come in
the *gilgul*, who are not capable of becoming fixed in a like
manner, all the more so [is this the case], that they must turn
to all sides in the *gilgul*. This was the case with Peretz; this
was the case with Boaz; this was the case with Ovad. With
all of them, the tree left the side of evil, and later clung to
the side of good. At first, 'Er, Judah's firstborn, was evil [in
God's eyes]' (Gen. 38:7), (and also Onan) and also Mahlon,
but not so much. With all of them, the evil was digested and
good could eventually come out. The one came out concerning whom it is written, 'and [David was] good-looking' and
God [was] with him' (1 Sam. 16:12, 18). Here the lower tree
stands in its place, and 'God reigns over the nations'.

The text explains that the story of Judah's descendants, Er, Mahlon, Ovad,
etc., is all about transformation of evil, so that in the end, *Elohim* can rule
over the nations.

בשירותא דכלא, מעקרא ויסודא עלאה, אשתרשו דרגין, ראובן שמעון לוי,
יהודה מה כתיב ביה (בראשית כט), הפעם אודה את יהו״ה, וכתיב ותעמוד
מלדת, היינו (ישעיה נד) רני עקרה לא ילדה, בגין דכד אתיליד יהודה, נפקת
נוקבא מתדבקא בדכורא, ולא הות על תקונהא אנפין באנפין, ולא אתכשרת
לאולדא

At the beginning of everything, the levels had their roots in a
high principle and foundation: Reuben, Shimon, Levi. What
does it say concerning Judah? 'This time I will acknowledge
God' (Gen. 29:35), and it is written 'and she stopped giving
birth'. This is [what is meant by] 'Rejoice, O barren one who
has not given birth' (Isa. 54:1), for when Judah was born,
the female came out attached to the male, and was not as
it should be, face-to-face, and she was not capable of giving
birth.

The overt reading of this unusual passage is that Judah was born as an androgyne, back-to-back, not face-to-face, and thus with no possibility of *zivug* or *tikun* and no possibility of giving birth. Luria and post-Lurianic readers interpret this passage as referring to *Malkhut* in her first undeveloped state, and in fact use it as a source text for the whole *tikun ha-nukva* (reparation of the feminine) theme which we will explore below.[86]

The simple meaning of the text indicates that this anomaly happened to Judah at his birth. The *Zohar* is basing itself on the midrashic passage which teaches that each of Jacob's sons was born with a twin sister; with Judah, says the *Zohar*, she was born attached to him.[87] Whatever the case, the identity between Judah and *Shekhinah* is clear.

כיון דנסר לה קודשא בריך הוא, ואתקין לה (ס״א אנפין באנפין), כדין אתכשרת לאתעברא ולאולדא. ובספרא דחנוך, ותעמוד מלדת לאו על לאה אתמר, אלא על רחל אתמר, ההיא דמבכה על בניה, ההיא דאשתרשת ביהודה

After God separated her, and prepared her, she was capable of becoming pregnant and giving birth. In the Book of Hanokh (Enoch) [it is written that the phrase] 'and she stopped giving birth' was not referring to Leah, but rather to Rachel (*Malkhut*), she who is weeping for her children, she who is rooted in Judah.

After the *nesirah*, she became capable of birth. The verse being interpreted is understood as referring to Rachel; who is deeply rooted in Judah, which is why she is identified in the *Zohar* as *Malkhut/Shekhinah*.

יה״ו ד״ה, ותעמוד מלדת, דהא לא אתתקנת. בקדמיתא דיוקנא דלעילא הוה כלא, ראובן, או״ר ב״ן, (בראשית א ג), ויאמר אלהי״ם יהי אור, ימינא אור (בן), שמעון, שמאלא אור, בההוא סיגא דדהבא בהדיה שם עון, לוי, חבורא דכלא, לאתחברא מתרין סטרין. יהודה נוקבא בהדי דכורא מתדבקת, יה״ו דא דכורא, ד״ה דא נוקבא דהות בהדיה

YHV DH—'and she stopped giving birth', for she was not yet fully developed. At first, everything was in the image above. Reuven (*R'VBN*)—*or ben* ('*VR BN*, 'light of the son') (Gen. 1:3). 'And God said, Let there be light'—the right [side] of light. Shim'on *ShM 'VN*—the left [side] of light, those dregs of the gold—*sham 'avon*, there is sin there. Levi—the connection of all, connected from both sides. Judah—*nukva* the female clinging to the male, *YHV* is the male, *DH* is the female that was with him.

The first three tribes are each what they are: right, left, and the combination of the two. But *Yehudah* is androgynous—*yehu* is the male, *dah* is the female.

ד״ה, אמאי ד״ה, אלא ד' אתדבקותא דרע בהדה, איהי דל״ת מסכנא איהי,
ואצטריך לאתבא בגלגולא, לאתעכלא ההוא רע ולמתבלי בעפרא, ולבתר
לצמחא בסטרא דטוב, ולנפקא ממסכנו לעתירו, וכדין ה', ועל דא יה״ו ד״ה

DH—why *dalet heh*? *Dalet* is the clinging of evil to her; she is *dalet* impoverished, she is poor, and must go through rebirth, so that this evil can be digested (recycled) and decompose in the earth, and then after to grow again on the side of good, and to go out from poverty to riches, and [then] it becomes *heh*, therefore [his name is] *YHV DH*.

Here we see highlighted again the connection between Judah and the side of evil.[88]

Judah's name shares the letters of the name of God but with one addition, the *dalet*. The *dalet*—often symbolizing '*dalat*' in the *Zohar*, meaning poor—expresses the *pegam*, the unrectified dimension of *Malkhut*. However, this dimension is exactly the Judah quality that holds everything together. Judah's *Shekhinah* quality makes room for and integrates all the dimensions. He is the fourth leg of the throne, lending it stability. *Dalet* is where evil clings to him/her, it must be transformed; it must go into the earth, and be reborn as good! Then it is reborn as the *heh*. What this means is that Judah is no less than the name of God, the *Shekhinah*, the unifying force of both his family and the cosmos.

יהודה אתה יודוך אחיך (שם מט ח), (ס״א כלהו אודן על שמא דא והיינו
וכו') היינו דאנן אמרין ברוך אתה, איהו ברוך, ואיהי אתה

Judah, you *atah* are praised by your brothers' (Gen. 49:8)—this is what we say: 'Blessed you' *atah*—he is 'blessed', she is 'you'.

Again Judah is the male and the female, but here, this unification of masculine and feminine is what we call forth when we bless God's name, *barukh
atah YHVH*, in the traditional blessing formula. This blessing subjugates
the Other Side and brings it into alignment. A radical implication of this
point is that when we say 'Blessed are You God', we are in effect saying
'Blessed is Judah, God'.

לכלהו בנוי לא אמר יעקב אתה, אלא לאתר דאצטריך, דא איהו אתה.
שמא דא (נ"א ודאי אתה) יודוך אחיך, כלהו אודן לך על שמא דא, ודאי
אתה יודוך אחיך, על שמא דא אסתלק ואתכפיא סטרא אחרא, בגין דכד
אתקרי ואדכר, הא נפקת סטרא אחרא בהדה

> Jacob did not say 'you' to all of his children; rather, only to
> the place where it was necessary, this one is [called] 'you'. This
> name, you, 'will be praised by your brothers'. They will all
> acknowledge you because of this name; certainly 'you will be
> praised by your brothers'. By this name the Other Side leaves
> and is subjugated, for when it is called and mentioned, the
> Other Side emerges with it.

When we call out and mention the name *Yehudah*, we call forth the *sitra ahra*.
This very process is what enables the *sitra ahra* to be purified and clarified:

כיון דאמרי אתה, שלטנו ורברבנו אית לה, וסטרא אחרא אתכפייא ולא
אתחזיאת תמן, ודאי בשמא דא אתרשים ואתבריר מסטרא אחרא, ודא
אסתלקו ושלטנו דילה, ותבירו וביש לסטרא אחרא

> When 'you' is said, she has authority and greatness, and the
> Other Side is *itkafiya* subjugated and cannot be seen there.
> Certainly through this name she is inscribed and *itbarer*
> clarified from the Other Side, and elevation and authority are
> hers, and brokeness and evil [come] to the Other Side.

By saying *atah*—that is, by creating *zivug* between *Tif'eret* and *Malkhut*—
the *sitra ahra* is subjugated *itkafiya* and clarified *itbarer*.

This passage is critical in that it introduces Judah's bisexual nature, and
more importantly, understands his feminine/*Malkhut* side as meaning that
he comes from the place where he is (literally) attached to the *sitra ahra*,
and that from this very ontology he derives his transformative power.

279

A Concluding Passage

Source 37: *Zohar Hadash* Midrash Rut *Ma'amar Zuhama Dehavya*

In our final source from the Zoharic genre of Wisdom of Solmon, which is messianic in intent, we return to the theme which we began, the rearranging of the letters of the Torah by Solomon. In the midrashic source we examined there, the letters successfully complain to God that Solomon wants to remove them, one by one, from the Torah. As we have noted above, Lainer's teacher Simcha Bunim re-reads this *midrash* positively as indicating that this rearrangement of letters was an intentional Solomon project.[89] The passage from *Zohar Hadash* bridges the two positions. This passage indicates that the messianic project of Solomon, whose goal was to expunge the taint of the snake (a *terminus technicus* for redemption), involved the rearrangement of the letters of the Torah.[90] This rearrangement was accomplished by Solomon through the *Songs of Songs*; according to *Zohar Hadash* this is what we mean when we say that in the time of Solomon the moon was always full.

ואע"ג דאברהם תקן מה דעבד אדם. וכן יצחק ויעקב וצדיקייא, עכ"ד זוהמא
דנחש לא פסקא עד דקיימו ישראל על טורא דסיני. ואהדרו אתוון בארח
מישר, ומנהון למפרע, חד מכאן, וחד מכאן. וכד סרחו, אהדרו בגופא
אחרא. אהדרו אתוון בגוונא אחרא. וכך אזל עלמא ברזין דאלפא ביתא, עד
דאתא שלמה. כיון דאתא שלמה, אשתכחין אתוון קיימין על קיומייהו. וכדין
כתיב, ותרב חכמת שלמה, וקיימא סיהרא בשלימותא, כדין אתגלי שיר
השירים בעלמא

[E]ven though Abraham fixed what Adam had done, and
similarly, Isaac and Jacob and the righteous, even so, the taint
of the snake did not cease, until Israel stood on Mount Sinai.
And the letters returned [to be] in a straight line, and some in
reverse, one from here and one from there. And when they of-
fended (sinned), they returned to another body; the letters to
another form. And so the world continued in the mysteries of
the alphabet, until Solomon came. Since Solomon came, the
letters were found standing in their place. Thus it is written,

281

'and the wisdom of Solomon waxed great' and the moon was established *bisheleimuta* in fullness, when the Song of Songs was revealed in the world.

The full moon in this passage represents the letters being rearranged in some way that heals the taint of the primordial fall symbolized by the snake. This did not happen on Sinai, which was apparently the beginning of the process. On Sinai the letters went in a straight line and in pairs, but when they sinned (presumably in the golden calf incident), the letters formed *gufa ahra*, another body, paralleling the use in the *Zohar* of the term *elohim aheirim*, other gods, which are the consequence of the fall of the *Shekhinah* into the *kelipot*.

CORDOVERO, LURIA, AND HASIDISM

At this point we turn, albeit much more briefly, to post-Zoharic sources which will help us map the major influences on Lainer's notion of *hokhmat Shelomoh*.

Firstly, we will look at a number of sources both from Isaac Luria and Moses Cordovero which show clearly that they received and incorporated the *Zohar*'s notion of the Wisdom of Solomon in their worldviews and teaching. The notion of Solomon's wisdom which they received from the *Zohar* was formulated by them in ways that are seemingly directly adapted by Mordechai Lainer of Izbica. We will also look at a few sources both in Luria and Cordovero which continue the theme of redeeming the sacred sparks in paganism.

Secondly, we look at earlier Hasidic teachings with two different intentions. First we shall see how different masters interpreted this tradition in accordance with their own orientation. Then we will show that within *Hasidut*, the Lurianic notion of *tikun ha-nukva*, the fixing of the *Shekhinah*, was an important theme for some of the key masters who influenced Lainer. We will focus especially upon the passage which we have already mentioned from Simcha Bunim of Przysucha. This text radically reframes the significance of the wives of Solomon, following the trajectory already found in Luria which was so greatly expanded and amplified in Izbica.

Cordovero

Source 38: *Pardes Rimonim* Shaar 22 Ch. 3

In the following passage Cordovero cites a parallel Zoharic passage to the one we analyzed from *Zohar* 1:249a (Source 20). That passage began with the image of the *Shekhinah* as a lioness and proceeded to unpack the distinction between David's *Shekhinah* project and that of Solomon, referred to as the Wisdom of Solomon.

והנה לא נכחיש כי כל ענין המרכבות הם תקוני השכינה ר"ל המלכות. ואל
הענין הזה ה' בחינות. הא' היא בחינת המלכות בערך קישוטיה ר"ל להשפיע
מהמדות העליונות שפע ולא שפע המזון ולא שפע צורך העולם אלא לתקן
הכלה שתהיה מקושטת בקשוטיה כמבואר בשער מהות והנהגה. והנה
הקישוטים האלה הם תיקונים אל הזווג לא הזווג ממש. והנה מזה הענין
והשפע הנשפע אל התיקון הזה אין ממנו עדיין תועלת כל כך עד היות הזווג
שאז תקבל השפע לזון ולפרנס עליונים ותחתונים. וזהו הטעם שהיה דוד
בעניות כמו שפי' בזהר פ' נח (דף ס"ג) בפסוק הקשיבה לישה מפני שהיו
כל ענייניו תיקונים כדי שתהיה מקושטת. ובימי שלמה היה הזיווג והיתה
הלבנה במילואה

And we cannot deny that the entire matter of the 'chariots' are adornments of the *Shekhinah*, that is, *Malkhut*. This includes five facets: One is the [state of] *Malkhut* as regards its adornments, meaning receiving from the higher attributes—not a plentitude of food, and not a plentitude for the sake of the world, but to adorn the bride so that she be adorned with her jewelry, as was explained...Now these adornments are in preparation for the *zivug*, not the *zivug* itself. There is not a great deal of purpose in this matter or in the plenty that is poured upon this aspect, until the actual *zivug*, when the plenty to satisfy above and below is received. This is why David was in poverty, as we find in the *Zohar* on *parshat Noah* (1:63), commenting on the verse 'Listen, o lioness': it is because everything [David] did was a *tikun* so that she would be properly adorned. And in the days of Solomon, there was *zivug*, and the moon was full.

285

Cordovero calls David's project the preparation for union, and Solomon's project *zivug mamash*—actual union. This union between *Malkhut/ Shekhinah*, says Cordevoro citing the *Zohar*, is what the sources mean when they say that in the days of Solomon the moon was always full.

Source 39: *Pardes Rimonim* Shaar 23 Ch. 13

Cordovero cites a Zoharic source which distinguished between two kinds of altar, an altar of copper and an altar of *adamah*, of earth. The altar, as is clear from this and other passages, is a *Shekhinah* image. The first type of altar—that of *nehoshet*—is connected to the *kelipot* and at times must nourish the *kelipot*. This it does, according to the *Zohar*, through the elongated form of the final *nun*, which goes beneath the line and reaches down, as it were, to the *kelipot*.

ומ״ש ואיהי איצטריכא למיזן לון, הכוונה כי היא נותנת מזון וחיות לכל,
לימין הקדושה ולסטרא דשמאלא. ולפי שאין ראוי לתת להם המזון הקדוש
נותן להם משמרי היין ומהעכירות כמו הם בלחמם הטמא. והנו״ן רומז
אל המלכות עצמה. ונודע כי המזבח הרומז למלכות נבוב לוחות היה והיו
ממלאים אותו באדמה. ואדמה נגזר מאדם שהוא בעלה. וסביב לה הקליפה
של נחש״ת. ועד שלא בא שלמה המע״ה היה מזבח הנחשת מטעם שהיתה
לבנה בחסרונה ולא היה הזווג אמתי כנודע. וכאשר נבנה בית המקדש של
מטה נבנה ב״ה של מעלה והי׳ לבנה במילואה והיה המזבח מאדמה כולו
[עט] להראות על לבנוניתה וכבר נפרדה ממנה קליפת התחש. והיה מלובן
בסוד הלובן להראות שכבר עברו ימי לבונה ונטהרה מהדמים ועומדת לבנה
בלבונה. וזה החילוק שבין מזבח אדמה למזבח נחשת

And as for what it says, 'she has to nourish them', the intention is that she gives food and life to everything, to the holy right and to the left side. And since it is not appropriate to give them the sacred food, they are given the dregs of the wine (yeast) and the dross, as they are with their impure bread. The *nun* hints at *Malkhut* itself. It is known that the altar indicates *Malkhut*—it was hollow, and was filled with earth. Earth *adamah* is taken from Adam, her husband, and she is surrounded by a shell of copper. Until Solomon came, the altar was made of copper, since the moon was lacking and the *zivug* was not complete, as is known. And when the sanctuary below was built, the Temple above was built, and the moon was full *levanah bemilo'ah*, and the altar was made solely from earth to emphasize its whiteness *livnunitah*, and that the skin of the *tahash* was already separated from it. And it was white, according to the secret of whiteness, to show that the days of her purification *libunah* had already passed, and she was purified from the blood, standing white (or, the moon standing) in her purity *levanah belibunah*. This is the difference between a copper altar and an altar made of earth.

Since it is inappropriate to give the *kelipot* holy nourishment, *Shekhinah*, which is the altar, feeds them from the *shemarei ha-yayin*, the dregs of wine. *Shemarei ha-yayin*, contrasts with *yayin meshumar*, properly aged wine. Yet it is the dregs which cause the wine to ferment, to become *yayin ha-meshumar* and not vinegar '*kehamar tav sheyativ al durdeya*', like good wine that sits on its dregs.

Cordovero continues with a teaching that this altar of copper which was in the tabernacle was filled with earth. Earth which is *adamah* is derived from Adam who is her husband. This is precisely parallel to the *Zohar* passage, which suggested that the altar was *Asheirah*, and that *Asher* and *Asheirah* were the divine couple of *Shekhinah* and *Tif'eret*. *Asher* and *Asheirah* are synomous with Adam and *adamah*. Of course Cordovero himself cites this *Zohar* passage on *Asheirah* and concludes, as we cited above, that *Malkhut* is indeed *Asheirah*. This is a clear precedent for Lainer's interpretation that Solomon intended to redeem the *Shekhinah* sparks from paganism, including those sparks connected with the pagan goddess *Asheirah*/Astarte to whom Solomon built sanctuaries in Jerusalem.

Returning to Cordovero and his discussion of the altar of copper, the copper indicates that before Solomon, although there was a level of *zivug*, the '*zivug* was not a true coupling, as is known'. But when Solomon's Temple was built, the parallel Temple above was built as well. After Solomon's Temple was built and the *mizbeiah*, the altar, was not merely filled with earth but was made completely from earth, then the *zivug* was perfected. Cordovero plays with the word white and moon, both from the same Hebrew root; the altar was plastered with white plaster to show its whiteness, but also in Hebrew its moon-ness. This would indicate that the altar, that is, the *Shekhinah*, had achieved a new level of erotic union with her lover *Tif'eret*. This is the accomplishment of Solomon and his Temple.

At the end of the passage, Cordovero points out that when she is drawing nourishment from her husband, that is to say when she is in *zivug*, she is called *mizbeiah Hashem*, God's altar, which in effect means the *Shekhinah* of *Hashem*. In this same fashion as we have seen, *retzon Hashem* in the *Zohar* and certainly in Izbica is a *Shekhinah* term, meaning technically the *Shekhinah* of *Hashem*, that is to say the *Shekhinah* when she is in *zivug* is called *retzon Hashem*. It is precisely this *Shekhinah* force which Solomon thought capable of guiding a person beyond the realm of law or *yamin* into the realm of *semol*, of eros which is no longer bounded by law. This is certainly how Lainer understands the *Zohar*. Although it is clear that Lainer is reading *Zohar* directly, rather than through the medium of Cordovero, it could not have been lost on him that Cordovero incorporates the core principle of the Wisdom of Solomon directly into his system.

Cordovero goes on to say that in Solomon's messianic time, the earth is purified; it is whiteness of the bride who is no longer a *nidah*, and people can therefore wear the white clothes of the holy bride, this may be an allusion to the purification of the *yetzer* of *'arayot* (sexuality), which as we saw was a theme in one of the several of the key passages in *MHs* on Judah and the desire for the unmediated embrace of *Shekhinah*.[91]

Luria

At this point we turn our attention to Luria, where we see three very clear themes that achieve prominence in Lainer in texts which could have served as his sources. In the first brief passage below, we see a clear recognition of the Wisdom of Solomon moon genre. In the second, we see what is most probably the source for both Simcha Bunim of Przysucha and Lainer's audacious re-interpretations of Solomon and his wives. In the third, the Wisdom of Solomon is given a very particular interpretation within the context of the Lurianic myth. We have a set of passages in Luria in which he identifies the Wisdom of Solomon—along with the full moon—with the process of *tikun ha-nukva*, the cosmic rectification of the feminine, which is a cornerstone of Lurianic theology.

Source 40: *Shaar Ma'amrei Rashbi* Peirush 'Al Zohar Shir Hashirim

Luria writes that the unique qualities of time which appear in Ecclesiates (written by Solomon according to tradition) are themselves the secret of the fullness of the moon.

והנה שמנה ועשרים עתי"ן שאמר שלמה ע"ה הם סוד מילוי הלבנה
וחסרונה הנמשך לה מצד הקליפה

> Now the twenty-eight times mentioned by Solomon are the secret of the filling of the moon and *hesronah* her lack (waning), which is drawn to her from the side of the *kelipot*.

This idea in Luria clearly resonates with Lainer. Fundamentally, this passage affirms the ontic identity between Solomon's wisdom and the moon in Luria.

Source 41: *Likutei Torah* Sefer Melakhim 1

One Izbica theme which has clear roots in Luria is his reframing of Solomon's relationship with his wives as a deliberate project whose goal is the redemption of the sacred sparks and their reintegration into the realm of the holy. This idea of Luria resounds clearly—first in Simcha Bunim of Przysucha, as we cite below (Source 43), and then in Lainer.

289

כוונת שלמה שלקח אלף נשים היתה לתיקון קליפת נוגה ולהשפיע בה כ"ב
עד שתחזור לקדושה והם סוד אלף יומין דחול ולכן לקח ג' מאות נשים וז'
מאות פלגשים ג' מאות נגד ג"ר וז' מאות בסוד ז' תחתונות וטעה כי עד
שיבא משיח א"א שיתקן וז"ש אמרתי אחכמה והיא רחוקה ממני

Solomon's intention in taking a thousand wives was to fix the
kelipah of *nogah*, and to influence it so strongly that it would
return to holiness—and they are the secret of 'a thousand
weekdays'.[92] He therefore took three hundred wives and seven
hundred concubines: three hundred for the three first [*sefirot*]
(*Keter Hokhmah Binah*) and seven hundred for the seven
lower ones (*Hesed* through *Malkhut*). He erred, for until the
Messiah comes, this cannot be rectified, which is indicated
by the verse 'I said I would become wise, yet it is far from me'
(Eccl. 7:23).

This passage was probably an important source for the Przysucha teaching about Solomon's wives. Solomon's project is said to be the work of the
Messiah. Though this project would seem to be extraordinarily risky, even
Sabbatean (to use the term anachronistically), Solomon here does not enter into the world of impurity, the realm of the three impure *kelipot*; rather,
he is operating in the less toxic zone of *kelipat nogah*, which rests between
the world of holiness and impurity.

Tikun Ha-nukva

In a very important set of sources, Luria significantly deepens our understanding of the Wisdom of Solomon, relating the Wisdom of Solomon directly to what Luria called *tikun ha-nukva*, the repair of the feminine. For Luria, the Wisdom of Solomon is actually a particular stage in the seven-stage process of *tikun ha-nukva*, which he outlines in several places in his writing.[93] This *tikun ha-nukva* theme was adopted in different guises by many of the Hasidic masters who were important sources for Lainer.

Luria's theory of *tikun ha-nukva* emerges from the two distinct midrashic traditions discussed in Source 8, which he freely conflates, extrapolating details from one to the other. The first source is the well-known text in the Babylonian Talmud which describes the moon complaining to God about sharing her glory with the sun. For Luria, *mi'ut ha-yarei'ah*, the diminishment of the moon, is the fundamental flaw in the cosmos which must be reversed and rectified. The second midrashic text conflated by Luria with the moon story is the story of the creation of the first, androgynous human, which is divided in two in order to be ultimately reunited at a higher level. This source delineates three distinct stages in the relationship between the first man and woman: the initial androgynous unity of male and female, which exist back-to-back in one body; the *nesirah* or separation of the male and female halves from each other; and finally, the ability of man and woman after they are separated to turn to face each other, *panim bepanim*, 'face-to-face'. These three stages, as we described above, correspond to the moon's evolution: the initial state corresponds to the state of the moon before she complains to God; this unity is broken when the moon becomes smaller as a consequence of her complaint; and ultimately, this unity will be restored at a higher level, represented by the moon in its fullness. Luria further divided these three stages into a total of seven stages, discussed below. It is one of these stages that is identified by Luria with *hokhmat Shelomoh*.

Source 42: *Eitz Hayyim* Shaar 36 ch. 1, 42

As we explained, Luria posits that in the eschaton the moon will attain her initial stature and even exceed it. Elaborating on the *Zohar*,[94] Luria tells the story of the relationship between the two *partzufim*, *Ze'ir Anpin* and *nukva*, or Man and Woman through these *midrashim*. *Ze'ir Anpin* is the *partzuf* at whose center is *Tif'eret*, and *nukva* is *Malkhut/Shekhinah*.

Eitz Hayyim, which records Luria's teachings, describes *nukva's* recovery from her diminishment, identifying seven stages, which are subdivided into the three stages discussed above, regarding the growth of the *partzuf* of *nukva* or 'Woman'—the personification of *Shekhinah* energy—in the context of her relationship with the *partzuf* of *Ze'ir Anpin* or 'Man'. At the end of the process of *tikun*, she stands in equal height to the masculine *partzuf*, *Ze'ir Anpin*. Until *tikun ha-nukva* is effected, she is unable to draw down the consciousness or *mohin* (lit. 'brains') which is hers and must receive this through the mediation of *Ze'ir Anpin*, while afterwards, she draws her consciousness directly from the great mother, from *Binah*.

In Luria's image, the degree of dependency is expressed in spatial terms. The shorter she is, the greater the degree of dependency on *Ze'ir Anpin*; the taller she is, the more she incorporates into her self and the more self-sufficient she becomes. Besides height, Luria applies a second evaluation to the level of *nukva's* growth and unfolding: the movement from a relationship that is back-to-back to one that is face-to-face. The messianic goal is for *nukva* to achieve an independent, face-to-face relationship, equal in stature, with *Ze'ir Anpin*.

The first three stages are back-to-back corresponding to the midrashic description of the androgynous human being. After *nesirah* takes place, *nukva* initially regresses back to a single point from which she grows in three successive stages, until she is once again of equal height to *Ze'ir Anpin*; this time, however, she is in a relationship to *Ze'ir Anpin* which is face-to-face. After the *nesirah*, even though *nukva* can turn towards *Ze'ir Anpin*, she cannot come face-to-face with *Ze'ir Anpin* until their statures become equal in the sixth and seventh stages. This entire process for Luria is essentially the cycle of *sihara*, the moon.[95]

A careful reading of *Eitz Hayyim* reveals that for Luria, the Wisdom of Solomon represents the sixth stage in this process. It is with this stage that Luria positions this process in historical time.

וז״ס מ״ש בזוהר אמור דקי״ב על בט״ו לחודש כי כדין קיימא סיהרא באשלמותא...וזהו בליל פסח שהוא בט״ו לחודש כי אז חזרה פב״פ עמו בבחי׳ ו׳ הנ״ל...ותיכף ירדה כבתחילה לכן אין הלל גמור בז׳ ימי הפסח

This is the secret of what is written in the *Zohar* on *parshat Emor* (3:112) on the fifteenth of the month, that then the moon is in her fullness…Such is the case on the night of Passover, the fifteenth of the month, for then she turns face-to-face with him, according to the sixth previously mentioned aspect…She then immediately returns to her former state.

Stage six, when *nukva* and *Ze'ir Anpin* achieve their first equality, is found only in fleeting moments, at least until *Shelomoh*, the time of *sihara be'ashleimuta*.

אח״כ מאז ואילך עד שבנה שלמה בית ראשון היתה בכל ימי שבתות פב״פ
בבחי׳ ו׳ כנ״ל ובכל ו׳ ימי החול היתה אב״א בבחי׳ ג׳ הנ״ל...ואח״כ כאשר
נבנה בית ראשון ע״י שלמה נתוסף עוד בה בחי׳ אחרת והיא כי בין בשבת
בין בחול לעולם היתה עמו פב״פ בחי׳ ו׳

After this, from then on until Solomon built the First Temple, she was face-to-face on all Sabbaths, in the aspect of [stage] six as mentioned above, while during the weekdays, she was back-to-back in the aspect of [stage] three mentioned above….When the First Temple was later built by Solomon, another aspect was added to her, and this is that, whether on Sabbath or weekdays, she was always face-to-face with him in the aspect of [stage] six.

Solomon is identified in this passage with stage six, in which the two *partzufim* are of equal height. While this stage is initially reached during the Exodus, it is achieved on a continual basis—that is to say not only on shabbat but also during the week—only at the time when Solomon builds the Temple, the time when the moon was always in its fullness. This, as we have seen in many sources, is the essential sign of Solomon's wisdom. Thus Solomon is identified by Luria with the state of being face-to-face; indeed it is the highest stage of being face-to-face that can be reached in pre-messianic history.

אמנם הבחינת ז׳ שהוא היות ב׳ מלכים משתמשין בכתר אחד כנ״ל לא
היתה כך לעולם עד לע״ל ואלו היה כן בבית ראשון לא היתה אומה ולשון
שולטת בנו כלל עוד

The seventh aspect, however, which is that of two kings sharing the same crown, as mentioned above, was not and will never be achieved until the future. If it had been so during the time of the First Temple, no nation or other tongue could ever again have ruled over us.

This notion of being face-to-face was absorbed by Mordechai Lainer, as we saw in volumes 1 and 2. He explictly adopts the face-to-face terminology of Luria's *tikun ha-nukva* in many different passage.[96] However, there are two very dramatic differences between Luria and Lainer. While Luria says clearly that the messianic stage, stage seven, is not accessible within pre-messianic history, for Lainer, stages six and seven to some extent collapse into each other. The sixth stage of *tikun ha-nukva* which is described as *panim bepanim*, face-to-face, is already messianic in its nature; unmediated face-to-face encounter with the *Shekhinah* is a genuine possibility within the present. There seems to be no need to wait for a seventh stage to follow it. Secondly, Lainer understands the notion of the level of face-to-face to refer not to the relationship between *Tif'eret* and *Shekhinah* within divin-ity, but to a direct relationship between a person and *Shekhinah*. Moving beyond the *kelalim* of *divrei torah* directly to *retzon Hashem* was for Lainer part of the great *tikun ha-nukva* project of Luria. Correspondingly, this project was for Luria the goal of the Wisdom of Solomon.

This is a protypical Hasidic absorption of Kabbalah, in which categories are psychologized and spiritualized. For Lainer, Luria's sixth stage is, in and of itself, messianic, with all of the radical antinomian implications that go with that, including the erotic motif of *ta'anug*, pleasure, which is a by-product of union, and access to *retzon Hashem* beyond the general principles of law. The notion of *panim bepanim* is taken out if its mytho-logical context in *MHs*. However, Lainer does not merely turn this into a metaphor, but rather he describes a living reality that can become manifest in any individual's life.

Simcha Bunim

Source 43: *Sefer Kol Mevaser vol. 1* Va'eira s.v. *ramatayim tzofim,* 15:42

Lainer received not only from the *Zohar* and Luria, but also from the teachings of those masters important to him in the Hasidic community as well. One of the most important sources for Lainer's understanding of Solomon's sin (or sinlessness) comes from his teacher Simcha Bunim. Simcha Bunim's teaching begins with a quote from the Talmud:

במדרש רבה (פרשה ו), נוח היה לו לשלמה לגרוף ביבין, ואל יכתוב עליו
(מלכים א יא) ויעש שלמה הרע בעיני ה' ולא מלא אחרי ה' כדוד אביו

In *Midrash Rabbah* (*Shemot* 6:1, Source 3 above) [it says:] Solomon would have preferred to have cleaned sewers rather than to have this verse written about him: 'And Solomon did evil in the eyes of God and was not fully after God like his father David' (1 Kings 11:6).[97]

Instead of the simple reading of this midrashic passage, in which Solomon acknowledges his folly in trying to determine the will of God based on his intuition even when it contradicts the letter of the law, Simcha Bunim cites the passage as evidence that Solomon was engaged in a deliberate spiritual project whose purpose was to be *menakeh bivin;* 'to clean out the sewers'— or literally, pipes—pipes being understood as a metaphor for the channels of effluence that Solomon sought to clear:

לפי פשוטו אינו מובן. ואמר הרר"ב זצ"ל הפירוש, כי שלמה המלך ע"ה רצה
לעשות תיקון העולם, לתקן חטא אדם הראשון, להוציא כל הניצוצות שנפלו
בחטא אדם הראשון מכל הרשעים. זה היה הכוונה בריבוי נשים, כידוע. אך
שלא עלתה לו, שלא הגיעה הזמן לתיקון זה על כן היה לו לגרוף הביבין, היינו
לתקן סתימת הצינורות של השפע מחמת מעשה הרשעים. היינו, גריפת ביבין.
שיהיו הצנורות נקיים, וילכו המים נחלים בלי עכוב. אבל לא שיכתוב עליו, ויעש
הרע. היינו, לתקן הרע בעיני ה', כי עשיה, הוא לשון תיקון. כמו שנאמר, ויעש
את הרקיע וגר, ופירש רש"י, לשון תיקון וחטא אדם הראשון נקרא רע בעיני ה'.
כי כל הגלות וכל הדברים לא טובים, המה בחטא הנ"ל. ודו"ק ויונעם לך

295

This cannot be understood according to its simple meaning. Rabbi Bunim explained that the meaning is that King Solomon, of blessed memory, wanted to heal the world, to repair the damage done by the sin of Adam, to redeem all the sparks that had fallen as a result of his sin. This was his motivation for taking many wives, as is well known. However, it was unsuccessful, as the time had not yet come for this *tikun*. Therefore, the meaning of 'he would have preferred to clean sewers' is [he hoped] to repair the conduits of divine energy that are blocked because of the misdemeanors of the wicked. This is what is meant by 'the cleaning of sewers', that the conduits be clean, so the water can flow without any obstruction. But not that it should be written concerning him, 'And he *made* evil'—it [really] means, to fix [that which is evil] in the eyes of God. For 'making' is language that means *tikun*, fixing, as it says, 'And he made the firmament', on which Rashi comments, '"He made" means He fixed'. And the sin of Adam is called 'evil in the eyes of God', for all of the exile and all things not good derive from that sin.[98]

Lainer was of course aware of this teaching and must have used it as a basis for his position that Solomon was engaged in a deliberate spiritual project that involved the violation of the law for the sake of a higher spiritual purpose, i.e. fulfilling the will of God. According to Rabbi Bunim, this spiritual project involved Solomon marrying many wives, who occasioned Solomon's engagement with paganism. This was not sin but was rather an act whose very essence was messianic and involved fixing that which is 'evil in the eyes of God', i.e the primal sin of Adam that caused the sparks to fall and be scattered throughout the universe. As is often the case with spiritual activism and agitation to bring about messianic consciousness, the reason it did not work is because it was before its time. Solomon, in fact, desired to clean out the sewers, that is to say, open the channels of divine energy that were stopped up, and allow for the free flow of divine eros throughout creation.

The Luria, Przysucha, and Izbica sources are all suggesting something else entirely from the Talmudic passage upon which this is based—that is, that a deliberate *Shekhinah* project was an integral part of the Wisdom of Solomon.

This is one of the immediate sources for the *MHs* passages describing Solomon's *Shekhinah* project, in which he marries many wives in order to incorporate the many faces of the *Shekhinah* into the holy. Lainer is more explicit than his teacher Simcha Bunim in emphasizing the feminine dimension of this project. For Lainer, it is about the *bat melekh* and the *nekeivot*, the daughter of the king and the females, who embody the essential spiritual power of the pagan cultures from which they emerge. We may, however, infer from Simcha Bunim that he also understands Solomon's project to be a *Shekhinah* project, because the phrase he uses—fixing the sin of the original Adam—is synonymous with *tikun ha-Shekhinah*.

It is also critical to note the distinction between Luria and Przysucha on one side and Lainer on the other. For the former, the *Shekhinah* project of Solomon was ultimately misguided because this is the work of the Messiah. Solomon commits the classic kabbalistic sin of attempting a spiritual project before its time, commonly referred to in the Lurianic context as *okhlei paga*, eating the fruit before it is ripe—another reference to the sin of eating from the tree of knowledge.

In Lainer this reservation about Solomon disappears and he becomes a model for the Judah archetype. In neither of the major passages which allude to Solomon and his wives does Lainer suggest Solomon was making a mistake in marrying the foreign women. For Lainer this was not only a deliberate *Shekhinah* project; it was a spiritually appropriate project.[99] This is of course highlights the recurrent messianic theme in *MHs*, which emphasizes time and again that it is possible after *berur* to fully access the redemptive quality of *'olam ha-ba* within *'olam ha-zeh*, not only in a spiritualized sense, but also in the sense of transcending the general principle of law in favor of the unmediated *retzon Hashem*, the will of God.

Other Hasidic Sources

We will now turn to look at other Chasidic sources on the Wisdom of Solomon. We will limit ourselves here to one modest objective: to demonstrate that in the period between Luria and Lainer the notion of a unique esoteric body of wisdom, referred to as the Wisdom of Solomon, was known and described in Hasidic literature. Within Hasidic texts one can discern two primary approaches to this esoteric body of knowledge. One echoes the Wisdom of Solomon tradition in the *Zohar* with all of its potentially radical implications. Within these texts the major motifs which appear in the *Zohar*, and later in Lainer, find expression. The image of the moon, Solomon's association with *hokhmah teta'ah* (which in the *Zohar* is a term for *Shekhinah*), the *yichud* or unification of higher and lower wisdom, the integration of *yetzer hara'*, and the wisdom of *benei kedem*, all resonate in these texts. The second approach is more conservative in nature and neutralizes the radical implications we find in other passages. Even in the first strain the radicalism never reaches the level of explicit expression found in Lainer. Often, as in the case of Ephraim of Sudilkov and Nachman of Bratzlav, the radical and conservative strains will appear in the writings of the same master, even in the same passage.

Source 44: *Degel Mahaneh Efrayim* Hayei Sarah s.v. o

In the beginning of this very long passage, Ephraim of Sudilkov gives a decidedly conservative reading of the Wisdom of Solomon, explaining that Solomon's wisdom is inferior because it is vulnerable to the *yetzer ha-ra'*.[100] He follows this reading, however, with a radical reading that views the Wisdom of Solomon in far more expansive terms, reminiscent of key *Zohar* passages that we have analyzed.

הגם שיש לפרש מכל חכמת בני קדם היינו מאותם החכמות עצמן של היצר הרע נתרבה החכמת אמת על דרך (אבות ד) איזהו חכם הלומד מכל אדם ואפילו מיצר הרע והבן זה ואין אנו בביאור זה כעת, ועל פי זה נבין מה דאיתא בזוה״ק כי בימי שלמה היה הסיהרא באשלמותא

299

It is also possible to explain 'from all the wisdom of the sons of the east' as meaning that through the very wisdoms of the evil urge true knowledge can increase, similar to what it says, 'Who is wise? He who learns from everyone' (*mAvot* 4:1)— even from the evil urge…Through this we can understand what is written in the holy *Zohar*, that during the time of Solomon, the moon was in its fullness…

Here Ephraim of Sudilkov (known as the 'Degel') suggests that the Wisdom of Solomon is not vulnerable to the *yetzer ha-ra*ʿ, but rather quite the opposite, the Wisdom of Solomon integrates the wisdom of the *yetzer ha-ra*ʿ and is fructified by contact with the *yetzer ha-ra*ʿ. It is through that very integration that *nitrabeh hokhmat emet* 'true wisdom expands'—alluding to the scriptural phrase *vateirev hokhmat Shelomoh*.

The Degel expands the well-known rabbinic dictum, 'Who is wise? He who learns from every person', to include the *yetzer ha-ra*ʿ. All of this, he says, is the intent of the *Zohar's* statement that 'in the days of Solomon the moon was in its fullness'. He then cites the continuation of the Zoharic passage, which talks about the fifteen generations from Abraham to Solomon, as a probable major source for Lainer's view of the Wisdom of Solomon.

In the continuation of the passage, the Degel asserts that the Wisdom of Solomon, while it might mean integration of *yetzer ha-ra*ʿ, also requires total control, *mashalah*, understood to mean control of the *kelipot*; indeed the very letters of *Shelomoh* are the same as and therefore allude to *mashalah*, dominion and mastery over the *kelipot*. This is roughly parallel to the idea in Lainer that one can only access the Wisdom of Solomon after *berur*.

ולהבין זאת כי אז היה סיהרא שהוא בחינת מלכות בשלימות כי מלכותו
בכל משלה פירוש בחינת מלכות דאצילות מושלת ומכניע כל הקליפות
דעשיה וזהו משלה אותיות שלמה...מעליונים עד תחתונים...ואפילו כל
הקליפות היו נכנעים תחת ידו והבן

And to understand this, [understand] that then the moon, which is *Malkhut*, was in completeness, for 'His kingdom rules over all' (Psalms 103:18). This means that the aspect of *Malkhut* of *Atzilut* has dominion and subjugates all the *kelipot* of ʿ*Asiyah*—this is 'mashalah', which has the same letters as

Shelomoh...[ruling] from the highest to the lowest...so that all the *kelipot* were to be subjugated under his hand.

In Ephraim of Sudilkov's conclusion, he asserts the Wisdom of Solomon is a stage of consciousness that is available to every person in every generation.[101]

וזהו ומלכותו בכל משלה שהיא מלכות שלימה ומושלת בכל כי קודם היחוד
נקרא פרוסה ואחר היחוד נעשה שלימה ובכל משלה ומכנעת כל הקליפות
והבן, וכן הוא בכל אדם ואדם ובכל דור

And this is what is meant by 'And his kingdom *mashalah* rules in everything': she is a complete *Malkhut* that rules over all. Before the *yihud*, she is called *perusah* (broken), and she becomes whole after the *yihud*, and rules over all and subdues the *kelipot*, and so it is for every person in every generation.

At the end of the passage, the Degel brings the entire conversation back to the *Shekhinah*. If the human being allows this integration of the *yetzer ha-ra*'— which gives him mastery over all the *kelipot*, he suffuses all of his limbs with holiness and fulfills the bibilical imperative 'your encampment will be holy'.

וכן היא באדם ממש כשממשיך חכמתו בכל האברים שלו ומקדש כולם וזהו
(דברים כג) והיה מחניך קדוש והיינו שכל האברים יהיו קשורים עם החכמה
הנקרא קודש ולא יראה בך ערות דבר שלא יראה שום קליפה וערוה נגד
השכינה

This is also the case with an actual person, when he draws his wisdom into all his limbs and sanctifies all of them. This is the meaning of (Deut. 23:15): 'And your camp will be holy'—that all the limbs will be tied to the *hokhmah* which is called holy; 'and no *eirvat davar* naked thing should be seen in you'—that no *kelipah* or lewdness be seen in the presence of the *Shekhinah*.

The reason that the camp must be holy is that no 'naked thing' should be seen in the presence of the *Shekhinah*. In effect what the Degel is suggesting is that a person who has internalized the Wisdom of Solomon–consciousness incarnates the *Shekhinah*, so that there is no aspect which is 'naked' of holiness. The human being, like the *mahaneh*, the encampment, becomes the place where the *Shekhinah* dwells. Here we see a soft allusion to acosmic humanism.

All of this, the Degel concludes, will be fully realized at the time of the coming of Messiah. Yet from the passage itself it would appear that this consciousness can be realized 'in every person and in every generation'. There is a pronounced tension here, also found in Lainer as to whether the consciousness of Solomon can be realized pre-eschaton.

Source 45: *Meor Eynayim* Bereishit

The early Hasidic master Menahem Nahum of Chernobyl, who was a contemporary of Ephraim of Sudilkov, also draws from the *Zohar* on the Wisdom of Solomon. In the following passage, Menahem Nahum explains the nature of Wisdom of Solomon–consciousness, citing the Zoharic passage, which we saw also cited in Cordovero, that identifies the Wisdom of Solomon with the unification of the two divine names of *Adonai* and *YHVH*. These two names for the *Meor Eynayim* represent upper and lower wisdom; uniting the lower wisdom with its higher sources is seen as the essence of the Wisdom of Solomon.

ובכל עבודות שלנו תורתינו ותפלתינו אכילתינו ושתייתינו נעשה יחוד זה וכל
העולמות תלוים בזה דהיינו יחוד הוי״ה ואדנ״י וכשהשני שמות משולבים
הוא יוד בראש יו״ד בסוף כזה יאהדונה״י דכולם בחכמה עשית וחכמה הוא
י׳ וחכמה הוא חומר הראשון של כל האותיות דבאורייתא ברא קודשא בריך
הוא עלמא

> And in all our works, our Torah and our prayers, our eating and our drinking, this *yihud* will be effected. And all the worlds are dependent on this, that is, the *yihud* of *YHVH* and *ADNY*. When the two names are combined, there is a *yod* at the beginning and a *yod* at the end, like this: *YAHDVNHY*, for 'all were made through *Hokhmah*', for *Hokhmah* is the *yod*, and *Hokhmah* is the first matter of all the letters, for God created the world with the Torah.

According Menahem Nahum of Chernobyl, it is precisely this *yihud* of names that brings about the union of the lower and higher wisdoms, which he refers to in the next part of the passage as *hokhmat Shelomoh*.

ונעשהי 'בסוף חכמה תתאה חכמת שלמה דהיינו בחינת אדנ"י הנ"ל שהוא
אלהותו יתברך שירד ונשתלשל למטה ומלובש בכל דבר שמלא כל הארץ
כבודו וכשעושה כל מעשיו לשם שמים הוא מקרב כל עניני העולם שהוא
חכמה תתאה אל החכמה עילאה שהוא הבורא יתברך המהוה כל העולמות

And the *yod* at the end becomes lower *hokhmah—hokhmat
Shelomoh*—which is the above-mentioned aspect of *ADNY*,
which refers to His Godliness that descended and unfolded
down and became engarmered in everything, for 'the whole
earth is filled with His glory'. And when [a person] does all
his deeds for the sake of heaven, he brings all the matters of
the world, which compromise lower *hokhmah*, close to higher
hokhmah, which is the Creator blessed be He that gives being
to all the worlds.

Towards the conclusion of the passage, Menahem Nahum raises the theme
of *yetzer ha-ra'* and its integration as essential to the Wisdom of Solomon.
When this *yihud* exists, the *Meor Eynayim* teaches, the *yetzer* ceases to exist
as a destructive force, for it has been integrated into the One:

כמאמר רז"ל אם פגע בך מנוול זה משכהו לבית המדרש וזהו וירא אלהים
וכו' כי טוב דהיינו שעושה יחוד כנ"ל אז ויבדל אלהים בין האור ובין החושך
הוא יצר הרע שאינו יכול להיות במקום שיש יחוד ואם לחשך אדם לומר
למה לי יצר הרע כלל זה אינו כי הלא אמרו רז"ל אלמלא יצר הרע לא הוה
חדוותא דשמעתא כי עיקר החשק והתענוג בא מצד יצר הרע וצריך להיות
כך בסוד שמאלו תחת לראשי שמתחלה צריך להיות מן היצר הרע ולכן
אמרו רז"ל לעולם יעסוק אדם בתורה ובמצות שלא לשמה וכו' דרך משל
כשיושב ללמוד מתחלה כשרוצה להתענג עצמו מן התורה שהוא תענוג כל
התענוגים נמצא הוא שלא לשמה בסוד שמאלו תחת לראשי ואחר כך בא
לבחינת וימינו תחבקני וזהו ויהי ערב ויהי בוקר היינו היצר הרע והיצר טוב
הוא יום אחד ושניהם צריכים כנ"ל

As the rabbis said, 'If this knave (the evil urge) meets you,
take him to the *beit ha-midrash*'. And this is the meaning of
'And God saw that it was good', meaning that he makes a
yihud, as mentioned above. Then 'And God separated between
the light and the darkness'. This is the *yetzer ha-ra'*, that cannot stay in a place where there is *yihud*. And if a person whispers to you saying, What do I need a *yetzer ha-ra'* for? This
cannot be, for the rabbis said, If not for the *yetzer ha-ra'*, there

303

would be no joy of learning. For pleasure and desire come primarily from the *yetzer hara'*, and this must be the case, as expressed in the secret of 'his left hand is under my head', that at first, it must come from the *yetzer ha-ra'*. This is why the rabbis said, 'A person should occupy themselves in Torah and *mitzvot* [even] not for its own sake, etc.' This is similar to a person who sits down to study. When he desires to take pleasure in the Torah, which is the pleasure of pleasure (i.e., the essence of pleasure), this is called 'not for its own sake'. This is the mystery of 'his left hand is under my head'. Only afterwards can he achieve the level of 'and his right hand embraces me'. This is what is meant by 'And it was evening and it was morning'—meaning the *yetzer ra'* and the *yetzer tov* make *yom ehad* 'one day', and both are necessary as explained above.

While Nahum's perspective is less radical then Ephraim of Sudilkov's, the basic outline of ideas remains the same. The *yetzer ha-ra'*, which is the side of *semol*, needs to be integrated. As we saw, this was a theme in the Zoharic passages on the Wisdom of Solomon. In the *Zohar* passage we read above,[102] Solomon's mistake was in thinking that the eros of the left side was sufficient and there was no longer any need for the *hesed* of the right side. Here Menahem Nahum of Chernobyl clearly affirms the necessity of both the left and the right.

Source 46: *Oheiv Yisrael* Shemot

The next passage is an exemplar of the radical strain in Chasidic interpretation of *hokhmat Shelomoh*. This passage from Abraham Joshua Heschel of Apt highlights the acosmic humanism that underlies both the Zoharic and Izbica reading of the Wisdom of Solomon. In the beginning of the passage, he states that this consciousness is part of the potential of every person in Israel. When this Solomonic consciousness is achieved, it causes an expansion of the divine consciousness; this is how he understands the kabbalistic *terminus technicus* of *gadlut ha-mochin*, expanded consciousness, which is the stage in which *katnut ha-mochin*, small mind, is transcended, and when the lines between human and divine consciousness begin to blur. Thus when it says *vateirev hokhmat Shelomoh*, 'the wisdom of Solomon waxed great', the master of Apt takes that to mean that the consciousness of God expanded.

ולכן כשישראל עושים רצונו ופותחין המקור של הנביעו עליונה. ובזה
נשלם רצון העליון ומחשבתו הקדומה. ובחי' זו נקראת גדלות המוחין,
היינו שהחכמה ומחשבה סתימא נתרבה ונתגדל. וזהו ותרב חכמת שלמה
מחכמת כל בני קדם, היינו החכמה של המלך שהשלום שלו נתרבה ונתגדל
מההוא שקיא

Therefore, when Israel does His will, and opens the source
of the higher flow, by this the higher will and first thought is
realized. This aspect is called *gadlut ha-mochin*, meaning that
wisdom and hidden (primal) thought grows and becomes
great. This is the meaning of 'And Solomon's wisdom waxed
greater than the wisdom of the children of the East'. Meaning
that the *hokhmah* of the King to whom peace belongs grows
and becomes great from that water source.

From a close reading of the entire passage it is clear that *gadlut ha-mochin*
does not mean only the expansion of divine consciousness. Rather, it also
means the expansion of human consciousness, which is by definition an
expansion of divine consciousness. This process includes in it the subjugation—not in the sense of destruction but in the sense of integration—of
all the parts of the evil, *ra'* into the good, *tov*.

These sources support our understanding of the Wisdom of Solomon as
an integrative unifying principle where the upper and lower wisdoms are
united, where the *yetzer ha-ra'*—synonomous with *teshukah* for the *Meor
Eynayim*—is integrated, where the names of God are merged and the moon
is in her fullness. This principle is expressed by human beings at a high
level of spiritual consciousness—not just by the *tzadik*—in the present.

Source 47: *Likutei Moharan* 2:91

The next passage, from Nachman of Bratzlav, affirms the integrative nature
of the Wisdom of Solomon and identifies it with the full moon. The goal
of Solomon's wisdom is indeed to integrate the higher and lower wisdoms,
the lower wisdom being the *Shekhinah*, as we have already pointed out.
However, Nachman introduces one critical caveat. Unlike the three preceding texts, which viewed the Wisdom of Solomon as democratic in the
sense of being open to anyone (i.e., any *hasid*) reaching a certain level of
consciousness, for Nachman the consciousness of Solomon achieved by
integration is the province only of the *tzadik*.

The section we quote from begins by saying that God does not desire the death of the wicked, but rather that through the *tzadik* they should be raised up to God. According to Nachman of Bratzlav, this is the meaning of the Talmudic teaching that 'when Moses died, God cried out, "...who will contend (lit., 'get up') *li* for me with evildoers?"'[103] This is part of the process, says Nachman, of tying together the lower and higher wisdoms:

היינו מי יקום ויעלה ויקשר בחינת לי היינו חכמה תתאה עם חכמה עלאה,
עם מרעים היינו שהוא מעלה החכמה תתאה מכל הרעים שבעולם,
ומקשרם להשם יתברך, ומעלה אותה לחכמה עלאה שזה בחינת לי, כי
הצדיק מגביה ומקשר חכמה תתאה לחכמה עלאה כנ"ל. ואזי מפגימת
הלבנה נעשה מלוי הלבנה

> This means, 'Who will arise and go up and join together', which is the aspect of *li*, meaning [joining together] lower *hokhmah* with higher *hokhmah*. The meaning of 'with evildoers' is that he elevates the lower *hokhmah* from all the 'evildoers' in the world, and connects them to God, and raises her to higher *hokhmah*, which is the aspect of *li* 'to Me'. For it is the *tzadik* who lifts and ties lower *hokhmah* to higher *hokhmah* as mentioned above. And then the filling of the moon is created through the blemish (lack) of the moon.

The lack in the moon is associated with evil, but it is this very lack which creates the conditions for unifying higher and lower wisdom, through which the moon is made full. All of this, continues Nachman, is the intention of *vateirev hokhmat Shelomoh*; the healing of the moon's blemish though the uniting of lower and upper wisdom. Note also that the verse he cites about the kings convening together refers to Joseph and Judah.

וזהו כי הנה המלכים נועדו עברו יחדו כד מלכים אזדמנו תרויהו ברעותא
חדא, כדין וכו' כולהו מארי דדינא אתכפין ואתעברו מעלמא וכו' כמו
שכתוב בזהר ויגש הנ"ל. ואזי הוא בחינת (מלכים א) ותרב חכמת שלמה
ותרגומו ואתרביאת סהרא דהיינו שנתמלא פגימת הלבנה וכנ"ל. ואזי
נמתקין כל הדינים ונתכפרין כל העוונות

> This is the meaning of 'For the kings have met, they crossed over together' (Psalms 48:5)—when both kings come together with one will, then etc...all masters of judgment are subdued and pass from the world (*Zohar Vayigash* 206b).

306

This is the aspect of 'And Solomon's wisdom grew', which in the Targum (Aramaic translation) is rendered as *ve'itrabi'at sihara* 'and the moon grew'—meaning that the moon's lack was filled. Then all the *dinim* were sweetened and all the sins were subjugated.

Unlike Lainer and the previous two sources, which hold out the possibility for anyone to achieve these spiritual heights, for Nachman of Bratzlav, this unification can only be achieved by the *tzadik*:

וכל זה על ידי הצדיק, שמקשר חכמה תתאה בחכמה עלאה על ידי שיחתו, שמלביש אור התורה בספורי דברים וכנ"ל

All this is through the agency of the *tzadik*, who ties higher *hokhmah* to lower *hokhmah* by his talk, for he engarments the light of the Torah though telling stories.

Nevertheless, the significance of the Wisdom of Solomon is the same: integration and unification, signified by the moon in its fullness.

We find in each of these sources the idea of an esoteric body of wisdom called *hokhmat Shelomoh*. This idea played a role in the Hasidic masters' conception of the goal and purpose of religious consciousness and the redemption. Solomon's wisdom was related to integration of the *yetzer ha-ra'* and the unification of lower with higher wisdom; the completion or fulfillment of the moon-*Shekhinah* and the unification of God's names. These sources represent one perspective on the Wisdom of Solomon in Hasidic thought. We have not focused on the opposing perspective, in which Solomon's wisdom was understood to be inferior or fundamentally flawed, since this perspective does not provide precedent for Lainer's own understanding.

As we saw in volume 2, Lainer took the concept of the Wisdom of Solomon several steps beyond even the most radical of readers. For Lainer, the Wisdom of Solomon served as the matrix for the Judah archetype, which included the notion of bypassing law and accessing the will of God directly, and the idea that *'olam ha-ba* is so accessible within our present reality that a human being can consciously experience his merging with divinity—these are the conditions for radical freedom. We now turn to Lainer's student, Tzadok of Lublin, where we find these themes amplified.

Notes for Texts of the Zohar

1 See Source 11 in volume 2.

2 See Source 1 above.

3 Not all Zoharic passages comparing Moses and Solomon share this perspective. In 3:181b, Solomon is clearly Moses' inferior, and is even regarded somewhat negatively. See below, endnote 1674.

4 E.g. Source 20 below.

5 This refers to the Talmudic legend found above, Source 8.

6 This is the first of several sources in this volume that focus in some significant way on the *mikdash* of Solomon. See also Sources 14, 22–24, and 31.

7 1 Kings 4:30 in the Christian Bible.

8 The *shekhinah* is united nightly with *kudsha berikh hu*, the Zoharic expression for the masculine face of God, the *sefirah* of *tif'eret*. This erotic union is aided and even participated in by the righteous who engage in the mystical study of Torah, particularly the members of the inner Zoharic circle itself. This genre of Zoharic sources describes a regular nightly occurrence, which is, according to the *Zohar*, part of the natural metaphysical order of the cosmos.

9 See *MHs vol. 1* Balak s.v. *ka'eit*.

10 1 Kings 5:12 in the Christian Bible.

11 See for example Tishby *Mishnat HaZohar* 1:402ff.

12 See for example Eliade, *Patterns*, 'The Moon and its Mystique', 157–187.

13 For a discussion of *binah kavu'a balev* in *MHs*, see 'The Second Quality of Will: Eros and the Will of God' in volume 1, and Source 12 in volume 2.

14 *Zohar* 3:128a.

15 For Lainer's use of the term, see, e.g., *MHs vol. 2* Ki Tavo s.v. *vehayah* (discussed in endnote 615 to volume 1).

16 Daniel 4:12 in the Christian Bible.

17 *Bara* literally means 'outside' or 'field'. However, it also suggests the word *bar* 'son' in Aramaic—i.e. 'animals of the son', or the word *bara* 'created' in Hebrew— i.e. 'animals he created'.

18 See 'The Matrix of Apotheosis' in Chapter 14 of volume 1.

19 *Mei-hokhmat* idiomatically means 'more than the wisdom', but can be translated literally as '*from* the wisdom'.

20 Note that *kedem* 'East' and the word for primordial share tha same root. The kings of Edom are interpreted by the *Zohar* as symbols of the original creation before this world. See next endnote.

21 This myth, from which Luria wove his cosmology of the shattering of the vessels, is more fully explicated by the *Zohar* in the *Idra Rabba* (3:135a–135b).

22 Compare the *Zohar* in *Sifra Detzni'uta* (2:176b): 'until they [male and female] were in balance, and they were face-to-face'.

23 Cf. the similar reading of *Zohar* 3:47b, in which greater wisdom comes through folly.

308

24 See for example *Zohar* 3:69a; see also Patai, 247–250.

25 See *Zohar* 1:149b (Source 14) and *Zohar* 1:248b (Source 18).

26 See esp. Sources 25 and 26.

27 See Source 23 in volume 2.

28 See Eisen, 'Ye Shall Be' 44–116.

29 *Lam. Rabbah* 9 and *Pesikta* 19.

30 *Vayikra Rabbah* 12:5 and *b Yoma* 69b.

31 *b Shabbat* 56b.

32 See Ginzberg, *Legends* 4:76; also n. 12 to this section for parallel and related texts. See further discussion below in the introduction to the wine sources (p. 782ff). See also on Solomon and paganism Josephus, *Antiquities* VIII 7.5, cited by Ginzberg.

33 *Pardes Rimonim* Shaar 23:1. See the related passage below, Source 39.

34 Scholar Jules Morgenstern (*Amos*) made this point in an obscure essay some sixty years ago. See also 'The Ark'. The relationship between *Asheirah*, cherubs, and later Kabbalistic manifestations of the feminine divine in the form of *shekhinah* constitutes the major thesis in Patai's *Hebrew Goddesses*.

35 See below Source 38 where Cordovero analyzes the meaning of these designations.

36 See esp. Sources 15 and 30. See also Sources 11, 14, 16, 25–28, 31, 34, 35 and 37.

37 See *MHs vol. 1* Vayeishev s.v. *vayehi Er*. See also the Jacob sources cited in Weiss 'Determinism'. The structural parallels with Lainer suggest that these Zoharic passages influenced him.

38 This source and others like it in the *Zohar* serve as a partial matrix for the Lurianic theory of *tikun ha-nukva* as being bound up with *shekhinah* beginning to receive its effluence directly from *nukva* and not through the medium of *Ze'ir Anpin*.

39 This theme would later be elaborated greatly in Luria. Since the possibility of *shekhinah* only receiving from the side of *gevurah* would be both terrifying and dangerous, Luria posited that *malkhut* received her *mohin* –at least until she had been refined through the historical process of *tikun ha-nukva*—indirectly through the *chasadim* of *Ze'ir Anpin*. See our discussion of Luria's *tikun ha-nukva* below p. 670ff.

40 These *tokfin* are the Zoharic shadow of the positive *tokfa* of the *shekhinah* archetype that became a central feature of the Judah archetype in *MHs* under the term *tekufot*.

41 This term of course also has messianic implications. The Messiah is described as 'poor and riding a donkey' (Zech. 9:9).

42 See the section 'Uncertainty' in volume 1, where we discuss the Zoharic passage cited by Lainer to explain the Binding of Isaac story. See *Zohar* 1:119b and 1:120a.

43 Adoniyahu, Solomon's brother and a rival to the crown, has been spared once by Solomon. Adoniyah then asks Batsheba to request from Solomon Avishag, one

of David's former wives, for a wife. Apparently to sleep with a wife of David would be to affirm Adoniyah's kingship over Solomon's—indeed this is precisely what Avshalom does in his rebellion (2 Kings 15 and 16).

44 An implicit acosmic humanism animates the Zohar text. My reading of this passage is that David's song is precisely what softens his inner self, which allows his *shekhinah* consciousness to expand and develop. David, by realizing his own 'inner *shekhinah*', brings the *shekhinah* herself to a state of fullness.

45 *Yamin* is specifically given this meaning in several passages below, including the next source (Source 21), and Sources 27 and 35.

46 See bSan. 20a; see also Ginzberg *Legends* 4:169–171.

47 *Maamar Omlalah Yoledet Hashiv'ah.*

48 See also Sources 27 and 35 on *yamin* as *mishpat*.

49 Also on this theme see Soures 14 and 34.

50 See *MHs vol.* 2 Proverbs s.v. *ki va'ar* (Source 11 in volume 2).

51 Though this passage is cited in *MHs* as referring to *sihara be'ashleimuta*, the actual text of this passage says that in the days of Solomon and the first Temple, *'alma be'ashleimuta*, 'the world was in completeness' and the moon was in *zivug* with the sun (which implies that it was full), but it does not use the phrase *sihara bisheleimuta*. However the intent of *'alma be'ashleimuta* in this *Pekudei* passage is used in the same manner as *sihara be'ashleimuta* to describe the nature of Solomon and his Temple.

The second passage that Lainer cites, from *Hukat* (3:181b–182a), does use the term *sihara bisheleimuta*. This passage represents a less radical strain in the *Zohar* than all the passages cited heretofore; indeed this passage ranges from reading Solomon neutrally to negatively. The text compares Moses and Solomon: Moses is *shimsha*, the sun, and Solomon is *sihara*. In the days of Solomon, says the *Zohar*, the moon rules, while in the days of Moses, the sun, which is superior to the moon, rules. The passage also implies that Solomon's level was attached to sin, stating that ומאן דאחיד סיהרא בלא שמשא עמלו תחת השמש ודאי ודא הוא חובא קדמאה דעלמא 'one who unites with the moon without the sun, "his labor is under the sun" literally, and this is the first sin in the world'. It would appear that either Lainer or the editor of *MHs* cited this passage simply because it supports the core idea that in the days of Solomon the moon ruled.

52 These are the tenets of the Oral Law that were only recorded 'outside' the *Mishnah*, though here in Lainer they stand for the entirety of the Oral Law. The word *beraita* derives from the word 'outside', *bar*.

53 See Source 6 above.

54 See also Cordovero's commentary on this passage, *Pardes Rimonim* Shaar 20 ch. 13.

55 See bPes. 50b and our discussion of Lainer's reading of this passage in the section 'Yihud Ha-sheimot (Unification of the Names)' in Chapter Fourteen, 'Model Four'.

56 The relation between shadow qualities usually kept hidden and the first Temple

of Solomon already appears in the early rabbinic literature. The Jerusalem Talmud (*ySan.* 29a) records that when David prematurely began the process of building the Temple, the water of *Tehom*, of the deep, threatened to overrun the world.

57 Jung, *Memories, Reflections, Dreams* 293–296.

58 E.g., Sources 14, 15, 17, as well as 29 below.

59 See Chapter 3 in volume 1.

60 Source 14 above.

61 See Source 16 and 23 above.

62 See e.g. *Zohar* 1:31a.

63 See Sources 4, 5 and 7. On Zoharic sources see for example Source 30 in this volume.

64 'Son of Man, say to the prince of Tyre…Your heart was exalted and you said, "I am God, on the seat of God I sat"…'

65 See *MHs vol.2* Shemini s.v. *yayin* 2 (Source 31 in volume 2).

66 'Higher sun', *shemesh 'ila'ah*, often refers to *tif'eret*; in this case, however, one could also read *sihara 'ila'ah* as *Binah* and *shemesh 'ila'ah* as *Hokhmah*.

67 To the non-Hebrew speaker: note that כל *kol* 'all' in this verse is unrelated to קול *kol* 'voice' below.

68 *Tif'eret* as *kol*, voice, corresponds to *malkhut/shekhinah* as *dibur*, speech.

69 See also Source 34 below.

70 See for example *MHs vol. 1* Vayehi s.v. *uvedam* (Source 24 in volume 2).

71 In terms of the history of ideas, this formulation is first used in *Hasidut*.

72 See Source 4 above.

73 *Shemot Rabbah* Naso 10:4; see Ginzberg, *Legends* 4:76.

74 See *Bereishit Rabbah* 5:9.

75 Abraham Isaac Kook (*Orot HaTeshuvah* 6:7) gives exactly this interpretation of the same rabbinic midrash. He explains that the significance of the tree being as sweet as the fruit is that the distinction between means and end, process and result, light and vessel, all fall away. The fundamental condition of the redemption of the *shekhinah* is that all activity is an end unto itself, and this eroticization is the redemption itself.

76 This is precisely how the *Zohar*, as read by Lainer, interprets the Binding of Isaac story. See comments on both passages in the section 'Uncertainty', volume 1.

77 We will see how this story was incorporated into the Lurianic understanding of *hokhmat Shelomoh* below.

78 See Source 44 in volume 2.

79 Compare this with the connection between a good eye, wine, and the Messiah described by Lainer (see the section 'The *Tovat 'Ayin* Sub-cluster' in volume 2.)

80 See Gafni 'On the Erotic'.

81 See also above, Source 20 and 21.

82 Source 33.

83 See also Source 25 above, which talks about oil and joy.

84 See above, Sources 9, 16, 23.

85 Luria in *Zohar Harakiya*, and those who interpret the *Zohar* in his wake, take this to mean that David, unlike those who preceded him, was totally immersed in the lower tree of *malkhut*, called in this nomenclature the world of *'Asiyah*.

86 See the section *'Tikun Ha-nukva'* below.

87 *Bereishit Rabbah* 87:8.

88 See above, Source 27, *Zohar* 1:236b–237a.

89 Source 43.

90 This *Zohar* passage is congruent with Lacan, who added to Freud the understanding that even the unconscious is ulitimately composed of language.

91 See *vol 1*. s.v. *dam anavim*.

92 This phrase appears numerous times in the Lurianic corpus, where it is attributed to the *Zohar*. It means most generally, the time of exile and the *kelipah* which dominates exile. See e.g. *Shaar Hapesukim* Sefer Mishlei 15.

93 See for example *Eitz Chayim* Heikhal Hanukva *Shaar Miut Hayareach* ch. 1.

94 *Zohar* 3:83a.

95 For a more detailed discussion of the feminine in Lurianic Kabbalah, see Jacobson, 'The Aspect'.

96 See the sections 'The Face-to-Face Encounter' (Chapter Fourteen, Model Four in volume 1) and 'The Face-to-Face Sub-cluster' ('The David Sources', volume 2).

97 Simcha Bunim quotes a different verse than the actual *midrash* uses, one which is essential to his interpretation because it includes the phrase 'did evil' *'asah ra'*.

98 *Sefer Kol Mevaser vol. 1* 15:42, Va'eira s.v. *ramatayim tzofim*.

99See Sources 1–4 in volume 2.

100 Ephraim of Sudilkov contrasts *hokhmat Shelomoh* with *hokhmah sheleimah*, 'complete' or 'whole' wisdom. Unlike *hokhmah sheleimah*, Solomon's wisdom is flawed. It is connected to the *yetzer ha-ra'* and to the passing pleasures of this world; indeed, he says dramatically, 'it is not wisdom at all'. The higher wisdom is not Solomon's but the wisdom of Torah—it is this wisdom and not the Wisdom of Solomon which increases. This interpretation is directly contradicted by the latter part of the passage which we analyze here.

101 This is in marked contrast to Nachman of Bratzlav, who while he will interpret the Wisdom of Solomon radically, also limits it to the *tzadik*, as we will see below.

102 Source 20.

103 *bSotah* 13b. The Talmudic text describes God exclaiming before the body of Moses as it is transported by angels to its resting place.

Part Two

TZADOK HAKOHEN OF LUBLIN

TZADOK HAKOHEN OF LUBLIN

Our core interpretation of the Wisdom of Solomon within Mordechai Lainer's oevre is born out definitively by an examination of the writings of Tzadok Hakohen from Lublin, Lainer's major student. The Wisdom of Solomon theme, which Tzadok clearly received from Lainer, as well as from earlier sources, is a prominent motif in his work. Tzadok Hakohen cites his master as referring explicitly to the term *hokhmat Shelomoh*. In Tzadok we find clear formulations of all the elements which mark Lainer's non-dual acosmic humanism: the Torah of the moon, the centrality of *teshukah*, a sympathetic examination of Solomon's relationship with his foreign wives, the metaphysics of name, explicit messianic motifs, nuanced engagement with paganism as a potential force of holiness, an understanding that it is possible to move beyond law to access God's unmediated will face-to-face, and a move towards integration of the darkness. All of these are recurrent themes in Tzadok's writings on the Wisdom of Solomon.

It is possible that the greater clarity with which Tzadok formulates some of these ideas, which are more obscure in Lainer, is due to the fact that he is writing himself, whereas *MHs*, as we have pointed out, is edited by Lainer's two grandchildren, who may have had an interest in hiding some of their grandfather's more radical teachings.

The passages we will examine validate our understanding that there is a clear stream of thought running through Lainer's teaching which is referred to as *hokhmat Shelomoh*. Moreover, the key dimensions of this body of thought in Tzadok are the same themes of acosmic humanism which we have shown to underlie the Judah archetype in *MHs*. It will furthermore become clear that Tzadok viewed his teacher as continuing the work Solomon in seeking to initiate messianic conciousness.

In the first source, we will focus on the thematic blurring of the distinction between the name of God and the name of man.[1] In this source, Tzadok conflates several of the key elements of the Judah archetype tradition he received from his teacher Mordechai Joseph. The themes of *rei'ah* (smell and intuition), of the Messiah, and of Solomon's deep desire to judge without witnesses, i.e. to access *retzon Hashem* without mediation, are all captured by the symbol of Solomon sitting on the throne of God.

Tzadok begins the passage by suggesting in the name of Lainer that the voices on Sinai were human voices expressing their core divinity.

דמ״ת היינו מפיות בני ישראל דאין קול בעולם זולת מה׳ מוצאות הפה ונא׳
נפשי יצאה בדברו וגו׳ שכללו כל חלקי נפשותם להש״י אז. ומצד כל כח
נפש יצא קול צעקה מיוחדת לאותו כח שהוא מכיר אמיתות הש״י ומתייחד
בו שע״ז הוא כל מתן תורה

> I heard about the voices at the Giving of the Torah, that they
> came from the mouths of the children of Israel, for there is no
> voice in the world other than the five issuances of the mouth,
> as it is said, 'my soul issued forth when he spoke' etc.—for
> they integrated all the parts of their soul in God then. And
> from the perspective of each soul's power, a singular cry went
> out through that power, which recognizes true reality of God
> and unites itself with it. For this matter is the entirety of the
> Giving of the Torah.

In the very next line Tzadok echoes the theme with which he began the passage, namely that every human being has their particular *mitzvah* which, implies Tzadok, is a function of the unique voice of every person.

ובודאי יש מצות מיוחדות שהם עצות מיוחדות לכל מדרגה שהוא עומד בה
איך להזדכך בה

> And there are certainly particular *mitzvot* that constitute
> unique advice for each level a person is at, [showing] how to
> be purified through it.

Tzadok later in the passage continues to unpack this idea in the vocabulary of acosmic humanism. The particular context is his explaining the unique nature of the Jewish people.

ע״ז נאמר ואמרו רק עם חכם ונבון וגו׳ שיודו על חכמת ישראל מצד עצמם
כענין שלמה המע״ה שהגיע למדריגה זו שביקש לדון בלא עדים (כמ״ש ר״ה
כא:) רק כענין משיח דמורח ודאין (סנהדרין צג:) שמעמיד על חכמתו

> Concerning this it says, 'And they will say, "Only a wise and
> understanding people"' (Deut. 4:6) etc., for they will admit to
> Israel's wisdom of themselves, as in the case of King Solomon,
> who reached this level, and sought to pass judgement without
> witnesses (bRosh 21b), just like the Messiah, who 'smells out'
> certainties (bSan. 93b), who relies on his [own] wisdom.

Here as in *MHs* the notion of being called by God's name is not a mere image, but a core expression of acosmic humanism.[2] The Wisdom of Solomon is expressed in his ability to bypass normative law. This ability is called by Tzadok, as it is by Lainer, *morei'ah vada'in*,[3] the ability to intuit the divine will, to literally 'smell certainty'. It is a function of the fact that the will and wisdom of Solomon and the will and wisdom of God overlap. Tzadok now weaves in the divinity of Solomon:

ורצונו שכן הוא האמת גם בחכמת הש״י לפי שנאמר וישב על כסא ה׳ הוא
דמות אדם שעל הכסא שזכה למדרגת יחידה דהיינו נקרא בשמו של הקב״ה

> This is the true [nature] even of God's wisdom, as it is written
> 'And he sat on the throne of God'—this is 'the image of man'
> on the throne (Ezek. 1:5, 26). For he merited the rung of
> *yehidah* (the highest level of soul, synonymous with divinity),
> which is the meaning of him being called by God's name.

For Tzadok, as for Lainer, the image of Solomon on the throne of God is not mere metaphor, but rather a realization and internalization on the ontological level of the *summum bonum* of religious service.

This unity between Solomon's wisdom and will and God's is what the biblical text means when it says that Solomon sits on God's throne;[4] this is what it means when it says that Solomon is called by God's name; this is the highest voice and level of the soul-*yehidah*, the place where the soul

317

experiences undifferentiated oneness with God. This is the level of acosmic humanism, described elsewhere by Tzadok as a place where there is no border, *ein lo gevul*,[5] a *terminus technicus* in Izbica for that which is ontologically real.

Source 49: *Peri Tzadik* Shemini Atzeret 38

In a second passage, Tzadok teaches that Shemini Atzeret is the day of Sukkot associated with Solomon.[6] Solomon is understood in this passage to represent the ultimate *berur* and *tikun* where all actions, even those which ostensibly are purely physical, are holy. This redemptive conciousness is then identified as being directly bound up with David and Solomon and particularly with the Temple. At the time of Solomon, the same level of *berur* was reached which in the future will be called Messiah son of David. At this level, all human action will be holy—a clear reflection of the acosmic humanism idea in Izbica. This passage is recorded by Tzadok Hakohen in the name of Simcha Bunim of Przysucha, the teacher of Lainer.

ביום השמיני עצרת תהיה לכם. ושמענו בשם הרה״ק מפרשיסחא זצללה״ה
שבשמיני עצרת הוא אושפיזא דשלמה המלך ע״ה, והוא על רמז כי תכלית
הבירור והתיקון של כל הימים הקדושים בתשובה ותפלה נשלם בשמיני
עצרת, ונתברר שכל מעשינו גם בדברים הגשמיים המה בקדושה. וזה ג״כ
בחינת שלמה המלך ע״ה, שבו נתברר כל העסק של דוד המלך ע״ה שתקן
הכל בכח תשובתו ותפלתו, כאמרם ז״ל (שבת ל.) שאמר לו השי״ת בחייך
איני מודיע, בחיי שלמה בנך אני מודיע וכו׳ כשדבקנו השערים וכו׳ ובאותו
שעה חיה היה דוד, והיינו שנשלם בו בחינת דוד מלך ישראל חי וקיים כמו שיהיה
תכלית הבירור בזה בימי משיח בן דוד לעתיד לבא

'On the eighth day, you shall have an assembly'. We heard in the name of the holy master of Przysucha, of blessed memory, that Shemini Atzeret is the day when King Solomon is the special guest, which alludes to the fact that the goal of the *tikun* and *berur* of all the holy days through returning and prayer is completed on Shemini Atzeret, when it becomes clear that all our deeds, also those that are of a physical nature, are all holy. This is also the aspect of King Solomon, for through him, the entire affair of King David was clarified, for he fixed everything by the power of his returning and his prayer. As the rabbis said, 'God said to him, I will not make it known in your (David's) life [that that sin was forgiven you], but I will make it known in the life of your son Solomon', etc. (*bShab.* 30a)…and at that moment, David 'lived', meaning that the aspect of 'David King of Israel lives and endures' was made complete in him, as will be the culmination of the *berur* in the days of Messiah the son of David in the time to come.

This overtly messianic Torah, which is so clearly connected to the Wisdom of Solomon genre, introduces important information relating to a passage we have already studied.[7] In that passage, the eighth day of Shemini Atzeret is explained in terms of moving from a back-to-back relationship with the *Shekhinah* to a face-to-face relationship. The strong association between Shemini Atzeret and Solomon here makes clear the correlation between the Wisdom of Solomon genre and *zivug 'im ha-Shekhinah*, uniting with the *Shekhinah* face-to-face.

Source 50: *Dover Tzedek* 4 s.v. *ushelomoh*

In our next source we see that the centrality of name is a consistent expression of acosmic humanism in the Wisdom of Solomon passages in Tzadok's writings. It is the source of the desire for *hitpashtut*, expansion or extension, which transcends ethics.

וכמשאז"ל שלמה ע"ש של הקב"ה נקרא פירוש כמו שנתבאר לקמן שהוא
רצה לפשט כל כך כח השם יתברך בנסתרותיו ששם אין שייך פירוד
דבחכמה שהוא נגד עולם האצילות שם הוא היחוד הגמור שאין פירוד ואין
שם רק הוא ושמו לבד ושלמה המלך ע"ה הוא ברזא דשמו שם אין רע כלל
כידוע ושם שפיר נקרא דוד עבדי ונבוכדנצר עבדי כי לשם אין מגיע הרע
כלל כידוע כי הרע הוא רק בהתפשטות

When the rabbis said that Solomon was called by God's name, it means…that he wanted to extend God's power so much in His hidden places, where there can be no separation. For in *Hokhmah*, which is parallel to the world of *Atzilut*, there is complete unity, no separation. Only He and His name alone are there. King Solomon is [patterned] in the secret of His name, where there is no evil (i.e., no separation) whatsover, as is well known. And in that place both David and Nebuchadnezzar can be called 'My servant', for evil does not reach this place at all, as is well known. For there is evil only where there is expansion.

319

At the level of Solomon, which is the level of the God's name, evil does not exist— not because it is transcended or eliminated, but because the illusion of its separation from the good is overcome. Though *hitpashtut* brings evil in its wake, Solomon desires through *hitpashtut* to extend God's power in the world to such a degree that evil is completely integrated. For Tzadok, this level of nonduality, beyond good and evil, is the level at which the separation between human and divine is equally erased. It is the overcoming of these two separations together that enables the radical freedom found in Tzadok and Lainer's acosmic humanism.

Source 51: *Tzidkat Hatzadik* 198

The next source, emerging directly from passages in *MHs*, weaves together many elements of the Judah archetype along with the underlying matrix of acosmic humanism. This notion expresses itself in many ways, including, again, the notion that the name of man merges with the name of God, as well as going beyond the principles of the law and accessing the divine will. Because of the length of this passage, we will analyze it in two parts.

The passage begins with a general statement that one who loves Torah will merit to have the Torah reveals her secrets to him in a passionate and erotic fashion.[8]

מי שאוהב את התורה התורה אוהבתו ג״כ כמ״ש בפר׳ הלא חכמה
תקרא...אני אוהבי אהב וגו׳ ומגלת לו כל סתריה ורזי התורה כמו החשוק
לחשוקו

> Whosoever loves the Torah, the Torah loves him, as it is
> written in the explanation [of the verses] 'Does not wisdom
> call?...I love those who love me' (Prov. 8:1, 17). and she re-
> veals all her mysteries and secrets of the Torah to him, just as
> 'what is desired is for the one who desires it'.

The same is true of the one who loves Israel, Tzadok will go on to say. This love itself engenders a radical empathy bordering on a kind of merging that reveals to Aaron the secrets of the all the souls of Israel.

It is as this point that Tzadok introduces the mystical notion of name. All the secrets of the world were revealed to Aaron by asking the *urim vetumim* (objects in the breastplate of the High Priest used for divination).

320

Usually it is understood that the name on the breastplate would in some way give an indication of the deep hidden truth needed to respond to the query. Tzadok Hakohen however, in agreement with his teacher, writes that the names of all Israel were engraved on Aaron's heart, thus he would feel a *belitah belev*, literally 'a protrusion in the heart', but more accurately a deep response which revealed the secret of the heart of the Israelite who came to the priest with questions. The name is the vehicle of revelation, for the name, writes Tzadok, is connected to the source *ma'aleh ma'aleh* at the height of divinity.

כי השם הוא שורש כח חיות נפשו במקורה ומקום אצילותה למעלה מעלה. וללב אהרן האוהב ישראל גלויים סודות כל הנפשות בשרשן. ועי״ז מתגלין לו כל חללי עלמא שהיו שואלין באורים ותומים והאותיות בולטין פי׳ שיש בליטה בלב להאוהב ישראל ע״י שמות בני ישראל לדעת רצון הש״י בהנהגת העולם דבר בעתו בכל דור ודור, שע״ז מורין נפשות ישראל שבכל דור הכלולין במקורן שמות האבות ושבטים החקוקים בצירוף תיבות שבטי ישורון

For the name is the root power of the life force of his soul in its source, and the place where it is emanated high high above. All the secrets of the roots of all the souls are revealed to Aharon, who loves Israel. In this manner all the spaces of the world would be revealed to him, for they would ask of the *urim* and *tumim*, and the letters would protrude. This means to say that there is a protrusion in the heart of he who loves Israel by means of Israel's names, to know God will in the conduct of the world, according to its time, in every generation. This matter teaches concerning the souls of Israel that in every generation included in their source the names of the patriarchs and the tribes that are engraved by combinations of the words of the tribes of Jeshurun.

It is this connection to the source *ma'aleh ma'aleh*, high above in divinity which allows *hanhagat ha-'olam* to be known in every time, for every person and in every generation.[9]

Now we arrive at the crux of the passage. Tzadok, in Lainer's name, sets up a distinction between Judah, that is, the Judah archetype, and the other tribes. The other tribes can either activate or not activate the ability to love; if they love then there is a level of merging with the other or with

Torah, and if they do not love then that level of merging does not take place. However, Judah is by his very essence merged with God. This is first and foremost expressed by the fact that Judah is called by the name of God, indicating that love of God and the consequent merging with God is *kavu'a*, fixed, a part of Judah's essence.

משא"כ יהודה שנקרא ע"ש של הקב"ה כמ"ש בסוטה (י) כי אהבת...
הש"י קבוע בו וכמו ששמעתי כי מי ששונא הנבחר משבט יהודה נק' שונא
ה' וכן נקראו שונאי דוד המע"ה משא"כ בשאר בשבטים כל א' כפי מעלתו
משבט יוסף השונאו נקרא שונא צדיק ומגד שונא תם ומלוי שונא ישראל כך
שמעתי. ולכן נקראו ישראל על שמו (כמ"ש בר"ר צח). וא' במגילה (יג) כל
הכופר בע"ז נקרא יהודי

Judah, on the other hand, is called by God's name, as it is written in *bSota* (10b), for God's love is *kavu'a* permanent in him. As I heard: Whoever hates the chosen one of the tribe of Judah is called 'enemy (lit., hater) of God', as the enemies of King David were called. This was not the case with the other tribes, where each one was called by his exemplary attribute. For the tribe of Joseph, his enemy was called 'enemy of the *tzadik*'. Of Gad, 'enemy of the unblemished one', and of Levi, 'enemy of Israel'—so have I heard. Israel is therefore called by his (Judah's) name (*Bereishit Rabbah* 98), and [this corresponds to what is] said in *bMegilah* (13a): 'Whosoever rejects idolatry is called a *Yehudi* (lit., a Judah-ite, i.e., a Jew)'.

To hate Judah says Tzadok is to hate God, because in some sense they are one and the same. *Shem* we have already seen in Lainer needs to be understood on two levels which are ultimately two facets of one prism. On the first level *shem* name refers to the name of God. On the second level it refers to the name of the person, in a very specific way. *Shem* is the unique story or soul print, in Lainer's nomenclature the unique *helek* and *shoresh*, of a person's soul. It is through deeply understanding that uniqueness, the *perat nefesh*, that a person can transcend *kelalei divrei torah* and touch *peratei divrei torah*, or what is generally referred to in Tzadok's writings as 'aveirah lishmah'.[10]

Source 52: *Tzidkat Hatzadik* 198–9 (part 2)[11]

Returning to the passage, Tzadok follows his teacher Lainer in asserting that the Talmudic statement in *Yoma* which says Judah cannot decide *hilkhata*, the law, refers only to the classical normative law, or what is referred to in Izbica as *kelalim*. However, Judah, about whom it says *mehokeki Yehudah*, is connected to *hukah*, which Tzadok identifies with the essential order of creation. This order is beyond law and governs the world.

לכן אמרו שם ביומא דגם בו נא' יהודה מחוקקי רק דלא מסיק כו' דודאי
המשפט מדה כנגד מדה הש"י מגלה לו סתריו אלא דזה אינו אליבא
דהלכתא פי' לשון הלכה היינו מלשון הכתוב זה הדרך לכו בו. ולענין הנהגת
העולם אמרו בב"מ (נט) לא בשמים היא ואין משגיחין בב"ק (ושם פו)
נחלקו במתיבתא דרקיע הקב"ה אומר כו' כי תושב"כ מן השמים נקרא
חקה חקקתי גזירה גזרתי כו'. וכן הבריאה דהוא מעשה הקב"ה נקרא חוקות
שמים וארץ וכן יהודה מחוקקי נתגלו לו חוקות הקב"ה

Tzadok suggests that only the oral law that is given over to the sages—concerning this oral law it says in the classic Talmudic passage, 'It is not in heaven'. However the written law, like the very order of creation, like *hanhagat ha-'olam*, is given over to Judah, who is *mehokek*, who is the perpetual lover of God and who therefore participates in the divine root of being.

At the climax of the passage, Tzadok cites the Talmudic case called *taku'a*. First, an explanation of this case of *taku'a* is in order. The source is a passage in *Tosefta*, where the issue is the prohibition of yoking a horse and a donkey or leading together on one rope.[12] The question at stake is, if the Torah prohibits using a horse and a donkey together, can one use a *pirdah*, which is the offspring of a horse and a donkey? The rabbis cites evidence from the biblical story of Adoniyahu's attempt to supplant his father David as king. Bathsheba together with Nathan goes to David to entreat him to crown Solomon as king. David grants their request and tells them to put Solomon on a *pirdah* (1 Kings 1:32–38).

The rabbis take this as proof that it is permitted to ride on or use a *pirdah*. To this suggestion, the *Tosefta* offers a response: *'Ein meishivin mitaku'a*, that is we can not learn from this story of Solomon riding on David's *pirdah* instructions what the law should be. We cannot learn from *taku'a* simply means that this is an exceptional case and for whatever reason it is not a model.

The *Tosefta* however responds to this rejection of David and Solomon as model by saying: 'David did that which was right in the eyes of God', i.e, David and Solomon and the case of *taku'a* are a model and need to be so considered.

At this point we turn to Tzadok himself, who cites this case and explains it in very dramatic terms. The whole point of the David and Solomon model is that it is based on a radical affirmation of *ratzon*. *Ratzon* even and perhaps especially when 'it has no *ta'am* reason at all' is an expression of *retzon Hashem*. This is the meaning according to Tzadok of the verse in Ecclesiastes, 'All that I have desired you have not held back from me' (Eccl. 2:10), which is explained by Tzadok to mean that Solomon's will was virtually identical with the divine will. Both of them are beyond reason, and human will can similarly be a commanding force, even (or especially) when it moves to nullify the law.

וכד״ש בתוספתא הובא בתוס׳ חגיגה (ב) על דוד ושלמה המע״ה אין למידין
מתקוע, שהוא עשה שלא כהלכה בלא שום טעם רק מפני שרצה בכך וסמך
על מה שהוא רוצה כך הוא אמיתות רצון הש״י ואין בו עבירה. ואע״פ שאין
בו שום טעם כי אין טעם לרצון וכמ״ש כל אשר שאלו עיני לא אצלתי וגו׳ אף
להפר תורה

Now Tzadok brings all of the sources together. The midrashic sources, which have Solomon sitting on God's throne, are for Tzadok and Izbica clear expressions of acosmic humanism; this is the matrix which allows Solomon to judge from his heart, *dinin shebelev*, without witnesses or appropriate warning; that is to say without the benefit of normative law.[13]

הגם שלא ידע טעם שיש בו עת לעשות לה׳ רק חוקה וכהלכתא הלכה
למשה מסיני בלא טעמא זה אינו מסקנא והלכתא להנהגת העולם ולכן
אמרו (ר״ה כא סע״ב) בקש שלמה המע״ה לדון בלא עדים והתראה. וכטעם
וישב על כסא ה׳ והרי על כסא ה׳ יושב הקב״ה רק האהבה הוא הדביקות
באותו דבר. ומי שאוהב התורה וישראל דבוק בהם ומי שאוהב הקב״ה שע״ז
יסד שלמה המע״ה כל ספר שה״ש הרי דבוק בו עד כביכול והיו לבשר אחד

All of this emerges from the fact that Solomon has attained a level of *deveikut* with God, symbolically becoming 'one flesh', *basar ehad*—a reference to Solomon's *zivug 'im ha-Shekhinah*, which was the underlying motif of the many of the Wisdom of Solomon passages in the *Zohar*.[14]

'Solomon was *taku'a*', says Tzadok, which he explains means that Solomon had arrived at the level of the Messiah and was able to violate the law. This immanent messianic state allowed Solomon to violate the law and ride on the *pirdah*. Similarly, Rabbi Yehudah Hanasi, who was descended from David and thus participates in the Judah archetype, also raised *pirdot*, according to Tzadok, to actualize his messianic conciousness.

ושלמה המלך ע"ה היה תקוע. פירוש תקוע עצמו לדבר הלכה לומר אני
ארבה ולא אסיר שחשב שכבר הגיע למדרגת משיח ולכן רכב על הפרידה
וכן רבי דאתי מדוד גידל פרדות לבנות והגם דהוא מלאך המות כנ"ל דזה
נקרא מיתה. מכ"מ הוא גידל והיי' דבר זה להעלות מדרגה זו גם כן כמו
שכתוב בפר' חלק אי מן חיי' ר' שמ' שהוא מדרגת משיח באותו דוד. והיינו
כי מדת שלמה המלך ע"ה הוא בהתפשטות חמודות עולם הזה כי היה אור
בהיר לפניו איך בכל מתפשט עצמות אלקותו ית' והכל נמשך מאמיתות
רצונו

He concludes the paragraph by saying that Solomon incarnated *hitapashtut*, the expanded conciousness which suffuses everything with *'atzmut Elokuto*, the essence of divinity, all of which derives from the clarity of true will which is divinty.

Source 53: *Dover Tzedek 4 s.v. veRabi Eliezer*

The notion in *MHs* that *hokhmat Shelomoh* is the matrix of the core notion that one can bypass general principles of law and access God's will resonates clearly in Tzadok.

וגם נגד התורה יש כח ביד חכמים למיגדר מילתא כטעם עת לעשות לה'
וזהו רק מצד החכמה ולא מצד הנבואה והוא מטעם כנ"ל כי בנבואה אי
אפשר להשיג יותר ממה שהשיג משה, ולכן אין קו' על מה שאז"ל (ילקוט
ישעי' ק נב) ע"פ ירום ונשא ממשה רבינו ע"ה והרי התורה לא תשתנה
ולעולם יהיה כתוב ולא קם נביא כמשה וז"ל אמרו בר"ה (כא סעב:) אבל
במלכים קם. פירוש מצד השגת המלכות כמשאז"ל (מגילה טו עא) על
ותלבש אסתר מלכות שלבשתה רוח הקודש שמצד רוח הקודש יוכל להיות
יותר והיינו מצד החכמה חכמת שלמה ולא מצד הנבואה

Here Tzadok is clear that *hokhmah* in the sense of *hokhmat Shelomoh* overrides even the prophecy of Moses which in this passage stands for the general principles of law. For the Wisdom of Solomon, teaches Tzadok, accesses *Malkhut*, unmediated *Shekhinah*, which reveals the will of God which is specific to the person and the time. When this happens, continues Tzadok, the possibility of *matir 'asurim*, that God can untie those that are bound up, that is to say, make the forbidden permitted, becomes real. This, according to Tzadok (in a curtailing of his teacher's radicalism)

325

does not happen until the future time, the time when we will no longer be in *ahorayim*, in relationship to the 'back' of divinity, but will be face-to-face with divinity. Indeed Tzadok cites here a classic biblical text which is a mantra-like rubric of the *tikun ha-nukva* genre in Hasidic thought, *nekeivah tesoveiv gever* 'the feminine will encircle the male' (Jer. 31:21), indicating the emergence of the divine feminine. This is the place where Solomon will surpass Moses.

וכנ״ל דאחורייים אין מבורר אף על פי של רבי עקיבא היה תוקף, מ״מ
אינו מבורר עד לעתיד, שאז אז״ל הקב״ה מתיר אסורים שתוגמר הנסירה
להיות אפין באפין ותהיה החכמה מבוררת שהיא חכמת השם יתברך ולא
מאחורייים, ואז יהיה חדשה דנקיבה תסובב גבר ותתעלה חכמת שלמה
למעלה במקום החכמה עילאה למעלה ממדרגת משה כטעם וירום ממשה

All of this of course, as Tzadok makes clear in many passages, is a function of acosmic humanism, which is the very essence of the Wisdom of Solomon, in which the borders between man and God are effaced so that man incarnates divine will. It is acosmic humanism which moves Solomon to want to bring everything under the realm of holy, or, more accurately, to clarify conciousness sufficiently so that one will realize that everything is already included in the holy.

Source 54: *Tzidkat Hatzadik* 249

As we might expect, the key themes of *teshukah* and the moon in her fullness are central to Tzadok's understanding of the Wisdom of Solomon.

ולכך שלמה המע״ה דבימיו סיהרא באשלמותא ולא הי׳ שום מונע נא׳
ככלות וגו׳ כל חשק שלמה וגו׳ שכל חשקו הי׳ נשלם ומובא לו. והוא הי׳
בתוקף החשק מכל הנבראים שע״ז חיבר שה״ש וכפי תוקף התגברות כח
החשק כך הוא משיג. כי החשק נקרא סוף מעשה שהוא מסיט ׳דנוק ומצד
החסרון הוא חושק למילוי והוא דבוק במחשבה תחלה וראשית מחשבת
הש״י שממנו שורש כל ההשפעות

Like his teacher Lainer, Tzadok is explicit in linking the Wisdom of Solomon with *teshukah* and *cheshek*. This *teshukah* derives from the side of *nukva* and it is the animating vitality of Solomon's wisdom. Tzadok then goes on to link *teshukah* and *hisaron*. Deep desire emerges from *hisaron*, from lack. Only if you understand your *hisaron* very deeply can you connect to the *teshukah* that upwells from it. This desire is not just a means, but an end: 'For desire is *sof ma'aseh* "the end (goal) of action"…and it at-taches to *mahshevah tehilah* 'the first thought', and the beginning of thought is God'. In terms of the symbol of the moon, the moon's state of lack is the state of *hisaron*, while the fullness of *teshukah* that comes from the *hisaron* is the moon in her fullness.

He completes the passage by attributing this Torah of *teshukah* to his teacher Lainer.

וכן מסט' דרע כאשר אין דבר מונעו .וכמו ששמעתי על שישק מלך מצרים
נקרא כן לשון תשוקה מצד עוצם תשוקתו להשיג רכוש דשלמה המע"ה
מצד זה עלתה בידו בימי רחבעם שכשהי' קצת חטא בישראל שלא הי' מדת
המשפט מעכבתו

According to Lainer ('as I heard'), Shisak the king of Egypt, whose very name means *teshukah*, was able to attain part of the property of Solomon because of his great desire for that attainment. The desire itself was a prime cause in its fulfillment.

Source 55: *Mahshevot Harutz* 20 s.v. *vekol*

This theme that *teshukah* is core to the Wisdom of Solomon is a recur-rent motif in Tzadok's writings. In the context of a passage discussing the metaphysical affinity between Ahasuerus of the Purim story and Solomon, Tzadok's discussion of *teshukah* leads him to Solomon's attempt to include pleasure (a corollary to desire in Lainer), within the realm of the holy. This Solomon sought to accomplish, at least in part, through his mar-riage to many wives. Tzadok—again in the wake of his master—is clear in understanding Solomon's marriage to the foreign women as being part of Solomon's deliberate *Shekhinah* project. At the end of this passage, Tzadok makes it clear that Solomon's project is attempting to reach, in Solomon's own time, full messianic consciousness.

כי הם תענוגי עולם הזה וגם לשלמה המלך ע"ה היה תענוגי עולם הזה ועושר
וכבוד של עולם הזה שלפי שעה שאינו קיים לעד. ודבר זה קלט ממלכי או"ה
שכבש דרך שלום. וזהו מהתחברות דנשים נכריות שחשב לתקן הכל שלא
יהיה מציאות לרע כלל כמו שעתיד להיות על ידי החוטר מגזע ישי דגר זאב
עם כבש

327

Solomon wants to bring everything into the holy; his model is himself. Just as he was able to realize acosmic humanism in his own person, he was convinced he could reveal the core divine identity of all of reality. This is what Tzadok refers to as Solomon's peaceful conquest of the world. This he refers to as *it'hapkha*, a classic term whose early sources date back to the *Zohar*, meaning the transformation of all that seems mundane and even ostensibly evil, in a way that reveals its innately sacred essence.

ושלמה המלך ע"ה חשב שיוכל להכניס הכל לקדושה כמו שהכניס כל
תענוגיו וחמדות גופו לקדושה כך יכניס כל הכחות הזרות שבכל העולם כולו
כשראה שנכבשו כולם ת"י בלא מלחמה רק על ידי לאתהפכא

At this juncture Tzadok moves in the direction implied in the *Zohar* and made explicit in Luria and Simcha Bunim. Solomon was ahead of his time. The world was not yet ready for the ultimate *tikun*, healing and fixing.

אבל עדיין לא הגיע זמן לתקן כל העולם כולו ועל ידי כן נשיו הטו את לבבו.
אף דלא פעלו חס וחלילה שום שינוי בלבו מכ"מ פעלו הטי' מה על ידי
שהיה"ל נטיי' לאהבתם כדי לתקנם ולא עלתה בידו מכ"מ היה בו נטי' של
אהבה לסט' דרע שלא נתקן עדיין

What is notable is that in Lainer this moment is only barely hinted at: 'When the Temple was completed, Solomon thought that *higi'a ha-'eit* the time had already come'.[15] Tzadok unlike Lainer, also suggests that Solomon sins, but reads his sin in the most understated of ways: 'his wives turned his heart, even though they did not work any change of his heart, God forbid'

Source 56: *Mahshevot Harutz* 20 s.v. *ve'azharta*

Tzadok expands his understanding of Solomon's marriage to many wives as a function of his acosmic humanism in the following passage, which begins with an explicit statement that Solomon's 'no-boundary consciousness' was the core both of his *Shekhinah* project and his marriage to the daughter of Pharoah.

ואזהרת לא ירבה לו נשים הוא פן יסורו את לבו הוא חשב דכפי רוחב לבו
דא"ל גבול אי אפשר להסיר כלל ובמצרים היה כל ג' אלו מצד הקלי" והרע
וע"ז נשא שלמה בת פרעה שחשב להכניע ולהכניס גם אותן כחות שמצד
הרע אל הקדושה. כי אין לך שום דבר רע שאין בו איזה צד כל דהוא לטוב
וזהו הני"ק שבו כשכשמעלין אותו להשתמש בו מצד הטוב הוא נכנס
לקדושה ונתבטל הרע מהעולם

328

The mistake Solomon made, continues Tzadok, was that his drive to include the pagan in the holy cannot be applied to idolatry, which is death. However in a paradoxical move typical of Tzadok, he suggests that Solomon wanted to revive the dead, and thus include even idolatry in the realm of the sacred.

אבל זהו בשאר דברים חוץ מע״ז דעכ״א סנהד׳ צ׳ א׳ בכל אם יאמר לך
נביא עבור על דברי תורה שמע לו חוץ מע״ז. כי בכל דבר יש מציאות
שיהיה צורך לכבוד שמים לפעמים לעבור על דברי תורה לצורך שעה דעז״נ
עת לעשות לה׳ הפרו תורתך וזהו מצד מציאות איזה צד טוב פעמים בכ״ד
רע. אבל בע״ז זה אינו כן שנק׳ מתים שאין בו שום ני״ק. ושלמה המלך ע״ה
חשב בכח חכמתו בתורה יוכל להכניס חיות גם במתים וכעין תח״ה דלעתיד
שהוא על ידי טל תורה דמחי׳ אותם כמו שכתוב סוף כתובות

In the next paragraph he again suggests that Solomon was mistaken—after all, not everyone merits resurrection.

וכפי הנראה ודאי באמת בת פרעה וכן שאר אותם נשים נכריות שזכו לידבק
באותו גוף קדוש דשלמה המלך ע״ה לא על חנם היה. ומסתמא היה בהם
איזה ני״ק שמחמתו הי״ל איזה שייכות לו אלא שהיה משוקע עדיין בתכלית
עומק דרע עד שלא היה אפשר להוציאו אז עדיין ואכלו פגה

At the end, Tzadok concludes that Solomon could not have been so dramatically wrong, and that there must be some core life, even in idolatry, which invited Solomon's attempt to redeem it. However, Tzadok concludes, Solomon was eating unripe fruit, for the world was not yet ready to rise.

Source 57: *Dover Tzedek* 4 s.v. *vehineih*

Integration of the fallen is a key theme in Tzadok's Solomon passages, as we see from the following text concerning the integration of *hokhmah hitzonit*. In particular, the Wisdom of Solomon raises and integrates the fallen sparks of Nebuchadnezzar. Concerning the holy sparks that fell, he writes:

שביררו מחכמה הנפילה דתורה שבעל פה שהיה ביד נבוכדנצר והעלוה
למקורה שהוא חכמת שלמה דטיפי שלמה המלך ע״ה לא נטו לחוץ על ידי
המסירת נפש למיתה כידוע בסוד נפילת אפים שעל ידי זה יוכל להעלות גם
מה שאין לו רפואה ותיקון על ידי זרע דמעלי שאמרו מלאכי השרת כו׳ ולא
הניחו להקב״ה שרצה להוציא אותו שורש מזרעו ממש שבזה היה תיקון

נגלה לשורש שלמה הגנוז בתוכו עד שלא יכלו אנשי כנסת הגדולה לטעון
נגדו

The sparks of fallen wisdom, which were 'in the hand of Nebuchadnezzar', are raised up to their sourse, which is the Wisdom of Solomon. Tzadok explains that 'by means of this it is possible to raise up even what has no possibility of healing or repair'. Nebuchadnezzar is of course a Solomon shadow figure in this passage. We similarly find Tzadok treating Hiram as a shadow figure of Solomon.[16] Lastly, we find that the Wisdom of Solomon is specifically defined by the integration of what is below it, hence it is called 'lower wisdom'.[17]

As we have seen, all of the important motifs which we have identified with the Wisdom of Solomon in *MHs* appear in Tzadok Hakohen's writings, often with greater clarity, and always in very clear relationship to the teachings of his master, Mordechai Joseph Lainer.

330

Notes for Tzadok Hakohen of Lublin

1 The end of this passage is also discussed in volume 1, in the section 'All is in the Hands of Heaven: A Humanist Agenda' in Chapter 9. We also analyzed a closely related segment of this same passage in the section 'Moses, Uniqueness, and Prophecy: A Radical Reading of Revelation' in Chapter 4.

2 See 'Called by the Name' in Chapter 9 of volume 1.

3 See cluster 2 in volume 2.

4 This theme is recurrent in Tzadok's writings. See also *Mahashevet Harutz* 20 s.v. *zeh*

5 See *Mahshevot Harutz* 20 s.v. *vekol*, as well as s.v. *vehineih*.

6 An allusion to this idea is already found in the Zoharic passages we learned in relation to Wisdom of Solomon. We saw in them that Bathsheba was seven and that Solomon, who is the son of Bathsheba, was implicitly identified as eight. Here again Solomon is identified with eight which is the eighth day of Sukkot, Shemini Atzeret. See Source 15 in this volume.

7 *MHs vol.* 2 Likutim Pinhas s.v. *bayom ha-shemini* (originally from *Sod Yesharim* Shemini Atzeret 18 s.v. *uvei'ur*, Source 21 in volume 2).

8 Cf. *Zohar* 2:99a–b.

9 The idea implicit in this passage of there being three arenas of revelation—the time, the person and the generation—is explicated several times in *MHs*. See for example *vol.* 1 Masei s.v. *kein mateh* 2, where Lainer gives his classic understanding of the relationship between the general principle of Law and personal revelation which accesses *retzon Hashem* beyond law, discussed in volume 1 in the section 'Freedom and Law'.

10 The term itself rarely appears in *MHs* and appears often in Tzadok. In Lainer the term does not appear because, ultimately, there is no *'aveirah*. Tzadok, unlike his teacher, seems to suggest that although the act is enjoined it still contains a dimension of sin which requires atonement. In this sense Tzadok, at least in terms of the Solomon genre, more accurately reflects the sensibility of earelier Zoharic sources which remain highly attracted and yet ambivalent towards Solomon. Lainer broke through that ambivalence and embraced the Solomonic model. Of course, even Lainer only applied this model to a human being who finished the difficult and almost super-human process of *berur*.

11 The remainder of the Tzadok passages are given in Hebrew and explained without being translated.

12 *tKelayim* 5:4.

13 For Lainer's use of this source see *MHs vol.* 2 Proverbs s.v. *ki va'ar* (Source 11 in volume 2).

14 See Sources 10–13 in this volume.

15 *MHs vol.* 2 Ki Tisa s.v. *elohei maseikhah* 1 (Source 4 in volume 2).

16 *Divrei Sofrim* Likutei Amarim 8 s.v. *usheloshah* and *Likutei Ma'amarim* 55b (also found in *MHs vol.* 2 Likutim s.v. *shama'ti*).

17 *Divrei Sofrim* Siyum Hashas s.v. *veyadu'a*. See also *Tzidkat Hatzadik* 249, where Tzadok suggests that the integration of *hokhmah hitzonit* was a particular stage in the unfolding of *hokhmat Shelomoh*. With the writing of Proverbs Solomon moved beyond this stage and no longer had need of *hokhmah hitzonit*.

INDEX-Selected Topics

acosmic humanism, synonymous with
  wisdom of Solomon xxv, 3, 43,
  66, 181
  activism 68, 80
  called by God's name 317
  as chauvinistic 5
  contemporary theological relevance
    reclaimed 5
  and David 87, 90, 94, 176
  David and Solomon 83, 90
  ein lo gevul (place where there is no
    border) 318
  freedom, radical 320
  hitpashtut (expanded conscious-
    ness) 178, 304, 319
  individualism, radical 91, 92, 94
  integration of darkness 315
  it'hapkha (transformation of all to
    reveal its sacred essence) 328
  Judah archetype 3, 178, 247, 315,
    320
  kingship motif 249, 261
  messianic motifs 181-4, 242, 255,
    315, 324, 326
  and *mikdash* 97
  the moon 117, 155, 315
  Moses and Solomon 56-7
  name, metaphysics of 72, 82, 87,
    91, 95, 237, 319-20
  no-boundary consciousness 40,
    117, 328
  paganism as spiritual force 315
  principles of nondual acosmic
    humanism xxv, 220
  Shekhinah 209
  Solomon's project 49, 64

Solomon's foreign wives, sympa-
    thetic perspective 315, 328
  synonymous with wisdom of
    Solomon *(hokhmat Shelomoh)*
    xxv, 304, 326
  tekufot (audacity, courage) 261
  Temple, first 235
  teshukah 44, 117, 315
  teshuvah 80-1
  truth higher than the law 178
  two hands 94, 96, 97
  unmediated divine will *(retzon
    Hashem)* beyond law 178, 315
  and wine 173, 176
  word of God 71
activism *(avodah)* 31, 53, 56, 67-8,
  70-1, 80, 237, 296
autonomy 147

bat melekh (daughter of the king) 13,
  43, 86, 110, 250, 297
Berur (clarification) xxvi, 27, 31, 85,
  192, 205, 225, 239, 297, 300,
  318-19
  of consciousness 113, 129, 131
  of desire 113, 116, 119, 121-23
  human actions 21, 56, 61-2, 70-1
  idolatry 116, 119
  and *menutzah* 139
  paganism 101-2, 119
  prayer 76
  sin 81, 273
  Solomon, David and Temple 318-19
  uniqueness 27, 44
  will of God 130, 205, 297

wine 129-30, 139
    see also Messiah
binah (intuitive understanding) 29,
    35, 110
Binah (Great Mother, the higher
    Shekhinah) 59, 109, 110, 179,
    209, 219, 230-1, 255, 264-5,
    267, 269, 271, 292
binah balev (wisdom in the heart) 35,
    84-5; see also yarei'ah moon
Bunim, Simcha 170-1, 178, 216, 281,
    283, 289, 295-7, 318, 328

called by the name of God 322
    see name of God
circles, igulim 4, 115
clarification see berur
consciousness
    expanded consciousness 137, 193,
        304; see hitpashtut
    levels of consciousness 5
    no-boundary consciousness 12,
        64, 328
Cordovero, Moses 170, 214, 283,
    285-6, 302

darkness 253, 260, 273, 303; see also
    integration and unification, of
    darkness
da'at kedoshim (knowledge of the
    holy) 36, 84
daughter of the king (bat melekh) see
    bat melekh
David 4-5, 37, 53-7, 57-66, 75, 77,
    83, 102, 109, 121, 122-4, 135,
    140-1, 147-9, 169 , 178, 184,
    189, 194-7, 205, 210, 221,
    223-5, 227, 229-30, 245, 247,
    256, 268-70, 273-6, 285-6, 295,
    318-19, 322-5
democratization of enlightenment

192, 340-1
dreams 24, 173
    Jacob's 202, 206
    Pharaoh's, from Genesis 263-4
    Solomon's 204-6, 213

ecstasy 10, 97, 101, 122, 145, 151-2,
    259
ein lo gevul (place where there is no
    border) 318
empowering acosmism 89
emet le'amito (inner truth) 33-4
eros xxv, 10, 16-17, 44, 125, 130, 146,
    151, 181-2, 191, 204, 228-30,
    235, 261, 269, 270-1, 288, 296,
    304, 334
evolution 197, 236, 291, 341-2
evolving 337

face-to-face 10, 75-81, 197-9, 276-7,
    291-4, 315, 319
feminine xxvi, 4, 13, 21, 30, 35, 53,
    75, 86, 88, 107, 109, 111-16,
    185, 214-15, 219, 231, 260,
    269, 275, 277, 279, 261, 291,
    297, 326, 334
freedom 5, 70-1, 265, 307, 320

Garden of Eden 201, 245, 252
Goddess 9-10, 11, 13-14, 19, 21, 34,
    36, 43-4, 84, 86, 88, 107, 111,
    113, 115, 151-2, 170, 186, 204,
    213, 215, 230, 287

hands of heaven 56-7
Hasidut 283
Hasidism 9, 63, 283
healing 239, 306, 328, 330
Heschel, Abraham Joshua 304

hisaron meyuhad (meyuchad) xxvi, 81, 273, 326-7

hisaron (shadow) 87, 136, 165, 202, 239, 326-7
  as essential role 15-16
  see also Pharaoh's daughter and Solomon

hitnas'ut (revelation of personal uniqueness) *see* uniqueness

hitpashtut xxv, 115, 136, 319-20

historic texts, foreshadowing of 170, 178-9, 183, 193, 204

hokhmat Shelomoh (wisdom of Solomon), essentially acosmic humanism 165, 169-70, 173, 178, 182, 184, 189, 191, 200, 204-7, 210-11, 302; *see also* acosmic humanism

humanism xxv, 65
  see acosmic humanism
  see nondual humanism

idolatry 4-5, 12, 18, 86, 97-8, 102-3, 106-9, 116-22, 147, 216, 255, 322, 329

igulim (circle) 4, 115

individuality 21, 28-31, 37, 64-5, 169

integral 5, 27, 33, 37, 110, 259, 296

integration and unification:
  breath as symbol of 241
  of darkness 189, 201, 204, 211, 239, 243, 247-8, 273, 315
  and eros 241-2
  of everything (*kol*) 239, 241
  divinity, two poles xxvi
  lower wisdom 299, 307, 329-30
  moon as symbol for 241, *see* moon in her fullness
  of names 307
  of paganism 11, 107, 212-13, 216, 315
  as redemption 107, 289, 307, 315
  of right and left 225, 230, 261, 303-4

Shekhinah project, energy of the feminine 107, 201-2, 205, 212, 216, 239, 241, 307

wisdom of Egypt, of the East 212-13

wisdom of Solomon, defining characteristic of 212, 235, 307, 329-30

yetzer hara' (inclination of evil, misuse) 299-301, 303-6, 307

Isaac and Solomon, a parallel 15-16

intuition 9, 21, 23, 30-1, 34, 39, 41, 61, 89, 17-11, 151, 295, 316

it'hapkha (transformation of all to reveal its sacred essence) 328

Jacob 124, 126, 184, 201-3, 206, 217-8, 220, 253, 256, 259, 277, 279, 281

Joseph 161, 191, 193, 225, 254, 264, 306, 322

joy
  unique Torah 131
  worldly pleasures and 17
  unique individuality 37
  and for the straight of heart there is 54-5, 139
  Isaiah 61:10 117
  like wine 131, 135, 144-5, 265-7
  moon, characteristic of, in its fullness 223, 241-2, 248
  integration with *Shekhinah* 241-2
  Judah and messianism, quality of 265-6
  din, relation to 265-7
  yetzer ha-ra', integration of 303-4

Judah archetype 3, 33, 118, 127, 130, 169-71, 210, 247, 321
  ayin tovah (a good eye) 135, 137
  berur 44, 122-3, 239

Judah archetype (con't.)
  binah balev (wisdom of the heart) 35
  da'at kedoshim (knowledge of the
    holy) 84
  David and 53-5, 77, 109, 121,
    135-6, 140, 148, 169, 247, 325
  divine name 54-5, 67
  divine will (retzon Hashem) 10, 21,
    27, 31, 36, 41, 54, 84, 113, 116,
    127-8, 169-71, 175, 178, 307,
    316, 320
  individualism, radical 67,169
  inner truth (emet le' amito) 33-4
  intuition 21, 34-5, 109, 316
  as king 127-8, 247, 259
  law 10, 21, 23, 26, 33-4, 151-2,
    297, 307, 320
  menutzah (overpowered by
    God) 148,169
  messianic consciousness 39, 137-8,
    247, 316, 325
  moon 34-6, 84, 135-6, 152, 217,
    224, 239, 247
  paganism 69, 102, 109, 116, 118,
    152
  and Solomon 27, 44, 169-71, 175,
    224, 247, 297, 316
  Unique Self 10
  uniqueness 21-2, 27, 44, 67,
    131,135
  wine, perception 122, 125, 131,
    247, 259
  wisdom of Solomon (hokhmat
    Shelomoh) 189, 247, 307
  see acosmic humanism 178, 247,
    315, 320
  see Shekhinah 247
Judah and Joseph 193
Jung 239, 270-1

kingship motif 249; see also Judah
  archetype, as king

ko'ah, unique (spiritual energy) 86
Kotzk, court of 91 n. 20, 155 n. 24

law:
  emet le'amito (truth higher than)
    xxv, 3, 17, 33-4, 44, 151-2
  hitpashtut, expansion of conscious-
    ness that allows transcendence
    xxv, 151, 192
  Holy of Holies 234-5
  Judah archetype's messianic quality
    3, 10, 21, 22-7, 30-1, 33-4, 37,
    151, 178
  mikdash, (temple) 233-5
  paganism 98, 116, 151-2
  Solomon's mistake 228-32, 269, 288
  spiritual intuition, smell 23-4, 30-
    1, 151-2, 253, 295
  spiritual leadership models 30
  two women and baby 176
  uniqueness and individuality 10,
    21, 31, 169
  will of God, unmediated (retzon
    Hashem) 9-10, 21, 27, 30-1,
    33-4, 61, 78, 141, 151-2, 169,
    178, 185, 193, 233, 294-7
Liebes, Judah (Yehuda) 46 n. 23
love 15, 37, 53, 58, 62,102, 112-13,
  140-1, 143, 192, 194-7, 207,
  209, 225-7, 225, 261, 267-271,
  287, 320-23, 334
lower wisdom (Malkhut/Shekhinah)
  212, 236, 299, 302, 305-6, 330
Luria xxvi, 4, 9, 16, 66, 75, 78, 81, 87,
  97, 165, 170-1, 185-6, 216, 277,
  283, 289-97, 328, 333-4

Men of the Great Assembly 32, 75,
  118-19, 121, 138
menutzah (overpowered by God) 3-4,
  125, 139-40, 142, 145-9, 151,

menutzah (con't.) 169, 264

Messiah 23-4, 26, 39, 250, 261-2, 265-6, 274, 290, 297, 302, 316-17, 318-19

messianic 13, 23, 26-7, 35, 39-41, 75, 79, 108, 138-9, 135-6, 151, 171, 179, 180, 245, 247, 260-1, 281, 288, 292-4, 296-7, 315, 319, 324-5, 327

mikdash (the Jerusalem Temple) 4, 53-4, 57, 189, 197-8, 233-6, 259, 286-7, 293

and acosmic humanism 10, 69

David and 54, 77, 109, 224

destruction of 222-4

eros 181, 182, 199, 204, 233

as eschaton 105-6

face to face 77, 293

Judah and 263

the moon 109, 116, 204, 233, 263, 267, 286-7, 293

paganism 18, 98, 106, 108-9, 120, 213-15, 259

the purpose of 77, 80, 108

redemption 107, 263, 318

the second Temple 234-5

Shekhinah 10, 43, 213, 224

Solomon 11, 18, 43, 108-9, 169, 182, 199, 204, 213, 224, 229, 233, 235, 263, 267, 287, 293, 328

with two hands 57, 69

moon (sihara)

and David 58, 83, 135-6, 205, 210, 225, 230

erotic motif 130, 196, 204, 233, 268-70, 287

Goddess-Shekhinah symbol 34-6, 84, 86, 88, 109, 127, 185-6, 204-5, 207, 251

hisaron (moon in her lack) 239

Israel and 88, 179, 184, 248-9

itpagma (diminished) 230

joy as characteristic 248

Judah archetype analogue 4, 34-6, 83-4, 126-7, 189, 225, 247, 251, 253, 257-8, 262-3

levanah moon 86, 88

paganism 86-7, 109, 210, 212

pagum (spiritually tainted) 232

retzon Hashem link 84, 151, 179, 185, 189, 239

secret of the Temple 233, 287

Shavuot (the giving of the Torah) 84

source of binah balev 84-5

suprarational consciousness 86

sun's relationship 83, 185-6, 233

stages of human consciousness 236

teshukah 86, 88-9

yarei'ah (moon) understanding in the heart 35, 43, 84-6

moon in her fullness (sihara bisheleimuta or sihara ba'asheleimuta)

da'at kedoshim (knowledge of the holy) equates 36, 43, 84, 189

field of apples 225

healing of hisaron 239

as ideal state 184-5

inclusiveness and integration 212-13, 217, 225-30, 240-4, 305, 307

messianic in nature 39, 179-81, 185, 262-3

nondual acosmic humanism 180

Solomon's wisdom, essence of 36, 43, 75, 83, 86, 89, 109, 130, 169, 179, 204-7, 211, 225-30, 256, 282, 286, 289, 305, 307

tikun ha-nukva (cosmic rectification of the feminine) 289, 291-3

wisdom of Egypt 212

Moses 21-31, 36, 65, 124, 132, 145-6, 173-4, 193-200, 306, 325-6

mystery of four 62

name 3, 36, 40, 43-4, 54, 58-67, 81,
    86, 99, 104-5, 111-12, 117, 128,
    146, 165, 184-5, 204, 209, 211,
    213, 214-5, 222, 240, 243, 249,
    273, 278-9, 288, 307, 315-22,
    327
names of God 44, 55, 65, 128, 236-7,
    249, 278, 316, 320, 322
    yihud (unification) of names 302,
    305
nondual humanism 220
    see acosmic humanism

'olam ha-ba (the world to come) 32,
    35, 86, 110, 271, 297

paganism 10, 11, 13-19, 43, 86-7,
    97-8, 101, 103, 105-10, 113,
    115-16, 119-20, 130, 151-2,
    169, 213-16, 283, 287, 296, 315
paradox 22, 27, 64-5, 115, 139, 147,
    260, 262, 329
pathology xxvi, 137, 165
Pharaoh's daughter and Solomon 13-
    18, 107-8, 213, 259, 328
prophecy 25, 174, 195, 325

rei'ah (smell) *see* intuition
retzon Hashem (will of God) 3, 9-10,
    21, 27-8, 30-2, 37, 40-44, 55,
    59-61, 78, 84-5, 100, 108-9,
    112-13, 116,125, 140-1, 145,
    147-8, 151-2, 169, 175, 178-9,
    185, 189, 193, 205, 217-18,
    222, 233, 239, 266, 288, 294,
    297, 316, 324
revelation 24, 34, 66, 68-9, 73, 79,
    117-18, 176, 213, 275, 321
Rosh Hashanah 36, 126, 135, 173, 193
Schatz-Uffenheimer, Rivkah 63

shadow:
    of acosmic humanism on Hiram
        242-3
    Jungian integration of 239, 270-1
    unique *see hisaron meyuhad*
    see hisaron
shadow figures, Solomon's 330
Shavuot (the giving of the Torah) 84
Shekhinah xxv-vi, 4, 9-11, 189, 193-
        200, 201-5, 214-16, 217-19,
        221-4, 224-32, 233, 235, 239,
        241, 244-5, 247-58, 259-65,
        266-8, 270, 273, 277-8, 282,
        283, 285-8, 292, 294, 301, 304,
        307, 319, 324-5
    Bat melekh as *terminus technicus* 13,
        14, 86
    as beautiful captive woman 87-8
    beyond the law 169
    Binah (the Great Mother), the
        higher *Shekhinah* 175
    as daughter of Pharaoh 16
    and David 58, 83, 149, 195
    divine will (*retzon Hashem*) syn-
        onym 9-10, 21, 27, 35, 55, 75,
        84, 109, 116, 141, 169
    embrace unmediated xxv-vi, 43,
        116-18, 121
    face-to-face relationship 75, 78-9
    higher and lower *Shekhinah*s 109-
        10
    as *hokhmat Shelomoh* (wisdom of
        Solomon) xxv, 4, 10
    Joshua, unique *Shekhinah* quality
        145
    as Judah archetype 10, 21, 27, 34,
        121-3, 125, 148
    Judah tribe 126-7
    a life force, divine, pantheistic 9, 10
    lower wisdom (*Malkhut/Shekhinah*)
        212, 236, 299, 302, 305-6, 330
    menutzah (overcome, seduced by
        God) 145, 148, 151

338

Shekhinah (con't.)
   mikdash, the sanctuary 182
   moon 34-6, 84, 86, 88, 109, 116,
      127, 185, 196
   Moses, an archetype 2, 145, 196-7
   pagan energy, sacred sparks 10-11,
      43, 109, 116
   Shekhinah-consciousness 21, 86,
      43, 55, 84, 86, 109
   Shekhinah project 11-13, 16, 18,
      43, 86, 88, 98, 107, 116, 189,
      213, 216, 224, 285, 296-7,
      327-8
   Solomon xxv-vi, 27, 193, 196,
      199-201
   symbol of divine identity within
      man 9
   symbol for God's immanence in
      world 9
   ti'uvta denukva (erotic passion of
      the feminine) 4
   two hands motif 58
   unique name as *Shekhinah* identity
      44, 55
   Vashti 121
   wine 125-7, 141, 148, 151
   without garments (levushim),
      beyond the law 69, 116-18, 122
      169
   yarei'ah, intuitive, messianic 34-35,
      86, 109
   Yisrael, the Community of Is-
      rael 111
   zivug (erotic merging) 191
Shemini Atzeret and face-to-face 78-9,
   318-19
silver, as desire 15
Sin 233-4, 244, 251, 278, 281-2, 307
   of Adam and Eve 244, 296-7
   of Amatzyah and Hi'el 100-1
   and David 54, 140, 148, 318
   of Israel 120, 141-2, 144-5, 198-9,
      202

of Judah 54, 132, 210, 251, 253-4
of Levi 146-8
of Menasheh 103
and Men of the Great Assembly
   118-20
and repentance 80-1
for the sake of God (*'aveirah
   lishmah*) 16
of Solomon 11, 15-17, 205-6,
   228-9, 297, 307, 328
and wine 132
sitra ahra (exterior, the other side)
   104-5, 202, 273, 279
Solomon and David 37, 53, 55, 81,
   83, 109, 195, 197, 221, 224,
   227, 247, 270, 318, 323-4
Solomon sitting on God's throne 179-
   80, 181, 185, 256, 316, 324
Solomon's wives 11-13, 18, 86, 107-8,
   178, 186, 189, 205, 213, 216,
   229-30, 315, 327-8, 283, 289-
   90, 296-7, 327-8
Song of Songs 29-32, 140, 181-2,
   198-200, 269, 282
soul print 63, 66, 152, 322, 338
story 218, 223-4, 254, 263, 276, 291,
   322-3, 327
   of Aaron and Elazar (his son) 55
   of Amatzyah, king of Judah 99
   of *bat melekh* 13
   the binding of Isaac 112
   the creation story with moon
      text 185-6
   of David and Bathsheba 140
   of David dancing, Ark and
      Temple 53-4
   the hero full of wine 131
   the Judah *menutzah* passage with
      King David the Jester of the
      King 148-9
   of Menasheh 102
   of moon's relationship with
      sun 184-5

story (con't.)
one's own 72-3, *see* soul print
the Purim story 138
of Rabbi Abba and Rabbi Shimon
206
of Rava's cane and Judah 34
of Solomon's dream theophany 173
of Song of Songs 30
of the spies 142-3
of two women and one baby 173,
176
of Vashti before King Ahaseurus
116
straight of heart 37, 54-5, 139
supra-rational *(lema'alah mida'ato)*
Judah archetype, quality of 137
messianic consciousness 131
levanah moon, Shekhinah-con-
sciousness 86

tekufot (sacred audacity) 55, 61, 70,
130, 143
of Judah 130, 261
name of God 55
will of God 61, 70
wine 143
the Temple, Jerusalem see *mikdash*
teshukah (desire) xxv, 151, 174-5, 189,
193, 199, 218, 239, 271, 288,
296, 304, 306, 316
central to acosmic humanism 16,
36, 89
of Ammonites 14
and David 59-60, 140
for face-to-face relationship with
God 75, 77
garments of the *Shekhinah* 69
God's desire to vindicate 68
God's desire for human activism 71
Goddess language and eros 130, 151
and *hisaron* 87, 107, 326-7
Isaac and Solomon, parallel 15-16

ko'ah (powers) of 118
called life 87
menutzah (surrendering desire to
God) 147-9
moon in her fullness 347
moon's essential power 88, 89
for nature of reality 113
pagan eros 10
pagan idolatry 4, 10, 110, 119-20,
122
and *ratzon,* unfolding divinity
within human heart 59-61
Shekhinah project 19, 86-7, 106-7,
115-18
Shekhinah unmediated 116-8,
121-2
as silver 15
for simplicity 122
surrender to God 73
Solomon and his wisdom 16,
326-7
Solomon and Pharaoh's daughter
15-16
Solomon's marriages 327
for spiritual service 16
story of beautiful woman captured
by Israelite warrior 87-8
in Tetragrammaton, in heart of
man 59-63, 66
for unmediated will of God *(ratzon
Hashem)* 10, 34, 147
Tetragrammaton 59-62, 105
teva (deep nature) 4, 98, 113, 115, 169
Tif'eret and *Malkhut* 191, 201, 203-4,
257, 279
tikun (healing, fixing) 75, 219, 274,
277, 285, 292
it'hapkha, Solomon's peaceful conquest 328
Solomon and the evil of Adam 296
Solomon and *Shemini Atzeret* 318
what the snake set wrong in
Eden 245

tikun ha-nukva (cosmic rectification of the feminine) 75, 283, 289, 291-2, 294, 326

Tishby, Isaiah (Tishbi) 3

tovat ayin (goodness of the eye) 135, 137-8

two hands 57-9, 63-4, 66-9, 72-3, 138

Tzadok Hakohen of Lublin xxvi, 5, 17, 165, 184, 242, 315, 318, 321, 327, 330

uncertainty 71, 222, 341

unio mystica 137

unique *helek* (vocation) 63, 169, 322

Unique Self 10, 335, 340-2

Unique shadow see *hisaron meyuhad*

unique Torah 131

uniqueness, personal *(hitnas'ut)* 21-2, 25, 28, 43-4, 64-6, 67, 72, 125, 131, 135, 322

upper and lower realms, wisdom (*'ila'ah* and *teta'ah*) 201, 236, 302, 305

Weiss, Joseph 63, 68, 139

Wilber, Ken 337-8

wine 4, 10, 122-52, 169, 189, 259-71, 286-7

and acosmic humanism 145, 148-9

clarified wine 129

connection with God 127-8

and David 139, 148-9

a higher level of perception 132-3, 135, 151

Judah archetype 122, 125-7, 135-6, 138, 148, 247, 259

menutzah 125, 139, 141, 145, 148, 151

and oil 270-1

and uniqueness 131, 135

and *Shekhinah* 135, 151

sin 132, 141-3

and *tekufot* 142-3

will of God see *retzon Hashem*

Wisdom of Egypt, of the East see paganism

yarei'ah moon 34-5, 43, 61, 64, 66, 83, 84-6, 109, 151-2, 185, 291

yetzer ha ra (desire, pleasures of the world) 299-300, 303-5, 307

zivug 'im ha-Shekhinah motif for Solomon 201, 252, 319, 324

Works Cited

Primary Sources

Abulafia, Abraham. *Hayyei Olam Haba.* Ed. Amnon Gross. Jerusalem, 1999. No short title

Abulafia, Abraham. *Or Hasekhel.* Ed. Amnon Gross. Jerusalem, 2001. No short title

Acre, Isaac of. *Meirat Einayim.* Jerusalem, 1993. No short title

Albo, Joseph. *Sefer Haikarim.* Tel Aviv, 1984. No short title

Alfasi, Yitzhak. *Sihot HaRan.* Jerusalem, 1998. No short title

Alter, Yehudah Arieh Leib of Gur. *Sefat Emet Im Likutim.* 5 vols. Jerusalem, no date. Short title: *Sefat Emet*

Azikri, Elazar Ben Moses. *Sefer Haredim.* Jerusalem, 2001. No short title

Azulai, Avraham. *Hesed LeAvraham.* Lvov, 1863. Short title: Hesed

Azulai, Hayyim Yosef David (Hida). *Tzavarei Shalal.* Jerusalem, 1995. No short title

Bacharach, Naftali. *Emek Hamelek*h. Amsterdam, 1648. Short title: *Emek*

Berdichev, Levi Yitzhak of. *Kedushat Levi Hashalem.* Jerusalem, 1972. Short title: *Kedushat Levi*

Berlin, Naftali Zvi. *Haemek She'elah*: Perush Lesheiltot DeRav Ahai Gaon. Jerusalem, 1986. Short title: *Haemek*

Braslav, Nahman of. *Likutei Mohoran.* Bnei Brak, 1972. No short title

Bunim, Simha. See Przysucha, Simha Bunim of.

Chernobyl, Menahem Nahum of. *Meor Einayim.* Jerusalem, 1975. No short title

Chernobyl, Menahem Nahum of. *Upright Practices. The Light of the Eyes.* Trans. A. Green. New York, 1982. Short title: *Upright*

Chernobyl, Mordechai of. *Likutei Torah.* Bnei Brak, 1983. No short titleCohen, David. *Kol Hanevuah.* Jerusalem, 1970. No short title

Cordevero, Moses. *Pardes Rimonim.* Jerusalem, 1962. No short title

Cordevero, Moses. *Shiur Komah.* Jerusalem, 1966. No short title

da Vidas, Elijah. *Reishit Hokhmah*. Ed. H. Y. Waldman. 3 vols. Jerusalem, 1984. No short title

Edwards, Betzalel Philip. *The Living Waters: The Mei Hashiloah: A Commentary on the Torah*. See Lainer, Mordechai Joseph. Short title: *The Living Waters*

Epstein, Kalonimus Kalman. Maor Vashemesh. 2 vols. Jerusalem, 1992. No short title

Gerona, Azriel ben Shlomo of. *Peirush Haagadot LeRav Azriel*. Ed. Isaiah Tishby. Jerusalem, 1982. No short title

Gikatilla, Joseph ben Avraham. *Shaarei Orah*. Offenbach, 1715. No short title

Hakohen, Tzadok. *Divrei Sofrim*. Bnei Brak, 1967. No short title

Hakohen, Tzadok. *Dover Tzedek*. Bnei Brak, 1956. No short title

Hakohen, Tzadok. *Kedushat Hashabat*. Jerusalem, 1994. No short title

Hakohen, Tzadok. *Mahshevot Harutz*. Bnei Brak, 1966. No short title

Hakohen, Tzadok. *Peri Tzadik. Jerusalem, 1959. No short title*

Hakohen, Tzadok. *Resisei Laylah*. Bnei Brak, 1969. No short title

Hakohen, Tzadok. *Sefer Hazikhronot*. Bnei Brak, 1956. No short title

Hakohen, Tzadok. *Takanat Hashavin*. Beit El, 1994. No short title

Hakohen, Tzadok. *Tzidkat Hatzadik*. Jerusalem, 1988. No short title

Hakohen, Yaakov Yosef. *Tzafnat Paane'ah*. Ed. Gedaliah Nigal. Jerusalem, 1989. No short title

Halevi, Yehuda. *Hakuzari*. Tel Aviv, 1978. No short title

Hanokh Hashelishi (*Heikhalot*). [No place of publication], 1791. No short title

Hayyat, Yehuda. *Commentary to Maarekhet HaElohut*. (attr. Peretz ben Yitzhak Gerondi.) Jerusalem, 1963. No short title

Hehasid, Yehudah ben Shmuel. *Sefer Hasidim*. Ed. Reuven Margaliot. Jerusalem, 1957. No short title

Horowitz, Isaiah. *Shenei Luhot Haberit*. Haifa, 1991. Short title: *Shenei*

Horowitz, YaakovYitzhak Halevi. *Zot Zikaron*. Jerusalem, 1992. No short title

Horowitz, Jacob Halevi (The Seer of Lublin). *Zot Zikaron.* In *Sefarim Hakedoshim mi Kol Talmidei HaBesht Hakadosh,* vol 2. Brooklyn, 1981. No short title

Ibn Gabai, Meir. *Avodat Hakodesh.* Jerusalem, 1963. No short title

Ibn Halawa, Bahya ben Asher. *Rabeinu Bahya Al HaTorah.* Bnei Brak, 1992. Short title: Rabeinu Bahya

Jaraslov, Zekhariah Mendel of. *Darkhei Tzedek.* New York, 1993. No short title

Josephus, Flavius. *Antiquities.* In *The Complete Works of Flavius Josephus.* Ed. William Whiston. Grand Rapids MI, 1960.

Kaplan, Aryeh. *Rabbi Nachman's Stories.* Jerusalem, 1985.

Kook, Avraham Yitzhak. *Arpelei Tohar.* Jerusalem, 1978. No short title

Kook, Avraham Yitzhak. 'Musar Hakodesh'. In *Orot Hakodesh.* No short title

Kook, Avraham Yitzhak. *Orot* series. Trans. and introduction, Bezalel Naor. Northvale, NJ, 1993. No short title

Kook, Avraham Yitzhak. *Orot Hakodesh.* 4 vols. Jerusalem, 1938-1990. No short title

Kook, Avraham Yitzhak. *Orot Hateshuvah.* Jerusalem, 1999. No short title

Koretz, Pinhas Shapira of. *Midrash Pinhas.* Warsaw, 1910. No short title

Lahover, Yeruham and Isaiah Tishby, trans. and eds. *Mishnat Hazohar.* Jerusalem, 1971. Cited as 'Tishby, Mishnat Hazohar'. No short title

Lainer, Gershom Henokh. 'Introduction (Hakdamah)' to *Beit Yaakov.* By Jacob Lainer. Short title: Beit Yaakov, Introduction

Lainer, Gershom Henokh. *Sod Yesharim.* Lublin, 1908.

Lainer, Hayyim Simhah. *Dor Yesharim.* New York, 1988. No short title

Lainer, Jacob. *Beit Yaakov.* Brooklyn, 1978. Introduction by G. Lainer. No short title

Lainer, Mordechai Joseph. *Mei Hashiloah.* Ed. Elhanan Reuven Golhaber, Yehudah Yosef Spiegelman. 2 vols. Vienna, 1860 (vol. 1). Lublin, 1922 (vol. 2). repr. Bnei Brak, 1995. Short title: *MHs.*

Lainer, Mordechai Joseph. *The Living Waters: The Mei Hashiloah: A Commentary on the Torah*. Ed. and trans. Betzalel Philip Edwards. Northvale, NJ, 2001. Short title: *The Living Waters*

Liadi, Schneur Zalman of. Seder Hatefilah. Warsaw, 1866. No short title

Liadi, Schneur Zalman of. *Shaar Hayihud Vehaemunah*. Bnei Brak, 2000. Short Title: *Shaar Hayihud*

Liadi, Schneur Zalman of. *Likutei Torah*. Brookline, MA, 1979. No short title

Liadi, Schneur Zalman of. *Sidur Tefilot Lekol Hashanah*. Berdichev, 1818. No short title

Liadi, Schneur Zalman of. *Likutei Amarim* (*Tanya*). Brooklyn: Kehot Publication Society, 1966. Short title: *Tanya*

Lintz, Gedaliah of. *Teshuot Hen*. Brooklyn, 1982. No short title

Lishensk, Elimelekh of. *Noam Elimelekh*. Jerusalem, 1960. No short title

Loew, Judah (Maharal of Prague). *Gevurot Hashem*. New York, 2001. No short title

Loew, Judah (Maharal of Prague). *Hidushei Agadot Maharal Miprag*. Bnei Brak, 1980. Short title: *Hidushei Agado*

Loew, Judah (Maharal of Prague). *Netzah Yisrael*. Bnei Brak, 1980. No short title

Luria, Isaac. *Sefer Hakavanot*. Venice, 1620. No short title

Luzzatto, Moshe Hayyim. *Daat Tevunot*. Jerusalem, 2006. No short title

Luzzatto, Moshe Hayyim. *Pithei Hoakhmah*. In *Shaarei Ramhal*. Tel Aviv, 1996. No short title

Maimonides, Moses. *Commentary to Mishnah*. Ed. Yosef Kapah. Jerusalem, 1968. No short title

Maimonides, Moses. *The Guide of the Perplexed*. Trans. Shlomo Pines. Chicago, 1963. Short title: *The Guide*

Maimonides, Moses. 'Hakdamah Leperek Helek'. In *Shalosh Hakdamot LehaRambam*. Jerusalem, 1995. No short title

Maimonides, Moses. *Mishneh Torah*. Jerusalem, 1954. No short title

Mei Tzedek. [Unavailable; cited in Gellman, 'The Denial'].

Mekhilta Derabi Yishmael. Jerusalem, 1954. Short title: *Mekhilta*

Mezerich, Dov Ber, Magid of. *Hayyim Vahesed*. Warsaw, 1891. No short title

Mezerich, Dov Ber, Magid of. *Magid Devarav LeYaakov*. Ed. R. Schatz-Uffenheimer. Jerusalem, 1976. No short title

Mezerich, Dov Ber, Magid of. *Or Haemet*. Bnei Brak, 1967. No short title

Mezerich, Dov Ber, Magid of. *Or Torah*. Brooklyn, 2004. No short title

Midrash Konen. In *Otzar Hamidrashim*. Ed. Naftali Greenbaum. Jerusalem, 2002. No short title

Midrash Tanhuma. Ed. Shlomo Buber. Jerusalem, 1972. Short title: *Tanhuma*

Midrash Rabah. Jerusalem, 1994. No short title

Mishnah. 12 vols. New York, 1953. Short title: E.g., *mAvot* 3:4

Modena, Aaron of. *Maavar Yabok*. Bnei Brak, 1990. No short title

Molho, Shlomo. *Sefer Hamefo'ar*. Jerusalem, 1989. No short title

Nahmanides, Moses ben Nahman (Ramban). 'Commentary on Job'. In *Kitvei Ramban*. Jerusalem, 1978. No short title

Nahmanides, Moses ben Nahman (Ramban). *Commentary on the Torah*. Trans. Charles Chavel. New York, 1974. Short title: Commentary

Nahmanides, Moses ben Nahman (Ramban). 'Torat Hashem Temimah'. In *Kitvei Ramban*. Ed. C. D. Chavel. Jerusalem, 1963. 1:162. No short title

Pesikta DeRav Kahana. New York, 1987. No short title.

Plotinus. Trans. A.H. Armstrong. Cambridge, MA, 1978-1988. Short title: *Plotinus*

Polnoye, Jacob Joseph of. *Ben Porat Yosef*. Koretz, 1781. No short title

Polnoye, Jacob Joseph of. *Ketonet Pasim*. Lvov, 1866. No short title

Polnoye, Jacob Joseph of. *Toldot Yaakov Yosef*. Jerusalem, 1962. No short title

Przysucha, Simha Bunim of. *Sefer Kol Mevaser*. Raanana, 1992.

Radomsk, Abraham Yesakhar Be'er Hakohen of. *Hesed le-Avraham*. Pietrkov, 1893. No short title

Rakatz, Y. K. K. *Siah Sarfei Kodesh*. 5 vols. Lodz, 1928-1931. Short title: *Siah*.

Safrin, Yitzhak Yehudah Yehiel of Komarno. *Ketem Ofir* (commentary to *Megilat Esther*). Brooklyn, 1995. No short title

Safrin, Yitzhak Yehudah Yehiel of Komarno. *Sefer Heikhal Haberakhah*. Lemberg, 1869. Short title: *Sefer Heikhal*.

Safrin, Yitzhak Yehudah Yehiel of Komarno. *Zohar Hai*. Jerusalem, 1971. Preface by Eliezer Tzvi of Komarno Safrin. No short title

Sefer Hatemunah. Tel Aviv: Zion, 1972. No short title

Sefer Yetzirah. Jerusalem, 1965. No short title

Shapira, Kalonymus Kalman. *Mevo Hashe'arim*. Jerusalem, 1966. No short title.

Shapira, Pinhas of Koretz. *Midrash Pinhas*. Warsaw, 1910. No short title

Sharabi, Shalom. *Nahar Shalom*. Tel Aviv, 1960. No short title

Shimon of Frankfurt. *Yalkut Shimoni*. Jerusalem, 1960 No short title

Shmuelevitz, Hayyim. *Sihot Musar*. Jerusalem, 1970-1973. No short title

Sifrei Bamidbar. Ed. H. S. Horovitz. Jerusalem, 1966. Short title: *Sifrei*

Soloveitchik, Joseph. *Besod Hayahid Vehayahad*. ***,1968. In untitled collection, vol. 2 of 4 vols. 1961-1975. Short title: *Besod Hayahid*

Soloveitchik, Joseph. 'The Community'. *Tradition* 17(2): 1978, 7-24. No short title

Soloveitchik, Joseph. *Halakhic Man*. Trans. Lawrence Kaplan. Philadelphia, 1983. No short title

Soloveitchik, Joseph. *On Repentance*. Jerusalem, 1980. No short title

Soloveitchik, Joseph. *Lonely Man of Faith*. New York, 1992. No short title

Soloveitchik, Joseph. *Reflections of the Rav*. Ed. Abraham Besdin. Jerusalem, 1979-1989. Short title: *Reflections*

Soloveitchik, Joseph. 'Uvikashtem Misham'. *Hadarom* 47, 1979: 1-83. Short title: 'Uvikashtem'

Steinsaltz, Adin. *Beggars and Prayers*. New York, 1979. No short title

Sudilkov, Moshe Hayyim Ephraim of. *Degel Mahaneh Efrayim*. Jerusalem, 1963. No short title

Talmud Bavli. 20 vols. Vilna, 1865. Short title: E.g., *bBer*.

Talmud Yerushalmi. 7 vols. Vilna, 1921. Short title: E.g., *yBer*.

Tikunei Zohar. Monroe, NY, 1992. No short title

Tishby, Isaiah. *Mishnat Hazohar*. See Lahover, Yeruham and Isaiah Tishby, trans. and eds. *Mishnat Hazohar*.

Tzemah, Yaakov ben Hayyim. *Zohar Harakiya*. New York, 1999. No short title

Vital, Hayyim. *Eitz Hayyim*. Jerusalem, 1904. No short title.

Vital, Hayyim. *Liqutei Torah*. Jerusalem, 1970. No short title.

Vital, Hayyim. *Peri Eitz Chayim*, Jerusalem, 1980.

Vital, Hayyim. *Sefer Hezyonot*. Jerusalem, 1954. No short title

Vital, Hayyim. *Shaar Hagilgulim*. Jerusalem, 1863. No short title

Vital, Hayyim. *Shaar Hakavanot*. Jerusalem, 1902. No short title

Vital, Hayyim. *Shaar Hamitzvot*. Jerusalem, 1974. No short title.

Vital, Hayyim. *Shaar Hapesukim*. Tel Aviv, 1962. No short title

Vital, Hayyim. *Shaar Maamarei Razal*. Jerusalem, 1988. No short title

Vital, Hayyim. *Shaar Ruah Hakodesh*. Jerusalem, 1963. No short title

Vitebsk, Menahem Mendel of. *Peri Haaretz*. Cracow, 1896. No short title

Volozhin, Hayyim of. *Nefesh Hahayyim*. Ed. Y. D. Rubin. Bnei Brak, 1989. No short title

Zhitomir, Zeev Wolf of. *Or Hame'ir*. Brooklyn, 1975. No short title.

Zloczow, Yehiel Mikhael of. *Mayim Rabim*. Brooklyn, 1979. No short title

Zohar. 3 vols. Ed. Reuven Margaliot. Jerusalem, 1984. No short title

Zohar Hadash. Brooklyn, NY, 1981. No short title

Monographs and Articles

Abbagnano, Niccola. 'Humanism'. In *Encyclopedia of Philosophy*, vol. 4. Ed. Paul Edwards. New York, 1967. 69-72. No short title

Abbs, Peter. 'The Development of Autobiography in Western Culture: From Augustine to Rousseau'. PhD Thesis, University of Sussex, 1986. Short title: 'The Development'

Abrams, Daniel. 'The Boundaries of Divine Ontology: The Inclusion and Exclusion of Metatron in the Godhead'. *Harvard Theological Review* 87, 1994. 291-321. Short title: 'The Boundaries'

Alfasi, Yitzhak. *Hahozeh MiLublin*. Jerusalem, 1969. Short title: *Hahozeh*

Aranoff, Yaffa. 'Abraham Joshua Heschel's Response to American Modernity'. MA Thesis, Hebrew University, 2000. Short title: 'Abraham'

Avivi, Yosef. *Binyan Ariel: Mevo Derushei Rabi Yitzhak Luria*. Jerusalem, 1987. Short title: *Binyan*

Bachofen, J. J. *Myth, Religion, and Mother Right: Selected Writings of J. J. Bachofen*. Trans. Ralph Manheim. Princeton, 1967. Short title: *Myth*

Barrett, William. *Irrational Man*. New York, 1958. No short title

Bartov, Yoav. 'Sin and the Will of God in the Process of Repentance in the Writings of Mordechai Joseph Lainer and Tzadok Hakohen of Lublin' (Hebrew). Senior Thesis, Efrat Community High School. Efrat, Israel, 2001. Short title: 'Sin'

Baumgardt, David. *Great Western Mystics*. New York, 1961. Short title: *Great*

Beckford, James. 'Religion Modernity and Postmodernity'. In *Religion: Contemporary Issues*. Ed. B. R. Wilson. London, 1992. 11-27.

Bellah, Robert N. *Habits of the Heart: Individualism and Commitment in American Life*. New York, 1986. Short title: *Habits*

Benayahu, Meir. *Sefer Toldot HaAri*. Jerusalem, 1963. No short title

Ben Dor, Yehuda. 'Normative Contradictions as Expressions of Radical Pluralism: An Analysis of Mei Hashiloah, Mordechai Lainer of Izbica'. Unpublished seminar paper, Hebrew University, 1997. Short title: 'Normative'

Ben-Sasson, Hayyim Hillel. 'Ishiyuto Shel HaGra [R. Eliyahu Meivilna] Vehashpaato Hahistorit'. *Tzion* 31, 1966: 39-86, 197-216. Short title: 'Ishiyuto'

Ben Shlomo, Yosef. 'Sheleimut Vehishalmut Betorat HaElohut Shel HaRav Kook'. *Iyun* 33(1-2), 1984: 289-309. Short title: 'Sheleimut'

Berger, David. ' "The Wisest of All Men": Solomon's Wisdom in Medieval Jewish Commentaries on the Book of Kings'. In *Hazon Nahum: Studies in Jewish Law, Thought, and History Presented to Dr. Norman Lamm on the Occasion of His Seventieth Birthday.* Eds. Yaakov Elman and Jeffrey Gurock. New York, 1997. Short title: 'The Wisest'

Berger, Peter. *Redeeming Laughter: The Comic Dimension of Human Experience.* New York, 1997. Short title: *Redeeming*

Berl, Hayyim Yehuda. *Rabi Avraham Yehoshua Heschel, HaRav MiApta.* Jerusalem, 1984. Short title: *Rabi Avraham Yehoshua Heschel*

Biale, David. *Eros and the Jews.* New York, 1992. Short title: *Eros*

Blejwas, Stanislaus A. 'Polish Positivism and the Jews'. *Journal of Jewish Studies* 46, 1984: 21-36. Short title: 'Polish'

Blumenthal, David. *God at the Center: Meditations on Jewish Spirituality.* San Francisco, 1988. Short title: *God*

Brill, Alan. 'Grandeur and Humility in the Writings of Simcha Bunim of Pryzsucha'. In *Hazon Nahum: Studies in Jewish Law, Thought, and History Presented to Dr. Norman Lamm on the Occasion of His Seventieth Birthday.* Eds. Yaakov Elman and Jeffrey Gurock. New York, 1997. 419-448. Short title: 'Grandeur'

Brill, Alan. 'The Mystical Path of the Vilna Gaon'. *Journal of Jewish Thought and Philosophy* 3(1), 1993: 131-151. Short title: 'The Mystical'

Brill, Alan. *Thinking God: The Mysticism of Rabbi Zadok of Lublin.* New York, 2002. Short Title: *Thinking*.

Buber, Martin. 'Spinoza, Shabbtai Zevi and the Baal Shem'. In *Buber, The Origin and Meaning of Hasidism.* Ed. and trans. Maurice Friedman. New York, 1960. 89-112. Short title: 'Spinoza'

Buber, Martin. 'Interpreting Hasidism'. *Commentary* 36, no. 3. September, 1963: 218-225. No short title

Buber, Martin. *Tales of the Hassidim.* Jerusalem, 1947. Short title: *Tales*

Buber, Martin. *Hasidism and Modern Man.* Ed. Maurice Friedman. New York, 1966. No short title

Buber, Martin. *The Origin and Meaning of Hasidism.* Ed. and trans. Maurice Friedman. Atlantic Highlands, NJ, 1988.

Burckhardt, Jacob. *The Civilization of the Renaissance in Italy*. Oxford, 1981. Short title: *The Civilization*

Campbell, Joseph. *The Masks of God: Primitive Mythology*. New York, 1959. Short title: *The Masks*.

Charlton, Chester. 'Christian Tradition and the Magical Wisdom of Solomon'. *Journal of the Palestine Oriental Society* 2, 1922: 1-24. Short title: 'Christian'

Dan, Joseph. *Al Hakedushah: Dat, Musar, Umistika Bayahadut Ubedatot Aheirot*. Jerusalem, 1997. Short title: *Al Hakedushah*

Dan, Joseph and Isaiah Tishby. 'Hasidut'. In *Ha'entziklopediyah Ha'ivrit*. Jerusalem and Tel Aviv, 1949-1995. No short title

Dan, Joseph. 'Metatron'. In *The Ancient Jewish Mysticism*. Ed. J. Dan.Tel Aviv, 1989. 108-138. No short title

Dan, Joseph. 'Metatron'. In *Hamistika Ha'ivrit Hakedumah*. Ed. J. Dan. Tel Aviv, 1989. 83-91. No short title

Dan, Joseph. 'The Name of God, The Name of the Rose, and the Concept of Language in Jewish Mysticism'. *Medieval Encounters* 2, 1996: 228-248. Short title: 'The Name'

Dan, Joseph. 'Samael, Lillith, and the Concept of Evil in Early Kabbalah'. *Association of Jewish Studies Review* 5, 1980: 32-37. Short title: 'Samael'

Day, John. 'Asherah in the Hebrew Bible and Northwest Semitic Literature'. Journal of Biblical Literature 105, 1986. 385-408. Short title: 'Asherah'

Derrida, Jacques. *Dissemination*. Trans. Barbara Johnson. Chicago, 1981. No short title

Dinov, Tzvi Elimelekh Shapira of. *Igra Dekala*. Przemysl, 1909. No short title

Dodds, E. R. 'Parmenides and the Neo-Platonic "One" '. *The Classical Quarterly* 22, 1928: 129-142. Short title: 'Parmenides'

Eco, Umberto. *Semiotics and the Philosophy of Language*. Bloomington, 1986. Short title: *Semiotics*

Eisen, Arnold. 'Re-reading Heschel on the Commandments'. *Modern Judaism* 9 (1), 1989: 1-33. Short title: 'Re-reading'

Eisen, Chaim. 'Ye Shall Be Like God: Hazal's Conception of the Yetzer Hara'. In. *The 1994 Book of Jewish Thought: A Journal of Torah*

Scholarship. eds. Eisen, Chaim and Moshe Sosevsky. New York, 1993. 44-116. Short title: 'Ye Shall Be'

Eliade, Mircea. *Cosmos and History: The Myth of the Eternal Return.* New York, 1959. Short title: *Cosmos*

Eliade, Mircea. 'Goddess Worship'. In *The Encyclopedia of Religion.* Ed. Mircea Eliade. NewYork, 1987. 6:35-58. No short title

Eliade, Mircea. *Patterns in Comparative Religion. Trans. Rosemary Sheed.* Lincoln, NB, 1996. Short title: *Patterns*

Eliade, Mircea. 'The Moon'. In *The Encyclopedia of Religion.* Ed. Mircea Eliade. New York, 1987. 10: 83-90. No short title

Elior, Rachel. 'Bein Ha"yesh" Leha"ayin"—Iyun Betorat Hatzadik Shel R. Yaakov Yitzhak Hahozeh MiLublin'. In *Tzadikim Ve'anshei Maaseh: Mehkarim Behasidut Polin.* Eds. Y. Bartal, R. Elior, H. Shmeruk. Jerusalem: Mosad Bialik, 1994. 167-218. Short title: *'Bein'*

Elior, Rachel. 'HaBaD: The Contemplative Ascent to God'. In *Jewish Spirituality II.* Ed. A. Green. 157-205. Short title: 'HaBaD'

Elior, Rachel. *Harut Al Haluhot: Hamahshavah Hahasidit, Mekorotehah Hamistiim Veyesodotehah Hakabaliim.* Tel Aviv, 1999. Short title: *Harut*

Elior, Rachel. 'Hazika Bein Kabala Lehasidut'. In *Proceedings of Ninth World Congress of Jewish Studies, Division C, Jewish Thought and Literature.* Jerusalem, 1986. 107-114 (Hebrew section). Short title 'Hazika'.

Elior, Rachel. 'Historical Continuity and Spiritual Change'. In *Gershom Scholem's Major Trends in Jewish Mysticism 50 Years After: Proceedings of the Sixth International Conference on the History of Jewish Mysticism.* Eds. P. Schaefer and J. Dan. Tubingen, 1993. 303-336. Short title: 'Historical'

Elior, Rachel. 'Iyunim Bemahshevet Habad'. *Daat* 16, 1986: 133-173. Short title: 'Iyunim'

Elior, Rachel. 'Luria's Kabbala, Sabbateanism and Hasidism: Historical Continuity and Spiritual Influence'. In *Kolot Rabim: Commemorative Memorial Volume to Professor Rivka Schatz-Uffenhemier (Jerusalem Studies in Jewish Thought* 13-14). Eds. J. Dan and R. Elior. Jerusalem, 1996. 560-585. Short title 'Kabbalat'

Elior, Rachel. 'The Paradigms of Yesh and Ayin in Hasidic Thought'. In

Hasidism Reappraised. Ed. A. Rapoport-Albert. 168-179. Short
title: 'The Paradigms'

Elior, Rachel. *The Paradoxical Ascent to God: The Kabbalistic Theosophy
of Habad Hasidism*. Trans. Jeffrey M. Green. Albany, NY, 1993.
Short title: *Paradoxical*.

Elior, Rachel. 'Temurot Bamahshavah Hadatit Behasidut Polin: Bein
Yirah Veahavah Leomek Vegavan'. *Tarbiz* 62, 1993: 381-432.
Short title: 'Temurot'

Elior, Rachel. *Torat Ahdut Hahafakhim: Hatei'osofiyah Hamistit Shel
Habad*. Jerusalem, 1992. Published in English as The Paradoxical
Ascent to God. Short title: *Torat Ahdut*.

Elior, Rachel. 'Messianic Expectations and Spiritualization of Religious
Life in the Sixteenth Century'. *Revue des Etudes Juives* 155, 1986:
35-49. No short title

Elior, Rachel. *Torat HaElohut Bedor Hasheini Shel Hasidut Habad*.
Jerusalem, 1982. Short title: *Torat HaElohut*

Elon, Ari. *Alma Di*. Tel Aviv, no date. No short title

Elqayam, Abraham. 'Sod Ha'emunah Bekitvei Natan HaAzati'. PhD
Thesis, Hebrew University, 1993. Short title: 'Sod'

England, I. 'Majority Decision and Individual Truth: The Interpretation of
the Oven of Achnai Aggadah'. *Tradition* 11(1, 2), 1975: 137-172.
Short title: 'Majority'

Etkes, Immanuel. 'HaBesht Kemistikan Ubaal Besorah Be'avodat
Hashem'. Tzion 61, 1996: 421-454. Short title: 'HaBesht'

Etkes, Immanuel. 'Shitato Upa'alo Shel R. Hayyim MiVolozhin'.
Proceedings of the American Academy for Jewish Research 38-39,
1970-1971: 1-45. Short title: 'Shitato'

Ezrahi, Ohad. *Olamot Hasafek*. Bat Ayin, 1995. Short title: *Olamot*

Ezrahi, Ohad and Mordechai Gafni. *Mi Mefahed MiLilit?* Ben Shemen,
2003. Short title: *Mi*

Ezrahi, Ohad. 'Shenei Keruvim'. In *Hayashan Yithadesh Vehahadash
Yitkadesh*. Jerusalem, 1997. No short title

Eybeschutz, Yohanan Levi. *Simha Bunim of Przysucha*. 1973. No short
title

Faierstein, Morris M. *All Is In the Hands of Heaven*: The Teachings of
  Rabbi Mordecai Joseph Leiner of Izbica. New York, 1989. Short
  title: *Hands*

Faierstein, Morris M. 'God's Need for the Commandments in Medieval
  Kabbalah'. *Conservative Judaism* 36, 1982: 45-59.Short title:
  'God's'

Faierstein, Morris M. 'Personal Redemption in Hasidism'. In *Hasidism
  Reappraised*. Ed. A. Rapoport-Albert. 214-224. Short title:
  'Personal'

Farber, Ginat Asi. 'Kelipah Kodemet Leperi: Leshe'elat Motza Hametafizi
  Shel Hara Bemahshavah Hakablit Hakedumah'. *Eshel Be'er Sheva*
  4, 118-134. Short title: 'Kelipah'

Feigelson, Miriam. 'The Theory of Mitzvot in the Theology of Mei
  Hashiloach'. Unpublished seminar paper for Prof. Rachel Elior,
  Hebrew University, 1996. Short title: 'The Theory of Mitzvot'

Fine, Lawrence. 'The Art of Metoposcopy: A Study in Isaac Luria's
  Charismatic Knowledge'. *Association of Jewish Studies Review* 11,
  1986: 79-101. Short title: 'The Art

Fine, Lawrence. 'The Contemplative Practice of Yichudim'. In
  Jewish Spirituality II. Ed. A. Green. 64-98. Short title: 'The
  Contemplative'

Forbes, Scott. Lecture. 'Conference on Freedom and Education'.
  Delivered at Brockwood Park, England. 10 Oct 1999. No short title

Gafni, Mordechai (Marc). 'Evolving Consciousness: The Return
  to Eden via the Redemption of the Snake in Hebrew and
  General Mysticism'. Unpublished work. Short title: 'Evolving
  Consiousness'

Gafni, Mordechai (Marc). 'On the Erotic and the Ethical'. *Tikkun*, March
  2003: 5–11.

Gafni, Mordechai (Marc). *The Mystery of Love*. New York, 2002. Short
  title: *Mystery*

Gafni, Mordechai (Marc). *On Eros and Holiness*. Forthcoming. Short
  title: *On Eros.*

Gafni, Mordechai (Marc). *Safek: Hashavat I Havada'ut Ke'erekh Ruhani.*
  Tel Aviv, 2001. Short title: *Safek*

Gafni, Mordechai (Marc). *Soul Prints: Your Path to Fulfillment*. New York, 2001. Short title: Soul Prints. Published in Hebrew as *Teviot Neshamah*. Tel Aviv, 2004. No short title

Gafni, Mordechai (Marc). *Teviot Neshamah*. See *Soul Prints*.

Garb, Yonatan. 'Hakoah Vekavanah Bakabalah'. PhD Thesis, Hebrew University, 2000. Short title: 'Hakoah'

Garb, Yonatan. 'Simhah Shel Mitzvah'. In *Renewed Jewish Commitment*. By Garb. Tel Aviv, 2004. 95-103. No short title

Geertz, Clifford. 'Religion as a Cultural System'. In *The Interpretation of Cultures*. By Geertz. New York, 1973. 87-125. Short title: 'Religion'

Gellman, Jerome. 'The Denial of Free Will in Hassidic Thought'. In *Freedom and Moral Responsibility: General and Jewish Perspectives*. Eds. B. Manekin and M. Kellner. Bethesda, MD, 1997. 111-131. Short title: 'The Denial'

Gellman, Jerome. *The Fear, The Trembling and The Fire: Kierkegaard and the Hasidic Masters on the Binding of Isaac*. Lanham, MD, 1994. 23-43. Short title: *The Fear*

Gellman, Jerome. 'Hasidic Existentialism?' In *Hazon Nahum: Studies in Jewish Law, Thought, and History Presented to Dr. Norman Lamm on the Occasion of His Seventieth Birthday*. Eds. Yaakov Elman and Jeffrey Gurock. New York, 1997. 393-417. Short title: 'Hasidic'

Ginzberg, Louis. *The Legends of the Jews*. Philadelphia, 1909-1966. Short title: *Legends*

Glatzer, Nahum Norbert. 'A Study of the Talmudic-Midrashic Interpretation of Prophecy'. In *Essays in Jewish Thought*. By Glatzer. Tuscaloosa, AL, 1946. 16-35. Short title: 'A Study'

Goldman, Eliezer. 'Zikato Shel HaRav Kook Lemahshavah Ha'eiropei'it'. In *Yovel Orot*. Eds. B. Ish-Shalom and Sh. Rosenberg. Jerusalem, 1978. 115-122. Short title: 'Zikato'.

Gottlieb, E. *Mehkarim Besifrut Hakabalah*. Tel Aviv, 1976. Short title: *Mehkarim*

Gottlieb, E. *Haketavim Haivriyim Shel Baal Tikunei Zohar Veraaya Mehemana*. Preface by M. Idel. Jerusalem, 2003. Short title: *Haketavim Haivriyim*

Green, Arthur. *Ehyeh: A Kabbalah for Tomorrow*. Woodstock, VT, 2002. Short title: *Ehyeh*

Green, Arthur. *A Guide to the Zohar*. Stanford, CA: Stanford University, 2004. Short title: *A Guide*

Green, Arthur. 'Hasidism: Discovery and Retreat'. In *The Other Side of God, A Polarity in World Religions*. Ed. Peter Berger. Garden City NY, 1981: 104-130. Short title: 'Hasidism: Discovery'

Green, Arthur. *Keter: The Crown of God in Early Jewish Mysticism*. Princeton NJ, 1997. Short title: *Keter*

Green, Arthur. 'Neo-Hasidism and Our Theological Struggles'. *Ra'ayonot* 4(3), 1984. 11-17. Short title: 'Neo-Hasidism'

Green, Arthur. 'Rethinking Theology: Language, Experience, and Reality'. *Reconstructionist* 54(1), 1988: 8-13. Short title: 'Rethinking'

Green, Arthur. *Tormented Master: A Life of Rabbi Nahman of Braslav*. Tuscaloosa, AL, 1979. Short title: *Tormented*

Green, Arthur. 'Typologies of Leadership and the Hasidic Zaddiq'. In *Jewish Spirituality II*. London, 1987. 127-156. Short title: 'Typologies'

Green, Arthur. 'Zaddiq as Axis Mundi in Later Judaism.' Journal *of the American Academy of Religion* 45(3), 1977: 327-347. Short title: 'Zaddiq'

Gruenwald, Ithamar. 'Maimonides' Quest Beyond Philosophy and Prophecy'. In *Perspectives on Maimonides: Philosophical and Historical Studies*. Ed. Joel Kraemer. Oxford, 1991. 141-157. Short title: 'Maimonides' Quest'

Hadari, Hayyim Yeshayahu. 'Shenei Kohanim Gedolim'. In *Me'et Latzadik: Kovetz Maamarim Al Rabi Tzadok Hakohen Umishnato*. Ed. Gershon Kitsis. Jerusalem, 2000. 77-95. Short title: 'Shenei Kohanim'

Hallamish, Moshe. 'Limekoro Shel Pitgam Besifrut Hakabalah: "Kol Hanofeah-Mitokho Hu Nofeah" '. *Bar Ilan Annual* 13, 1976: 211-223. Short title: 'Limekoro'

Hallamish, Moshe. *Mevo Lakabalah. Sidrat Hillel Ben Hayyim – Sifrei Yesod Bemada'ei Hayahadut*. Jerusalem, 1991. Short title: *Mevo*

357

Hallamish, Moshe. 'Mishnato Haiyunit Shel Rabi Schneur Zalman MiLiadi'. PhD Thesis, Hebrew University, 1976. Short title: 'Mishnato'

Hallamish, Moshe. 'Mitzvah Ahat'. In *Mishe'ibud Leg'eulah: Sefer Zikaron LeMoshe Bari*. Jerusalem, 1996. 222-235. Short title: 'Mitzvah'

Hallamish, Moshe. 'The Teachings of R. Menahem Mendel of Vitebsk.' In *Hasidism Reappraised*. Ed. A. Rapoport-Albert. 268-287. Short title: 'The Teachings'

Hallamish, Moshe. 'Torat Hatzedakah Bemishnat Rabi Schneur Zalman MiLiadi'. *Daat* 1, 1978: 121-139. Short title: 'Torat'

Hallamish, Moshe. 'Yahas Shel Hamekubalim Leumot Haolam'. *Jerusalem Studies in Jewish Thought* 14, 1998: 289-311. Short title: 'Yahas'

Handelman, Susan. *Slayers of Moses*. Albany NY, 1982. Short title: *Slayers*

Hellner-Eshed, Melila. 'Al Sefat Hahavayah Hamistit Bazohar'. PhD Thesis, Hebrew University, 2001. Short title: 'Al Sefat'

Heschel, Abraham Joshua. *God in Search of Man*. New York, 1966. Short title: *God in Search*

Heschel, Abraham Joshua. 'God, Torah and Israel'. In *Theology and Church in Times of Change: Essays in Honor of John C. Bennett*. Eds. E. LeRoy Long, Jr. and Robert Handy. Philadelphia, 1970. Short title: 'God, Torah'

Heschel, Abraham Joshua. *The Prophets*. New York, 1962. No short title

Heschel, Abraham Joshua. *The Theology of Ancient Judaism* (Hebrew). 2 vols. New York, 1961, 1965.

Heschel, Abraham Joshua. *Torah Min Hashamayim Baaspaklariah Shel Hadorot*. 3 vols. Jerusalem, 1995. Short title: *Torah Min Hashamayim*

Hundert, Gershon David. 'An Advantage to Peculiarity? The Case of the [Jews in the] Polish Commonwealth'. Association *of Jewish Studies Review* 6, 1981: 21-38. Short title: 'An Advantage'

Huxley, Aldous. *The Perennial Philosophy*. New York, 1945. Short title: *The Perennial*

Hyman, James. 'Meaningfulness, the Ineffable, and the Commandments'. *Conservative Judaism* 50(2-3), 1998: 84-99. Short title: 'Meaningfulness'

Idel, Moshe. *Absorbing Perfections: Kabbalah and Interpretation.* New Haven, 2002. Short title: *Absorbing Perfections*

Idel, Moshe. 'Adam and Enoch According to St. Ephrem the Syrian'. *Kabbalah: Journal for the Study of Jewish Mystical Texts* 6, 2001: 183-205. Short title: 'Adam'

Idel, Moshe. 'The Book that Contains and Maintains All'. In Idel, *Absorbing Perfections.* 111-136. Short title: 'The Book'

Idel, Moshe. 'The Concept of the Torah in Heikhalot Literature and Its Metamorphoses in Kabbalah'. *Jerusalem Studies in Jewish Thought* 1, 1981: 23-84. Short title: 'The Concept'

Idel, Moshe. 'Defining Kabbalah: The Kabbalah of Divine Names'. In *Mystics of the Book: Themes, Topics, and Typologies.* Ed. R.A. Herrera. New York, 1993. 97-122. Short title: 'Defining'

Idel, Moshe. 'Enoch is Metatron'. In *Hamistika Haivrit Hakedumah.* Ed. Joseph Dan. Tel Aviv, 1989. 151-170. No short title

Idel, Moshe. 'From Italy to Safed and Back'. In *Messianic Mystics.* Moshe Idel. 154-183. Short title: 'From Italy'

Idel, Moshe. 'Hamahshavah Haraah Shel HaEl'. *Tarbiz* 49, 1980: 356-364. Short title: 'Hamahshavah'

Idel, Moshe. 'Hanokh Tofer Minalim Hayah'. *Kabbalah* 5, 2000: 265-286. No short title

Idel, Moshe. *Hasidism: Between Ecstasy and Magic.* Albany, NY, 1995. Short title: *Hasidism.*

Idel, Moshe. 'Hermeticism and Judaism'. In *Hermeticism and the Renaissance.* Ed. I. Merkel and A. Debus. Washington, 1988. 59-76. Short title: 'Hermeticism'

Idel, Moshe. *Kabbalah: New Perspectives.* New Haven, CT, 1988. Short title: *Perspectives*

Idel, Moshe. 'Martin Buber and Gershom Scholem on Hasidism: A Critical Appraisal'. In *Hasidism Reappraised.* Ed. Ada Rapoport-Albert. 389-403. Short title: 'Martin Buber'

Idel, Moshe. *Messianic Mystics.* New Haven, CT, 1998. Short title: *Messianic*

359

Idel, Moshe. 'Metatron: He'arot Al Hitpat'hut Hamitos Bayahadut'. *Eshel Be'er Sheva* 4, 1996: 29-44. Short title: 'Metatron: He'arot'

Idel, Moshe. *The Mystical Experience in Abraham Abulafia*. Trans. Jonathan Chipman. Albany, NY, 1987. Short title: *The Mystical*

Idel, Moshe. 'On Oral Torah and Multiple Interpretations in Hasidism'. In Idel, *Absorbing Perfections*. 470-481. Short title: 'On Oral'

Idel, Moshe. 'On the Concept of Zimzum in Kabbalah and Its Research'. *Jerusalem Studies in Jewish Thought* 10, 1992: 59-112. Short title: 'On the Concept'

Idel, Moshe. ' "One from a Town, Two from a Clan"—The Diffusion of Lurianic Kabbala and Sabbateanism: A Re-Examination'. *Jewish History* 7: 2. 1993: 79-104. Short title: 'One'

Idel, Moshe. *Perakim Bekabalah Nevu'it*. Jerusalem: Akademon, 1990. Short title: *Perakim*

Idel, Moshe. 'Preface' to Faierstein, *All Is In the Hands of Heaven*. ix-xii. Short title: 'Preface'

Idel, Moshe. 'Radical Forms of Jewish Hermeneutics'. In *Absorbing Perfections*. 250-271. Short title: 'Radical'

Idel, Moshe. 'Universalization and Integration: Two Conceptions of Mystical Union in Jewish Mysticism'. In *Mystical Union and Monotheistic Faith: An Ecumenical Dialogue*. Ed. Moshe Idel and Bernard McGinn. New York, 1989. 27-57. Short title: 'Universalization'

Inge, W. R. *The Philosophy of Plotinus*. 2 vols. London, 1948. No short title

Ish-Shalom, Binyamin. 'Dat, Teshuvah Veheirut Haadam Bemishnat HaRav Kook'. In *Yovel Orot*. Ed. Ish-Shalom and Shalom Rosenberg. Jerusalem, 1978. 295-329. Short title: 'Dat'

Ish-Shalom, Binyamin. *Haguto Shel HaRav Kook: Bein Rationalism Umistikah*. Tel Aviv, 1990. Short title: *Haguto*

Jabes, Edmond. 'Key'. Trans. Rosmarie Waldorf. In *Midrash and Literature*. Ed. Geoffrey H.Hartman and Sanford Budick. New Haven, 1986. 349-360. No short title

Jacobs, Louis. *Hasidic Prayer*. New York, 1987. No short title

Jacobs, Louis. *Religion and the Individual*: A Jewish Perspective. Cambridges, 1992. Short title: *Religion*

Jacobs, Louis. 'The Uplifting of the Sparks in Later Jewish Mysticism'. In *Jewish Spirituality*. Ed. Arthur Green. 99-126. Short title: 'The Uplifting'

Jacobson, Yoram. 'The Aspect of the "Feminine" in Lurianic Kabbalah'. In *Gershom Scholem's Major Trends 50 Years After: Proceedings of Sixth International Conference on the History of Jewish Mysticism*. Ed. P. Schager and J. Dan. Tubingen, 1993. 239-255. Short title: 'The Aspect'

Jacobson, Yoram. 'Galut Vegeulah Behasidut Gur'. *Daat* 2/3, 1978-1979: 175-215. Short title: 'Galut'

Jacobson, Yoram. *Mikabalat HaAri Ad Lahasidut*. Tel Aviv, 1984. Short title: *Mikabalat*

Jacobson, Yoram. 'Torat Haberiah Shel R. Schneur Zalman MiLiadi.' *Eshel Be'er Sheva* 1, 1976: 307-368. Short title: 'Torat'

Jaeger, Werner. *Humanism and Theology*. Milwaukee, 1943. Short title: *Humanism*

Kallus, Menahem. 'The Theurgy of Prayer in Lurianic Kabbalah'. PhD Thesis, Hebrew University, 2002. Short title: 'The Theurgy'

Kamenetz, Rodger. *Stalking Elijah: Adventures With Today's Jewish Mystical Masters*. New York, 1997. Short title: *Stalking*

Kaplan, Aryeh. Inner Space. Jerusalem, 1990. Short title: Inner Kaplan, Edward. 'Metaphor and Miracle: Abraham Joshua Heschel and the Holy Spirit'. *Conservative Judaism* 46(2), 1994. 3-18. Short title: 'Metaphor'

Katz, Steven T. 'Language, Epistemology, and Mysticism'. In *Mysticism and Philosophical Analysis*. Ed. Katz. New York, 1978. 22-74. Short title: 'Language'

Kaufmann, Walter. *Critique of Religion and Philosophy*. New York, 1958. Short title: *Critique*

Kaufmann, Walter, *Existentialism From Dostoyevsky to Sartre*. New York, 1976. Short title: *Existentialism*

Keegan, Robert. *The Evolving Self*. Cambridge, MA, 1982. Short title: *The Evolving*

Keen, Sam. *Hymns to an Unknown God*. New York, 1995. Short title: *Hymns*

Klein-Braslavy, Sara. *Shelomoh Hamelekh ve-haEzoterizm Hafilosofi Bemishnat HaRambam.* Jerusalem, 1996. Short title: *Shelomoh*

Koestler, Arthur. *Insight and Outlook: An Inquiry into the Common Foundations of Science, Art and Social Ethics.* London, 1949. Short title: *Insight*

Krishnamurti, J. *Action: A Selection of Passages from the Teachings of J. Krishnamurti.* Ojai, CA, 1990. Short title: Action

Lamm, Norman. *Torah Lishmah.* Jerusalem, 1972. No short title

Landy, Francis. 'The Name of God and the Image of God and Man'. *Theology* 84, 1981: 164-170. Short Title: 'The Name'

Langdon, Stephen. *Tammuz and Ishtar: A Monograph Upon Babylonian Religion And Theology.* Oxford, 1914. Short title: *Tammuz*

Langer, Jiri. *Nine Gates.* Trans. Stephen Jolly. London, 1961. No short title

Laytner, Anton. *Arguing with God: A Jewish Tradition.* Northvale, NJ, 1994. Short title: *Arguing*

Lever, Amira. 'Paradoxical Principles in the Writings of Tzadok HaCohen of Lublin'. MA Thesis, Touro College, 1993. Short title: 'Principles'

Levin, J. L. *Haadmorim Meilzbica.* Jerusalem, no date. Short title: *Haadmorim*Levinger, Yaakov. 'Imrot Autenti'ot Shel HaRebi MiKotzk'. *Tarbiz* 56(1), 1986: 109-135. Short title: 'Imrot'

Levinger, Yaakov. 'Torato Shel Harebi MiKotzk Le'or Ha'imrot Hameyuhasot Lo Al Yidei Nehdo Reb Shmuel MiSokachov'. *Tarbiz* 55(4), 1986: 413-431. Short title: 'Torato'

Lewis, C. S. *The Discarded Image: An Introduction to Medieval and Renaissance Literature.* Cambridge, UK, 1994. Short title: *The Discarded*

Liebes, Yehuda. 'Hamashiah Shel Hazohar'. In *Haraayon Hameshihi BeYisrael: Yom Iyun Leregel Melo'ot Shemonim Shanah LeGershom Scholem.* Jerusalem: Israel Academy of Sciences and Humanities, 1982. 87-236. Short title: 'Hamashiah'

Liebes, Yehuda. 'Hamitos Hakabali Shebefi Orpheus'. In *Sefer Hayovel LeShlomo Pines*, vol. 1. (*Jerusalem Studies in Jewish Thought* 7, 9) 1998-1990, 425-459. Short title: 'Hamitos'

Liebes, Yehuda. 'Hibur Bileshon Hazohar LeRav Wolf Ben Rav Yehonatan Eybeschutz Al Havurato Ve'al Sod Hageulah'. *Kiryat Sefer* 1, 1982: 148-178. Short title: 'Hibur'

Liebes, Yehudah. 'Lidemuto, Ketavav, Vekabalato Shel Baal Emek Hamelekh'. *Jerusalem Studies in Jewish Thought* 11, 1993: 101-137. Short title: 'Lidemuto'

Liebes, Yehudah. 'Myth versus Symbol in the Zohar and in Lurianic Kabbalah'. In *Essential Papers on Kabbalah*. Ed. Lawrence Fine. New York, 1995. 213-219. Short title: 'Myth'

Liebes, Yehudah. *Sod Haemunah Hashabta'it.* Jerusalem, 1995. Short title: *Sod*

Liebes, Yehudah. 'Shabbtai Zevi's Religious Faith'. In *Studies in Jewish Myth and Messianism*. By Liebes. 107-113. Short title: 'Shabbtai'

Liebes, Yehudah. *Studies in Jewish Myth and Jewish Messianism*. Trans. Batya Stein. Albany, NY, 1993. Short title: *Studies*

Liebes, Yehuda. 'Zohar Ve'eros'. *Alpayim* 9, 1994: 67-119. No short title

Lipshitz, Chaim. *Roeh Orot: Shirat Haadam, Shirat Hateshuvah Bemishnat Maran HaRav Avraham Yitzhak Hakohen Kook.* Jerusalem, 1975. Short title: *Roeh*

Loevinger, J. *Ego Development*. San Francisco, 1977. Short title: *Ego*

Loewenthal, Naftali. 'Reason and Beyond Reason in Habad Hassidism'. In *Alei Shefer: Mehkarim Besifrut Hahagut Hayehudit: Mugashim Likhvod HaRav Alexandre Safran (English title: Alei Shefer: Studies in the Literature of Jewish Thought Presented to Rabbi Dr. Alexandre Safran)*. Ed. Moshe Hallamish. Ramat Gan, 1990. 109-126 in English section of book. Short title: 'Reason'

Lowenthal, Tali. 'The Apotheosis of Action in Early Habad'. *Daat* 18, 1987: v-xix. Short title: 'The Apotheosis'

Lovejoy, Arthur. *The Great Chain of Being*. Cambridge: Harvard University Press, 1964. Short title: *The Great*

MacIntyre, Alasdair. *After Virtue*. Notre Dame, 1981. No short title

MacIntyre, Alasdair. *A Short History of Ethics*. Notre Dame, IN, 1996. Short title: *A Short History*

Macy, Jeffery. 'Prophecy in al-Farabi and Maimonides in the Imaginative and Rational Faculties'. In *Maimonides and Philosophy: Papers Presented at the Sixth Jerusalem Philosophical Encounter, May, 1985*. Ed. S. Pines and Y. Yovel. Norwell, MA, 1986. Short title: 'Prophecy'

Magid, Shaul. *Hasidism on the Margin: Reconciliation, Antinomianism, and Messianism in Izbica/Radzin Hasidism*. Madison, 2003. Short title: *Hasidism*

Mahler, Raphael. *Hasidism and the Jewish Enlightenment: Their Confrontation In Galicia and Poland In the First Half of the Nineteenth Century*. Trans. Eugene Orenstein, Aaron Klein, and Jenny Machlowitz Klein. Philadelphia, 1985. Short title: *Hasidism*

Matt, Daniel. 'Ayin: The Concept of Nothingness in Jewish Mysticism'. In *The Problem of Pure Consciousness: Mysticism and Philosophy*. Ed. Robert K. C. Forman. Oxford, 1990. 121-160. Short title: 'Ayin'

Meeks, Wayne. 'Moses as God and King'. In *Religions in Antiquity: Essays in Memory of Erwin Ramsdell Goodenough*. Ed. Jacob Neusner. Leiden, 1968. 354-371. Short title: 'Moses'

Meir, Benayahu. *Sefer Toldot HaAri*. Jerusalem, 1967. Short title: *Sefer Toledot*

Meroz, Ronit. 'Hebeitim Betorat Hanevuah HaLurianit'. MA Thesis, Hebrew University, 1980. Short title: 'Hebeitim'

Moore, George Foot. History of Religions. 2 vols. New York, 1914. Short title: History Mopsik, Charles. 'Union and Unity in the Kabbalah: The Proclamation of the Divine Unity and the Male/Female Couple'. In *Sex of the Soul: The Vicissitudes of Sexual Difference in Kabbalah: Sources and Studies in the Literature of Jewish Mysticism* 15. Ed. and foreword by Daniel Abrams. Los Angeles, 2005. 1-149. Short title: 'Union'

Morgenstern, Arie. 'Tzipiyot Meshihiyot Likrat Shnat Heh-Taf-Resh (1840)'. In *Meshihiyut Ve'eskatologiyah*. Ed. Zvi Baras. Jerusalem, 1983. 343-364. Short title: 'Tzipiyot'

Neuman, Erich. *The Great Mother: An Analysis of the Archetype*. 2nd ed. Princeton, 1963. Short title: *The Great*

Nigal, Gedaliah. 'Hasidic Doctrine in the Writings of Rabbi Elimelekh of Lishensk and His Disciples'. PhD Thesis, Hebrew University, 1972. Short title: 'Hasidic'

Pachter, Mordechai. 'Acosmism and Theism: R. Hayyim Volozhin's Concept of God' (Hebr.: 'Bein Akozmizm Lete'izm—Tefisat HaElohut Bemishnato Shel R. Hayyim Volozhin'). In *Mehkarim Behagot Yehudit.* Ed. Moshe Idel, Devorah Diament, and Shalom Rosenberg. Jerusalem, 1989. 139-157. Short title: 'Acosmism and Theism'

Pachter, Mordechai. 'Igulim Veyosher'. *Daat* 18, 1987: 59-90. No short title

Pariz, Yitzchak Dov. 'Ha"Kohen" MiLublin: Oseh Hashalom Betorotav'. In *Me'et Latzadik: Kovetz Maamarim Al Rabi Tzadok Hakohen Umishnato.* Ed. Gershon Kitsis. Jerusalem, 2000. 147-162. Short title: 'HaKohen'

Patai, Raphael. *The Hebrew Goddess.* Detroit, 1990. No short title

Pedaya, Haviva. *Hashem Vehamikdash Bemishnat Rabi Yitzhak Sagi Nahor.* Jerusalem, 2001. Short title: *Hashem*

Pedaya, Haviva. 'Pegam Vetikun Shel HaElohut Bekabalat Rabi Yitzhak Sagi Nahor'. In *Hakenes Habeinleumi Letoledot Hamistikah Hayehudit.* Ed. Joseph Dan. Jerusalem, 1987. 157-285. Short title: 'Pegam'

Piekarz, Mendel. *Bein Idiologiah Lemetsiut: Anavah, Ayin, Bitul Mimitsiut Vedevekut Bemahshavtam Shel Rashei Hahasidut.* Jerusalem, 1994. Short title: *Bein*

Piekarz, Mendel. *Biyimei Tzemihat Hahasidut: Megamot Raayoniyot Besifrei Derush Umusar.* Jerusalem, 1978. Short title: *Biyimei*

Piekarz, Mendel. *Studies in Braslav Hasidism.* Jerusalem, 1972. No short title

Polen, Nehemiah. 'Miriam's Dance: Radical Egalitarianism in Hasidic Thought'. *Modern Judaism* 12, 1992: 1-21. Short title: 'Miriam's Dance'

Pritchard, J. B., ed. *Ancient Near Eastern Texts Relating to the Old Testament.* Trans. W. F. Albright. 3rd ed. Princeton, 1969. Short title: *Ancient*

Putnam, Robert D. *Bowling Alone: The Collapse and Revival of American Community.* New York, 2000. No short title

Rabinowicz, Z. M. *Rabbi Simhah Bunim MiPeshishah.* Tel Aviv, 1944. Short title: *Rabbi*

Rakover, Nahum. *Ends Justify Means.* Jerusalem, 2000. Short title: *Ends*

Rapoport-Albert, Ada. 'God and the Tzadik as Two Focal Points of Hasidic Worship'. *History of Religions* 18, 1979: 296-325. Repr. in *Essential Papers on Hasidism*. Ed. G. D. Hundert. New York, 1991. Short title: 'God and the Tzadik'

Rapoport-Albert, Ada, ed. *Hasidism Reappraised*. Portland, OR, 1996. No short title

Rosenberg, Shalom. 'Hashivah Legan Eden: He'arot Letoledot Haraayon Hageulah Harestorativit Befilosofiah Hayehudit Biyimei Habeinayim'. In *Haraayon Hameshihi BeYisrael: Yom Iyun Leregel Melo'ot Shemonim Shanah LeGershom Scholem*. Jerusalem, 1982. 37-86. Short title: 'Hashivah'

Rosenberg, Shalom. 'Hitgalut Matmedet: Sheloshah Kivunim'. In *Hitgalut, Emunah, Tevunah*. Ed. Moshe Hallamish and Moshe Schwarcz. Ramat Gan, 1976. 131-143. Short title: 'Hitgalut'

Rosenberg, Shimon Gershon (Shagar). 'Teshuvah Kekabalah Atzmit: Iyun Bemishnat Hateshuvah Shel R. Tzadok'. In *Me'et Latzadik: Kovetz Maamarim Al Rabi Tzadok Hakohen Umishnato*. Ed. Gershon Kitzis. Jerusalem, 2000. 193-209. Short title: 'Teshuvah'

Ross, Tamar. 'Hamahshavah Ha'iyunit Bekitvei Mamshihav Shel Rav Israel Salanter Betenuat Hamusar'. PhD Thesis, Hebrew University, 1986. Short title: 'Hamahshavah'

Ross, Tamar. 'Musag HaElokut Shel Harak Kook'. Daat 8, 1982: 109-128; 9, 1982: 39-70. Short title: 'Musag'

Ross, Tamar. 'Perakim BeTorat HaRav Kook: Leket Mekorot'. Unpublished manuscript. Jerusalem, 1991. Short title: 'Perakim BeTorat'

Ross, Tamar. 'Shenei Peirushim Letorat Hatzimtzum – Rav Hayyim MiVolozhin VeRav Schneur Zalman MiLiadi'. *Jerusalem Studies in Jewish Thought* 2, 1982: 153-169. Short title: 'Shenei'

Ruderman, D. B. 'The Italian Renaissance and Jewish Thought'. In *Renaissance Humanism: Foundation, Forms and Legacy*, vol. 1. Ed. Albert Rabil. Philadelphia, 1988. 382-433. Short title: 'The Italian'

Ruerup, R. 'The European Revolution of 1848 and Jewish Emancipation'. In Revolution and Evolution: 1848. In *German-Jewish History. Schriftenreihe wissenschaftlicher Abhandlungen des Leo Baeck Instituts 39*. Ed. Werner E. Mosse, Arnold Paucker and Reinhard Ruerup. Tubingen, 1981. 1-53. Short title: 'The European'

Sack, Bracha. Beshaarei Hakabalah Shel Moshe Cordevero. Beer Sheva, 1995. Short title: Beshaarei

Safran, Bezalal. 'Maharal and Early Hasidism'. In *Hasidism, Continuity or Change*. Ed. Bezalal Safran. Cambridge, MA, 1988. 47-144. Short title: 'Maharal'

Safran, Bezalal. 'Rabbi Azriel and Nahmanides: Two View of the Fall of Man'. In *Rabbi Moses Nahmanides (Ramban); Explorations in His Religious and Literary Virtuosity*. Ed. Isadore Twersky. Cambridge, MA, 1983. 75-106. Short title: 'Rabbi'

Sagi, Avi. *Elu Ve'elu: A Study on the Meaning of Halachic Discourse*. Tel Aviv, 1996. Short title: *Elu Ve'elu*

Sasson, Gilad. *Melekh Vehedyot: Yahasam shel Hazal Lishelomoh Hamelekh*. PhD thesis, Bar Illan University, 2004. Short title: *Yahasam*

Schatz-Uffenheimer, Rivka. 'Autonomiah Shel Haruah Vetorat Moshe'. *Molad* 21, 1963: 554-562. Short title: 'Autonomiah'

Schatz-Uffenheimer, Rivka. *Hahasidut Kemistikah*: Yesodot Kvi'atistiyim Bamahashavah Hahasidit Bame'ah ha-18. Jerusalem, 1980. Short Title: *Hahasidut*

Schatz-Uffenheimer, Rivka. *Hasidism as Mysticism: Quietistic Elements in Eighteenth-Century Hasidic Thought*. Trans. Jonathan Chipman. Princeton, 1993. Short title: *Hasidism*

Schatz-Uffenheimer, Rivka. 'Hayesod Hameshihi Bemahshevet Hahasidut: Hayesh Tzivyon Meshihi Histori Leraayon Hageulah Bahasidut?' *Molad* 1, 1967: 105-111. Short title: 'Hayesod'

Schimmel, Annemarie. *Mystical Dimensions of Islam*. Chapel Hill, NC, 1978. Short title: *Mystical*

Schneider, Susan. *Kabbalistic Writings on the Masculine and the Feminine*. Northvale, NJ, 2001. Short title: *Kabbalistic Writings*

Schochat, A. 'Al Hasimcha Behasidut'. Zion 16. 1951: 30-43. No short title

Scholem, Gershom. 'The Concept of Kavvanah in the Early Kabbalah'. In *Studies in Jewish Thought: An Anthology of German Jewish Scholarship*. Ed. A. Jospe. Detroit, 1981. 162-180. Short title: 'The Concept'

Scholem, Gershom. 'Devekut, or Communion with God'. In *The Messianic Idea*. 203-226. By Scholem. Short title: 'Devekut'

367

Scholem, Gershom. 'Gilgul: On the Transmigration of Souls'. In *On the Mystical Shape of the Godhead*. By Scholem. 197-250. Short title: 'Gilgul'

Scholem, Gershom. 'Isaac Luria and His School'. In *Major Trends*. By Scholem. 244-286. Short title: 'Isaac Luria'

Scholem, Gershom. *Jewish Gnosticism: Merkabah Mysticism and Talmudic Tradition*. New York, 1960. Short title: *Jewish Gnosticism*

Scholem, Gershom. *Kabbalah*. New York, 1974. No short title

Scholem, Gershom. 'The Kabbalah of R. Jacob and R. Isaac Cohen'. *Mada'ei Hayahadut* 2, 1927: 165-293. Short title: 'The Kabbalah of'

Scholem, Gershom. 'Leheker Kabalat R. Yitzhak Ben Yaakov Hakohen. Part B: Hitpat'hut Torat Ha'olamot Bekabalat Harishonim'. *Tarbiz* 3, 1932: 59-92. Short title: 'Leheker'

Scholem, Gershom. *Major Trends in Jewish Mysticism*. New York, 1961. Short title: *Major Trends*

Scholem, Gershom. 'Martin Buber's Interpretation of Hassidism'. *In The Messianic Idea*. By Scholem. 227-250. Short title: 'Martin Buber'

Scholem, Gershom. 'The Meaning of the Torah in Jewish Mysticism'. In *On the Kabbalah*. By Scholem. 32-86. Short title: 'The Meaning'

Scholem, Gershom. *The Messianic Idea in Judaism and Other Essays in Jewish Spirituality*. New York, 1971. Short title: *Messianic Idea*

Scholem, Gershom. 'The Name of God and the Linguistic Theory of the Kabbalah'. *Diogenes* 79, 1972: 59-80, 164-194. Short title: 'The Name'

Scholem, Gershom. 'The Neutralization of the Messianic Element in Early Hassidism'. In *The Messianic Idea*. By Scholem. 176-202. Short title: 'The Neutralization'

Scholem, Gershom. *On the Kabbalah and its Symbolism*. Trans. Ralph Manheim. New York, 1969. Short title: *On the Kabbalah*

Scholem, Gershom. *On the Mystical Shape of the Godhead: Basic Concepts in the Kabbalah*. Trans. Joachim Neugroschel. Ed. and revised by Jonathan Chipman. New York, 1991. Short title: *On the Mystical Shape*

Scholem, Gershom. *Origins of the Kabbalah*. Ed. R. J. Z. Werblowsky. Trans. Allan Arkush. Philadelphia and Princeton, 1987. Short title: *Origins*

Scholem, Gershom. *Pirkei Yesod Behavanat Hakabalah Usemalehah*. Trans. from German by Y. Ben-Shlomo. (English translation: *On the Kabbalah and its Symbolism*). Jerusalem, 1976. Short title: Pirkei

Scholem, Gershom. 'Redemption through Sin'. In *The Messianic Idea*. By Scholem. 78-141. Short title: 'Redemption'

Scholem, Gershom. 'Reflections on Jewish Theology'. In *On Jews and Judaism in Crisis: Selected Essays*. By Scholem. Ed. Werner J. Dannhauser. New York, 1976. 261-297. Short title: 'Reflections'

Scholem, Gershom. *Reishit Hakabbalah*. Jerusalem, Tel Aviv, 1948. (English translation of the German is *Origins of the Kabbalah*). Short title: *Reishit*

Scholem, Gershom. 'Religious Authority and Mysticism'. In *On the Kabbalah*. By Scholem. New York, 1965. 5-32. Short title: 'Religious'

Scholem, Gershom. 'Revelation and Tradition as Religious Categories in Judaism'. In The *Messianic Idea*. By Scholem. 282-303. Short title: 'Revelation'

Scholem, Gershom. 'Tsaddik: The Righteous One'. In *On the Mystical Shape of the Godhead. By Scholem*. 88-140. Short title: 'Tsaddik'

Scholem, Gershom. *Sabbetai Sevi, the Mystical Messiah*. Trans. R. J. Z. Werblowsky. Princeton, 1973. Short title: *Sabbetai Sevi*

Scholem, Gershom. 'Shekhinah: The Feminine Element in Divinity'. In *On the Mystical Shape of the Godhead*. By Scholem. 140-149. Short title: 'Shekhina'

Scholem, Gershom. 'Sitra Achra: Good and Evil in Kabbalah'. In On the Mystical Shape of the Godhead. By Scholem. 150-197. Short title: 'Sitra'

Seeman, Don. 'Martyrdom, Emotion and the Work of Ritual in R. Mordechai Joseph's Lainer's Mei ha-Shiloach.' *Association of Jewish Studies Review* 27(2), 2003: 253-279. Short title: 'Martyrdom'

Shagar. See Rosenberg, Shimon.Shapira, Abraham. 'Shetei Darkhei Geulah Bahasidut Be'aspaklariyah Shel Martin Buber'. In *Massu'ot: Mehkarim Besifrut Hakabalah Ubemahshevet Yisrael, Mukdashim Lezikhro Shel Ephrayim Gottlieb*. Eds. M. Oron and A. Goldreich. Jerusalem, 1994. 426-429. Short title: 'Shetei'

Shochat, Azriel. 'Al Hasimhah Bahasidut'. *Zion* 16: 1951, 30-43. No short title

Shragai, S. Z. *Benetivei Hasidut Izbica-Radzyn*, 2 vols. Jerusalem, 1972. Short title: *Benetivei*

Silman, Yohanan David. *Kol Gadol Velo Yasaf: Torat Yisrael Bein Sheleimut Lehishtalmut*. Jerusalem, 1999. Short title: *Kol*

Silman, Yohanan David. *The Voice Heard at Sinai: Once or Ongoing?* Jerusalem, 1999. Short title: *The Voice*

Sokol, Moshe. 'Personal Autonomy and Religious Authority'. In *Rabbinic Authority and Personal Autonomy*. Ed. Sokol. Northvale, NJ. 169-216. Short title: 'Autonomy'

Soloveitchik, H. 'Three Themes in Sefer Hasidim'. *Association of Jewish Studies Review* 1. 1976: 311-358. Short title: 'Three Themes'

Sperber, Shmuel. 'Al Yesod Hachidush'. *Daat* 18, 1988: 111-114. Short title: 'Al Yesod'

Sterne, Laurence. *Sentimental Journey*. Ed. Herbert Read. London, 1929. Short title: *Sentimental*

Stone, Merlin. *When God Was A Woman*. New York, 1976. Short title: *When*

Strauss, Leo. *Persecution and the Art of Writing*. Glencoe, IL, 1952. Short title: *Persecution*

Suzuki, D. T. *Essays in Zen Buddhism*. 3 vols. London, 1970. Short title: *Essays*

Suzuki, D. T. *Studies in the Lankavatara Sutra*. London, 1968. Short title: *Studies*

Taylor, Charles. *Ethics of Authenticity*. Cambridge, MA, 1991. No short title

Taylor, Charles. *Hegel*. Cambridge, 1975. No short title

Taylor, Charles. Sources *of the Self: The Making of the Modern Identity*. Cambridge, MA, 1989. Short title: *Sources of the Self*

Tillich, Paul. 'The Two Types of Philosophy of Religion'. In *Theology of Culture*. Ed. R. Kimball. New York, 1959. 10-29. Short title: 'Two Types'

Tishby, Isaiah. *The Doctrine of Evil in Lurianic Kabbalah*. New York, London, 2002. Short title: *The Doctrine*

Tishby, Isaiah. *Hikrei Kabalah Usheluhotehah: Mehkarim Umekorot*, 3 vols. Jerusalem, 1982-1992. Short title: Hikrei

Tishby, Isaiah. 'Kudsha Berikh Hu Orayta Veyisrael Kula Had—Mekor Ha'imrah Bepeirush Idra Raba LaRamhal'. *Kiryat Sefer* 50, 1975: 480-492. Reprinted in *Hikrei Kabalah Usheluhotehah: Mehkarim Umekorot*. By Tishby. 941-960. Short title: 'Kudsha'

Tishby, Isaiah. *Mishnat Hazohar*, 2 vols. Jerusalem: 1961. No short title

Tishby, Isaiah. *Paths of Faith and Heresy*. Ramat Gan, 1964. No short title

Tishby, Isaiah. *Torat Hara Vehakelipah Bekabalat HaAri*. Jerusalem, 1942. Short Title: Torat

Tishby, Isaiah. *The Wisdom of the Zohar: An Anthology of Tex*ts. 3 vols. Trans. D. Goldstein. London, Washington, 1991. Short title: *The Wisdom*

Tishby, Isaiah. 'Yahaso Shel Rav Avraham Azulai Lekabalat HaRamak Ulekabalat Ha'Ari'. *Sefunot* 1(16), 1980: 191-203. Reprinted in Tishby, Hikrei Kabalah Usheluhotehah. 255-267. Short title: 'Yahaso'

Twersky, Isadore. 'Some Non-Halachic Aspects of the Mishneh Torah.' *In Jewish Medieval and Renaissance Studies*. Ed. A Altman. Cambridge,MA, 1967. 95-119. Short title: 'Some'

Urbach, Ephraim E. 'Halakhah Venevuah'. *Tarbiz* 18, 1947: 1-27. Short title: 'Halakhah'

Urbach, Ephraim E. 'Matai Paskah Hanevuah?'. *Tarbiz* 17, 1946: 1-11. Short title: 'Matai'

Urbach, Ephraim E. *The Sages: Their Concepts and Beliefs*. 2 vols. Trans. I. Abrahams. Jerusalem, 1979. Short title: *The Sages*

Weiss, Joseph. 'Contemplation as Self-Abandonment in the Writings of Hayyim Haika of Amdura'. In *Studies in Eastern European Jewish Mysticism and Hasidism*. By Weiss. Ed. D. Goldstein. Oxford, 1985. 142-154. Short title: 'Contemplation'

Weiss, Joseph. 'Contemplative Mysticism and "Faith" in Hasidic Piety'. *Journal of Jewish Studies* 4, 1952: 19-29. Short title: 'Contemplative'

Weiss, Joseph. 'Determinism'. See Weiss, Joseph, 'Torat Hadeterminizm'.

Weiss, Joseph. 'The Kavvanot of Prayer in Early Hasidism'. In *Studies in Eastern European Jewish Mysticism*. By Weiss. Ed. D. Goldstein. Oxford and New York, 1985. 95-125. Short title: 'The Kavvanot'

Weiss, Joseph. 'A Late Jewish Utopia of Religious Freedom'. In *Studies in Eastern European Jewish Mysticism*. By Weiss. Ed. D. Goldstein. Oxford, 1985. 209-248. Short title: 'A Late Jewish Utopia'

Weiss, Joseph. *Mehkarim Behasidut Braslav*. Ed. Mendel Piekarz. Jerusalem, 1974. Short title: *Mehkarim*

Weiss, Joseph. 'The Saddik—Altering the Divine Will'. In Studies *in Eastern European Jewish Mysticism*. By Weiss. Ed. D. Goldstein. Oxford, 1985. 183-193. Short title: 'The Saddik'

Weiss, Joseph. 'Torat Hadeterminizm Hadati LeR. Yosef Mordechai Lerner [sic] Meilzbica'. In *Sefer Yovel LeYitzhak Baer.* Eds. S. Baron, B. Dinur, S. Ettinger, and I. Halpern. Jerusalem, 1961. 447-453. Short title: 'Determinism'

Weiss, Joseph. 'Via Passiva in Early Hassidism'. In *Studies in Eastern European Jewish Mysticism*. Ed. D. Goldstein. Oxford, 1985. 69-94. Short title: 'Via Passiva'

Werblowsky, R. J. Z. *Joseph Karo, Lawyer and Mystic*. Philadelphia, 1977. Short title: *Joseph*

Werblowsky, R. J. Z. 'The Safed Revival and its Aftermath'. In Jewish Spirituality II. Ed. A. Green. New York, 1989. 7-33. Short title: 'Safed'

Wilber, Ken. 'A Developmental View of Consciousness'. Journal of Transpersonal Psychology 11(1), 1979. 1-21. Short title: 'A Developmental'

Wilber, Ken. *Boomeritis: A Novel That Will Set You Free.* Boston, 2002. Short title: *Boomeritis.*

Wilber, Ken. *The Eye of the Spirit.* Boston, 1997. Short title: *The Eye*

Wilber, Ken. *The Marriage of Sense and Soul.* New York, 1998. Short title: The *Marriage*

Wilber, Ken. *No Boundary: Eastern and Western Approaches*. Boston, 1979. Short title: *No Boundary*

Wilber, Ken. 'The Pre/Trans Fallacy'. *ReVision* 3(2), 1980. 51-73. No short title

Wilber, Ken. *Sex, Ecology, Spirituality: The Spirit of Evolution*. Boston, 1995. Short title: *Sex, Ecology*

Wilensky, M. Idel, *Studies in Jewish Thought. Jerusalem*, 1989. No short title

Wilensky, Sara Ora Heller. 'Joseph Weiss, Letters to Ora'. In *Hasidism Reappraised*. Ed. A. Rapoport-Albert. 10-41. Short title: 'Joseph'

Wilson, Bryan. *Religion in Sociological Perspective*. Oxford, 1978. Short title: *Religion*

Wolfson, Elliot. *Abraham Abulafia—Kabbalist and Prophet: Hermeneutic Theosophy and Theurgy*. Los Angeles, 2000. Short title: *Abraham*

Wolfson, Elliot. *Along the Path: Studies in Kabbalistic Myth, Symbolism, and Hermeneutics*. Albany NY, 1995. Short title: *Along*

Wolfson, Elliot. 'Beautiful Maiden Without Eyes: Peshat and Sod in Zoharic Hermeneutics'. In *Midrashic Imagination*. Ed. Michael Fishbane. Albany, NY, 1993. 155-203. Short title: 'Beautiful'

Wolfson, Elliot. 'Circumcision and the Divine Name: A Study in the Transmission of Esoteric Doctrine'. *Jewish Quarterly Review* 78, 1987: 77-112. Short title: 'Circumcision and the Divine Name'

Wolfson, Elliot. 'Circumcision, Vision of God, and Textual Interpretation: From Midrashic Trope to Religious Symbol'. *History of Religions* 27, 1987. 189215. Short title: 'Circumcision, Vision of God'

Wolfson, Elliot. 'Female Imaging of the Torah: From Literary Metaphor to Religious Symbol'. In *From Ancient Israel to Modern Judaism: Intellect in Quest of Understanding. Essays in Honor of Marvin Fox*. 4 vols. Eds. Jacob Neusner, E. Frerichs, and N. Sarna. Atlanta, 1989. Vol. 2 271-308. Short title: 'Female'

Wolfson, Elliot. 'Forms of Visionary Ascent as Ecstatic Experience in Zoharic Literature'. In *Gershom Scholem's Major Trends in Jewish Mysticism 50 Years After: Proceedings of the Sixth International Conference on the History of Jewish Mysticism*. Ed. P. Schaefer and J. Dan. Tubingen, 1993. 209-235. Short title: 'Forms'

Wolfson, Elliot. 'The Hermeneutics of Visionary Experience: Revelation and Interpretation in the Zohar'. *Religion* 18, 1988: 311-345. Short title: 'The Hermeneutics'

Wolfson, Elliot. 'Light Through Darkness: The Ideal of Human Perfection in the Zohar'. *Hebrew Theological Review* 81(1), 1988: 73-95. Short title: 'Light'

Wolfson, Elliot. 'The Mystical Significance of Torah Study in German Pietism'. Jewish Quarterly Review 84(1), 1993: 43-78. Short title: 'The Mystical Significance'

Wolfson, Elliot R. *Through a Speculum That Shines: Vision and Imagination in Medieval Jewish Mysticism*. Princeton, 1994. Short title: *Through*

Wolfson, Elliot. 'Walking as a Sacred Duty: Theological Transformation of Social Reality in Early Hasidism'. In *Hasidism Reappraised*. Ed. A. Rapoport-Albert. 180-207. Short title: 'Walking'

Wolfson, Eliot. 'Woman–The Feminine as Other in Theosophic Kabala: Some Philosophic Observations on the Divine Androgyny'. In *The Other in Jewish Thought and History: Constructions of Jewish Culture and Identity*. Eds. L. J. Silberstein and R. L. Cohn. New York, 1994. 166-204. Short title: 'Woman–The Feminine'

Wolfson, Harry Austryn. *Hallevi and Maimonides on Prophecy*. Philadelphia, 1942. Short title: *Hallevi*

Yasif, Ely. *Sipur Haam Haivri*. Jerusalem, 1994. Short title: *Sipur*

Yovel, Yirmiyahu. *Spinoza and other Heretics*. Princeton, 1988. Short title: *Spinoza*

Zaehner, R. C. Mysticism, Sacred and Profane: An Inquiry Into Some Varieties of Praeter-Natural Experience. Oxford, 1957. Short title: Mysticism

ABOUT THE AUTHOR

Marc Gafni, D.Phil., Scholar-in-Residence and Director of the Center for World Spirituality, is a philosopher and public intellectual who is leading the emergence of the World Spirituality movement, based on what Gafni has termed the Democratization of Enlightenment. At the core of his teachings is what he calls the Enlightenment of Fullness, the linchpin of which is Unique Self Teachings, a breakthrough technology with the potential to change the source code of the human experience. The Unique Self teaching is now being adapted in leading treatment centers, universities, private schools and spiritual centers all over the world. In each of these fields serious work is being done by leaders to bring Gafni's teaching to bear in a way that redefines the field. For example, the Castlewood Treatment Centers are now working on a revolutionary approach to addiction and treatments based on Unique Self teaching, which extends and transcends traditional 12-step work.

Over the past 30 years, Dr. Gafni has developed many educational programs and workshops rooted in traditional wisdom and yet fully adapted to the needs of the contemporary world. His acclaimed writings and standing-room-only lectures are known for their unique mix of profound teaching and transmission, open-hearted compassion and love, intellectual rigor. Depending on the night, he might include stand-up comedy or storytelling.

An iconoclastic artist and provocative visionary, Dr. Gafni has led spiritual movements and learning communities as well as created and hosted the leading Israeli television program, on ethics and spirituality. Now, he is focusing on bringing his passion, brilliance, and ability to the World Spirituality Institute, which he initiated together with Ken Wilber, Mariana Caplan, Sally Kempton, Warren Farrell and John Mackey. World Spirituality is a new framework for meaning aimed at the highest possible integration of pre-modern religions, modern scientific principles, and post-modern philosophies based on Integral principles. More than an interfaith movement, and beyond perennial philosophy, World Spirituality thinkers are blazing new evolutionary paths for realizing authentic self-discovery and evolving the source code of human meaning and values.

Dr. Gafni has written seven books including the national bestseller *Soul Prints*, which won awards including the NAPRA Nautilus Award for Best Spirituality Book of 2001, and the critically acclaimed book *The Mystery of Love*, which focused on Kabbalah and Eros. Both books were published by Simon & Schuster, and *Soul Prints* was also made into a National PBS special. Both books were made into audio series. All of Gafni's books are being re-issued by Integral Publishers. Gafni is presently writing a major new work on World Spirituality together with Ken Wilber. In a series of dialogues with His Holiness the Dalai Lama, Ram Dass, Moshe Idel, Deepak Chopra, Surya Das, Gabriel Cousens, Michael Murphy and many others, he advanced the radical notion that all of Hebrew wisdom may be properly understood as a form of evolutionary panentheism whose intended goal is the greatest depth of enlightenment for the greatest possible span of humanity.

Dr. Gafni's forthcoming book, *Your Unique Self: The Radical Path to Personal Enlightenment*, challenges the conventional wisdom of enlightenment and suggests a fundamental evolution of the source code of enlightenment thought. It is the culmination of years of research into Western and Eastern enlightenment traditions and many hours of conversations with cutting-edge thinkers and spiritual teachers from diverse lineages and traditions. His other forthcoming books include *Towards Integral Religion: Dance of Tears, Between Certainty and Uncertainty: The Future of Faith*, and *World Spirituality based on Integral Principles* co-authored with Ken Wilber. Collectively, these works elucidate the Enlightenment of Fullness.

The themes of Dr. Gafni's early books have been transcended and included in this new paradigm, based on Integral principles with Unique Self at its core. The World Spirituality movement brings the Enlightenment of Fullness into practice in real world communities, creating a vibrant and fulfilling context of meaning for people around the globe who can no longer locate themselves in the religious traditions or who no longer feel that one religion can be their exclusive home. The Unique Self principle reconciles Eastern and Western approaches to enlightenment in an elegant, exciting, and original way. Together with Mariana Caplan, Sally Kempton and other leading teachers, he is shaping a revolutionary way to understand the nature of human existence, a new paradigm which could very well re-make today's spiritual landscape.

Dr. Gafni, born Marc Winiarz, is the son of Kehath Winiarz and Claire Subar, survivors of the Holocaust. He earned his doctorate from Oxford University in England and today he lives in the greater San Francisco area. He is the father of four children. He is the director of the Center for World Spirituality and teacher in residence at the Venwoude Spiritual Community in Holland and at the Shalom Mountain Wisdom School in New York. He occasionally forays into the corporate boardroom and leads widely-acclaimed seminars for CEOs.